REPERTORY GRID TECHNIQUE
AND PERSONAL CONSTRUCTS

Repertory Grid Technique and Personal Constructs

Applications in Clinical & Educational Settings

Edited by Nigel Beail

BROOKLINE BOOKS
Cambridge, MA

© 1985 N. Beail
Published in the USA and dependencies,
Central and South America by
Brookline Books, 29 Ware Street,
Cambridge, Massachusetts 02138

Library of Congress Cataloging in Publication Data
Main entry under title:

Repertory grid technique and personal constructs.

   Bibliography; p.
   Includes index.
   1. Repertory grid technique. 2. Personal
construct theory. 3. Psychological tests.
4. Educational tests. 5. Psychodiagnostics.
I. Beail, Nigel, 1956–
BF698.8.R38R46   1985   155.2′8   85-10939
ISBN 0-914797-16-6

CONTENTS

LIST OF CONTRIBUTORS

Nigel Beail

Department of Clinical Psychology
St Luke's Hospital
Crosland Moor
Huddersfield, West Yorkshire
HD4 5RQ

Sue Beail

Department of Social Service
Pudsey Town Hall
Pudsey
Leeds, S28

Shelagh Brumfitt

Department of Linguistics
University of Sheffield
Sheffield
S10 2TN

R.J. Butler

Department of Psychology
High Royds Hospital
Menston
Ilkley, West Yorkshire
LS29 6AQ

Eric Button

Department of Psychiatry
Royal South Hants Hospital
Graham Road
Southampton
SO9 4PE

Robert Davies

MRC/ESRC
Social and Applied Psychology Unit
University of Sheffield
Sheffield
S10 2TN

Bryn D. Davies

Department of Community Studies
Brighton Polytechnic
Falmer
Brighton
BN1 9PH

Keren Fisher

Royal National Orthopaedic Hospital
Brockley Hill
Stanmore, Middlesex
HA7 4LP

Sheila Harri-Augstein

Centre for the Study of Human
Learning
Brunel University
Uxbridge, Middlesex
UB8 3PH

Terry Honess

Department of Psychology
University College
Cardiff
CF1 1XL

Steven Mendoza

65 Yeldham Road
London
W6 8JQ

Judith Middleton

Department of Psychology
University of Surrey
Guildford, Surrey
GU2 5HX

Bernadette O'Sullivan

16 Whitebeam Road
Clonskeagh
Dublin, 14
Eire

Estelle M. Phillips

School of Education
The Open University
Walton Hall
Milton Keynes
MK7 6AA

Harry G. Procter

Department of Psychology
Tone Vale Hospital
Norton Fitzwarren
Taunton, Somerset
TA4 1DB

Anthony Ryle

Department of Psychiatry
St Thomas's Hospital
London, SE1

Maureen J. Sheehan

Psychology Department
Friern Hospital
Friern Barnet Road
London
N11 3BP

Brian Stanley

Department of Clinical Psychology
Stanley Royd Hospital
Aberford Road
Wakefield, West Yorkshire
WF1 4DQ

Laurie F. Thomas

Centre for the Study of Human
Learning
Brunel University
Uxbridge
Middlesex
UB8 3PH

Susan Vicary

Department of Psychology
North East London Polytechnic
The Green
London
E15 4LZ

David A. Winter

Napsbury Hospital
London Colney
Nr St Albans
Herts.
AL2 1AA

D.M. Yorke

Centre for Educational Development
and Training
Manchester Polytechnic
Elizabeth Gaskell
Hathersage Road
Manchester
M13 0JA

FOREWORD

When George Kelly outlined repertory grid technique some 30 years ago, he presented it as essentially an addendum to, and illustration of personal construct theory. Certainly, he thought well of his invention, both as a clinical and a research tool, though he waxed just as enthusiastic about his elaboration of self-characterisation methods. Centrally, he seems to have looked to repertory grid technique to illustrate, in vivid and practical form, what he saw as the primary undertaking of psychology: to develop an understanding of the way in which persons interpret their experience. Repertory grid technique was important for Kelly, but important only in relation to the theory from which it was derived. Thus, he profoundly shocked one statistical enthusiast for repertory grid method by describing it, in conversation, as 'an excrescence of personal construct theory'.

As history would have it, the presentation of repertory grid technique came at the height of the traditional battle between 'objective' and 'subjective' testers. This battle was variously fought under the banners of 'nomothetic' versus 'idiographic' or wider labels such as 'scientific' versus 'humanistic'. It raged between the devotees of standardised and mechanically scored tests of the questionnaire type, yielding numerical scores on prescribed traits, and the enthusiasts for projective-type tests which allowed for free-ranging responses from the subject and equally free-ranging interpretations by the tester. The 'objectivists' dismissed their opponents as unscientific witch doctors while the 'subjectivists' retorted with accusations of mechanical triviality. To those unhappy with both stances repertory grid technique came like a gift from the gods. On the one hand, forms of grid did permit subjects to work with material drawn from their own experience and to comment on such material in their own personal terms. Yet at the end of the day, systems of grid analysis yielded numbers which allowed comparisons to be made and hypotheses, clinical or general, to be tested. So, from the very beginning, repertory grid technique held fascinations which were, in part, independent of Personal Construct Theory, though they echoed Kelly's ideology.

A further historical development, which caught up with repertory grid technique, was the elaboration of the computer, the coming of the age of every subject with its own factor analysis. Strangely, this turned the grid into a swift and handy tool while generating complexities of analysis so elaborate that it became difficult to see the connection between the final scores and the original thoughts and dreams of the subject who completed the grid.

Where the grid was used directly in relationship to the psychology of personal constructs it seemed destined to monopolise the theory. Neimeyer, in his socio-historical analysis of grid literature, could trace only a handful of construct theory studies that had not used the grid as their prime experimental method.

At least two fair statements can be made about the development, to date, of grid method. First, the grid has powerfully drawn the attention of psychologists to the central importance of persons' interpretations of their worlds, and thereby forced them to take heed of the central tenets of Personal Construct Theory. Secondly, grid method is a Frankenstein's monster which has rushed away on a statistical and experimental rampage of its own, leaving construct theory neglected, stranded high and dry, far behind. Current and future work using grid methods can be looked at as supporting one or other of these tendencies.

The value of this book is that it displays the subtlety and range of grid method *in the context of the psychology of personal constructs* and as a way of elaborating Kelly's central themes. Kelly explicitly valued both theories and methods for their fertility, for their richness in generating insights. The essays and studies in this book are fertile: fertile in crossing the arbitrary boundaries of clinical, educational and general psychology; fertile in making the grid a method which can unite psychologist and subject in a communal exploration; fertile in posing new forms of inquiry, not simply providing stock answers to old questions.

Kelly had his own sense of foreboding about future uses of the grid matrix. He wrote

as I think of the uses to which the matrix might be put, I find myself a little depressed. Suppose someone would surreptitiously put 'stimuli' instead of persons along one margin of the matrix, and 'responses' instead of constructs along the other.

If that should ever happen I am sure I would feel that I had been brought back, full circle, to where I started.

Hopefully the grid studies here described and considered, will help us extend rather than constrict Kelly's invention.

D. Bannister

ACKNOWLEDGEMENTS

I would like to thank Rosemary Barnitt and Hazel Carter for introducing me to Repertory Grid Technique and for encouraging me to use the method in my research. I am grateful to Don Bannister for his encouragement and many hours of useful discussions. Much of the work on this book was completed whilst I was at the Department of Clinical Psychology, Stanley Royd Hospital, Wakefield. I would particularly like to thank Eileen Greaves of that Department for her invaluable secretarial assistance. I am grateful to Sharon Sidhu for providing secretarial help during the final stages.

1 AN INTRODUCTION TO REPERTORY GRID TECHNIQUE

Nigel Beail

George Kelly developed a theory about how people make sense of themselves and the world around them. He presented his theory in his major work *The Psychology of Personal Constructs* (Kelly, 1955). A central notion of his theory is that all women and men are scientists — each of us having our personal ideas, philosophies and theories about the world. He did not mean that we are by profession scientists, but that on the basis of our personal theories we, like the professional scientist, develop hypotheses, test them out, revise them, and develop our theories to make sense of our experiences. Thus, we come to understand the world in which we live by erecting a personally organised system of interpretation or constructs of experienced events. The system is personal in that we all make our own interpretations of our experiences. But we too can share a view and appreciate someone else's interpretation or construction of events. Each interpretation or construct is an abstraction which subsumes some aspect of a repeated event or set of events of which the person is aware. A construct is our way of distinguishing similarity from difference — thus a construct is essentially a discrimination which a person can make. A construct is not simply a verbal label. We begin construing from birth, and therefore long before we have developed the capacity to give verbal labels. We also construe many aspects of our experience such as art, music, taste and smell without applying verbal labels to these. Kelly also felt it more useful to see constructs as bipolar to emphasise the fact that we affirm and negate something at the same time. Thus, when I say psychology is an *interesting* subject I am not saying it is *interesting* as distinct from being *yogurt*, *grass like*, or *tasty* or many other things. What I am saying is that for me it is an *interesting* subject and *not* a *boring* one. Our constructs are not a chaotic jumble, but are organised into a system. They are linked, related and integrated into a complex hierarchical structure or system containing many sub-systems. Through our system of

1

personal constructs we are able to predict and control our interpersonal world. Thus they are our guidelines for living.

Repertory grid technique is the methodological component of Personal Construct Theory. Kelly devised the grid as a method for exploring personal construct systems. It enables the investigator to elicit personal constructs and examine the relationships between them within a specific domain — no one grid is capable of eliciting the entire construct system. The method is like a form of interview with a skeletal structure providing results which can be recorded in a matrix. It has three main components: (i) 'elements' which define the area of construing to be investigated; (ii) 'constructs' which are ways that the person groups and differentiates between the elements; and (iii) 'linking mechanism' which shows how each element is judged on each construct. Kelly's (1955) original Role Construct Repertory Test, from which all subsequent forms of grid derive, was designed to elicit a representative sample of personal constructs upon which an individual relies to interpret and anticipate the behaviour of significant people in their life, and to assess the way in which they relate their constructs to one another. The grid is a flexible methodology, but all grids are designed so that statistical tests can be applied to a set of comparisons each person makes. When using grid methods we are assuming that the mathematical association between two constructs for a given person reflects the psychological relationship between them for that person. The purpose of grids is to inform us about the way in which our system of personal constructs is evolving and its limitations and possibilities. It is a way of standing in the shoes of others, to see the world from their point of view, to understand their situation, their concerns.

Repertory grid technique is a flexible methodology, but despite this administration generally proceeds in five stages:

1. Eliciting elements
2. Eliciting constructs
3. Completing the grid
4. Analysis
5. Interpretation

For the purpose of exposition of these stages, I shall illustrate with an example, the case of John.

John was a resident in a mental handicap hospital. He was a moderately mentally handicapped man in his twenties whom I was seeing for individual psychotherapy. At the time there was much talk in the hospital about John's future, particularly future placement in the community. John had become very concerned about this and wanted to talk about it at every session. He went through a list of places where he had lived and worked. At times it was difficult to follow what John was saying, and I became confused as to which place he was talking about. So, to help me conceptualise his experiences, I decided to use the grid format to structure the conversation.

Eliciting the Elements

The elements are chosen to represent the domain in which construing is to be investigated. They can be significant people in a person's life as in Kelly's original exposition of the technique. They can be works of art (Chapter 17), radio programmes (Chapter 16), selves (Chapter 8), how others see me (Chapter 9), occupations (Chapter 21) and so on. In each case the elements determine the focus of the grid.

To elicit the elements for John's grid I asked him to start with the first place he worked or lived after leaving school and then all the moves after that. In all, eleven elements were elicited, and these were written along the top of the grid (see Figure 1.1).

There are various ways of generating elements. They can simply be supplied by the investigator. For example, I could have gone through John's records and listed all the places he had worked and lived. Alternatively, elements can be generated by providing role or situation descriptions. Kelly provided 24 role descriptions such as, a teacher you liked, an intelligent person, a successful person and so on. For John I could have provided situational descriptions such as 'a place you were happy', 'a place you disliked'. But John had already 'defined a pool' that being places I have lived and worked. Similarly, the investigator can define a pool he or she would like to investigate such as 'occupations'. After defining the pool or area of interest the elements are elicited through discussion (see, for example, Chapter 18).

There are two important points that should be kept in mind

when selecting the elements to be used in the grid. First, the elements should be representative of the area to be investigated. For example, with John a grid which did not include his parents' home would be rather suspect as it would exclude a very major part of his life experience. Secondly, the elements should be within a particular range as constructs apply to only a limited number of people, events or things. In John's case I wanted to include some elements in his grid which represented alternative places in which he might live in the future — for example, 'living with a landlady'. However, John had no idea of what this would be like and could not even guess. Thus, the element is outside the range of his existing construct system and therefore cannot be included in the grid. Therefore, it is important to note, particularly when you are supplying elements, that the subject needs to be given the opportunity to say that they cannot construe a particular element.

Eliciting the Constructs

When we administer a grid we are basically saying to the subject 'Construe me these elements'; or 'How do you see these things?'. Kelly devised several ways of going about this. The best known is the minimum context card form or triadic method. This method involves presenting to the subject triads of elements with the question 'In what important way are two alike and thereby different from the third?', and then 'In what way does the third element differ from the other two?', or 'What is the opposite of that characteristic?' As many triads of elements are presented to the subject as the investigator thinks appropriate — there are no fixed rules. Kelly also suggested that triads could be presented in 'sequential form' by systematically changing one element each time. One element can also be retained in every triad. Kelly suggested the retention of the 'self' element and called this elicitation procedure the 'self-identification form'. However, any element could be retained. A different method of questioning is the personal role form. Here triads are presented with the question 'Suppose that the three of you were all together by yourselves for an evening — what kind of place would it be?'; 'What would happen?' and so on. It is important to note that there is no reason why three elements need to be used. It is quite reasonable to use two elements for elicitation or more than three as in a little used procedure described by Kelly called the 'full context card form'. In this form all the elements are written on cards and spread out in front of the subject. They are asked to think of important ways in which groups of elements are alike. If the elements are people the less structured personal role form questions can also be used.

Constructs can also be elicited by Kelly's Self-characterisation Method. Here the subject is asked to write a character sketch of himself or herself in the third person as if they were the principal character in a play. They are asked to write about themselves from the point of view of a close friend who knows them intimately and very sympathetically. The ways in which the subject describes himself in this sketch are constructs which can be used in a grid.

For many people constructs may be more forthcoming through less structured conversation. This is particularly so for children and mentally handicapped people. After eliciting John's elements I presented one triad, but he could not understand this. I took one element away and asked whether the two places were similar in any way. He proceeded to talk about what it was like at one place and then went on to talk about the other. I followed on by asking him to talk about each place in turn. For each construct that emerged during the conversation I asked for its opposite. In all, nine constructs were elicited, and these were written down the side of the grid (see Figure 1.1).

Types of Construct

When eliciting constructs from John he would frequently say that a place was 'alright'. However, when I asked him 'What do you mean, "alright"?' in one case he meant 'it wasn't boring' and in another 'the people were caring'. Thus, the first construct elicited did not fully reflect what John meant and further probes were necessary. This kind of problem was recognised by Hunt (quoted in Kelly, 1955), who drew up the following list of constructs which might not be particularly useful and may need further probing.

Construct Type	Example
Excessively permeable	They are both men
Excessively impermeable	Machinist/overlocker
Situational	Lives in Wakefield

Superficial	They both have blonde hair
Vague	They are both OK
Constructs which are a direct product of the role title	They are my parents/she is my sister

What may be vague or superficial to the investigator might be very important to the subject. When such constructs are elicited they should be noted prior to making use of any further probes.

Supplying Constructs

There has been quite a debate over whether one can supply constructs and about how elicited constructs compare with provided ones. I do not intend to reproduce the arguments here, and I would refer the interested reader to the reviews of the subject by Adams-Webber (1979, pp. 23-7) and Fransella and Bannister (1977, pp. 19-20, 106-7). From a practical point of view there may be many occasions when the investigator may want to supply constructs in part or in full. But whatever is supplied by the investigator is itself the subject of the subject's personal construing. Thus, the person will attach his or her own meaning to your label. So what is important is that the supplied verbal label be meaningful to the subject.

Completing the Grid

John's grid contains a list of elements along the top and constructs down the side. The next step is to sort the elements in terms of the constructs. There are several ways of doing this.

Dichotomising

In Kelly's original format, once a construct was elicited, the subject was required to place a tick under every element which had that characteristic, for an example see below.

	Self	Mother	Father	Brother	Sister	Friend	Ideal Self	
Happy		√	√		√	√	√	Sad
Loving							√	Selfish

Kelly assumed that we would distribute our elements roughly equally between the two poles of the construct. However, this is not always the case. Sometimes the distribution could be lopsided or skewed such as Loving-Selfish in the example. The methods of analysis suggested by Kelly for grid data could not cope with lopsided rows so Kelly suggested that they be removed before analysis. As an alternative to this Bannister (1960) suggested that the subject should be asked to divide the elements between the two poles of each construct. This is called the split half method. Whilst this procedure removes the problem of skewed distributions it imposes considerable constraint on the subject. Dichotomising also does not allow for shades of grey; as in the example you can be sorted as being either happy or sad whereas you could be anywhere along that construct dimension. This problem and the lopsidedness problem is less apparent when the elements are rank-ordered.

Rank Ordering

Ranking elements were originally used as an alternative to dichotomising as it removed the problem of skewed distributions. Ranking simply involves placing the elements in order between the two construct poles. For example:

	Self	Mother	Father	Brother	Sister	Friend	Ideal Self	
Happy	7	4	5	6	3	2	1	Sad

Ranking provides much greater discrimination than the dichotomous method, but it may force the subject to indicate differences between elements where really there is no difference. There is also a tendency when ranking to judge the element in terms of likeness to one pole of the construct, without giving full consideration to the other pole. The procedure also becomes more difficult as the number of elements increases.

Rating Scales

The most popular method of completing grids is by rating scales. With this method each element is rated on a scale defined by the two construct poles. This method allows the subject greater freedom when sorting the constructs and does not force them to make discriminations which do not exist. The scales usually have five or seven points, for example:

	Self	Mother	Father	Brother	Sister	Friend	Ideal Self	
Happy	7	4	4	5	4	1	1	Sad

However, the scale can be of any size. It can also be presented in the form of visual analogues. Here the two poles of the construct are placed at either end of a line of say 10 cm with no calibration. The subject indicates where along the line the element would be placed. The score is then derived by measuring how far along the line the element is placed.

For completing John's grid I opted for a three-point rating scale. For John his elements were either one pole (1) or the other (3) or a bit of both (2). John's completed grid is shown in Figure 1.1.

Implications Grids

The implications grid was developed by Hinkle (1965). This grid contains no elements like the other forms. The method examines what meaning each construct has for the subject in terms of the other constructs. Thus, for this grid form the constructs are drawn not only down the side of the grid but also along the top.

For details of Hinkle's original instructions see Bannister and Mair (1976, Chapter 3) or Fransella and Bannister (1977, p. 43). I have found these instructions rather cumbersome and prefer the style of questioning used by Honess (1978). This involves asking 'if a person is x will they also be y'. Honess used a three-point scale: 'very likely' (1), 'may or may not' (2) or 'very unlikely' (3), for scoring the grid, as in the example on page 10.

Figure 1.1: John's Grid

ELEMENTS

3		ATC	PWA	PWL	SSH	P	HHH	WARD	MHL	W	PH	PHP		1
		Adult training centre	Psychiatric ward (acute)	Psychiatric ward (locked)	Social services hostel	Prison	Halfway house (hostel)	Mental handicap hospital (ward currently on)	Mental handicap hospital (locked ward)	Workshop currently attending	Parents' home	Parents' home in the past		
1	Boring	3	2	3	3	3	3	1	3	1	1	2		Not boring
2	Did not enjoy	3	2	3	3	3	3	1	3	1	1	3		Enjoyed
3	Felt upset/depressed	1	3	3	3	3	3	1	3	1	1	3		Did not feel upset
4	Nobody bothered about me	3	3	3	1	3	3	1	2	1	1	2		Caring
5	Learnt nothing	2	3	3	3	3	3	2	1	1	2	3		Learnt from experience
6	Don't like	3	3	3	3	3	3	2	3	1	1	3		Liked
7	Did not help me feel clear	3	3	3	3	3	3	1	3	1	2	3		Helped me feel clear
8	Felt confused	2	2	3	3	3	3	1	1	1	1	3		Not confused
9	Felt annoyed/mad	1	2	3	2	3	3	1	3	1	1	3		Not mad

	Kind	=	Spoilt	Generous	Intelligent	Honest	Sincere	Bad-tempered
Happy	1	3	2	1	2	1	1	13

Equivalence of Grid Forms

We assume that the various ways of scoring a grid will produce equivalent results. There have been a few studies which have compared one grid form with another. These studies indicate that grids of various forms cannot be considered identical either in terms of perceived task or in terms of their results (Fransella and Bannister, 1977). Only one study, by Beail (1983), has compared all the major grid forms with each other for a single case. He found that the correlations between the forms were not very high (range +0.41 to +0.68). He also compared their principal component plots. There were similarities between these in that a group of constructs formed a cluster in all plots, but a second group of constructs were plotted in a variety of ways from a tight cluster, therefore implying they are in some way equivalent constructs, to three unrelated isolates, therefore implying that they are not equivalent. These differences may affect clinical interpretation of grid data. Thus, further study in this area is clearly needed as the answer to why the various forms are not equivalent is not clear.

Computer Elicitation of Repertory Grids

It is also possible to elicit a repertory grid with the aid of the computer. PEGASUS (Thomas and Shaw, 1977; Shaw, 1980) is an interactive program which elicits a grid using a conversational heuristic. The program elicits elements and then elicits constructs using the triadic method. The elements are sorted using a rating scale. As the grid is built up it can also analyse it and provide a continual commentary on the patterns in the responses. A smaller version of PEGASUS, BELLEROPHON (a rider on Pegasus) is also available (Burton, 1983).

Analysis

Now that our grid is complete the next step is to perform some form of analysis on it in order to clarify the information in it as an aid to interpretation.

Examination of the Raw Grid

Prior to carrying out any form of sophisticated analysis the investigator should examine the raw grid. If we look at John's grid (Figure 1.1) we can see that he is construing some places in similar terms to others. For example, the ward where he currently lives, the workshop and his parents' home, are all construed in a positive light, whereas the two hostels he lived in, the prison and the locked psychiatric ward are all construed in negative terms.

Focusing the Raw Grid

Further clarification of the patterning in the grid can be achieved by using a procedure developed by Laurie F. Thomas called FOCUSing (for examples see Chapters 13 and 18). This method involves reordering the rows of constructs and the columns of elements to put like with like. Thus, the raw data are simply clarified without any complicated analyses.

Measuring Association Between Constructs and Between Elements

According to Kelly (1955, p. 307), the degree of similarity between constructs (or elements) can be given by a mathematical expression. Therefore the next step in the analysis of a grid is to compute 'similarity matrices' or 'correlation matrices' between rows of constructs and element columns. This procedure can be carried out by hand or by computer. Various measures of association (similarity and distance) have been employed with grid data to represent the degree of relationship in numerical terms. Here only the more commonly used measures will be reviewed.

Measures of Association for Dichotomous Data. For dichotomous data Kelly used a simple measure of association called the matching score. This is a measure of the extent to which elements selected or rejected as classifiable under one construct are selected or rejected under another. However, Phillips (1973) argues that matching scores are highly inappropriate for measuring association between rows of dichotomous data. First, the value of the matching score varies according to the number of elements in the grid. This is resolved by dividing the matching score by the number of elements — thus, the score is normalised for its range. The resultant statistic is usually referred to as the Simple Matching Coefficient. A second and more serious problem arises out of Kelly's assumption that people will allot roughly half of their elements to each pole of the construct. Difficulties are encountered when only one or two elements are allotted to one pole. Such lopsided rows can give rise to misleading matching scores or simple matching coefficients. Indeed, all measures of this kind (for a review see Sneath and Sokal, 1973) will tend to give misleading values when rows are lopsided.

Phillips (1973) states that the *phi* correlation coefficient is the correct measure. Also Leach (1979) states that Kendall's *tau.b* gives a way of measuring the relationship between constructs which does not have any of the problems associated with Kelly's matching score. For dichotomous data, however, the absolute values of *tau.b* and *phi* are equivalent. These measures have the advantage of being statistically more precise, but they take a lot longer to compute by hand than the simple coefficients.

Measures of Association for Rank-order Data. For rank-order data a measure of association between construct rows can be derived by computing either Spearman's *rho* or Kendall's *tau*. These are very time consuming to compute by hand.

Measures of Association for Ratings Data. For three-point scales we can calculate a matching score similar to that described by Kelly (1955). Procter (1978) suggests that for two rows matches between identical ratings are scored 1, mismatches (between highest and lowest ratings) are scored 0 and matches with the middle rating is scored 0.5. These are then summed to give a measure of association between two rows. This score can also be normalised for range. Like Kelly's matching score it is a quick method for deriving a measure of association by hand. But it also has all the problems associated with Kelly's measure.

Bannister and Mair (1968) suggest the 'difference score' as a measure of association which can easily be computed by hand for ratings data. This score is simply derived by subtracting the ratings for each element and summing these. Alternatively, the differences can be squared prior to summation.

Of the more sophisticated measures of association used for ratings data the most widely employed, particularly in computer analysis, is Pearson's product moment correlation coefficient. Its computation by hand is very lengthy. Pearson's r has been criticised 'because the correlation is unity whenever two profiles are parallel, irrespective of how far they are apart' (Everett, 1974). A group of measures called metrics or distances are more sensitive, they are also easier to compute by hand. An example is the distance measure derived from the city block metric for the analysis of relationships between constructs in a repertory grid (described in Shaw, 1980).

Exhibiting the Patterns and Structure in the Grid

The matrices of similarity or distance scores tells us how the constructs/elements are related to each other. These matrices can be summarised by various procedures, some of which provide graphical or diagrammatic presentation of the grid. These pictorial summaries reveal the main relationships between the constructs and elements, and aid interpretation and the communication of the results to others. Two main methods have been employed: factor analysis and cluster analysis.

Factor Analysis. Kelly developed a method of non-parametric factor analysis which can be applied to matrices of matching scores. Kelly described this method fully (Kelly, 1955) so that grid users could analyse their own grids by hand. The method differs from conventional factor analysis as it reveals patterns of relationships between constructs, and additionally identifies the particular elements associated with each pattern. A computer program was written for this method of analysis (Kelly, 1964), but little use has been made of it in Britain, probably because in the same year Slater (1964) made available a program which analysed grids into their principal components called INGRID. Grid users could send their grids to Slater who, with the backing of the Medical Research Council, would analyse them free of charge. Such a service is still available, but it is now organised more locally. Most universities also have INGRID on their computer. INGRID has been, and still is, the main program used to analyse individual grids. I chose this method to analyse John's grid (Figure 1.2), and there are many further illustrations of this program's application throughout this book.

The INGRID program output is fairly lengthy. It provides information on the relationships between constructs, elements and constructs with elements, and a principal components analysis. Principal components analysis involves transforming an original set of variables into a set of hypothetical variables which are uncorrelated. The first hypothetical variable or component is derived in such a way that it accounts for the maximum variance, the second component accounts for the maximum variance subject to being uncorrelated to the first, and so on.

When using INGRID the most popular method of displaying the data is to draw these first two components orthogonal (at 90°) to each other, and then, using the loadings as co-ordinates, plotting the constructs or elements in relation to the two axes. This gives a two-dimensional plot displaying relations between constructs and a similar plot for elements. Slater (1977), however, argues that both sets of results can be combined into a single diagram. He suggests that the points for the elements are found in the usual way by taking their loadings as co-ordinates. To show the relations between constructs, Slater suggests we draw a circle with its centre at the origin at a convenient radius around the element distribution. The loadings of the constructs define axes crossing the radius, and their contrast or opposite poles are shown projecting from the circumference. The resultant diagram shows the relations among the elements and among the constructs and, according to Slater's (1977) model, the relations between constructs and elements as well. John's grid has been plotted in this way (see Figure 1.2).

Slater has also developed a spherical co-ordinate model. This enables grid data to be plotted onto a globe. For further details of this method and INGRID see Slater (1976, 1977). Principal Components Analysis and Factor Analysis are also available in a number of standard computer program packages which were not designed for grid analyses. An example which is used by two contributors to this book (Chapters 7 and 8) is sub-program FACTOR in the Statistical Package for the Social Sciences (Nie, *et al.*, 1975).

An alternative to factor analytic solutions is multidimensional scaling, which is a somewhat similar analysis to principal

Figure 1.2: John's Elements and Construct Plotted Along Their Two Main Principal Components (INGRID)

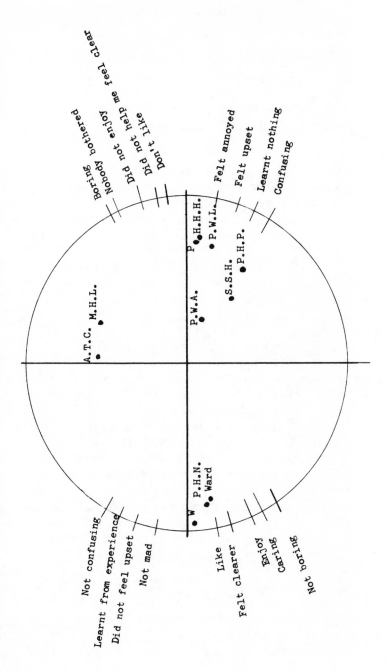

components analysis. However, this type of analysis assumes the data to have ordinal properties. Thus, in the final solution the original relations between constructs is retained, but the actual distance is not. Various multidimensional scaling computer programs have been applied to grid data (for an example see Van der Kloot, 1981); however, no particular program has been developed for the analysis of grids and no particular program has become more favoured than others.

Cluster Analysis. In 1965 Bannister suggested a simple method for deriving a two-dimensional representation of grid data called the Anchor Method. This is a method of cluster analysis. Originally presented so that clinicians could derive a pictorial presentation of the grid data by hand, the method involves taking the construct which correlates most highly with all other constructs and using this as the first axis. The construct which correlates the next most highly with all other constructs, but is not correlated with the first, is taken as the second axis. All other constructs are plotted in relation to these two using their relationship scores ($r^2 \times 100$) as co-ordinates. A fully worked example of this form of analysis is presented in Fransella and Bannister (1977, pp. 34-6). This method is also available on a computer program called GAB (Higginbotham and Bannister, 1983). Indeed, in the clinical setting GAB has become a very popular method of analysis as it is available on most micro-computers, thus enabling on-the-spot analysis rather than sending the grid off to be analysed by INGRID.

The FOCUS method of analysis described earlier is also available on computer (Thomas and Shaw, 1976). The FOCUS program re-orders the grid to put like with like for construct rows and element columns. It also computes distance scores between all construct pairs and all element pairs. Following this a two-way hierarchical linkage analysis is carried out, thus clustering the data and illustrating this by a tree diagram attached to the re-ordered grid. This procedure can also be carried out by hand (for details see Chapter 18). The FOCUS program can also apply a method called SPACED which takes the FOCUSed grid and separates the rows and columns according to the degree of likeness between adjacent lines. This helps indicate clusters of elements which are construed similarly and clusters of constructs which are operating on groups of element similarity (for an illustration see Chapter 18).

In some cases a method called Q-Analysis may be appropriate. This procedure splits each construct into two. For example, the construct Happy-Sad becomes Happy-Not Happy and Sad-Not Sad. Distance measures are computed and a form of hierarchical cluster analysis is carried out. The rationale for the appropriate application of Q-Analysis is presented in Chapter 17, with an example.

There are many more ways of analysing individual repertory grids by hand or computer than can be mentioned here. In published studies INGRID has been by far the most popular method of analysis. It is probably the analysis of choice for most practitioners too. But the availability of microcomputers in the clinical setting has resulted in the GAB program becoming very popular. The FOCUS method has also become more popular as it too is available on microcomputer.

The question as to which method provides the best form of analysis is open to debate. There have been very few studies comparing the results of the different programs for the same grid. Fransella (1965) compared Bannister's Anchor Method with Slater's INGRID for a single case and found a close correspondence between the two solutions. Shaw and Gaines (1981) compared INGRID, FOCUS and Q-Analysis for a single case, and concluded that the results did not differ in any meaningful way. Van der Kloot (1982) compared INGRID with multi-dimensional scaling (HOMALS) for one case, and re-analysed Kelly's (1955) original case example of the grid by HOMALS to compare it with Kelly's non-parametric factor analysis. He concluded that the three methods were comparable.

Thus, these few case studies suggest that the various methods available tend to give similar results. The method you choose to analyse your grid will in part depend on your own preference for presentation of data and also what facilities are available to you. Whichever method you use it is always advisable to check your results against the similarity matrices and the raw grid.

Comparing and Averaging Grids

There may be occasions where we want to compare grids (for examples see Chapters 3, 9, 10 and 22) or combine grids (for examples see Chapters 5 and 7) in order to make generalisations about certain groups. Since devising methods for computer analysis of individual grids the authors of INGRID, FOCUS and GAB have developed programs to compare and average a number of grids. Slater (1977) has developed the Grid Analysis Package, Thomas and his co-workers at the Centre for the Study of Human Learning have developed a variety of programs based on FOCUS, and Higginbotham and Bannister have developed options on the GAB program to compare and average based on the Anchor method. Some of these programs and their purpose are summarised in Table 1.1.

Although these programs claim to do similar things, they do not necessarily do it in the same way. For example, when combining grids aligned by row and column the Slater program

Table 1.1: Computer Programs for Analysing Grid Data

Purpose	Programs		
	GAP (Slater, 1977)	CSHL (Thomas *et al.*)	GAB (Higginbotham and Bannister, 1983)
Individual grid analysis	INGRID	FOCUS	GAB
Comparison between two grids	DELTA	MINUS	Option available
Averaging grids aligned by constructs and elements	SERIES	—	Option available
Extraction of commonality of a series of grids aligned by elements only	PREFAN	SOCIOGRIDS	Option available
Extraction of commonality of a series of grids aligned by constructs only	ADELA	—	Option available

computes the average for each cell, and submits this grid of average ratings to principal components analysis. Higginbotham and Bannister, on the other hand, average the similarity matrices of relationship scores ($r^2 \times 100$) and then carry out the Anchor Analysis. Unfortunately the two procedures do not seem to produce the same results (for an illustration see Beail, 1984).

Making Sense of the Results

Repertory grid technique enables us to investigate the system of constructs through which we experience life, and categorise and make use of our experience. Guidelines on how to interpret the results produced are rather difficult to produce as interpretation will depend on how the grid was designed, produced and the purpose for which it was used — this point is well illustrated throughout this book. In general, however, all methods of analysis attempt to reveal patterns of relationship between entities in the grid. In particular, we can look at how the constructs are interrelated, how the elements are related to one another, and some methods reveal how the constructs and elements relate to each other.

It is important to remember that when we look at someone else's grid we are using our own experience, our own constructs, to make sense of it. This will be influenced by our professional training, whether we be psychologists, psychiatrists, speech therapists, teachers or priests. Our theoretical beliefs will also affect how we interpret what we see in a grid. Although grids were developed as the methodological component of personal construct theory there seems to be no reasons for not using them from the viewpoint of another theoretical position. However, one would expect the interpretation of the results to differ to some degree. Thus, we use our own construct system to interpret another's. But, as Kelly (1955) points out the grid enables us to

> Look beyond words. We can study contexts. For example, does the client use the word affectionate only when talking about persons of the opposite sex. Does he apply the term sympathetic only to members of his own family or persons who have been described as 'intimate'?

The answers to questions such as these may give us an understanding of the interrelations of our client's terminology, and provide us with a better understanding of his or her position which no dictionary could offer.

The graphical presentation of John's analysed grid (Figure 1.2) shows that his constructs are very highly interrelated. Other workers who have used grids with people with mental handicap have found their subjects to have a small number of highly interrelated clusters of constructs (Barton, Walton and Rowe, 1978; Oliver, 1980; Wooster, 1970). In John's case the elements appear to be construed in terms of one major dimension which has a strong positive pole and a strong negative pole. The elements fall into three groups; one group being positively construed, one group being negatively construed and two falling into neither cluster. The grid shows that this aspect of John's life experiences have been fairly horrific. The three elements being construed positively are the places he has lived and worked in during the last twelve months only. The results also show that on discharge from hospital John would want to move back to his parents' home and would be very unwilling to accept a place in a hostel.

This is a fairly simple use of grid method. I used it as an aid to structure the conversation between John and myself. It became clear through the process of completing the grid how John viewed the different places and where he would and would not consider living in the future. Submitting the raw grid to computer analysis was in fact unnecessary for my own purposes. However, for the purpose of communicating results to colleagues the graphical presentation of the data provides a convenient visual summary.

This book provides a wealth of information on the various ways of interpreting grid data in a range of clinical and educational settings. Some contributors examine relations between all entities in the grid, some focus on the elements only, some on constructs only and others look at relations between specific elements and constructs. A variety of repertory grid indices have also been developed which indicate some underlying relationships, structures and processes. For reviews of some of these measures see Adams-Webber (1979) and Fransella and Bannister (1977). Several of the authors in this book have employed indices as an aid to interpret their findings.

Further information about the meaning of a construct can be obtained through investigations which take us beyond the grid. Hinkle (1965) developed a procedure he called laddering. This involves eliciting constructs and then asking the person to say by which pole of each construct they would prefer to be described and why. The answer given is another construct superordinate to the first, to which the same question is asked, and so on, for each new construct until the person cannot, or will not, produce any more. Hinkle argued that each construct elicited was superordinate to the first, and thus when all constructs in the grid are laddered one would expect some to have the same superordinates.

Another way of exploring the meaning of a construct is by eliciting increasingly subordinate constructs for each construct in the grid. This is done by pyramiding (Landfield, 1971) which involves asking the subject to tell you more about someone who is X. The reply is another construct subordinate to the first to which the same question is asked. This procedure is applied to both poles of a construct thus producing a kind of pyramid of subordinate constructs.

Both laddering and pyramiding help the investigator to explore the organisation of the construct system beyond the grid. Another technique of interest is that described by Procter and Parry (1978) for exploring the biography of a construct. To do this each construct in the grid is laddered (Hinkle, 1965) until one or more superordinate constructs are produced. The person is then asked to think back to the point in his life when the construct first emerged. Then the construct's ancestor is examined by asking 'From what earlier construct did this one evolve at that time?'. When the earlier construct has been elicited the biography of this one is traced in the same way. They suggest that life experiences associated with the construct should also be discussed.

These are just three methods for examining personal constructs beyond the grid, and there is scope for many more. A point to bear in mind when exploring personal construct systems is that 'There is nothing sacrosanct about the tabular form of the grid' (Thomas, 1979).

Conclusions

In 1955 Kelly presented a method — repertory grid technique — for exploring the essence of his theory — personal constructs.

Since then a variety of grid forms have been developed. This has included the development of a range of elicitation procedures, scoring procedures and methods of analysis. In this chapter I have outlined the basic steps of grid design, administration and analysis. It is important to remember that the repertory grid is a flexible and diverse methodology and not a standardised test with a set procedure. The British Psychological Society (1981) have published a statement on psychological tests. In this statement they describe tests as assessment techniques yielding ratings or scores derived from procedures clearly described in the test manual, and based on adequate standardisation data. Repertory grid technique does not meet these requirements. Whilst there is a manual available (Fransella and Bannister, 1977) this manual, like this chapter, outlines the diversity of the technique. In contrast, a test manual specifies a set or standardised way of administering the test. Unlike tests, grids do not have norms. However, the grid method has formed the basis of a standard clinical test (Bannister and Fransella, 1966) and some clinicians have begun to collect normative data (see, for example, Chapter 12). But such exercises are the exception rather than the rule.

A requirement of a good test is that it is reliable and valid. With there being one way of administering a test reliability and validity can be established. However, for grids the issue is far more complex as there are so many ways of constructing one (for discussions see Fransella and Bannister, 1977; Slater, undated; and Chapter 23).

Repertory grid technique is a flexible instrument appropriate to the investigation and exploration of personal construct systems. The method is not a handy or convenient tool, as administration can be quite a lengthy affair. But they yield valuable data in a variety of contexts, and this is what has made the method so attractive to clinicians and educationalists. After 30 years of existence the method is still growing in popularity.

This chapter has been limited in scope in that the method has been illustrated through the administration of a one-off grid with a single case. Whilst using grids in this way is probably the largest use of the method it is by no means the only use. The scope of the technique is now illustrated throughout the rest of the book.

References

Adams-Webber, J.R. (1979) *Personal Construct Psychology: Concepts and Applications*, Wiley, Chichester

Bannister, D. (1960) 'Conceptual Structure in Thought Disordered Schizophrenics', *Journal of Mental Science, 106,* 1230-49

—— (1965) 'The Rationale and Clinical Relevance of Repertory Grid Technique', *British Journal of Psychiatry,* III, 977-82

—— and Fransella, F. (1966) *Grid Test of Thought Disorder,* Psychological Test Publications, Barnstable

—— and Mair, J.M.M. (1968) *The Evaluation of Personal Constructs,* Academic Press, London

Barton, E.S., Walton, T. and Rowe, D. (1976) 'Using Grid Technique with the Mentally Handicapped' in P. Slater (ed.), *The Measurement of Intrapersonal Space by Grid Technique, vol. 1,* Wiley, Chichester

Beail, N. (1983) 'Equivalence of Grid Forms: A Case Report', *British Journal of Medical Psychology, 56,* 263-4

—— (1984) 'Consensus Grids: What About the Variance?', *British Journal of Medical Psychology, 57,* 193-5

British Psychological Society (1981) 'Psychological Tests: A Statement by the British Psychological Society', British Psychological Society, Leicester

Burton, A.M. (1983) BELLEROPHON, details available from the author, Department of Psychology, University of Nottingham

Everett, B. (1974) *Cluster Analysis,* Heinemann, London

Fransella, F. (1965) 'The Effects of Imposed Rhythm and Certain Aspects of Personality on the Speech of Stutterers', unpublished PhD thesis, University of London

—— and Bannister, D. (1977) *A Manual for Repertory Grid Technique,* Academic Press, London

Higginbotham, P.G. and Bannister, D. (1983) 'The GAB Computer Program for the Analysis of Repertory Grid Data', 2nd edition. Available from D. Bannister, High Royds Hospital, Menston, Ilkley, West Yorkshire

Hinkle, D. (1965) 'The Change of Personal Constructs from the Viewpoint of a Theory of Construct Implications', unpublished PhD thesis, Ohio State University

Honess, T. (1978) 'A Comparison of the Implication and Repertory Grid Techniques', *British Journal of Psychology, 59,* 305-14

Kelly, G.A. (1955) *The Psychology of Personal Constructs, vols. 1 and 2,* Norton, New York

Kelly, J.V. (1964) 'A Program for Processing George Kelly's Repertory Grids on the IBM 1620 Computer', unpublished manuscript, Ohio State University

Landfield, A.W. (1971) *Personal Construct Systems in Psychotherapy,* Rand McNally, Chicago

Leach, C. (1979) *Introduction to Statistics: A Non-parametric Approach for the Social Sciences,* Wiley, Chichester

Nie, N.W., Hull, C.H., Jenkins, J.G., Steinbrenner, K. and Bent, D.H. (1975) *Statistical Package for the Social Sciences,* McGraw-Hill, New York

Oliver, C. (1980) 'Repertory Grid Technique and Mentally Handicapped Children: An Exploratory Study', BSc dissertation, Loughborough, University of Technology

Phillips, J.P.N. (1973) 'The Use and Analysis of Repertory Grids: Discussion' in *Repertory Grid Methods,* The British Psychological Society Mathematical and Statistical Psychology Section, Leicester

Procter, H.G. (1978) 'Personal Construct Theory and the Family: A Theoretical and Methodological Study', PhD thesis, University of Bristol
—— and Parry, G. (1978) 'Constraint and Freedom: The Social Origins of Personal Constructs' in F. Fransella (ed.), *Personal Construct Psychology*, 1977, Academic Press, London
Shaw, M.L.G. (1980) *On Becoming a Personal Scientist*, Academic Press, London
—— and Gaines, B.R. (1981) 'Recent Advances in the Analysis of a Repertory Grid', *British Journal of Medical Psychology, 54*, 307-18
Slater, P. (1964) *The Principal Components of a Repertory Grid*, Vincent Andrew, London
—— (ed.) (1976) *The Measurement of Intrapersonal Space by Grid Technique, vol. 1*, Wiley, Chichester
—— (ed.) (1977) *The Measurement of Intrapersonal Space by Grid Technique, vol. 2*, Wiley, Chichester
—— (undated) 'The Reliability and Significance of a Grid', unpublished manuscript, St George's Hospital Medical School, London
Sneath, P.H.A. and Sokal, R.R. (1973) *Numerical Taxonomy: The Principles and Practice of Numerical Classification*, Freeman, San Francisco
Thomas, L.F. (1979) 'Construct, Reflect and Converse: The Conversational Reconstruction of Social Realities' in P. Stringer and D. Bannister (ed.), *Constructs of Sociality and Individuality*, Academic Press, London
—— and Shaw, M.L.G. (1976) *FOCUS manual*, Centre for the Study of Human Learning, Brunel University
—— and —— (1977) *PEGASUS Manual*, Centre for the Study of Human Learning, Brunel University
Van der Kloot, W. (1981) 'Multidimensional Scaling of Repertory Grid Responses: Two Applications of HOMALS' in H. Bonarius, R. Holland and S. Rosenberg, *Personal Construct Psychology: Recent Advances in Theory and Practice*, Macmillan, London
Wooster, A.D. (1970) 'Formation of Stable and Discrete Concepts of Personality by Normal and Mentally Retarded Boys', *Journal of Mental Subnormality, 16*, 24-8

PART ONE

EXPLORING PERSONAL CONSTRUCT SYSTEMS

Kelly devised repertory grid technique as a method for exploring personal construct systems. Thus, any use of this method is concerned with exploring constructs, so the rest of this book and not just this section has this as its central concern. In this section we focus on how the exploration of personal constructs can provide valuable information in clinical practice and research. In Chapter 2 R.J. Butler provides an up-to-date account on the way grids can be used to explore children's personal constructs in order to understand their difficulties. Brian Stanley (Chapter 3) illustrates how grids can be used to investigate alienation in young offenders. In Chapter 4 Eric Button presents both case material and research findings where grids have been used to investigate the personal constructs of women with anorexia nervosa and obesity. Finally, in Chapter 5, Bernadette O'Sullivan presents some of her research an agoraphobia in which she used grids with the same element titles and supplied constructs to generate group data. Some of the advantages and disadvantages of this procedure are discussed.

2 TOWARDS AN UNDERSTANDING OF CHILDHOOD DIFFICULTIES

R.J. Butler

Kelly (1955) is well known for his suggestion that if you want to know something about someone, you should ask him. In adult-adult conversation this may prove productive; but what happens when we have before us a child?

Our adult-framed questions, rather than enabling us to understand the child, as O'Reilly (1977) suggests, often lead us to a familiar question-and-answer routine which tends to end nowhere. Questions which particularly focus on the 'area of concern' are typically even less productive, being predictably met with 'don't know' responses by the child. It may be the case that the 'area of concern' is meaningful only to the parent or whoever brings the child along to the clinic. The child may be problematic to others but sees himself as easy to understand (Jackson and Bannister, 1985). For the child who does not construe himself as a problem, questions concerning his 'problematic' behaviour will be meaningless. There is no reason why a child should see such an interview as other than irrelevant (Ravenette, 1977). It is as if in terms of Kelly's sociality corollary (Kelly, 1955) the clinician fails to construe the construction processes of the child, and in so doing fails in the search for an understanding of that child.

Are we then to give up asking questions of the child? Are the alternatives any more helpful? Exploring the area of concern with parents who share with the clinician an understanding of the 'problem' is one alternative often offered by behavioural management approaches. Here the child's view is neglected. On the other hand, falling back on traditional methods of assessment, in an endeavour to understand children's behaviour is rejected by Salmon (1976) because such precise information-gathering forces the child to fit predetermined dimensions which may well be irrelevant to the child's particular outlook. For the child the task is often meaningless.

Our attempts at understanding children has to begin with how they view the world in their own terms. For the construct theorist a child is construed as a 'scientist', having theories about his world and himself. His behaviour, though often a puzzle to us, has meaning. Our quest as psychologists is to discover ways of understanding how a child makes sense of his world. The repertory grid is one of a number of ways offered by Personal Construct Theory which lead to an exploration of the subjective world of the child. This chapter hopes to consider ways of using repertory grids with children. Especially for the younger child, modifications to the usual grid procedures (see Fransella and Bannister, 1977) are required.

Salmon (1976) has outlined the major principles in introducing a grid to a child:

(1) We can present the grid, for what it is — a way of trying to understand how the child sees things. We do not have to mask our intentions as we might in using formal assessments.
(2) There are no right or wrong answers, and how one child responds will not necessarily be the same as how others might respond.
(3) Most children find the tasks asked of them to be interesting and unusual. If we are sensitive in our design, the child should not be faced with a task beyond his capability. He may have to think long and hard, or consider issues he previously gave little thought to, but generally where the question is relevant, a child tackles it with enthusiasm and in the end, often with some surprise over the furtherance of his awareness.

Selecting Elements

Two factors are relevant: the child's age or his ability to deal with verbal labels, and the question(s) we are attempting to explore. As elements we may choose:

People
Where we might be interested in the child's construing of interpersonal relationships, elements might include parents, siblings, other relatives or peers. We might be interested to see how the child construes himself amongst his contemporaries and use roles such as friend, someone I dislike, someone I sit next to in class, a popular figure, someone good at sport, someone who

gets into trouble and so on. Social roles such as teacher, nurse, therapist, and doctor would also be valid where interest is focused on the child's construing of particular social environments.

It is worth noting that children's constructs about people may have restricted ranges of application. Family members, for example, may be construed in a completely different way from peers or figures in a school context, so care should be taken to ensure that a child is not asked to apply a construct to the sort of element he would not normally use it on.

Situations

These may be events or relationships. Significant events for a child who might have, for example, problems in reading, could be doing homework, reading in class, doing maths, interfering with other's work, playing out, starting a fight and so on. Events have a temporal nature so where we might hope to investigate how a child, for example, construes his difficulties in attending school, elements could be: getting ready for school; leaving the house; walking to school; arriving at school; waiting for the bell; registration; being in assembly; doing classwork. Relationships can take the form of the child's self in relation to significant others. For example, being with mum; being with dad; being away from mum; being with my best friend and so on.

Self

For children these tend to take the form of 'self' and 'ideal', either in terms of a person labelled by the child as most like he would like to be, or more generally a title 'how I'd like to be'. Mancini, Pallini and Donato (in press) in studying the development of self-knowledge, supplied 14 elements concerned with self-construing to children as young as 8. These included as well as 'like I am', and 'like I would like to be', 'like others see me' and 'like I was three years ago'. Further self elements may arise from other expectations of the child, e.g. 'how mum expects me to be', 'how teachers think I should be'.

For younger children, perhaps below the age of 7 or 8, where verbally presented labels may be too abstract, concrete material then proves a necessity. Elements can be represented by models (where the child selects from a range, those he finds appropriate), pictures, photographs or the child's own sketches of people and situations. As Salmon (1976) suggests, young children will more readily make judgements where elements can be physically moved about, allowing a visual representation of the child's choices of element allotment.

Eliciting Constructs

Kelly's triadic method proves a difficult conceptual task for most children, and experiments by Ravenette (1968) and Salmon (1967) suggest it may do less than justice to the repertoire of constructs possessed by young children. The triadic comparison tends not to produce psychological constructs although these can be demonstrated, by other approaches, to exist in the child's construct system. We have to turn to other methods we can more fruitfully use in our attempts to discover the child's construing.

Descriptive Exercises

Asking a child to tell us something about significant people in his life or the elements in the grid, gives an idea of the constructs he is using to establish meaning. These descriptions may be taped, or dictated to the therapist. Salmon (1976) discussed how during conversation with a child we need to establish the real meaning of a distinction made by a child who may use a word very differently from how an adult may use it. Salmon advised using requests such as 'Tell me a bit more about that', and questions such as 'How would you know if a thing was . . . ?' to explore the child's meaning. Jackson and Bannister (1985) asked children to write descriptions of themselves as if written by someone who knew them well, so it was in the third person, and began, for example, 'Susan Smith is . . .'. Care should be taken to ensure the child does not construe such exercises as similar to tests they might be presented with at school.

Contrasting Exercises

Wolff and Barlow (1979) used dyadic comparisons where a child is presented with pairs of elements and asked to mention all the differences that can be seen between the two elements. Different pairs of elements are next selected and the procedure repeated. Constructs may also be elicited by asking a child to discover similarities between two elements. For example, a child may say that a best friend and himself both play good tricks on others. We then seek the other pole of the construct with requests such as 'Tell me what kids who don't play good tricks on others are like', or questions such as 'How would you describe someone who didn't play good tricks on others?' The responses might be 'doesn't play tricks', 'they're boring' or 'they play naughty tricks'. In this way we begin to establish dimensions of meaning for a child.

Categorisation

With a young child or one who finds verbal expression difficult we might encourage the sorting of elements into groups, of 'those which go together', and having formed groups we ask the child to try and find a way of describing the groups. This is then repeated with a new set of groups until the child cannot find new classifications. As Salmon (1976) suggests, this may result in an 'untidy' elicitation as a child may produce a number of groups in any one sorting whilst using several different constructs simultaneously. Asking a child to divide the elements into one of only two groups, to then label may sharpen up the method.

Self-evaluation

This technique explores how a child believes he is understood by others. Taking the elements as people we ask the child 'Who do you think knows or understands you best?' If, for instance, he should say his mother, our line of questioning would go, 'Let's say I didn't know you at all. If I were to meet your mother and I asked her to describe you, what might she say? What three things do you think your mother would say about you?' Invited to give three descriptions, even the most tentative of children give at least one. The procedure is repeated for other elements or people the child brings to the discussion. A child may also be asked the same question of someone he dislikes, a pet, or of himself, e.g. 'If I were to meet you for the first time and knew nothing at all about you, what three things might you tell me about yourself'.

For Christine, a girl of 10 referred by an educational psychologist because of preoccupations over her sister's death, self-evaluation was chosen at our initial interview as a means of both understanding her construing and her perceptions of how she thought she was seen by others. The following are a selection of her responses:

Mum   1. has had many shades of hair
          2. she calls me an automatic dishwasher which has broken down
          3. doesn't smile often

Dad   1. I wear glasses
          2. I like being on my own

Friend   1. likes to play with me
          2. very clever
          3. doing well at school

Teacher 1. there are only a couple of other girls as clever
          2. shy at times
          3. thinks about things a lot

Self   1. like listening to music
          2. watch TV on my own. I don't like horror films
          3. like ice cream

Sister (who had died of *spina bifida* before Christine herself was born)
          1. like her to be down here, but she'd be in pain
          2. think I might have all the diseases she had
          3. I'd like to be with her but I'd like the rest of my family to be with me

From this, constructs were apparent. Christine gave the contrast poles e.g.

very clever	—	stupid
feels shy	—	brave
thinks about things a lot	—	doesn't think
plays on own	—	plays with friends

Elements in addition to self, friends, disliked individuals, someone who wasn't shy and so forth, included 'what my sister might have been like'. The grid subsequently showed Christine had idealised her sister ('how I'd like to be' and 'what my sister might have been like' were very highly correlated).

Christine found the exercise illuminating, and for the first time was able to find a way of discussing her sister through which her illness, death and loss to the family became meaningful. Christine found her preoccupation lessened, and started to work hard at school as a result.

Portrait Gallery

This is a technique of Ravenette's (1980) for studying the elaboration of feelings. It produces a wealth of material concerning the child's sense of experience and will lead to the elicitation of constructs.

We start with two simple drawings, depicting a happy and a sad face. We begin by asking the child, 'Which is the happy face?', which is then labelled. Next, the child is invited to tell of three reasons why the face might be happy. Following this response we move to the second face and ask in comparison with the first face, 'What could this face be?' This is labelled accordingly (most children will say 'sad') and the child is asked for three reasons again as to why the face might be sad. A face outline, without details, is then drawn and the child asked, 'We have drawn a happy face and a sad face. What else could a face be?' For example, 'frightened' might be a response and it is so labelled. The child is asked to fill in the details: 'Can you draw a frightened face?', for which a further three reasons why a face might be frightened are sought. Now a further face outline is drawn and the child asked, 'That face was frightened, but if it wasn't frightened what could it be?' 'Brave' might be a reply, so the child is encouraged to draw this in the face outline and asked for three reasons as to why the face might be brave. This form of drawing and questioning is continued until the child can think of no other faces. Faces pertaining to the child's problem, or 'like you' can be supplied. Constructs are evident directly by the child's contrasts (e.g. frightened — brave) and also through examination of the underlying reasons.

Roland, a 7½-year-old boy diagnosed as having Asperger's syndrome (Wing, 1981), was introduced to the Portrait Gallery. The following is a sample of his replies:

happy	*sad*
1. plays with his dad's calculator	1. doesn't learn sums
2. learns sums	2. doesn't learn anything
3. learns problems	3. has no toys

naughty
(drawn with a slight smile)
1. got into trouble and his mum would be cross
2. swears and acts silly
3. if he nagged his mum for a calculator

normal
(elicited as a contrast)
1. gets what he wants
2. not naughty
3. doesn't act silly

upset
1. if someone's awful to him
2. smacked for being naughty
3. being bullied

no contrast elicited

Constructs drawn from this included:

acts silly	—	doesn't act silly
gets bullied	—	sticks up for himself
learns problems	—	doesn't learn anything

Supplying Constructs

There are circumstances where we may offer predetermined constructs to a child. This may arise:

(1) where we wish to understand a particular area of a child's construct system. Ravenette (1977) describes the case of a 15-year-old boy where eight prescribed constructs were used in a grid to explore his construing of family and peers. Supplied constructs included 'least likely to have friends — most likely to have friends', 'most likely to understand other boys — least likely to understand other boys', and 'mother would choose him to be like — mother would not choose him to be like'.

(2) in research where comparisons between the way children construe aspects of their experience are examined. Jackson and Bannister (1985) in comparing the development of self-construing across age, sex and whether they were problematic to the teacher, supplied eight constructs: good tempered, clever, like I'd like to be as a person, easily frightened, like I am as a person, hard to understand, lazy, and like I used to be as a person.

Supplying constructs in this way seems to depart form Kelly's principle that in grids we should use the person's own dimension of meaning. However, as Bannister and Mair (1968) point out, in a sense we cannot provide constructs, we are only able to provide verbal labels, to which the child attaches his own construct.

Precautions need to be taken however, when we opt to supply constructs:

(1) we should ensure the dimension is meaningful for the child. This involves selecting constructs which are part of the child's 'sub-cultural language system' (Jackson and Bannister, 1985). We can check this by way of asking the child if he knows anybody who would be described by either or both poles of the construct. If he cannot, then the construct may not have a focus of convenience for the child. A second check can be made on the applicability of the verbal label. Children often use a different vocabulary from adults, so for example adults often describe encopresis in terms of 'soiling', yet children will use words such as 'dirties', 'messes', 'poos' or 'big jobs'. Verbal labels should be chosen for familiarity to the child.

(2) both poles of the construct should be supplied, as Wooster (1970) demonstrated that children do not necessarily attribute a conventionally agreed opposite to a given verbal label. Presenting one pole only leaves the child free to provide the opposite pole, and therefore possibly transforming the construct into something quite different from what we had in mind. Asking children to make judgements on the construct 'clever' for example, without providing its opposite pole leaves us uninformed as to whether the child discriminated in terms of 'intelligence', 'cheekiness' or some other dimension.

Element Allotment

We arrive now at the point where the child is asked to distribute elements along constructs. There are basically three forms this can take, the choice largely, although not exclusively, determined by the child's age. The younger the child, the simpler should be the sorting task, is the general rule.

Categorisation

The child is asked to judge each element as belonging to one pole, to the contrast pole or to neither. Salmon (1976) suggests choosing the latter category can mean several things; uncertainty, an intermediate position between the poles or that the element is outside the range of convenience of the construct. Which of these alternatives is the case can usually be discovered by asking the child as he makes the categorisation.

Ranking

For children 7 and over, rank ordering elements is usually within the child's capacity. Salmon (1976) suggests a maximum of eight elements for the young child, increasing up to ten for children 10 years and older. Ranking elements from those most readily subsumed under the emergent pole of the construct (Fransella and Bannister 1977) is fine for some children. Others, however, find difficulty in allotting particularly the last remaining elements. Ravenette's (1968) modification usually overcomes this. He invites children to select the elements in turn, first from the emergent pole, e.g. 'Who would you consider, out of all the people, to be the most kind?', followed by selection of the contrast pole, e.g. 'Who would you consider the most mean?' By removing those elements already selected, selection from alternative poles of the construct in this way ensures the child is constantly aware of the dimension along which judgements are made.

Rating

For children there are three considerations to make in using rating:

(1) the size of the scale: the younger the child, the fewer the number of rating categories is the general rule. A three or five-point scale is sufficient for children under 10.

(2) the use of verbal labels to define points along the scale, rather or in addition to numbers. A 'don't know' category should also be available for the child. Where numbers alone are used, it is advisable to check occasionally with the child that he is judging between the contrast poles, e.g. 'So mum is kind?', 'Dad is not as kind as mum then?' etc.

(3) physical allotment of the elements along the construct is often preferable for young children. This can be made available to the child in a number of ways. The construct can be drawn on a card with the poles labelled. The child would then be free to

place the elements (objects, pictures, etc.) spatially along the construct as he so wishes. Alternatively, the child could be asked to mark the construct where he believes the element to be judged. This can lead to a rating or ranking score. An element would be rated as its position on an equally divided scale, a rank on its position in relation to all other elements along the scale. For younger children, again, the points along the construct can be represented by boxes, verbally labelled, into which the child can place elements.

The procedures so far have challenged the child to allot elements along constructs according to their judgements of the elements, e.g. 'who's the most kind?' (rank) 'where would your best friend be along the dimension from clever to stupid?' (rate).

Self-evaluation grids on the other hand ask a different question: How does a child think he would be judged by the elements? It is a way of understanding how a child believes himself to be seen by others.

Mark, an 8-year-old boy with encopresis did a self-evaluation grid after constructs had been elicited using the self-evaluation method. He was invited to place the elements (written on cards) along the construct, in a way which represented how he imagined they thought of him. The following is a sample of Mark's grid:

	1	2	3	4	5	6	7	
HAPPY	brother friend self therapist	cousin			mum	teacher	dad	SAD
NAUGHTY		mum			teacher	cousin	dad brother friend self therapist	GOOD
KIND	friend dad self therapist	brother cousin teacher					mum	UNKIND
POOS HIS-SELF	mum dad brother therapist						self teacher friend cousin	DOESN'T POO HIS SELF

Grid Analysis

Analysing children's grids requires the same principles as operate for adult's grids. This may involve anything from inspection of the 'raw' data to using computer programs for obtaining principal component analysis. Two case studies will be discussed to demonstrate how grids might be used in a clinical setting.

Shirley

Shirley, a girl of 12, was referred by her GP because of anxieties about going to school. This consisted of abdominal pain and sleepless nights prior to school days. She would discuss the difficulty with no one, and if a conversation turned to the subject of school, Shirley became quiet and tearful.

Both parents accompanied Shirley to the first session. She was sullen and withdrawn, her mother demonstrative and eager to answer for the child, whilst father acted as support for mother. What emerged from our initial discussion was the parents saw the focus of concern as within school, e.g. that Shirley wanted to avoid school because of fears she might make errors in class and with her homework. Shirley's view was difficult to assimilate because of her tearfulness and unwillingness to talk.

At our next session I saw Shirley on her own, and suggested a grid as a way of helping us understand how she saw what was troubling her. She agreed once the procedure was explained to her, and she saw it did not require her to engage in extensive verbal dialogue. I asked her to write down on separate cards those situations pertaining to school she found most difficult. These were Shirley's *elicited elements*:

1. Asking a question in class
2. Being at school
3. Doing homework
4. Asking for help in a lesson
5. Going to school

I then suggested I wrote some situations on cards which she could comment on if she liked. These were *supplied elements*:

6. A trip to the dentist (This was included as an anchor element, being assumed to be an anxiety provoking situation.

This was familiar to Shirley, being a regular attender at the dentist.)
7. Being with friends (Shirley had a few friends whom she felt quite possessive about.)
8. Being on my own (seven and eight were supplied so that we could explore how Shirley construed herself in relation to her peers, and examine the hypothesis that anxieties about school might be related to social withdrawal.)

The final three elements were supplied to explore another side of attending school, i.e. leaving home. Some of mother's earlier comments had suggested a 'clinginess' about Shirley's behaviour.

9. Being with Mum
10. Being with Dad
11. Being away from Mum

Shirley accepted these elements, and between appointments I asked if she could write down three things about each element. She arrived at the next appointment with a wealth of information, having done her 'homework'. From this we were able to *elicit constructs*. Common themes were abstracted and the contrast poles sought.

Happy	—	Unhappy (this was supplied and included as a buffer construct)
Makes me worry	—	Don't worry
Nervous	—	Feel alright
I enjoy	—	I don't enjoy
Feel different from others	—	Feel the same as others
Avoid	—	Don't avoid
Successful	—	Unsuccessful
Feel uncomfortable	—	Feel at ease
Feel like crying	—	Don't feel like crying
Self-conscious	—	Not self-conscious

Shirley was asked to *rank* the elements along each construct in turn. The grid was then analysed using Slater's INGRID program for principal component analysis (Slater, 1977). Figure 2.1 shows the elements plotted in component space.

Figure 2.1: Principal Component Analysis: Shirley

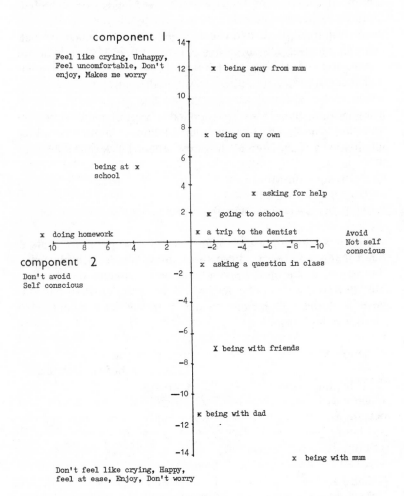

Component 1 seems to describe Shirley's anxieties in terms of her relationships. She feels at her best when with parents, particularly Mum and at her worst when away from Mum. This issue of 'attachment' and the hypothesis that Shirley's anxieties over school were to do with separation from parents, was discussed with Shirley and her parents, who came to see it as acceptable. When we tried to explore why it was an issue for Shirley at the present time, a history of separation emerged. Shirley's father had worked away from home for a number of years when Shirley had been a little girl. He was now contemplating employment again overseas, which would mean leaving the family for long periods. In addition, Shirley's mother had recently taken up politics and become a county councillor, which meant spending an increasingly greater amount of time away from Shirley. It was noticeable that Shirley's stomach aches and sleeplessness was at its most severe on the eve her mother left home for a two-day conference. For Shirley then her anxieties over going to school appeared to revolve around her concerns over separation from her parents. Therapy then became an issue of developing peer-group attachments coupled with a re-framing of her relationship with parents along a dimension of independence.

Component 2 in Figure 2.1 is concerned with avoidance. Shirley appears to describe events to do with school along this dimension. Avoidance is coupled with not being self-conscious. Shirley strives to act in a way which will not draw attention to herself. Within the expectation and structure of school culture Shirley is able to survive adequately. So long as she does her homework and does not ask for help in class she does not draw attention to herself.

Jane

Jane, a girl of 11, was referred by her GP. Her mother had become concerned over letters the school were sending, describing Jane's behaviour in school as aggressive and asocial. Jane is an only child of a one-parent family, her father having died when she was 4 years old. Jane discussed her school life in a relaxed and open way. She had never felt happy at school, having few friends and not being stretched academically. She had won a scholarship at 11 to attend an all-girls independent school in the same town, and soon discovered a similar pattern of concern. Jane found the curriculum inflexible and unstimulating, failed to form stable friendships and remained socially isolated.

The construction of a grid began with *eliciting* those individuals Jane believed knew her well. An *evaluation* was then undertaken where Jane was invited to talk about how she imagined the individuals might describe her. For example, Jane thought Eleanor (described as a best friend from her previous school) would describe her as restless, friendly and a good laugh. She described herself as a good worker, sensible and responsible. Contrast poles were sought for these descriptions forming *constructs*. These were:

sensible	—	silly/messes around
responsible	—	irresponsible
restless	—	lazy
good worker	—	doesn't pay any notice
good laugh	—	boring
naughty	—	does what she's told
interesting	—	boring
friendly	—	aggressive
cheeky	—	sensible
never stops talking	—	never talks

Elements from the grid included her best friend (from previous school), a girl she met at Guides, a girl from her present school who had recently tried to include her in things, someone she disliked, and her uncle (aged 16), all of whom were *elicited* during evaluation.

Jane was invited to think of someone who seemed to enjoy school. She named two girls, one who was very good at classwork, another who was very popular. Both were included. Five further elements were supplied. These were:

As I am at school
As I am when not at school
How I'd like to be
What teachers expect me to be like
What mum expects me to be like

The elements were *rated* on the constructs using a seven-point scale, an exercise Jane enjoyed and completed with no difficulty. The grid was analysed using Higginbotham's and Bannister's GAB program (1983), and plotted according to Bannister's cluster method.

Figure 2.2: Construct Analysis: Jane

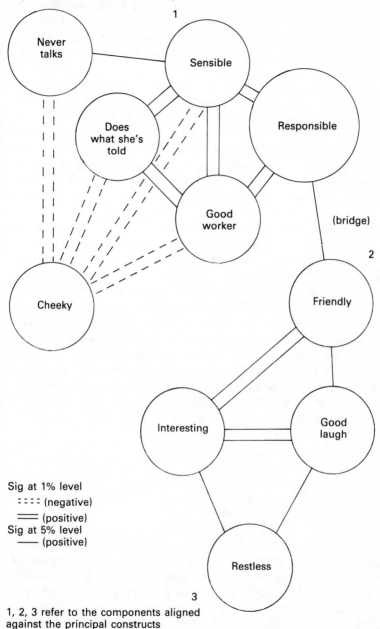

Figure 2.2 shows Jane to have two major constructions sub-systems linked by the construct responsible — irresponsible. In addition, Figure 2.3 suggests Jane sees herself as responsible, which is how she would like to be and what others expect of her. Being responsible would seem to be central in Jane's core role construing.

Examining the way Jane has allotted elements to the constructs indicates there is agreement in her ideal and what teacher's expect of her on the construct good worker — doesn't pay any notice. However, to achieve her ideal of being a good worker would imply being sensible, does what she's told, is not cheeky and indirectly never talks (Fig. 2.2). This is also what Jane feels her teachers and mother would expect of her, but is not how she sees herself or how she would like to be. Jane is a nonconformist. Becoming a good worker would imply potential threat to her core role construing.

Although Jane is capable of doing well at school, and ideally would like to, because teachers expect this of her, she reacts against it. A similar pattern emerges in cluster 2, where Jane perceives she would ideally like to be more friendly, but recognises that this is what teachers and mother expect of her. To remain reactionary then means acting more 'aggressively', and thus Jane remains without many friends. Jane's concern over her school work and lack of social relationships are a result of her need to be seen as nonconforming. Jane accepted this hypothesis. She wanted to be a good worker and friendly, but did not want to be seen as doing what teachers in particular expected of her. Nonconforming for Jane also avoided being called a 'creep' by her contemporaries.

Conclusions

Investigations of childhood difficulties take a number of forms. Some inhibit or deny the child expression, others assume or impose meaning on the child's behaviour through observation or assessment. Personal Construct Theory offers a way of understanding how the child establishes meaning on his world. The repertory grid allows us to explore how the child construes his difficulties and problems. Understanding a child's construing

Figure 2.3: Jane: Allotment of Supplied Elements on Constructs

```
                              Ratings
                     1   2   3   4   5   6   7

                    XI
                    TM  O
2. Responsible      ├────────────────────────────┤  Irresponsible

                    TM  X   O   I
1. Sensible         ├────────────────────────────┤  Silly/messes around

                    TI  M   X   O
4. Good worker      ├────────────────────────────┤  Doesn't pay any notice

                    TM      O   I   X
6. Does what        ├────────────────────────────┤  Naughty
   she's told

                        XIO             M   T
9. Cheeky           ├────────────────────────────┤  Sensible

                        T   M       I   X   O
10. Never talks     ├────────────────────────────┤  Never stops talking

                    TM  I   O   X
8. Friendly         ├────────────────────────────┤  Aggressive

                    I   MO  X   T
7. Interesting      ├────────────────────────────┤  Boring

                    IO  M   X       T
5. Good laugh       ├────────────────────────────┤  Boring

                    X       MO  TI
3. Restless         ├────────────────────────────┤  Lazy
```

X As I am at school
O As I am when not at school
I Ideal (how I'd like to be)
T What teachers expect me to be like
M What mum expects me to be like

forms the beginning of psychotherapy. As Kelly (1955) said of the therapist-client situation

> so that it can be a genuinely cooperative effort, each must try to understand what the other is proposing and each must do what he can to help the other understand what he himself is ready to try next. They formulate hypotheses jointly.

References

Bannister, D. and Mair, J.M.M. (1968) *The Evaluation of Personal Constructs*, Academic Press, London

Fransella, F. and Bannister, D. (1977) *A Manual for Repertory Grid Technique*, Academic Press, London

Higginbotham, P. and Bannister, D. (1983) *The GAB Computer Program for the Analysis of Repertory Grid Data*, available from D. Bannister, High Royds Hospital, Menston, Ilkley, W. Yorks

Jackson, S.R. and Bannister, D. (1985) 'Growing into Self' in D. Bannister (ed.), *Issues and Approaches in Personal Construct Theory*, Academic Press, London

Kelly, G.A. (1955) *The Psychology of Personal Constructs, vols I and II*, Norton, New York

Mancini, F., Pallini, S. and Donato, A. Personal Communication, 'Development of Some Aspects of Self-knowledge: A Kellyian Study'

O'Reilly, J. (1977) 'The Interplay Between Mothers and Their Children: a Construct Theory View' in D. Bannister (ed.), *New Perspectives in Personal Construct Theory*, Academic Press, London

Ravenette, A.T. (1968) 'The Situations Grid: A Further Development in Grid Technique with Children', unpublished manuscript, London Borough of Newham

—— (1977) 'Personal Construct Theory: an Approach to the Psychological Investigation of Children and Young People' in D. Bannister (ed.), *New Perspectives in Personal Construct Theory*, Academic Press, London

—— (1980) 'The Exploration of Consciousness: Personal Construct Intervention With Children' in A.W. Landfield and L.M. Leitner (eds), *Personal Construct Psychology Psychotherapy and Personality*, Wiley, Chichester

Salmon, P. (1967) 'The Social Values and Conformity Behaviour of Primary Schoolboys in Relation to Maternal Attitude', unpublished thesis, University of London

—— (1976) 'Grid Measures with Child Subjects' in P. Slater (ed.), *The Measurement of Intrapersonal Space by Grid Techniques, vol. 1*, Wiley, Chichester

Slater, P. (1977) *The Measurement of Intrapersonal Space, vol. 2*, Wiley Chichester

Wing, L. (1981) 'Asperger's Syndrome: a Clinical Account', *Psychological Medicine, 11*, 115-29

Wolff, S. and Barlow, A. (1979) 'Schizoid Personality in Childhood: A Comparative Study of Schizoid, Autistic and Normal Children', *J. Child Psychol. Psychiat., 20*, 29-46

Wooster, A.D. (1970) 'The Pragmatic Meaning of Relational Terms', *Primary Mathematics, 8(3)*, 137-45

3 ALIENATION IN YOUNG OFFENDERS

Brian Stanley

Alienation and Delinquency

Studies of delinquency have traditionally polarised between the empirical investigations of psychology based on personality theory, and the theoretical formulations of sociology based on discussions of social and cultural forces. Taylor (1968) has argued for the importance of both perspectives in contributing to our understanding of the problem, and has suggested that this polarity may be bridged if social scientists begin to use interpretative concepts which are common to both levels of analysis. According to Taylor, the concept having the potential to elucidate the widest range of delinquency phenomena is 'alienation'.

This concept has been used extensively throughout the social sciences to describe patterns of social relations. In psychological terms, however, it is best thought of as describing clusters of related attitudes concerning the self and the social environment. These attitudes are commonly described in one of two ways: *social alienation*, or feelings of estrangement which may be experienced in relation to other people, particularly significant others; and *self-alienation*, or feelings of separation which can occur between aspects of one's identity, particularly actual self and ideal self (see King (1968), for example). Clearly, this distinction can never be completely intact whilst individuals continue to remain part of a social milieu. It is, however, a convenient distinction to draw if only on the grounds of clinical utility.

Alienated Construing in Young Offenders

Several studies have tried to examine the nature of alienated construing in young offenders. For example, Hayden, Nashby and Davids (1977) demonstrated that a group of maladjusted

47

boys had poorly differentiated interpersonal construct systems which impaired their social adjustment. Bhagat and Fraser (1970) found that a group of young Scottish offenders evaluated each of a variety of concepts (e.g. self, ideal self, mother, father etc.) more negatively than did a control group, thus demonstrating 'an adverse view of self and environs'.

In a study of thirty-nine delinquent boys, Noble (1971) found both forms of alienation to be significantly more pronounced than for a control group. The delinquent boys appeared to lack suitable male identification figures, perceiving themselves as being less like their fathers and best friends and, indeed, wishing to be even less like such figures. More recently, Miller and Treacher (1981) replicated Noble's finding, and in a further study found that a group of delinquent boys perceived significant adults to be less adequate role models than did a control group. The delinquent group saw themselves as being more like their significant adults at present, although, as in Noble's study, they wished eventually to be less like them.

Noble additionally found that the delinquent group experienced a greater actual/ideal self-discrepancy than did the control group. Such self-alienation was also the subject of a later analysis of adolescent car theft by Kelly and Taylor (1981), who hypothesised that successful thefts served to reduce the driver's actual/ideal self-discrepancy but to increase that of his passenger.

The broad conclusion to be drawn from these few studies is to support the view that young offenders do appear to experience difficulties characterised by self and/or social alienation. However, two problems remain for the clinician or educationalist who wishes to apply such findings to the individual case: how should we operationally define both self and social alienation and, having defined them, how can we measure change which may result from therapeutic initiatives?

In another context, Makhlouf-Norris has developed several operational definitions of alienated construing, which also have implications for the measurement of change (Makhlouf-Norris and Jones, 1971). These definitions are derived from a self-identity plot of elements which we shall now describe.

Construction of a Self-identity Plot

The self-identity plot (see Norris and Makhlouf-Norris, 1976) is constructed in the following manner:

(1) A representative pool of elements is formed to elicit relevant constructs using the method of self-identification (Kelly, 1955, p. 219). This method is the basic triadic procedure, except that each presentation of elements always contains 'actual self' as one of the three elements to be construed.

(2) Having elicited sufficient constructs, the elements are then rated on a semantic differential-type scale from 1 to 7.

(3) The resulting matrix (constructs × element ratings) is then subjected to a form of principal components analysis (INGRID) devised by Slater (1972).

The advantage of this analysis is that the similarities between elements or constructs can be assessed precisely. In the representation that is built up of the person's construct system, the elements diverge outwards from a central point, and the actual distance of each can be measured and compared to the overall 'expected distance' between two random elements. These ratios of actual/expected distances are calculated by INGRID and printed out as 'distances between elements'.

The element ratios have a minimum of 0, a mean of 1, and rarely exceed 2. Thus, a pair of elements with a distance close to 0 are construed as virtually identical. Conversely, two elements separated by a distance approaching 2 are construed as being unlike each other. Elements having a distance score close to 1 are essentially unrelated to each other.

(4) In order to examine the degree of alienation perceived by an individual, two axes are drawn using actual self (abscissa) and ideal self (ordinate), each having a range of 0 to 2. The remaining elements are plotted against these two axes using their distance scores on each as co-ordinates.

(5) A fifth central area is also identified between the co-ordinates 0.8 and 1.2 on each axis. This represents the area of independence which surrounds 1. Elements which fall into this area are essentially unrelated to actual/ideal self, as opposed to being either like or unlike them. (Although this area was originally chosen arbitrarily by Makhlouf-Norris, a later study by Norris and Makhlouf-Norris (1976) demonstrated that 92 per cent of randomly derived element distances fell into this area.)

(6) For self-alienation, the separation between actual self (AS) and ideal self (IS) is greater than 1.2, and no more than two non-self elements are further away from ideal self. For social alienation, the entire area within a distance of 0.8 from either self

contains a maximum of two other non-self elements.

We shall now briefly present two examples which may serve to illustrate the clinical utility of the above procedure when employed with young offenders.

Example 1: Self-alienation

Peter was admitted to the Young Offenders' Unit of a northern psychiatric hospital, having assaulted the warden of a local hostel. He had been resident there as a result of dozens of bogus self-referrals to hospital casualty departments requiring overnight stays in hospital. Peter considered his parents to be the main victims of his activities insofar as he was constantly letting them down. The picture presented by his Probation Officer was, however, of a rather disinterested uncaring family who were unaffected by Peter's actions.

On admission Peter completed a repertory grid to construct a self-identity plot. The following elements were agreed upon: father (1); mother (2); probation officer (3); people in my neighbourhood (4); liked friend (5); lads on the unit(6); staff on the unit (7); me as I am now (8); me as I would like to be (9); me as other people see me (10); me as I pretend to other people (11); hostel warden (12).

The following constructs were elicited:

A. explains things properly/doesn't explain things properly
B. understands me/doesn't understand me
C. in trouble/stays out of trouble
D. rash/cool headed
E. loves me/doesn't love me
F. can talk to/can't talk to
G. can control himself/can't control himself
H. quiet/argumentative
I. won't speak his mind/nothing to lose
J. knows himself/mixed up
K. same wavelength/doesn't understand

Most constructs loaded on the first few components (Component I = 62.68%; Component II = 20.03%; Component III = 5.90%; Component IV = 3.43%) which represents a rather undifferentiated construct system as discussed by Hayden *et al.* (1977). This could be an artifact of the element pool from which the constructs were elicited, as this predominantly reflects an opposition of self and authority. It is, nevertheless, highly representative of Peter's social world at that time.

A self-identity plot was constructed from the element distances (Figure 3.1).

Figure 3.1: Peter: Self-identity, Plot I

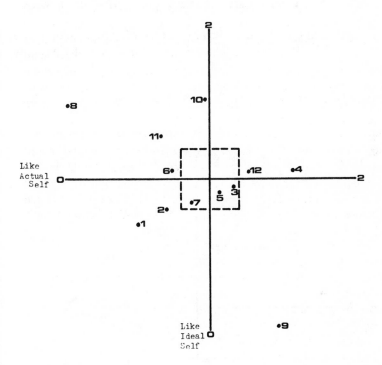

This plot conforms to our definition of self-alienation in that the actual/ideal self distance is greater than 1.2 (i.e. 1.483) and no more than two other elements are further away from the ideal self (i.e. social self (10)).

For Peter, the link between actual and ideal self seems to be provided by his parents (1,2). This partly corresponds to Miller and Treacher's (1981) finding that current significant adults are perceived as similar to actual self. However, unlike Miller's and Treacher's subjects, Peter also perceived his parents as identification figures, judging by their proximity to ideal self. His social self (10) is clearly an unsatisfactory role for him: it is unlike his ideal self (9), indifferent to his actual self (8) and corresponds closely to his false self (11). Apart from the lads on the unit (6) the remaining elements are either unlike him (12,4) or indifferent figures (3,5,7).

Further appreciation of Peter's degree of self-alienation may be gained by substituting false self (11) for ideal self (9) as the

Figure 3.2: Peter: Actual Self/False Self, Plot I

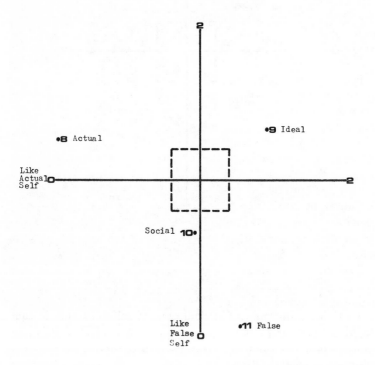

ordinate. The justification for this derives from Winnicott's (1965) description of self-alienation as a split between 'true self' and 'false self'. False self, he suggests, is built up on the basis of compliance and, when treated as genuine by either the individual or the social environment, the result is a growing sense of futility and despair. If we now plot Peter's self-elements against actual and false self it is clear that his self-presentation in social relationships is largely a façade, and one which he construes as far from ideal (Figure 3.2).

This situation constituted the main treatment goal during Peter's stay on the unit. During this time both self and observer behaviour-rating scales (Jesness, 1984) demonstrated Peter's gradual improvement in communication, self-control, rapport and self-confidence.

Nine months after the first grid a second was completed using the same elements and constructs. The correlation between the two grids was 0.52 (using Slater's (1968) DELTA program), which suggests some degree of change. Most of the change was accounted for by changes in Peter's use of certain constructs whose emergent poles were: can talk to; knows himself; explains things properly; understands me. In addition, there were changes in the rankings of the following elements: father (1); mother (2); liked friend (5); staff on unit (7); me as I am now (8); me as I would like to be (9); me as I pretend to other people (11).

The second self-identity plot (see Figure 3.3) shows a reduction in the degree of self-alienation in that the actual/ideal distance is less than 1.2 (i.e. 0.912). Peter's parents (1,2) now occupy less prominent roles in his life with new role models beginning to emerge in his friend and the unit staff (5,7). His social self (10) is still unlike his ideal self but is now closer to actual self. False self (11) is now more differentiated from actual self.

The plot of actual/false self (Figure 3.4) demonstrates that Peter's ideal self and social self are far more closely related to actual self than before and less influenced by false self.

Example 2: Social Alienation

David was admitted to the Young Offenders Unit after having assaulted a young girl and been found stealing underwear from clothes lines. He was very unwilling to discuss these offences, and remained virtually mute towards staff members for several

Figure 3.3: Peter: Self-identity, Plot II

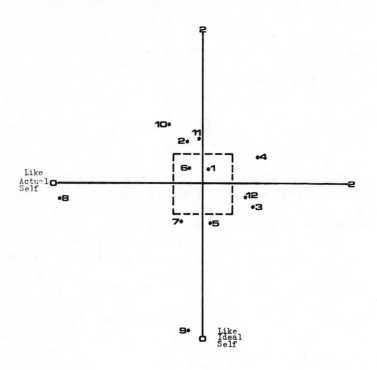

months. The Probation Officer reported that David's family were greatly disturbed by what had happened and were anxious to help if possible.

The following elements were used to elicit David's grid: father (1); mother (2); lads on the unit (3); staff on the unit (4); people in my neighbourhood (5); me as I am now (6); me as I would like to be (7); me as other people see me (8); me as I pretend to other people (9); brother (10); sister (11); liked uncle (12).

The following constructs were elicited:

A. not bothered what I do/tries to make me do things
B. argue with/don't argue with
C. tries to cover things up/doesn't need to cover things up

Figure 3.4: Peter: Actual Self/False Self, Plot II

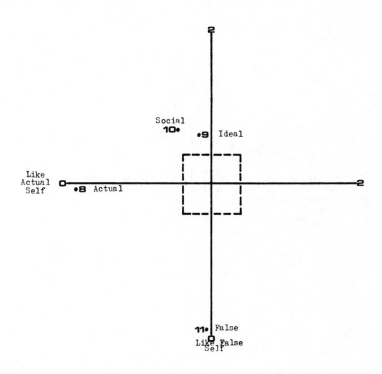

D. satisfied/not satisfied
E. does what he or she wants to do/has to conform
F. makes demands on me/doesn't make demands
G. fairly easy going/difficult to get on with
H. well-mannered/bad-mannered

When David's grid was analysed using INGRID, Component I was found to account for 23.31 per cent of the variance; Component II accounted for 20.19 per cent; Component III accounted for 17.16 per cent; and Component IV accounted for 12.44 per cent.

A self-identity plot was drawn up from the element distances, and is shown in Figure 3.5.

Figure 3.5: David: Self-identity, Plot I

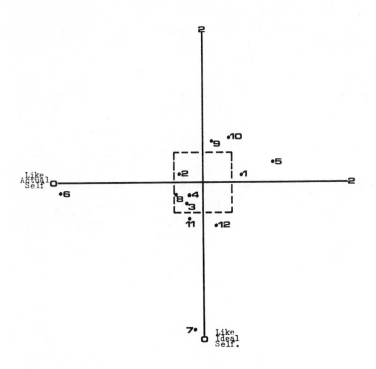

This distribution of elements is characteristic of our definition of social alienation as the entire area within 0.8 of both actual self and ideal self has no more than two elements. Makhlouf-Norris and Jones (1971) have referred to this as 'actual self isolation' and 'ideal self isolation'. David knows what he is not, but cannot identify what he is; he knows what he does not want to be, but not what he wishes to become. Apart from his sister (11) and uncle (12), David's social world appears to be empty in terms of figures with whom he can identify.

This position can be further emphasised by replotting the elements using actual self and social self as axes (Figure 3.6).

Here we can see a closer correspondence between actual self and social self, and a greater degree of separation from the

Figure 3.6: David: Actual Self/Social Self, Plot I

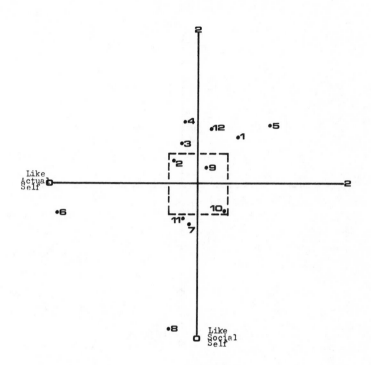

remaining elements than in Figure 3.5. The closest element to social self is ideal self (7), which triangulates with actual self to exclude the remaining elements and heighten the sense of self convergence.

The main approach taken with David during his stay on the unit involved examining both the nature of this self-convergence and exploring his perceived sense of social alienation. Progress was extremely slow due to David's reticence, but after thirteen months both self and observer behaviour-rating scales (Jesness, 1984) began to show improvements in friendliness, involvement, communication, sociability and responsibility.

At this stage a second grid was completed using the same elements and constructs as before. The correlation between the

Figure 3.7: David: Self-identity, Plot II

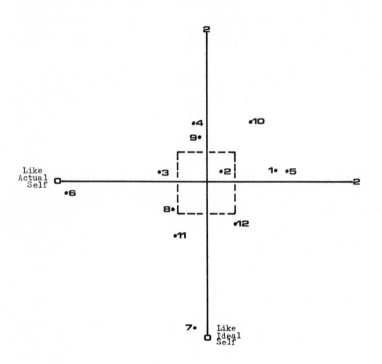

two grids obtained from the DELTA program was 0.54, which indicated that most of the change between the two grids could be accounted for by changes in David's use of the constructs whose emergent poles were: not bothered what I do; makes demands on me; does what he/she wants to do; argue with. In addition, changes occurred in the rankings of the following elements: mother; staff on the unit; false self; lads on the unit; ideal self; social self.

The second self-identity plot (Figure 3.7) demonstrated slight improvement in David's perception of significant others. Lads on the unit (3) and social self (8) are now perceived as being closer to his actual self; whilst sister (11), uncle (12, and social self (8) are beginning to approach ideal self.

Figure 3.8: David: Actual Self/Social Self, Plot II

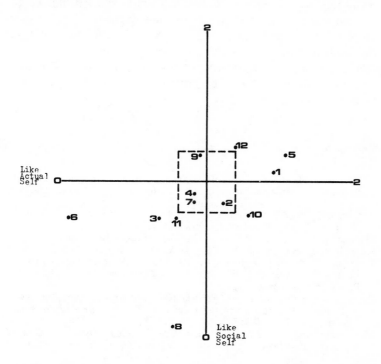

If we replot the elements using social self as the ordinate (Figure 3.8), we can see that the heightened self-convergence which formerly excluded other elements has somewhat lessened, with lads on the unit (3), sister (11) and brother (10) now perceived as more similar to social self.

Progress with David was slow and change was relatively slight, but the nature of the change achieved was quite encouraging. Admission to the unit, with its close proximity peer group and high staff ratio, appears to have begun to alter David's pronounced social alienation in a positive way, permitting him some degree of integration, and a reduction in his degree of self-convergence.

Summary

Taylor (1968) has argued that alienation is a crucial concept for social scientists to employ in their attempt to unify complementary approaches to the study of delinquency. This chapter illustrates the application of Maklouf-Norris' self-identity plots to the clinical study of alienation in young offenders. Using this method, it is possible to produce operational definitions of self and social alienation, and to derive an indication of change for both phenomena.

References

Bhagat, M. and Fraser, W.I. (1970) 'Young Offenders' Images of Self and Surroundings: A Semantic Enquiry', *British Journal of Psychiatry, 117*, 381-7

Hayden, B., Nashby, W. and Davids, A. (1977) 'Interpersonal Conceptual Structures, Predictive Accuracy, and Social Adjustment of Emotionally Disturbed Boys', *Journal of Abnormal Psychology, 86*, 315-20

Jesness, C. (1984) *Jesness Behaviour Checklist*, NFER-Nelson, Windsor

Kelly, D. and Taylor, H. (1981) 'Take and Escape: A Personal Construct Study of Car "Theft" ' in H. Bonarius, R. Holland and S. Rosenberg (eds), *Personal Construct Psychology: Recent Advances in Theory and Practice*, Macmillan Publishers Ltd, London, pp. 231-9

Kelly, G.A. (1955) *Psychology of Personal Constructs vol. 1*, Norton, New York

King, P. (1968) 'Alienation and the Individual', *British Journal of Social and Clinical Psychology, 7*, 81-92

Makhlouf-Norris, F. and Jones, H.G. (1971) 'Conceptual Distance Indices as Measures of Alienation in Obsessional Neurosis', *Psychological Medicine, 1*, 381-7

Miller, K. and Treacher, A. (1981) 'Delinquency: A Personal Construct Theory Approach' in H. Bonarius, R. Holland and S. Rosenberg (eds), *Personal Construct Psychology: Recent Advances in Theory and Practice*, Macmillan Publishers Ltd, London, pp. 241-50

Noble, G. (1971) 'Some Comments on the Nature of Delinquents' Identification with Television Heroes, Fathers and Best Friends', *British Journal of Social and Clinical Psychology, 10*, 172-80

Norris, H. and Makhlouf-Norris, F. (1976) 'The Measurement of Self-identity' in P. Slater (ed.), *Explorations of Intrapersonal Space*, John Wiley & Sons, Chichester

Slater, P. (1968) 'Summary of Output from DELTA', unpublished manuscript, St George's Hospital, London

—— (1972) 'Notes on INGRID '72', unpublished manuscript, St George's Hospital, London

Taylor, L.J. (1968) 'Alienation, Anomie and Delinquency', *British Journal of Social and Clinical Psychology, 7*, 93-105

Winnicott, D.W. (1965) 'Ego Distortion in Terms of True and False Self', in *The Maturational Processes and the Facilitating Environment*, Hogarth Press, London

4 WOMEN WITH WEIGHT ON THEIR MINDS

Eric Button

During the past decade there has been a growing awareness that women, at least during adolescence and early adulthood, are more likely than their male counterparts to get into difficulty concerning eating and weight control. Although obesity is fairly common in both sexes in 'Western' society, anorexia nervosa and bulimia nervosa are disorders mainly confined to females. For example, in a recent study a student of mine carried out on a college population, it was found that 5 per cent of females, but no males, exhibited a 'subclinical' form of anorexia nervosa (Button and Whitehouse, 1981). Although I have elsewhere discussed the possible theoretical basis of this particular vulnerability of females (Button, 1983), my aim here is to consider the use of grid technique as a tool for exploring such problems: although the approach is equally applicable to men, in my experience people referred for psychological help with this kind of problem are mainly young women.

To my knowledge, the first report of grid technique with such problems, was Crisp's and Fransella's (1972) case studies of two young women with anorexia nervosa. They suggested that it was only when weight ceased to be of central importance in defining the self that patients improved clinically. A similar argument was also applied to the obese (Fransella and Crisp, 1970) with, in both cases, the theory advanced that resistance to change may be related to the 'meaningfulness' of life as an 'anorexic' or an obese person. On the basis of this theoretical stance, Fay Fransella initiated a research project to be supported by The Medical Research Council. I was fortunate to work on this project at the Royal Free Hospital in London between 1973 and 1976. The main research tool was implications grids, both with anorexic and obese females at various stages during and after treatment. I also carried out my own separate longitudinal study of anorexic patients using conventional rated grids, partly because of the greater range and ease of analysis compared with implications grids. The results from these studies have been described in

Button (1979, 1980, 1983) and Fransella and Button (1983).

My aim here, however, is to share with you some of the *clinical* insights that grids have provided me with this kind of problem, although I will also briefly summarise some of the research findings. My focus will be mainly on 'self' construing. I would like to begin with two examples from my rated grid study of a sample of anorexics treated on an in-patient basis at the Royal Free Hospital. The treatment regime (along the lines described by Russell, 1964) was mainly directed at the nutritional level, and my aim was to monitor the psychological changes contingent upon weight change. Grids were completed shortly after admission (whilst emaciated), as well as at discharge and at two follow-up points.

Two Anorexia Nervosa Case Studies

Jean

Jean was 26 and single. When she was admitted to the Royal Free Hospital, she weighed 33 kg (5 st 2 lb) (62 per cent of 'standard weight' for age and height). The anorexic problem was of long standing, she having had several previous hospitalisations during her teens. As well as showing the typical anorexic bahaviours, she also had marked obsessional traits, as well as a tendency to depressive and suicidal symptoms. Like all the patients in my research, Jean completed grids in which a number of selves were supplied as elements (e.g. 'Me at my thinnest'), as well as a number of constructs (e.g. 'slim-fat') also supplied by me. I also elicited a sample of personal constructs from each subject. The grids were analysed by Slater's Grid Analysis Package (Slater, 1977).

Principal components analysis of Jean's grid (Figure 4.1) revealed a very large first component (accounting for 83 per cent of the variance).

This might be described as a virtually one-dimensional picture. Everything associated with being 'anorexic' is negative ('not responsible human beings', 'discontent', 'not sensible', 'don't know what wants out of life', 'ill', 'not good company', 'no goal in life' and 'lacks self respect'). In sharp contrast, an optimistic view of life at normal weight is presented in which she would be 'a responsible human being', 'good company' and so forth. It is

Figure 4.1: Component Diagram Derived from INGRID
Analysis of Jean's Grid

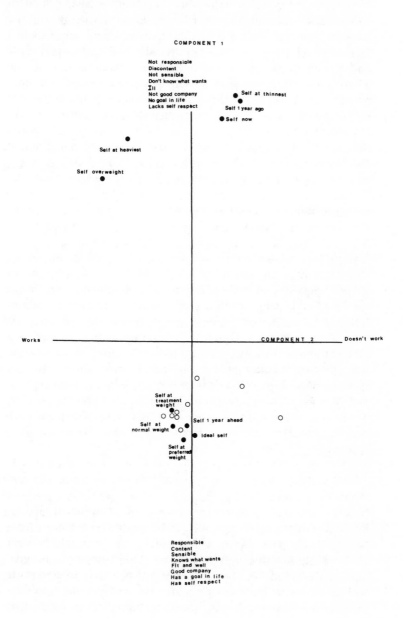

notable that the other people in her life are not differentiated from each other, all being construed in idealised terms. She thus sees herself as isolated, with others regarded as having the ideal characteristics she might gain if she could get her weight right. It is clear, however, that Jean has no personal experience of this. Before developing anorexia nervosa she had been overweight, and it is clear that this is also looked back on in negative terms. Thus, her positive image of herself at 'normal weight' is a hope, or perhaps more accurately, a fantasy. This is borne out by the fact that in the diagram we can see that thinness is extremely, and therefore more definitely, construed whereas her possible life in the future at 'normal weight' is less extremely defined and, therefore, associated with more uncertainty. In short, she seems to know a lot about life as an anorexic, but a lot less about what life might be like if she abandoned it. What little she does know is arguably rather unrealistic, with an expectation that just being the right weight gives people respect, contentment and so on. You may not be surprised to hear that Jean's outcome after leaving hospital was poor. Although the treatment regime was successful in getting her to a 'healthy weight' (49 kg (7 st 10 lb), 92 per cent of standard weight on discharge), she rapidly lost weight after leaving hospital and was soon admitted to another hospital in her home town in a very precarious physical and mental state. Thus although 'co-operating' with the treatment, she was unable to carry through its implications. I would argue that she had failed to anticipate what life would really be like. Getting to a 'healthy' weight didn't bring her respect and the ability to get on with people etc. Faced with the prospect of likely anxiety, if not predictive 'chaos', it is not surprising that she should retreat to the more familiar territory of her life as an anorexic.

Anna

Anna was a 23-year-old single young woman who was transferred to the Royal Free from an acute medical ward of another hospital. On admission she weighed 32 kg (5 st) (55 per cent of 'standard weight'). Anna was brought up in a middle-class, closely-knit, Jewish family in London. Unlike many 'anorexics', her problems did not start in her teens, but at age 20 after she had left home to study at university. Her first year was cut short by a serious physical illness, but she returned to restart her first full year and it was in her second term that she met a young man, Mark, who she described as 'everything I'd never known before': he was non-Jewish and from a Yorkshire farming background. She was immensely taken up with him and 'fell head over heels' for him. She spent most of her time trying to please him, which eventually led her in the direction of slimming. This got out of hand and turned into anorexia nervosa. She failed to hold on to Mark, but went further and further into weight control, until she eventually became so emaciated, weak and depressed that she was brought home by her parents and was forced to give up university. At that time she had an appointment with a psychiatrist, but she resisted help, having been put off by the sight of a mental hospital. She managed to 'muddle through', however, and she put on some weight and worked as a sales executive at a hotel. She put as much energy into this as she had done with her dieting: she spent all her time working, with no boyfriends or friends outside the hotel. Following a promotion, she became frightened about her capabilities and again turned to calorie control and rapidly lost weight, leading to her admission to the Royal Free.

Anna's first grid is quite different from Jean's (Figure 4.2). A much more 'multi-dimensional' picture is revealed, with the first component accounting for only 44 per cent of the total variance. As we can see, the elements and constructs are much more evenly dispersed, with the first component being rather different from Jean's. The main contrast is between 'Jewish' and 'close to family' as opposed to 'non-Jewish' and 'separate from family'. Her former boyfriend Mark seems to symbolise the non-Jewish end, whereas she sees herself and her father at the Jewish end. In contrast to Jean, this first component is, thus, not really about being the right weight. She does not see herself as changing much on this dimension, although she doesn't seem entirely happy with the close family way of life associated with her religion. Her 'ideal self' is neutrally positioned on the dimension. Anna seems to be in a dilemma about this way of life: the 'loadings' of some of the other constructs on this dimension provide some clues. Although Mark's way of life seems more carefree ('accepts life as it comes') it also means you 'can't be so attached', you can only understand superficial people', you have 'no sense of responsibility for life' and you are 'more inclined to hurt people'.

Figure 4.2: Component Diagram Derived from INGRID Analysis of Anna's Grid

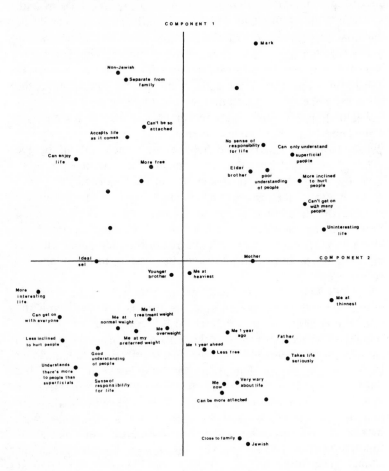

Interview with Anna revealed that as a child she had always been the 'good girl', particularly in her father's eyes and she had always tried to please him. It had seemed that she had tried to apply similar constructs with her boyfriend, feeling that in order to hold his affection all she had to do was please him. Although this seemed to have worked and brought the rewards of affection and attachment with her father, it didn't seem to work with Mark. Now she seemed to have retreated to the world of her family, although she was clearly not entirely happy with it, particularly since her parents were in a considerable degree of discord and she felt she wanted to be able to make them happy.

The second component is more like Jean's first dimension in that 'Me at thinnest' is contrasted with 'ideal self'. Ideally, she would like, amongst other things, to 'have an interesting life' and 'get on with everyone', but like her father, and to a lesser extent her mother, she has a most uninteresting life as an anorexic and can't get on with many people. Interestingly, Mark also fares rather poorly on this dimension, again suggesting dilemmas arising out of her experience of him. Like Jean, she hopes that things might be better at a normal weight, but it is significant that this contrast is not the major dimension of construing for Anna.

Anna's response to treatment was a rather stormy one. After initial weight gain, her weight started to slide whilst in hospital and she was discharged at 42 kg (6 st 9 lb) (73 per cent of 'standard weight'). She went back to her parents' home, but within 24 hours had been re-admitted following an overdose. She later told me that she was struck by the impossibility for her of living at home and enduring her parents' arguments. During the next few months in hospital she was anything but conforming and showed quite a rebellious strand to her behaviour. Her relationship with her parents now became the focal point of treatment and she had regular sessions with a psychologist colleague of mine. Her parents were also given some help in tackling their marital problems, thus taking some of the pressure off Anna. Although during this period she lost weight and showed more anorexic behaviour, the theme of therapy was now concentrated on helping her to find some way of being herself and to learn to handle her relationships in new ways. A series of grids during the follow-up period of my research were able to chart the process of change. The full details of this personal construct case study can be found in Button (1980). One feature of this process of change, however, deserves particular mention. The construct concerned with attachment showed a lot of change in its implications during the coming months and years. For instance, on admission, being more attached was highly correlated with being less free. By the time of her second discharge from hospital, however, a moderate correlation in the opposite direction was found. By the later follow-up assessments, however, these constructs were independent of each other. This is, perhaps, indicative of the extent to which relationships were a difficult matter for Anna, and how she was reconstruing this area of life in the light of her new experience and therapeutic guidance.

Following several months of psychological help she was eventually able to set up her own home and develop friendships and interests as well as finding a satisfying job. When seen for follow-up three years later, Anna clearly was more optimistic although also realistic about some of the difficulties she faced in her life. In describing herself as 'blown by storms', she was acknowledging her emotional vulnerabilities, but was no longer locked in to trying to achieve things through the superficial matter of weight.

Some Research Findings about Anorexia Nervosa

The above two clinical case descriptions provide some insights into the various personal meanings that can be associated with anorexia nervosa. Although the grids were helpful in providing clinical insights with these individuals, they also offered a methodology relevant to the exploration of the aetiology and possible recovery from anorexia nervosa. This work has been described elsewhere (Button, 1980, 1983; Fransella and Button, 1983), but I would like to refer briefly to some of the findings.

(1) From the implication grid study of anorexics we derived measures of meaningfulness of 'thinness' and 'normal weight', much as Fay Fransella had done with her research on the treatment of stutterers (Fransella, 1972). By using the number of implications in grids as a measure of 'meaningfulness', we were able to show that those with previous admissions to hospital for anorexia nervosa had less 'meaningful' construct sub-systems for construing people than those on their first admission. There was also evidence that the greater the meaningfulness of 'normal weight', the greater the likelihood of their weight being maintained after discharge.

(2) The rated grid study showed, as particularly exemplified in the first case study above, that 'self at thinnest' was much more extremely defined compared with the other 'self elements'. For the group as a whole, return to a normal weight left the patients with a much less clearly defined view of themselves than when

they had been thin. There were also a number of prognostic implications, with relatively 'one dimensional' construing (as typified by Jean) being predictive of a poorer outcome. Improvement was also associated with a cyclical process of 'tightening' and 'loosening' of construing, whereas relapsers maintained consistently tighter construing. Finally, it was shown that those who improved defined themselves less extremely, suggesting that they were more able to construe themselves 'propositionally'.

Obesity

Although it would generally be acknowledged that obesity is multi-factorially determined, there is general recognition that in many individuals, psychological factors can play a part both in the causation and maintenance of the problem. One of the most striking features of obese people is that though they often react to social pressure by dieting, they are extremely resistant to *permanent* weight loss. Fransella (1972) noted that stuttering was also notoriously resistant to change, and she produced some evidence from a grid study that this may be related to a greater 'meaningfulness' of their familiar life as a stutterer as compared with becoming fluent. She extended this argument to the obese person, for whom she suggested life was more meaningful as a fat person than as a slim one.

In addition to the studies of anorexics described above, we therefore also carried out an analogous longitudinal study with obese subjects. Implication grids were applied serially to a group of obese women, who were either receiving a behavioural or a personal construct approach to treatment. Both 'normal weight' and 'overweight' grids were obtained and a measure of 'meaningfulness' based on the number of implications in each type of grid was derived. Contrary to our hypothesis, there was no evidence that the two types of grid differed in 'meaningfulness' (Button, 1979). It was possible, of course, that our chosen measure was not a good one. My interpretation, however, was that our subjects may have had quite an elaborate idea of what it may have been like to be 'normal weight'. Their view of it, however, may have been over-idealised and inconsistent. In my clinical work with overweight people I have, therefore, turned to

examining the content of their constructions surrounding slim-
ness, rather than just focusing on the more structural measure of
'meaningfulness'.

I would like to illustrate the way a grid can help to identify
content of constructions blocking change in obesity by another
individual case.

I was asked if I might be able to help Sally, a 24-year-old
nurse, who was referred to me by her GP. She was about 17
stones (108 kg) in weight (about twice her 'ideal weight') and had
been overweight since a child. She felt she should lose weight
because of the effect it was having on her personal life and her
health. She described how she'd been on diets but easily lost
interest, and felt she needed someone to be strict with her. In
order to try and clarify where her difficulties may lie, I completed
a rated grid with Sally on the basis of 24 constructs elicited from
11 elements. The elements included 3 'self' elements: 'Me'; 'Me
ideally'; 'Me if I was 9 stones' (57 kg). Thus, there were just 8
'other' elements, and it was striking that with the exception of
her brother there were no males, which was perhaps indicative of
her lifestyle which seemed to centre on her mum and her nursing
colleagues who were all female.

Sally's first component (39 per cent) (Figure 4.3) contrasts
mainly her 'ideal self' with a disliked female colleague of
hers, Mary. The most important construct was 'over-rates self-
realistic', with Mary considered to over-rate herself. Other
'negative' construct poles were 'dive straight in', 'talk behind
people's backs', 'only interested in what they have to say' and
'unreliable'. In contrast, Sally would ideally like to be 'realistic
about herself', to 'give things more consideration', to 'say things
to people's faces' to 'listen' and to be 'reliable'. It is interesting
that her mother also loads highly on the positive end of this
dimension. This fits with the fact that she still lives with her
mother, and although not entirely satisfied with the situation, is
reluctant to leave home. Other people who load 'negatively' are a
friend and her brother (who is older than her and has left home).
Interestingly, her present 'self' is construed neutrally on this
component so that she sees some room for improvement. The
general theme, however, is quite clear: she seems to be saying
that she must not over-rate herself but must be 'realistic'. You
may already, perhaps, be anticipating some of the problems with
this construct. For instance, does being 'realistic' hold her back

from extending herself as a person? Let us examine the second component and see if this provides any clues. Here we see that 'self' is defined more extremely and contrasts with her brother, whom she would be more like (albeit less extremely) if she was her 'ideal self' and at 9 stones (57 kg) in weight. To be like her brother would mean to 'have lots of possibilities', 'will take a chance', 'ambitious', 'successful' and 'thin'. In contrast she, and somewhat less extremely, her mother, 'have only limited

Figure 4.3: Component Diagram Derived from INGRID Analysis of Sally's Grid

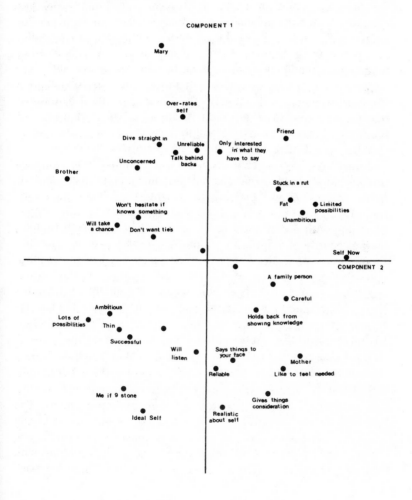

possibilities', are 'careful', 'unambitious', 'stuck in a rut' and 'fat'. On the face of it, becoming slim would seem to hold distinct 'possibilities' for Sally. But does she really want to be like her brother, which is what seems to be implied by becoming thinner? I think not.

In addition to the negative construing of her brother on the first component, closer examination of the second component reveals that also associated with the thin end of the component are 'unconcerned', 'doesn't want ties with the past', 'won't hesitate if they know something' and 'dives straight in'. Her ratings of her 'ideal self', however, indicate that she would prefer the opposite poles of these constructs: 'like to feel they're needed'; 'a family person'; 'tend to hold back from showing knowledge' and; 'gives things more consideration'. Thus, although having the appeal of success and so on, becoming thinner also implies for Sally giving up her family ties and also risking taking on interpersonal qualities, such as 'diving in', which she evaluates negatively. It is perhaps, not insignificant that there appear to be no 'models' amongst Sally's elements of the kind of ideal person who is both successful and 'realistic'.

When I fed back to her the above picture derived from the grid analysis, she quickly recognised the implications of the results and she added that she may become 'career minded' and likely to 'bowl people over' if she became thin. It is, therefore, not difficult to see why she should have been having difficulty in persisting with a diet and that she couldn't bring herself to give up the security of living with her mother. I discussed with her the therapeutic implications of her dilemma and felt that we had reached a good starting point for counselling. It may come as no surprise to you, however, to hear that after completing the grid, Sally did not keep her subsequent appointments and didn't reply to my letters. It is unfortunate that I did not get the opportunity to fully pursue the implications of the grid with Sally, but this example is a reminder of the fact that grids can sometimes reveal uncomfortable or even painful issues, which a person may not wish to face.

Concluding Comments

I hope that this brief illustration of the use of grids in eating disorders conveys something of the kind of psychological issues which can surround such problems. Although common difficulties involving interpersonal and sexual relationships were evident, we were able to gain some insight into the idiosyncratic ways in which they expressed their hopes and dilemmas. We were also able to see the importance of their perception of key people in their lives. Such information can be invaluable in directing psychotherapy, whether it be a matter of reconstruing a well-construed figure (e.g. an 'awful' father or an idealised mother) or in using more ambiguous people as a basis for 'elaboration'. I would like to emphasise, however, that the clinical analysis of grid material is by no means a straightforward instant matter. In the present state of the art, our techniques of grid analysis only provide us with a mathematical representation, and it is left to us to provide a *psychological* intepretation. This takes time, but this is only right and proper if we are to take our clients seriously, rather than being over-anxious to arrive at a neat stereotypic formulation of the problem. Finally, whilst grids can be one particularly effective form of communication, they are not everyone's cup of tea, and I can recommend conversation as an admirable alternative way of exploring constructs!

References

Button, E.J. (1979) 'The Threat of Weight Change', paper presented at the 3rd International Congress on Personal Construct Theory, Breukelen, The Netherlands

—— (1980) 'Construing and Clinical Outcome in Anorexia Nervosa', unpublished PhD thesis, University of London

—— (1983) 'Construing the Anorexic' in J. Adams-Webber and J. Mancuso (eds), *Applications of Personal Construct Theory*, Academic Press, Toronto

—— and Whitehouse, A. (1981) 'Subclinical Anorexia Nervosa', *Psychological Medicine, 11*, 509-16

Crisp, A.H. and Fransella, F. (1972) 'Conceptual Changes During Recovery from Anorexia Nervosa', *Brit. J. Medical Psychology, 45*, 395-405

Fansella, F. (1972) *Personal Change and Reconstruction*, Academic Press, London

—— and Button, E.J. (1983) 'The "Construing" of Self and Body Size in Relation to Maintenance of Weight Gain in Anorexia Nervosa' in P.L. Darby (ed.), *Anorexia Nervosa: Recent Developments in Research*, Alan Liss Inc., New York

—— and Crisp, A.H. (1979) 'Conceptual Organisation and Weight Change', *Psychosom. Psychother. 18*, 176-85

Russell, G.F.M. (1964) 'Anorexia Nervosa. Investigation and Care of Patients in a Psychiatric Metabolic Ward', *Nursing Times*, 3 July

Slater, P. (1977) *The Measurement of Intrapersonal Space by Grid Technique, vol. 2, Dimensions of Intrapersonal Space*, Wiley, Chichester

5 THE EXPERIMENT OF AGORAPHOBIA

Bernadette O'Sullivan

George Kelly (1969) proposes that human behaviour is an experiment which 'takes on additional meaning when one sees it as a contrast, a denial, an abandonment of alternatives, or as a choice which has left other possibilities unexplored'. Thus, if human action can be described as an experiment involving predictive hypotheses then, as Kelly indicates, the negative as well as the positive implications of these hypotheses are integral features of the experiment. It was within this context that a study on agoraphobia was completed. An aspect of this study is discussed in this chapter. Agoraphobia is construed as an experiment by the client which denies certain alternatives while affirming others. These alternatives, or constructs, many of which have verbal dimensions, are believed to be specific to each person, but with many themes shared by agoraphobic persons generally. The similarities between such clients have been well documented.

Certain issues, delineated by previous research as being relevant predictive hypotheses about agoraphobia, are explored in this chapter using the repertory grid technique. Data from the agoraphobic subjects are analysed on the INGRID and SERIES programs (Slater, 1977) and are compared to those from anxiety-state and non-client subjects.

Observations on Agoraphobia

Agoraphobia has been researched extensively and discussed in both the public and professional media for many years. There have been a number of positive treatment developments although uncertainty remains, particularly regarding aetiology (Mathews, Gelder and Johnston, 1981). There is agreement on the many commonly noted features of agoraphobia as a clinical presentation (Marks, 1969), and a growing acceptance of a re-definition which recognises fear of fear, rather than fear of open spaces or public places, as central to the need to avoid (Goldstein and Chambless, 1978; Mavissakalian and Barlow, 1981). Discussion continues about the accuracy of viewing agoraphobia as a discrete syndrome or indeed within a medical model framework (Hallam, 1978, 1983). This becomes more relevant when it is noted that persons diagnosed as anxiety-state are similar to agoraphobic persons in most aspects that have been measured excepting the sex ratio. In clinical populations agoraphobic females greatly outnumber agoraphobic males, whilst the sex ratio for anxiety-state is usually reported as being more equal (Mathews *et al.*, 1981).

A high degree of dependency has frequently been postulated as a feature of agoraphobic persons prior to the development of clinical symptoms (Terhune, 1949; Andrews, 1966; Shafer, 1976). Such dependency, with the related effects of avoiding autonomy, initiative and assertiveness, has also been the reason preferred for the preponderance of women in the clinical presentation of agoraphobia. The latter is described by Fodor (1974) as 'an exaggerated version of the stereotypic feminine role' resorted to in the face of the realistic stresses of adult life. However, where it has been sought, evidence has not been found to suggest that dependency was a significantly more likely occurrence in agoraphobic subjects than in matched normal controls (Buglass *et al.*, 1977), nor in neurotic subjects generally (Roth, Garside and Gurney, 1965).

Self-assertion has also been described as 'especially impossible for the phobic individual *within* the context of his dependent relationship' (Andrews, 1966). It has been further suggested by Goldstein and Chambless (1978) that, as a result of adverse childhood experiences, agoraphobic persons have difficulty both in the expression of feelings and in the appropriate recognition of emotional experiences. These authors reported that therapists' ratings of clients at the commencement of treatment indicated that agoraphobic clients were significantly more likely to be seen as lower in emotional expressiveness and aggressiveness than were specific phobic clients. A lack of emotional expressiveness was also observed by Liotti and Guidano (1976) in a group of male agoraphobic clients.

The data to be reported on here pertain to some of those subjects who participated in a more extensive study on agoraphobia. The latter was undertaken as an exploration of the value of a personal construct theory perspective on this clinical presentation. There was a particular emphasis on those issues of personal and interpersonal construction which may be pertinent to an understanding of agoraphobia and which have been summarised above.

Methodology

Subjects

Twelve married female agoraphobic clients, referred from a number of different clinical settings in the Dublin area, participated in the phase of the study to be reported on in this article. Twelve anxiety-state married female clients were referred from the same clinics. A non-client group, closely matched with the agoraphobic subjects in terms of age, sex, marital and educational and socio-economic status, were contacted through informal sources. There were no significant differences between the three groups on the matching criteria.

Measure

A rank-ordering format of the repertory grid technique was completed by each subject. Constructs and elements were included in this grid pertaining to the themes of agoraphobic fears, independence, assertion, sex-role attributes and approval by parental and spouse figures. These were all themes, as outlined above, which have been argued or noted to have especial pertinence in agoraphobia. Administration of each grid took approximately three-quarters of an hour and constituted part of a more extensive interview.

Procedures

Fourteen role-title elements were used to rank-order twelve supplied constructs. Both lists are given in Table 5.1. Supplying constructs and using a rank-ordering format allowed for ease of administration and comparisons although both are limiting in the information that may then be available regarding a subject's anticipatory predictions.

Analyses

Analyses of the data derived from these completed grids using

Table 5.1: Element Role-titles and Supplied Constructs Used in this Repertory Grid

---

Elements (each one being identified by the subject with the name of an acquaintance)

1. A sexually attractive man
2. A masculine man
3. A good father
4. A good husband
5. A good mother
6. A good wife
7. A person approved of by your father
8. A person approved of by your mother
9. A person approved of by your spouse or closest boyfriend
10. A sexually attractive woman
11. A feminine woman
12. Me as I would really like to be
13. Me as I used to be
14. Me now

Constructs

1. Experiences fear if out of home alone
2. Will give a differing point of view even if it angers the person closest to them
3. Able to verbally express a need for affection to the person closest to them
4. Will verbally express impatience at others' mistakes to those making the mistakes
5. Will verbally express a point of view if he or she has a strong opinion about it
6. Sympathetic
7. Is able to negotiate a share in important decision-making within the family
8. Once knows what the job requires, likes to be in charge
9. Likely to experience fear if walking across an open space alone
10. Sensitive to the needs of others
11. Most like what I would like to be like
12. Most like me now

---

the computer programs of INGRID and SERIES (Slater, 1977) will be reported on here.

The SERIES program provides a consensus or average-grid from a number of grids, where the latter are aligned in terms of constructs and elements. The consensus-grid is a listing of the average scores on all of the elements on each construct-dimension. While obtaining such a grid does facilitate the making of comparisons between groups, it nevertheless limits the available data. This is so because it necessitates the use of supplied rather than elicited constructs, and it focuses attention away from the individual-subject onto a group-average score. Recognising these limitations, it was judged that useful comparative information would, however, be indicated through obtaining an average-grid for each group.

Each consensus-grid was analysed using the INGRID program. This provided correlational data on constructs; scores indicating the relationships between elements; and a principal component analysis of the construct and element data. This analysis indicated the dispersal of constructs and thus their relationships to each other, in terms of all of the elements that were ranked in the grid, and also the dispersal of the elements in terms of the constructs which were used to rank them. It identified the independent dimensions or components which can be described according to those elements and constructs with the highest loadings on them. Slater (1977) writes that the principal component form of analysis was developed

> merely as a method for simplifying the records of a large number of correlated variables . . . by reducing them to a possibly smaller number of independent measurements, ordered from largest to least according to the amount of variation they recorded.

Whilst many more independent dimensions may be derived from a matrix of data, usually the greatest amount of variance will be accounted for by the first two or three components or dimensions. Ignoring the other components can result in a loss of information, but unless the percentage of variance accounted for by the first three components is small, it is not always practicable to consider much more than the first three components.

Results

It was noted that the first three components of the principal component analyses of the consensus-grids accounted for a high percentage of the variance in all cases: (80.73 per cent — agoraphobic group; 86.70 per cent — anxiety-state group, and 88.61 per cent — non-client group).

Those constructs and elements which were indicated as having the highest weighting (i.e. a vector value equal to or greater than ± 0.30) on the first component, extracted for each of the three groups, are detailed in Table 5.2. In view of the arguments regarding the importance of interpersonal relationships in agoraphobia, the loadings of those elements referring to parental and spouse approval are also noted when each of the components are discussed.

It is indicated that for all three groups the first component described aspects of the 'present self'. Thus, for the agoraphobic group it was primarily descriptive of the 'self' as somebody who experiences agoraphobic fears. This was indicated as not resembling the 'ideal self'. Most of the other constructs and elements had considerably lower loadings on this component.

Although approval by spouse related positively to this agoraphobic component, the actual value of the loading was low. Parental approval had negligible loadings and was therefore indicated as not very relevant to these agoraphobic subjects.

The emphasis of the anxiety-state group, on Component 1, was not on fears but on nurturant, female-role, attributes as descriptive of the 'self' and indeed of the 'ideal self'. The pattern for the non-client group was similar to that of the anxiety-state group for this component.

Parental or spouse approval was not indicated as of great importance for the anxiety-state group in defining this self-descriptive component. Parental approval, in the guise of an implication of lack of approval by the father figure for the 'self' (present or ideal), was indicated as relevant on this component for the non-client group.

In Table 5.3 are described those constructs and elements which had vector values equal to or greater than ± 0.30 on Component 2 for each of the three groups. The values for the parental and spouse approval elements are also given. Component 2 suggested a differing elaboration of essentially the ideal self for all three groups. Thus, for the agoraphobic group the 'ideal self', indicated on Component 1 to be dissimilar to the 'present' (agoraphobic) self, is here described in terms of the 'past self'. The picture is one of an interest in being nurturant with a rejection of interpersonal assertion. It is interesting to note that a good-father type was differentiated from a masculine man. This suggests, perhaps, a willingness in this agoraphobic group to identify in the past and, ideally, with paternal-type activities or

Table 5.2: Vector Values on Component 1 of the Principal Component Analyses of the Three Groups

	Agoraphobic group	Present-self component Anxiety-state group	Non-client group
Elements	+0.69 Self now −0.49 Ideal self	+0.58 Sexually attractive man −0.49 Ideal self −0.38 Good mother −0.36 Self now	+0.49 Self now +0.45 Ideal self −0.47 Sexually attractive man
	−0.06 Approval by father −0.02 Approval by mother −0.15 Approval by spouse	+0.13 Approval by father +0.09 Approval by mother −0.03 Approval by spouse	−0.34 Approval by father −0.02 Approval by mother −0.01 Approval by spouse
Constructs	+0.63 Open space fear (C9) +0.54 Out of home fear (C1) +0.49 Self now (C12)	−0.49 Sympathetic (C6) −0.46 Ideal self (C11) −0.41 Sensitive (C10) −0.38 Self Now	+0.46 Sensitive (C10) +0.44 Self now (C12) +0.43 Sympathetic (C6) +0.44 Ideal Self
Percentage variance accounted for by this component	52.80	39.77	54.32

attributes, but not with the interpersonal assertion more usually associated with male rather than with female roles. Interestingly, while the vector values were not high, it was indicated that movement towards the 'ideal self' was construed as likely to meet with paternal approval and spouse disapproval.

The anxiety-state group differed from the agoraphobic group on this component in that the 'ideal self' was indicated as being dissimilar from the allied 'past and present self'. The 'ideal self' was here associated with interpersonally assertive behaviours and, unlike the 'present and past self', was not construed as fearful. Approval by spouse or parental figures did not appear to be of great relevance here for the anxiety-state group.

The non-client group who, on Component 1, indicated a concordance between the 'present' and 'ideal self' now further elaborated the 'ideal self' as similar to the masculine man role, capable of taking charge and of being non-fearful. Noting the vector values on this component for the 'present and past self' (i.e. −0.12 and −0.33 respectively), suggests that this non-client group construed progress towards independence to have been made, but not to the extent that was considered ideal.

Component 3 yielded some further information, and the data are given on Table 5.4. It would appear that independence (as represented by constructs 5 and 7) was construed by the agoraphobic group as not entirely outside the ranges of convenience of either the 'ideal self' or of nurturant behaviours. What were indicated as unacceptable were attributes associated by this group with the masculine man and sexually attractive man role-elements. Data from Component 2 would suggest that these attributes may relate to interpersonally assertive actions, particularly of a negative kind.

Despite a close alignment between the 'present and past self' for the anxiety-state group, Component 3 indicated that there was a construction of the 'past self' which resembled more good-father qualities than female-role qualities, and which also had a higher level of, particularly, paternal approval associated with it. Experiencing fears was more closely associated with female familial roles.

Component 3 data for the non-client group provides a little more elaboration of the construction of the 'ideal self'. The latter had already been indicated as likely to be independent, but the vector values on this component would suggest that assertion

Table 5.3: Vector Values on Component 2 of the Principal Component Analyses of the Three Groups

	Agoraphobic group	Ideal-self component Anxiety-state group	Non-client group
Elements	+0.44 Past self +0.44 Ideal self −0.40 Good father −0.30 Masculine man	+0.63 Self now −0.53 Ideal self +0.34 Past self	+0.51 Masculine man +0.39 Ideal self
	+0.26 Approval by father −0.03 Approval by mother −0.20 Approval by spouse	−0.14 Approval by father +0.09 Approval by mother −0.05 Approval by spouse	+0.10 Approval by father −0.11 Approval by mother +0.09 Approval by spouse
Constructs	−0.54 Express opinion (C5) −0.44 Give differing view (C2) −0.47 Express impatience (C4) +0.36 Sensitive to others (C10)	−0.40 Express opinion (C5) −0.39 Express impatience (C4) +0.39 Out of home fear (C1) −0.37 Give differing view (C2) +0.33 Self now	−0.62 Out of home fear (C11) −0.55 Open space fear (C9) +0.35 In charge (C8)
Percentage of variance accounted for by this component	15.88	36.53	27.15

Table 5.4: Vector Values on Component 3 of the Principal Component Analyses of the Three Groups

	Agoraphobic group	Anxiety-state group	Non-client group
Elements	+0.49 Masculine man −0.43 Sexually attractive man +0.25 Approval by father −0.10 Approval by mother −0.21 Approval by spouse	−0.49 Feminine woman −0.39 Good mother −0.36 Good wife +0.33 Good father +0.32 Past self +0.28 Approval by father +0.14 Approval by mother +0.08 Approval by spouse	+0.69 Ideal self −0.44 Me now −0.33 Masculine man −0.17 Approval by father −0.04 Approval by mother −0.17 Approval by spouse
Constructs	−0.58 Ideal self (C11) −0.42 Negotiate in decisions (C7) −0.38 Express opinion (C5) −0.37 Sympathetic (C6) −0.35 Sensitive (C10)	−0.66 Open space fear (C9) −0.54 Out of home fear (C1)	+0.53 Ideal self (C11) −0.47 In charge (C8) −0.43 Express impatience (C4) −0.39 Self now (C12)
Percentage of variance accounted for by this component	12.05	10.40	7.14

involving, for example, the expression of impatience, was not desirable.

Summary

In summary, therefore, principal component analyses of the averaged (consensus) grids, for each of the three groups of married females being reported on here, suggested that there were patterns of constructions or predictive hypotheses which differed between the groups. These, in turn, highlighted certain features about the agoraphobic subjects.

Thus, while the non-client group alone indicated a construction of the 'present self' as independent, the agoraphobic group's data pointed to just such a construction of the 'ideal self' and indeed of the 'past self'. This would tend to corroborate, therefore, the finding by Buglass and her colleagues (1977) of a similarity between agoraphobic and normal subjects in terms of premorbid dependency.

Interpersonal self-assertion (and emotional expressiveness) was construed as not descriptive of the 'present self' of either of the client groups. The difference between them lies in how the 'ideal self' is construed, i.e. the anxiety-state group indicate a willingness to incorporate such assertion and the agoraphobic group reject it. The emphasis in this repertory grid was on the expression of negative feelings. The data suggest agreement with the indications noted in other studies of difficulty amongst agoraphobic subjects related to assertion, but perhaps of a particular kind, i.e. expression of negative feelings. There was no indication that such assertion was particularly affected by spouse or parental approval for any of the three groups.

Identification with female familial roles was seen as of particular relevance only in the anxiety-state group. Qualities more usually associated with female roles, i.e. sensitivity to others' feelings and sympathy, were stressed by all three groups and indicated as important in the construction of the 'ideal self'. Thus, evidence was not forthcoming that the agoraphobic subjects exhibited a more stereotypic feminine-role identification than the subjects from either of the other two groups.

Conclusion

Only limited information can be obtained from an analysis of data such as described here, and particularly where attention is on group averages rather than on intra-individual relationships. Nevertheless, the patterns obtained were informative of particular constructions which have a relevance to an understanding of agoraphobia.

References

Andrews, J.D. (1966) 'Psychotherapy of Phobias', *Psychological Bulletin, 66,* 544-80

Buglass, D., Clarke, J., Henderson, A.S., Kreitman, N. and Presley, A.S. (1978) 'A Study of Agoraphobic Housewives', *Psychological Medicine, 7,* 73-86

Fodor, I.G. (1974) 'The Phobic Syndrome in Women: Implications for Treatment' in V. Franks and V. Burtle (eds), *Women in Therapy: New Psychotherapies for A Changing Society,* Brunner/Mazel, New York

Goldstein, A.J. and Chambless, D.L. (1978) 'A Reanalysis of Agoraphobia', *Behaviour Therapy, 9,* 47-59

Hallam, R.S. (1978) 'Agoraphobia: A Critical Review of the Concept', *British Journal of Psychiatry, 133,* 314-19

—— (1983) 'Agoraphobia: Deconstructing a Clinical Syndrome', *Bulletin of the British Psychological Society, 36,* 337-40

Kelly, G.A. (1969) 'Ontological Acceleration' in B. Maher (ed.), *Clinical Psychology and Personality. The Selected Papers of George Kelly,* John Wiley & Sons Inc., New York

Liotti, G. and Guidano, V. (1976) 'Behavioural Analysis of Marital Interaction in Agoraphobic Male Patients', *Behaviour Research and Therapy, 14,* 161-2

Marks, I.M. (1969) *Fears and Phobias,* Academic Press, New York

Mathews, A.M., Gelder, M.G. and Johnston, D.W. (1981) *Agoraphobia: Nature and Treatment,* Tavistock, London

Mavissakalian, M. and Barlow, D.H. (1981) *Phobias: Psychological and Pharmacological Treatment,* Guilford Press, New York

Roth, M., Garside, R.S. and Gurney, C. (1965) 'Clinical-statistical Enquiries into the Classification of Anxiety States and Depressive Disorders', *May & Baker Conference Proceedings,* Leeds, pp. 175-87

Shafer, S. (1976) 'Aspects of Phobic Illness — A Study of 90 Personal Cases', *British Journal of Medical Psychology, 49,* (3), 221-36

Slater, P. (ed.) (1977) *The Measurement of Intrapersonal Space by Grid Technique, vol. 2,* Wiley, Chichester

Terhune, W. (1949) 'The Phobic Syndrome: A Study of 86 Patients with Phobic Reactions', *Archives of Neurology and Psychiatry, 62,* 162-72

PART TWO

CONSTRUCTS AND DISABILITY

In this section the theme of exploring personal construct systems is continued but in the domain of 'constructs and disability'.

Bannister (1981) points out that the most significant corollary of personal construct theory for those directly involved in working with people with disabilities is the sociality corollary. This states 'to the extent that one person construes the construction processes of another he/she may play a role in a social process involving the other person'. Thus, whether helper or researcher it is not enough to know about a disability or to sympathise. What is needed is understanding of the personal viewpoint of the person with a disability.

Very little has been written about personal constructs and disability. Even less has been reported where grids have been used with people with a disability to explore the meaning of disability. In this section there are three chapters, each reporting exploratory work using grids with people who are disabled. Shelagh Brumfitt discusses in Chapter 6 the use of grids with people who have restricted communication. She then reports the findings of her own pioneering work using grids with people suffering from aphasia. Keren Fisher reports in Chapter 7 on her work using grids in the context of understanding the adjustment problems of patients following the amputation of a limb. In Chapter 8 Nigel Beail discusses some of the problems that may be encountered when using grids with people who are severely physically disabled. He provides an illustration to show how grids can be used with this population, and suggests how other clinicians and researchers can elaborate upon this.

Reference

Bannister, D. (1981) 'Construing a Disability' in A. Brechin, F. Liddiard and J. Swain (eds), *Handicap in a Social World*, Hodder & Stoughton, London

6 THE USE OF REPERTORY GRIDS WITH APHASIC PEOPLE

Shelagh Brumfitt

Introduction

The condition of aphasia is described. The emotional reactions to this disorder of communicative ability will be discussed in terms of the aphasic person suffering a major loss. Grief as the reaction to loss is discussed in Personal Construct Theory terms. The use of repertory grid technique with people with restricted communication is discussed, and a study investigating the use of repertory grids with aphasics is reported.

The Condition of Aphasia

Many descriptions of aphasia have been recorded in the past (Riese, 1977), but it is only in the later part of this century that specialised interest has focused on the condition. A valuable definition of this disorder is given by Goodglass and Kaplan (1976). 'Aphasia refers to the disturbance of any or all of the skills, association and habits of spoken or written language, produced by injury to certain brain areas which are specialised for these functions'. A more personal, but illuminating definition is offered by Dahlberg, a psychiatrist who suffered aphasia himself, and who described it as a 'disease of verbal intercourse' (Dahlberg and Jaffe, 1977).

The aphasic problem occurs as a result of trauma to the brain such as by cerebral vascular accident, head injury, cerebral tumour or viral infection. By far the most common causes are cerebral vascular accident and head injury. Both these incidents are acute and totally unpredictable. Speech therapists see these aphasic patients following the cerebral incident and work with each person individually over a long period of time helping them to regain their communication skills. Some of these patients will regain all of their ability to communicate. A great many will be

89

left with problems in all language modalities that are unhelped by present approaches. At the same time these patients will have associated problems that are part of the brain-damage pattern — possible paralysis, visual deficits, memory problems and perceptual difficulties. All of these other difficulties may, like aphasia, potentially be remediated; but many may remain with the person forever.

The linguistic features of the aphasic condition vary greatly from person to person. Part of the speech therapist's role is as a diagnostician, assessing the individual's ability to communicate via a battery of tests (Porch, 1967; Schuell, 1965; Goodglass and Kaplan, 1972). Aphasics vary in the amount of language that they can understand and in the amount that they can expressively produce. Linguistically, their expressive difficulties can be seen to occur at three levels of language production: phonologically, syntactically and semantically. This is the current approach to understanding the breakdown of language (Lesser, 1978; Taylor Sarno, 1981).

These three levels of linguistic difficulty can be seen in the following way in the patient. First, that the aphasic person may be seen to struggle with finding the correct name for something. He may cope functionally with this by giving up, talking about the subject instead of stating what the subject is, or providing an alternative to his target word (the alternative being a real word or a non-word). The aphasic may also struggle with sequencing sentences and be reduced to telegrammatic-style communications (/'shops, shops, chocolate?'/ for 'I want to go to the shops and get some chocolate'.) The third level which may be affected involves organising the sounds in a word whereby the aphasic may get into difficulties and produces paraphasias because of this (e.g. mɪʃɪŋ mɪʃin* for 'washing machine' — without phonetic script, this would read as 'mishing misheen'). These levels of difficulty may occur alongside each other or as separate, individual features of the aphasic's problem.

Whatever the precise linguistic features are, however, all adult aphasics do share the same experience of having been efficient communicators in their past. They also share the same uncertain future because as yet there is no accurate predictor of how much linguistic recovery there will be.

One of the ironies of the aphasic condition is that it becomes so difficult for patients to be able to describe the experience of losing communication skills. Literature focusing on the personal experience appears to offer two approaches to the discussion of the problem. Many people who have suffered aphasia and made a good recovery, have attempted to describe it (Lordat, quoted in Riese, 1979; Scott Moss, 1972; Wulf, 1973; Hodgins, 1968). Professionals who work with aphasics have similarly attempted to describe the aphasic's reactions (Benson, 1973; Lebrun, 1978; Broida, 1979; Brumfitt and Clarke, 1983). Thus, there is evidence which is from the person's internal experience and other evidence which comes from external observation.

A Major Loss for the Aphasic

Whether aphasic or professional, there seems to be no doubt that the experience can be viewed as a major event in the life of the aphasic and as a major loss.

Patients who are suffering from brain damage particularly lose a lot of control over their lives. Mobility and much physical independence may be lost. If the patient is aphasic too, then the major and conventional forms of communication are blocked. Often the description of the aphasic's loss of communication skills is inadequate as it can be seen as a generalisation which may obscure the complexities of the loss. These complexities in the loss, such as problems with expressing anger, everyday needs, emotional needs and teasing and joking in intimacy are described in Brumfitt and Clarke (1983). Certainly, the loss in the quality of a personal relationship cannot be overestimated (Müller and Code, 1983; Kinsella and Duffy, 1978).

If the aphasic suffers a major loss in this way, a useful perspective on his reaction to the loss is in the grief reaction. The process of grief has been further described by both Bowlby (1980) and Murray-Parkes (1975). Murray-Parkes offers seven features of bereavement reaction to encompass the process of grief, and these will be discussed in relation to the aphasic predicament.

(1) *The Process of Realisation.* Clearly, it is essential for the aphasic's steps in rehabilitation that he move satisfactorily through this process so that there is some realistic understanding of what has happened to him. Often the speech therapist helps the aphasic through this process as the extent of his communication problem becomes apparent through therapy.

(2) *Alarm Reaction.* Often aphasic patients complain of waking in the night with feelings of extreme fear. Relatives also complain of the patient being unable to settle.

(3) *Urge to Search for and Find the Lost Person.* This can be related to the aphasic's search for his old self — the person he was before suffering the brain damage. Often the aphasic wants to talk about this 'past self' by bringing objects and photographs that relate to his old self.

(4) *Anger and Guilt.* This is noted to occur particularly towards those who seem to be trying to force the bereaved or aphasic patient into acceptance of his loss. This may often be directed at the speech therapist, who by assessment methods may well be indicating to the aphasic patient the extent of his handicap. Aphasics often feel real guilt at what has happened to them and may rationalise it as a punishment for something bad they did in the past, or else see it as validation of the bad person they feel they really are.

(5) *Feelings of Internal Loss of Self or Mutilation.* Clearly, to lose communication skills has an impact in all social relationships. The aphasic cannot function in the same way and thus his old self is damaged.

(6) *Identification Phenomena.* Often the aphasic makes great efforts to identify with aspects of his old self, by spending time with workmates (although he cannot work himself), carrying round some object that identifies him as he used to be (certificates of qualifications etc).

(7) *Pathological Variants of Grief.* In people who had lost spouses and who were referred for psychiatric help, Murray-Parkes noted that two types of reaction were presented which constituted atypical grief: (i) the tendency for grief to be prolonged; (ii) the tendency for the reaction to bereavement to be delayed. These two reactions have relevance for the aphasic in terms of the patient who has extreme difficulty in adjusting to his handicap. He may suffer in the ways previously outlined, but without movement or change. For the aphasic who is delayed in responding to his loss, this may be a physical phenomena (diaschisis — where the brain physically is thrown out of gear and needs time to function — Lebrun, 1978), but also a means of subconsciously defending himself from letting the feelings come through.

A Personal Construct Approach to Grief

Kelly (1955) stated that, 'one's deepest understanding of being maintained as a social being is his concept of his core role'. Each person depends on validation of core roles as a means by which to maintain a consistent view of himself. If the core roles were not consistent it would be difficult for the person to have any sort of sense of self. Clearly, individuals need to have some sense of self that they recognise. If an event occurs which causes a breakdown of the core roles then the person may be pushed into total psychological disorder.

Certainly, a person's construction system is never completely at rest. Kelly describes the person as a 'form of motion'; we are obviously continually evolving. However, within this natural movement core roles stay the same unless an event is so major as to cause reconstruing in a major way.

The impact of becoming aphasic is seen as an event that is of the magnitude to affect core-role construing. The dimensions of transition as described by Kelly (1955) relate to core-role reconstruing and these are clearly relevant to the process of grief. As previously discussed, grief is composed of many features, and it is clear that the newly aphasic person who is forced to reconstrue may experience the following:

guilt — the awareness of dislodgement of the self from one's core-role structure (Kelly, 1955)

threat — the awareness of imminent comprehensive change in one's core structure (Kelly, 1955)

fear — the awareness of an imminent incidental change in one's core structures (Kelly, 1955)

anxiety — the recognition that the events with which one is confronted lie outside the range of convenience of one's construct system (Kelly, 1955)

sadness — an awareness of the invalidation of implications of a portion or all of the core structure (McCoy, 1977)

anger — an awareness of invalidation of constructs leading to hostility (McCoy, 1977)

Many people would intuitively define grief as sadness, and certainly McCoy's definition of sadness accommodates a lot of the concept of grief. However, what is particularly important about grief is the range of feelings experienced with a grieving person moving in and out of predominant anxiety, guilt, anger or sadness. There is a need to form a definition which allows for all those dimensions to exist.

Importantly in grief, one major element is lost. If 'oneself as a speaker' is considered as an element the following definition can be seen to apply to the process of grief and thus to the aphasic experience: 'an awareness that one's core constructs are in the process of change by invalidation of their implications through loss of one of the elements'.

Use of Repertory Grids with People who have Restricted Communication

In the past there has been very little use of this method of finding out about a person's construct system, when the person is aphasic. Bannister and Fransella (1971) discuss the use of the Grid Test of Thought Disorder with aphasic patients, where it was found that they scored near the tight end of the tight-loose dimension.

Riedel (1970) presented an investigation of personal constructs using what he described as non-verbal tests with neuropsychiatric (chronic pyschotic) and non-psychiatric medical patients. Although clinically different from the aphasics, Riedel proposed that the limited expressive speech of the psychotic patients warranted a new approach to the investigation of construing. Mancuso and Sarbin (1972) were highly critical of this approach mostly because of what they saw as Riedel's misunderstanding of psychoses, but also because of Riedel's assumption that his use of circle tokens could be made to 'stand for' a person's construct of self. Riedel used symbols to represent elements, and placed the symbols in relation to each other to represent the person's construal of closeness/distance, quality/inequality and other interpersonal constructions. Ziller, Megas and De Cencio (1964) used a similar approach with patients who have had electro-convulsive therapy (ECT) and other neuropsychiatric patients and then neuropsychiatric patients and normal subjects, where the subjects were required to arrange circles representing the self and other relevant people on a felt board.

If this approach of using symbols to represent elements were used with aphasics some difficulties might occur in getting the aphasic to understand the idea of a token representing the self — for two reasons. One, that some aphasic brain-damaged people suffer difficulties with spatial ability; and two, because the symbolic activity involved in letting an object 'stand for' something else is quite complex and may be even more difficult than a straightforward struggle with language.

Gordon (1977) used a repertory grid technique with profoundly deaf teenagers. They were asked to rank eight elements along ten supplied constructs. All constructs were communicated by sign. Thus, signing language was used in place of verbal language.

Hence, approaches to the repertory grid have been developed which have attempted to take account of different sorts of problems with communication.

Investigation of Use of Repertory Grids with Aphasics

I decided to use repertory grids with a group of moderate to severe aphasic patients to explore whether this was a feasible approach with this sort of patient, and whether it would reveal and perhaps confirm some of the aspects about grief previously discussed. Seven patients were included in this group, six men and one woman, all of whom had suffered a cerebral vascular accident (CVA) at least 7 months previously. Exact length of time since onset, age and occupation can be found in Table 6.1.

Table 6.1: Comparative Ages, Occupations and Time Since Onset of CVA

Subject	Age	Time since onset of CVA	Occupation
A	39	1 yr 8 mth	Engineer
B	61	1 yr	Cremation worker
C	78	11 mth	Retired
D	55	1 yr 2 mth	Steel worker
E	72	1 yr 6 mth	Housewife
F	48	1 yr 3 mth	Joiner
G	61	8 mth	Sales manager

The subjects used ranged in age from 39-78 years, with a mean age of 59.1 years. The length of time since the cerebral vascular accident ranged from 8 months to 1 year and 8 months, with a mean length of 1 year 1 month.

All these patients had very restricted language (see appendix for an example of a patient's speech in conversation). In order to maintain a conversation the therapist had to give many prompts in order to keep it going at all. Within a four-minute recorded conversation there is a particularly high rate of verbal exchange between therapist and patient, and much of the patient's responses are mere acknowledgements of the therapist's attempts to guess what the target speech is (see Table 6.2).

Table 6.2: Therapist and Patient Interaction in a Four-minute Conversation

Subject	Therapist's questions	Therapist's responses (including 'mm')	Patient's responses	Patient's questions
A	5	4	7	
B	33	9	36	
C	8	7	15	
D	43	13	42	
E	20	5	23	1
F	24	13	30	
G	21	7	19	

This group's understanding of language is also very restricted. The therapist's comments have to be simple and concrete. Because of this it was unlikely that this group of patients would be able to make sense of the linguistically complex elicitation procedure in the traditional repertory grid. Therefore it was decided to devise some means of making the grid less of a verbally focused exercise.

In consequence, the number of elements used was restricted to 8 elements for six of the group and 7 elements for Mr C, who had very restricted social contact. The elements used were as follows:

1. Past self
2. Self when struggling to talk now
3. Self when not talking now

4. Ideal self
5. Spouse
6. Child/brother/sister
7. Someone you feel sorry for
8. A friend

Mr C used the same elements 1-4, but then used:

his mother (dead some years before)
his speech therapist
his doctor

In terms of eliciting constructs, one solution would have been to supply the constructs. However, the problem then arises of not knowing whether the verbal label supplied is a meaningful label to the patient. Aphasics frequently recognise a word as one that they know, and in a vague, elusive way have a 'feeling of knowing' the word. Yet, actually, they are unable to process the word sufficiently to actually understand the meaning of it. There was a possibility then that the therapist could construe the patient as understanding the supplied label and that might have been incorrect.

Hence, it was decided to use a visual stimulus to help the aphasic select his own label and thereby his own construct. Pairs of photographs were therefore presented to each patient. They were selected from advertisements in magazines and all had scenes depicting some sort of human condition. It was felt important to include photographs which might elicit constructs about health vs handicap, loneliness vs being involved with people.

Grid Construction

All seven subjects managed to produce grids. The number of constructs which they were able to produce ranged from 5 to 7. On two occasions, two subjects had to be cued for elicitation of a construct label. (This is a speech therapy approach where a stimulus is given which aids production of a word — e.g. 'a person who smiles and laughs a lot is . . .'. The narrowing of the semantic field in this way appears to help dysphasics sometimes). For the rest of the elicitation procedure the subjects were able to struggle for themselves until they produced a label that was

Figure 6.1: Subject A's Grid

3	2	1	Past self	Self when talking now	Self when not talking	Ideal self	Wife	Mother	Sister	Son
Laughing		Not laughing	3	1	1	3	3	1	3	3
Happy		Not happy	2	1	2	3	2	2	3	3
Ill		Not ill	1	3	3	1	1	3	1	1
Not angry		Angry	1	1	2	1	1	1	1	1
Young		Old	3	2	2	2	2	1	1	3
Normal		Not so normal	3	1	2	2	3	1	3	3

satisfactory to them. See Figure 6.1 for an example of a grid completed by someone with aphasia.

Results from Analysis of Grids by INGRID

The raw grids in this study were analysed by the INGRID program (Slater, 1977). The features of particular interest will be reported below.

Distances Between Elements. When self element distances were ranked (see Table 6.3) and the Friedman Two-way Analysis of Variance applied (Siegel, 1956), it was clear that these distances represented a group pattern. Of particular interest is the closeness between the two elements 'past self' and 'ideal self' which was represented in all subjects. This is a useful finding in relation to the discussion of grief. As the grieving person mourns the loss of the previous self, this self becomes a yearned and longed-for identity and thus is idealised. So, it makes sense that the aphasics would construe qualities in their past pre-CVA self as being the ideal qualities to be sought after.

Amount of Variance in Components. Individual grids vary in how much variance is accounted for by each component. Of particular interest is the amount of variance accounted for by Component 1. Although there is, at present, no hard evidence to suggest

Table 6.3: Aphasic Group, Comparison of Element Pairs

Subject	PS/ST Distance score	Rank order	PS/SNT Distance score	Rank order	ST/SNT Distance score	Rank order	PS/IS Distance score	Rank order	ST/IS Distance score	Rank order	SNT/IS Distance score	Rank order
A	1.303	2	1.555	1	0.603	5.5	0.603	5.5	1.255	3	1.101	4
B	1.183	4.5	1.183	4.5	1.183	4.5	1.183	4.5	1.673	1.5	1.673	1.5
C	1.128	2	0.798	4.5	1.128	2	0.000	6	1.128	2	0.793	4.5
D	0.988	3.5	0.988	3.5	1.398	1	0.000	6	0.988	3.5	0.988	3.5
E	0.948	4.5	0.948	2.5	0.000	5.5	0.000	5.5	0.948	2.5	0.948	5.5
F	0.933	4	1.373	2	0.852	5	0.762	6	1.204	3	1.570	1
G	0.847	3.5	0.847	3.5	0.000	6	0.692	5	1.094	1.5	1.094	1.5
Main distance	1.05		1.1		0.738		0.463		1.18		1.17	

Note: Elements: PS = past self; ST = self talking now; SNT = self not talking now; IS = ideal self.
Friedman Two-way Analysis of Variance
$Xr^2 = 18.3$
$P = \sim 0.001$

average amounts it would seem that most grids range from 30 to 60 per cent in Component 1. Table 6.4 gives the amount of variance for Component I and Component 2. The great amounts shown for some of the subjects in Component 1 are unusual.

Table 6.4: Amount of Variance (Per Cent) Accounted For by the Two Main Principal Components

Subject	Component 1	Component 2
A	76	14
B	50	30
C	66	25
D	56	44
E	59	24
F	71	14
G	67	19

In this particular group, subjects A, F, G and C represented a very unusual sample. The amounts for subjects A (76 per cent) and F (71 per cent) are especially large and indicate that both people interpret the world by means of a certain set of constructs for a lot of the time.

Individual Grids

To illustrate the possible clinical usefulness of repertory grids, two individuals will be discussed in more depth in relation to their own results from the grid.

Subject A. This man was aged 39 years at the time of the grid administration and had suffered a CVA 17 months previously. He had worked as an engineer before becoming ill, but was now too handicapped to work at all (he had a right hemiplegia, agnosia, apraxia and aphasia). His emotional reaction to his predicament had been expressed to his own speech therapist and he was able to communicate some of this bewilderment over his position to her. He had responded to his difficulties in the initial stages by refusing to go out, and it had needed help from the speech therapist before he would venture into any sort of social life. He had a supportive wife, but she was as bewildered as he was by the confusing array of problems he experienced because of the apraxic and agnosic element in the brain damage.

The important construct relationships are presented below in a diagrammatic form (0.6 and above is taken as a significant construct relationship).

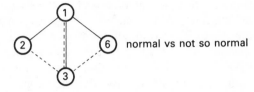

laughing vs not laughing

happy vs not happy   normal vs not so normal

ill vs not ill

....   negative correlation

_____   positive correlation

==============   perfect correlation (1.000)

As noted in Table 6.4, the amount of variance accounted for by the Component 1 is 76 per cent and only 14 per cent in Component 2. As previously stated, this amount of variance accounted for in Component 1 is very unusual. The constructs which were shown to carry heavy loadings in Component 1 were 1, 2, 3 and 6, to which are the constructs presented diagrammatically above as being significantly correlated. Thus, it would seem that subject A saw much of this world in terms of discriminating between being ill, not laughing, normal and happy. Of special interest is the fact that constructs 1 and 3 are perfectly correlated, so that for subject A being not ill means you can be laughing whereas being ill means you cannot be laughing.

What is particularly interesting in this system is the restricted construing. Subject A construes much of his world in terms of the construct discriminations mentioned above. This implies a constellatory way of construing. Kelly (1955) states that it is often 'economical' for people to use a constellatory means of construing in everyday situations. However, if this sort of construing takes place exclusively, it then becomes difficult for the person to recognise or to experiment with other constructs which fail to fit into that constellation. This may cause a problem in rehabilitation for this subject if he fails to elaborate his construing.

With reference to the elements considered in subject A's grid, his construal of 'past' and 'ideal self' are close. There is some evidence that he does discriminate between 'self talking' and 'self not talking' although the distance is small (0.603). However, of note is the element distance between 'past self' and 'self not talking now' (1.555 and considered as 'rare' by Tutton, 1972). Because the two elements of 'self talking now' and 'self not talking now' were included in the grid, it was hoped to tease out the person's discrimination between himself as an active disabled speaker as opposed to himself not speaking at all (therefore not having to recognise this disabled communication). Surprisingly then, this subject actually construed a great distance between his old self and his present self when not talking. It may be that the state of 'not talking' represented more intensely to him his present predicament and the vastness of the distance between that state and what he was before his stroke.

This subject's particular aphasic problem represented a breakdown in language at the semantic level. This sort of problem means that the person has difficulty in mentally gaining access to the lexicon even before attempting to articulate a word. Thus, for this man to have got communication going at all may have felt like something very positive.

Alternatively, this subject may have made a rather concrete interpretation of the two element labels 'self talking' and 'self not talking', which meant that he understood 'self not talking' to literally mean his aphasic communication. Thus, it would make sense for this to be greatly distant from his construction of his 'past self'.

Subject G. Subject G was a man who had suffered a CVA 6 months previously. He had recovered physically, but still had marked aphasic problems. He had been working up to the time of his stroke as a sales manager in a well-known electrical firm. His wife and son provided good support, but he was finding difficulty in accepting that he might never return to work.

There is a very tight relationship of constructs here. Correlations are notably high on all of these (0.8 and above for constructs 1+2, 1+4, 1+5, 1+6, 5+6; perfect correlation on constructs 2+4). Constructs 2+4 which show this perfect correlation are difficult to make sense of with the amount of information available. What is implied from this correlation is that being

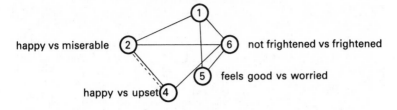

healthy vs handicapped

happy vs miserable

not frightened vs frightened

feels good vs worried

happy vs upset

Diagram of Significant Construct Relationships for Subject G

⋯⋯⋯⋯⋯⋯   perfect correlation between two constructs

happy means being happy and being miserable means being upset. Clearly, the elicitation of the constructs was not taken far enough. The limits of this subject's language meant that his one word responses had to be accepted for what they were. To use a technique of pyramiding or laddering would have been impossible.

In this grid 67 per cent of variance is taken out by the first component. Like subject A, this is a large amount and very unusual. In terms of the constructs which are closely related, subject G sees a major part of his world in terms of healthiness, feeling good, being happy and not frightened; or in contrast being handicapped, frightened, miserable, upset or worried. An expected way to view the world in view of this person's difficulties but a very restricted way.

Of interest in the way that the elements are construed, is the fact that this person construes his son and ideal self as identical. This brings into question whether the son now embodies all the qualities that subject G has lost and thus these qualities have become those that he now yearns for and idealises.

The elements of 'self talking now' and 'self not talking now' are also construed identically. It may be that this subject recognises his plight of the present in a totally negative way so that talking or not makes no difference to the dreadfulness of it all.

Conclusions

The results showed a consistent pattern, in that all subjects construed themselves differently in the present as compared to the past. This group also had three examples of people who construed their 'past selves' as identical to the 'ideal selves' which justifies the assumptions put forward by the brief model of Murray-Parkes in terms of the searching for the lost self.

It was hoped to establish a definite distinction between 'self talking' and 'self not talking'. The results were surprising in that two subjects (E and G) construed the two elements identically. As suggested in the individual review of subject G, this may have been because their present state felt complete and talking or not talking were equally bad.

Certainly, the subjects in this study presented as constricted construers. This may be an important feature in rehabilitation. If the CVA patient constricts in order to cope with the chaos around him, positive change from the state of being a disabled person may be difficult.

Using Repertory Grids with Aphasic Patients

By definition the plight of the aphasic patient may be uncommunicable. But it is clear that certainly a greater depth of understanding of the aphasic's construct system can be gained by the use of the repertory grid.

Even with severely disabled aphasics, some construct labels can be obtained providing the patient has access to some small range of vocabulary. The size and extent of the grid has to be limited but it may indeed represent only too well the limitations of the aphasic's world.

A final point has to be made about pre-verbal and non-verbal construing. It would seem that the aphasic still has the potential to construe in this way. Frequently pre- and non-verbal construing relates to bodily sensations, the 'gut reactions' that are difficult even for a normal speaker to articulate. The aphasic may have to non-verbally reconstrue his own body which may now be hemiplegic, and this needs to be acknowledged too.

The aphasic is not a person, therefore, who only has constructs which reflect the level of his language ability. There may well be a useful means of construing which is inaccessible via spoken language strategies.

Appendix

Subject A in Conversation with the Therapist

Th. /I'm going to 'show you some 'pictures/ I 'want you to 'try and 'tell me the 'names. What's 'that?/

Pt /'That 'there/ It's . . ./ It's 'what you . . ./ It's 'one of 'these here . . . (long pause)

Th. /Why can't you 'tell me what it is?/

Pt /Because it 'won't 'come./ It 'blocks it'self out/,

Th. /How a'bout if I 'tell you 'what it 'is and then you re'peat it/ It's a chair/ chair/

Pt (long pause. Thumps table) /'Chair/.

Th. /'Good/ /'What's that?/

Pt /It's 'that/ (waves hand) (Oh./

Th. /'Try it a'gain / after me / 'Hand /

Pt /'No its . . . /

Th. /'Does it 'help if I 'say it or 'does it confuse you?/

Pt /'Some/ Sort of 'built up/ But 'that/. You're just 'saying it and 'nothing it's not, it's not./ It's like 'stuck 'there but it 'doesn't come through/ It's like 'stuck there and there's nowhere for it to come out/.

Th. /Mm. What's that?

Pt /It's what I've 'come in this 'morning./

References

Bannister, D. and Fransella, F. (1971) *Inquiring Man: The Theory of Personal Constructs*, Penguin, London

Benson, D. (1973) 'Psychiatric Aspects of Aphasia', *British Journal of Psychiatry*, *123*, 555-66

Bowlby, J. (1980) *Loss, Sadness and Depression. Attachment and Loss: Vol. 3*, Penguin, London

Broida, H. (1979) *Coping with Stroke*, College Hill Press, San Diego, California

Brumfitt, S.M. and Clarke, P.R.F. (1983) *An Application of Psychotherapeutic Techniques to the Management of Aphasia* in C. Code and D.J. Müller (eds), Aphasia Therapy Edward Arnold, London

Codey, C. and Müller, D.J. (1983) *Aphasia Therapy*, Edward Arnold, London

Dahlberg, C.C. and Jaffe, J. (1977) *Stroke — a Doctor's Diary of his Recovery*, G. McLead Ltd, USA

Goodglass, H. and Kaplan, E. (1972) *The Assessment of Aphasia and Related Disorders*, Philadelphia: Lea & Febiger

Gordon, A. (1977) 'Thinking With Restricted Language: a Personal Construct Investigation of Prelingually Profoundly Deaf Apprentices', *British Journal of Psychology, 68*, 253-5

Hodgins, E. (1968) *Episode: Report on the Accident Inside My Skull*, Atheneum, New York

Kelly, G. (1955) *The Psychology of Personal Constructs Volumes 1 and 2*, Norton and Co, New York

Kinsella, G. and Duffy, G. (1978) 'The Spouse of the Aphasic Patient' in 'The Management of Aphasia' in *Neurolinguistics, vol. 8*, Swets & Zeitlinger, Amsterdam

Lebrun, Y. (1978), 'The Inside of Aphasia' in 'The Management of Aphasia' in *Neurolinguistics*, vol. 8, Swets & Zeitlinger, Amsterdam

Lesser, R. (1978) *Linguistic Investigations of Aphasia*, Edward Arnold, London

Lordat, J. (1983) 'Auto Observation of Aphasia' in W. Riese (ed.), *Selected Papers on the History of Aphasia*, Swets & Zeitlinger, Amsterdam

McCoy, M. (1977) 'A Reconstruction of Emotion' in D. Bannister (ed.), *New Perspectives in Personal Construct Theory*, Academic Press, London

Mancuso, J.C. and Sarbin, T.R. (1972) 'Schizophrenia, Personal Constructs and Riedels Constructs', *Journal of Abnormal Psychology, 79*, 148-50

Murray-Parkes, C. (1975) *Bereavement*, Penguin, London

Porch, B. (1967) *The Porch Index of Communicative Ability*, Consulting Psychologists Press, USA

Riedel, W. (1970) 'An Investigation of Personal Constructs Through Non-verbal Tasks', *Abnormal Psychology, 76*, 173-9

Riese, W. (1977) 'Selected Papers on the History of Aphasia' in *Neurolinguistics, vol. 7*, Swets & Zeitlinger, Amsterdam

Schuell, H.R. (1965) *The Minnesota Test for the Differential Diagnosis of Aphasia*, University of Minnesota Press, Minneapolis

Scott Moss, C. (1972) *Recovery With Aphasia*, University of Illinois Press, Illinois

Siegel, S. (1956) *Non-parametric Statistics for the Behavioural Sciences*, McGraw Hill, New York

Slater, P. (1977) *Explorations of Intrapersonal Space*, Wiley, Chichester

Taylor Sarno, M. (1981) *Acquired Aphasia*, Academic Press, London

Tutton, E. (1972) 'Analysis of Distance Between Elements' in 'Notes on INGRID 1972', P. Slater, St George's Hospital, London

Wulf, H.H. (1973) *Aphasia, My World Alone*, Wayne State University Press, Detroit

Ziller, R.C., Megas, J. and De Cencio, D.D. (1964) 'Self Social Constructs of Normals and Acute Neuropsychiatric Patients', *Journal of Consulting Psychology, 28*, No. 1, 59-63

7 REPERTORY GRIDS WITH AMPUTEES

Keren Fisher

A recent Medline literature search (Jan. 1984) revealed that only 37 papers were available that had attempted to describe the self-image of seriously injured people. Of these, a mere six dealt with amputation subjects, and only one, Weiss, Fishman and Krause (1970) had employed recognised psychological testing procedures. Unfortunately, this was an unusual use of the Bender Gestalt (Bender, 1938), and the results were not sufficiently reliable to warrant the use of the test on individual patients. Murray-Parkes (1973) has used visual analogue scales to allow patients to rate themselves on three supplied components (Pain insensitive/Sensitive, Adaptable/Rigid, Perfectionist/Slapdash) and related them to subsequent phantom pain, but was unable to demonstrate very high correlations. Although Caine (1973) suggests that about half of the patients who undergo an amputation later require some form of psychological help, there seems to have been very little systematic assessment of the problems that interfere with successful rehabilitation.

On the face of it, it seems reasonable to ask about factors affecting self-esteem, and in a group of rehabilitation patients who had sustained various disabilities through disease or accidents, Katz, Shurka and Florian (1978) used the Semantic Differential (Osgood, Succi and Tannenbaum, 1957). This would seem to lead us into an appropriate area of study until we realise the Semantic Differential was completed by *other people* (school children), and measures of 'self' esteem were attributed to the same wheelchair patient seen on video tape with several different explanations of the cause of injury. Those children who were given a war-veteran explanation rated 'self' esteem higher than others who were told that the cause was a road or work accident, or polio. Fortunately, this finding was confirmed when 56 disabled patients were asked to rate their own self-concept. Using the Tennessee Self-concept Scale (Fitts, 1965), the same authors discovered that self-esteem was higher among the war veterans than among those disabled for other reasons, even if the success of rehabilitation was the same.

Not a single published study could be traced that used the repertory grid technique to examine the change in self-image occasioned by severe injury. This is quite surprising considering its popularity with emotional disorders generated by the loss of a spouse or adaptation difficulties to other problems such as stuttering (Fransella, 1972). It is true that Cunningham (1977) thought that the repertory grid was unsuitable for physically disabled subjects and abandoned it, but in fact it has unique properties for answering questions about the self before and with the disability, or in the ideal world, and only two of the current sample were unable to co-operate. These subjects objected to the idea of focusing on their emotional reactions at all (preferring to 'forget' them), rather than rejecting the grid in particular.

The advantage of the grid technique is that it is ideographic and as such has particular value in describing an individual's unique experience, thus overcoming some of the objections to ready made standardised tests that contain irrelevant items or are impossible to answer accurately from the 'myself before my accident' standpoint. However, it has also proved possible to use some of the elements and constructs as universal ideas and thus to look at group analysis, which is able to describe the differences between groups divided on physical grounds. Thus, individual grids on amputation subjects have been able to help answer the following questions all in one operation:

(1) How has this person's self image changed as a result of his/her amputation?
(2) What are the particular aspects (if any) of this person's experience that are giving rise to psychological disorders and which can be incorporated into a psychotherapeutic programme?
(3) Do amputation subjects have anything psychologically in common with each other?
(4) Does the outcome of rehabilitation aimed at physical independence relate to the patients' psychological functioning?

Subjects

In order to qualify for inclusion in the study the patients must:

(1) Give consent

(2) Have lost a limb as a result of accident or illness

(3) Be available for assessment at least one year after the amputation

(4) Be in the 'young traumatic' group rather than the 'elderly vascular' group (by far the largest number of amputation subjects could not be selected on this variable).

Out of 18 patients who fulfilled these criteria two refused to complete the procedure, two were excluded because of inadequate data in the grid, and two had major family problems rendering the procedure of low priority to them. This left twelve patients with a mean age of 33 years and a mean time from amputation of 25 months. Two of these had above-elbow, six had above-knee and four had below-knee amputations. Eight sustained their injuries in accidents, one had a tumour, one had vascular disease of early onset, and two patients requested amputation following repeated unsuccessful knee operations to repair instability.

After a minimum of one year from amputation the subjects were divided by the surgeon's opinion into two groups. Group One were successfully rehabilitated on the physical criteria of being able to employ their time usefully (returning to work or former household duties wherever possible) and not requesting frequent clinic appointments because of amputation-related symptoms. Group Two failed to reach these criteria and are considered the unsuccessful group. There are six patients in each group who do not differ in any important way in distribution of sex, age, time elapsed since amputation or site of amputation.

Procedure

The repertory grid was administered in the usual standard format, though not all of Kelly's (1955) 24 roles could be used. As far as possible elicitation was favoured, but after the first four subjects when a common pool of four constructs was found, these were supplied at the end of the procedure if they or their synonyms had not been produced. The patients were also asked to use the elements 'myself now', 'myself in the ideal world' and 'myself before the amputation', but all other elements were produced by the individual.

When all possible elements had been produced by the patients, construct elicitation was carried out by the triadic method retaining 'myself now' in every presentation. The number of constructs elicited varied from eight to fourteen, but all patients produced or had supplied 'successful vs not', 'happy vs depressed', 'adapted vs not' and 'independent vs dependent'. The only exception to this was one patient who saw independent and successful as opposite poles of the same construct. She is described in Case Study 2.

The patients were then asked to complete the rating form by deciding which end of the construct was appropriate for each element in turn, and how much it applied. Thus, if element 1 is very successful the rating would be 1), if very unsuccessful the rating would be 7). Each individual grid was then analysed by SPSS FACTOR program PAI, with Varimax rotation, elements and constructs being treated separately (Nie *et al.*, 1975).

The important variables for describing the most obvious issues in psychological adjustment were a monolithic construct system and self-alienation (negative correlation of actual and ideal selves). Figure 7.1 shows an example of a well-integrated individual's element plot. Figure 7.2 shows a non-integrated patient. Note the difference in distance between actual self, ideal self and self before amputation.

Makhlouf-Norris and Norris (1972) described a non-neurotic construct system as articulated which allows the subject to shift easily between two or more sets of ideas by means of the linking construct (see Figure 7.3 for an example). In this case the subject is able to differentiate characteristics of people in her life, but at the same time to have flexibility and a sense of cohesion in her predictions of others' behaviour. She can see that people she expects to behave in an ambitious, strong and optimistic way are not necessarily the most caring or likeable people she knows, but she can admire both sorts. In contrast to this a monolithic system reflects rigidity which does not allow for change. Figure 7.4 shows an example. Here, the subject has a tight construing pattern in which people are all seen as either possessing all these 'good' characteristics or not. They cannot be anything instead of argumentative or not, fit or not, happy or not etc. so the patient himself has had to try and fit his changed self into this inflexible

Figure 7.1: Element Plot of Well-integrated Subject

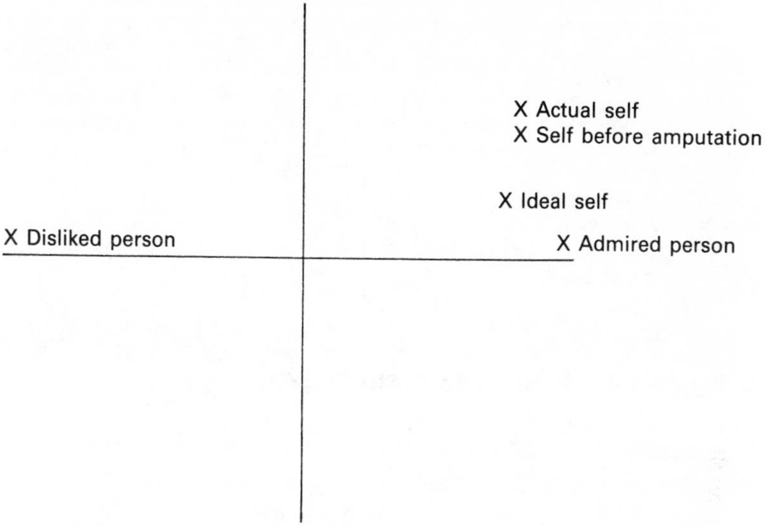

X Actual self
X Self before amputation

X Ideal self

X Disliked person   X Admired person

Figure 7.2: Element Plot of Subject with Self-alienation

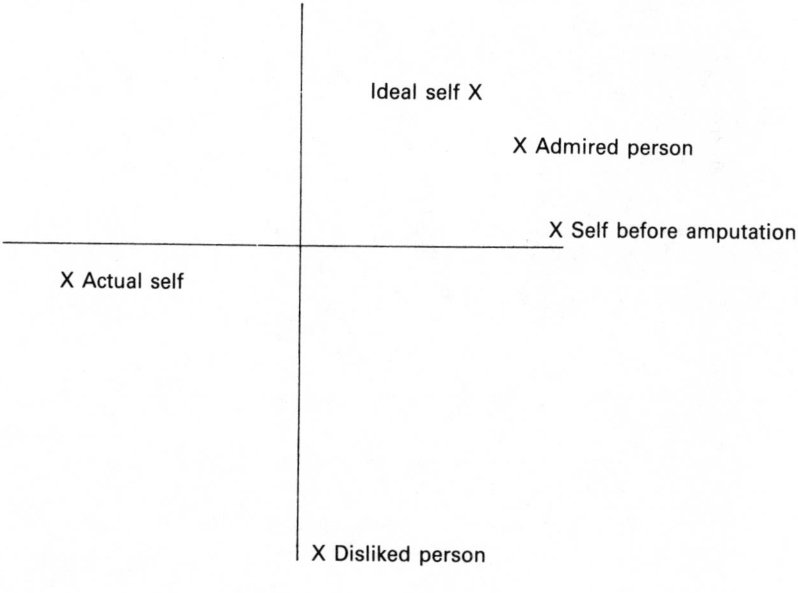

Ideal self X

X Admired person

X Self before amputation

X Actual self

X Disliked person

Figure 7.3: Articulated Construct System

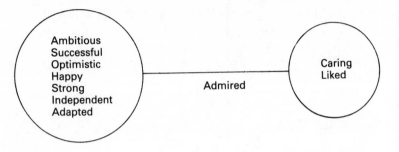

Figure 7.4: Monolithic Construct System

pattern. The result has been that he has not apparently noticed that he has changed since his construct system does not really allow for this eventuality (see Case Study 1).

Figure 7.5: A Segmented Construct System

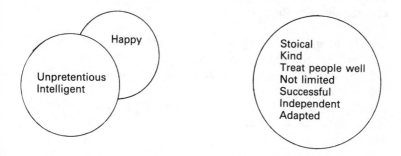

A third alternative pattern in construing behaviour is the segmented system in which groups of ideas are separate from one another but have no linking construct (see Figure 7.5). Here, the patient has divided his thinking into two distinct groups of people. Those who are unpretentious, intelligent and happy cannot in general also be stoical, kind or successful. He expresses a certain confusion about his self-image in relation to these ideas and consequently is indecisive about his life goals. While his ideal self is kind, stoical and independent it is also unintelligent. This is at variance with his measured intelligence, but fits with his difficulty in committing himself to a vocational training to achieve a stimulating job.

By and large, the commonest construct system in the amputation sample is monolithic irrespective of the success of rehabilitation and self-integration.

Results

The successful and unsuccessful groups' ratings on self elements (actual self, self before amputation, ideal self) on the four common constructs, happy, successful, adapted and independent were compared by Mann-Whitney U test to see if there were any significant differences between the groups in terms of their perceived success, happiness, adjustment or independence.

Table 7.1 summarises their results, and it can be seen that these variables do not statistically significantly relate to outcome of rehabilitation, though on this very small data sample, some trends seem to be apparent. There are certain hypotheses worth testing following these results:

(1) The actual self is somewhat depressed following an amputation whether the physical outcome is successful or not.
(2) The ideal self is seen as more happy and more independent in the unsuccessful group.
(3) The former selves are less successful, happy and independent in the unsuccessful group.

Table 7.1: Mann-Whitney U Tests of Raw Ratings for Actual, Ideal and Former Selves on the 4 Common Constructs, Successful and Unsuccessful Groups Compared

Construct	Element	U	P
	Actual	11	0.15
Successful	Ideal	15	0.35
	Former	11	0.15
	Actual	17	0.46
Happy	Ideal	12	0.19
	Former	10	0.12
	Actual	18	0.53
Adapted	Ideal	15	0.35
	Former	13	0.24
	Actual	13	0.24
Independent	Ideal	12	0.19
	Former	10	0.10

Since the Group 2 means for the ideal selves are close to 1 (i.e. the rating suggesting the greatest amount of success and adjustment) it may be that one of the contributing factors to unsuccessful rehabilitation is holding unrealistic beliefs about what one should be like. The unsuccessful group seem to have a lower opinion of themselves even before their accidents, and so it is not surprising that their adjustment to the amputation has been affected.

Two other elements were found which were common to all the records. These were an admired person and a disliked person, and correlation coefficients were computed between the self elements (actual/ideal, actual/former and ideal/former), and between the self and non-self elements (actual/admired, actual/disliked, ideal/admired, ideal/disliked etc.). Table 7.2 summarises the results of this analysis for the successful and unsuccessful groups. This indicates that for the successful group 'myself before the amputation' was very like 'myself as I would like to be' ($r = 0.87$), 'myself now' is not very like 'myself before' ($r = -0.15$) or 'myself as I would like to be' ($r = -0.41$), which implies a significant degree of self-alienation even with satisfactory mobility and occupation of time.

Table 7.2: Correlation Coefficients Between Self and Common Non-self Elements, Successful and Unsuccessful Groups Compared

	Actual	Ideal	Former	Admired	Disliked
Successful group					
Actual		−0.41	−0.15	−0.04	−0.64
Ideal			0.87	0.78	−0.11
Former				0.89	0.00
Admired					0.00
Unsuccessful group					
Actual		−0.08	−0.70	−0.29	−0.80
Ideal			0.33	0.31	0.15
Former				0.36	0.70
Admired					0.79

In the unsuccessful group the striking feature is that the former self is quite like the disliked person ($r = 0.70$) suggesting a pre-existing degree of self-dissatisfaction. Self-alienation is still apparent, though the negative correlation between the actual and ideal selves is smaller ($r = -0.08$) than in the successful group. The finding that those people who fail to make satisfactory progress with physical rehabilitation saw themselves as like disliked people even before their amputations, fits with the implications of the analysis of the raw ratings, that they were less successful, happy and independent before, than the others.

Large-scale investigation of these hypotheses is worth under-taking so that if they are confirmed, relevant psychotherapeutic measures (cognitive therapy or personal construct therapy) can be offered earlier to these patients. It may then be possible to potentiate physical rehabilitation and reduce frequent consulta-tion for amputation-related symptoms for which no medical or prosthetic intervention seems appropriate.

A summary of the frequency of the two main indications of psychological difficulty (self-alienation and a non-articulated construct system) is given in Table 7.3. This shows, not surprisingly, that self-alienation is more frequent in the unsuccessful group, but that a non-articulated construct system is common irrespective of success of rehabilitation. It may be the case that tightening of the construct system has occurred in response to this potentially traumatic procedure, or that pre-existing monolithic systems are adaptable.

Table 7.3: Summary of Frequency of Abnormal Responses

	Successful group %	Unsuccessful group %
Self-alienation	33	66
Non-articulated constructs	66	81

Illustrative Case Studies

Case Study 1

Mr B age 52 was referred for a solicitor's report to help assess the factors involved in settling a compensation claim for damages following a road traffic accident. Mr B had been riding a motorcycle when he was hit by a carelessly driven car and sustained serious injuries to his left leg. This later came to below-knee amputation, and about a year afterwards Mr B was sent for psychological assessment at the surgeon's instigation to include evidence of assumed psychological trauma in his final settlement. When seen, Mr B really had no complaints. He had returned to his firm, but as a bookkeeper (having been previously qualified), rather than the storeman he had been before, and was involved in organising events at his local cycle club where before he had been an active participant. Otherwise Mr B had 'taken up where he left off', and thought that nothing had changed about his self-image. He denied being depressed and had a Beck Depression Inventory (Beck, 1978) score of zero. The element plot of his grid certainly corroborated this as there is no distance at all between his actual and former selves, and on the first factor of his analysed scores, which seems to be a disliked-admired dimension, he sees all his self elements and most people in his social setting as at the ideal end. On the second factor, which could be described as a reasonable-unreasonable dimension, all his self elements and most of the others have very low loadings (see Figure 7.6). His construct system, however, is monolithic (see Figure 7.7).

This indicates that Mr B has a tight construing system in which change is very difficult. It is, of course, not possible to say whether this was a premorbid characteristic or was acquired in the year since his accident, but his assertion that he felt in no way

Figure 7.6: Case Study 1, Element Plot

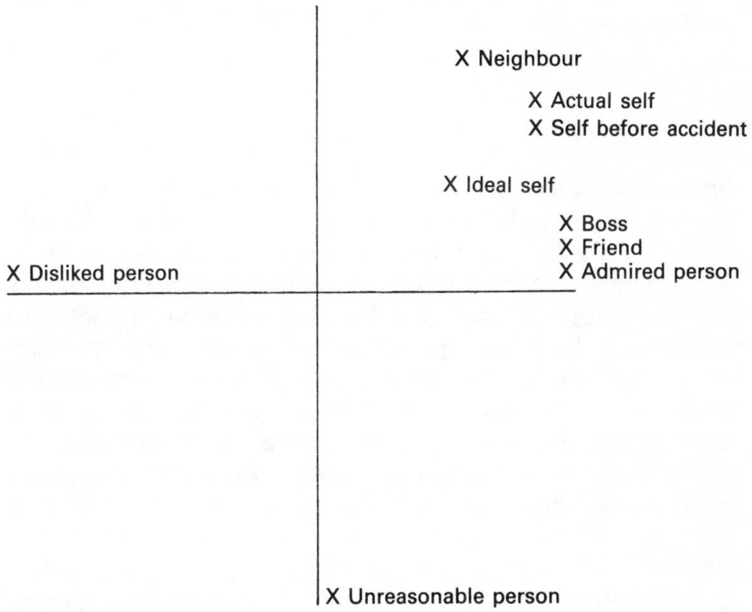

Figure 7.7: Case Study 1, Construct System

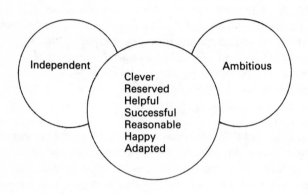

different indicates that he had previously adapted to his life in this way, and found it successfully reduced difficulties with self-esteem. While the monolithic system is said to be neurotic and in this patient's case may represent denial, there was never any evidence before or since that Mr B experienced psychological problems with adjusting to his amputation and it seems unnecessary to invent any. Beck *et al.* (1979) has stated that only people with a predisposition to depression experience it in response to a crisis, and it seems that the grid has behaved as a valid cross-check to this assertion. With Mr B's full approval a report to this effect was sent to the solicitor.

Case Study 2

In contrast to Mr B, Ms D, although also in the successful group from the point of view of physical rehabilitation, had numerous psychological problems. She had also sustained a motorcycle accident. She had been a pillion passenger at the age of 15 and had unstable leg fractures resulting in a below-knee amputation some time later. Ms D's first assessment was carried out a year after her amputation, but nearly three years after her accident. She freely expressed her emotional difficulties, though asserted from the beginning she did not believe anyone could help her with them. It is interesting that the constructs she immediately produced were to do with relationship problems such as 'disliked by others', 'finds it hard to tolerate people', 'bitter' and 'unkind'. She distinctly saw 'independent' and 'successful' as being polar opposites, and laddering shed some light on this. She saw being independent as implying 'not having people around excessively', 'avoiding people getting on your nerves', 'not getting bored with people', whereas 'successful' meant 'other people like you' and 'can sit and talk'. While her ideal self scored highly at the independent end she saw her actual self as less independent because she attracted sympathy, and was liked by people but only because of her disability. Her construct system was monolithic with two unrelated ideas. These were the independent/successful dichotomy and kind/unkind (see Figure 7.8).

She therefore appeared to be expressing difficulty with how she could construe kind people. They were not necessarily happy, easy-going or liked by others. Her report suggested that kind people were the ones who 'got on your nerves', and were 'boring', and to extract herself from this she chose to be independent of relationships rather than successful in them. This clearly indicates a degree of psychological dysfunction which needed further attention. Her element plot showed self-alienation with a moderately large negative correlation between her actual and ideal selves (-0.5), and as can be seen in Figure 7.9 these elements form the extremes of the first component. The second component seems to consist of an admired idea with her most admired and least admired elements lying close to its ends. Her mother (deceased), father and her boyfriend take up intermediate positions along this dimension.

Another interesting feature of this patient's plot is that her before-accident self lies between her ideal self and her most disliked person. This again shows some confusion as to how successful she had ever been at interpersonal relationships. Her

Figure 7.8: Case Study 2, Construct System

X Independent/successful   X Kind

raw rating on 'liked by others' for her former self was moderately 'not liked'. This undoubtedly reflects a certain element of adolescent conflict, but she was unwilling to explore it further.

She then seemed to become inextricably involved in a self-fulfilling prophecy, and soon after she abandoned the relationship with her previous boyfriend (who had been driving the motor cycle at the time of the accident) because of embarrassment and bitterness, she seized the opportunities offered by a young man at work. Not surprisingly, she needed the reassurance that she was still sexually attractive in spite of the amputation, but unfortunately she quickly became pregnant.

When seen for a final report some four years after the amputation her self-esteem was very low, her actual and ideal selves correlating -0.87. At this stage 'myself before the

Figure 7.9: Case Study 2, Element Plot of First Grid

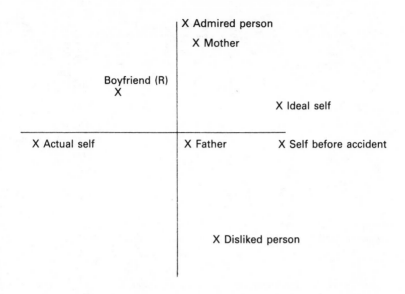

accident' has moved much closer to her ideal self, suggesting that her problems then were as nothing compared to how they are now. Her previous boyfriend has moved nearer her ideal self, however, so it seems some resolution of her antipathy to her friends is occurring. 'Myself in 5 years time' (a new element introduced to test her assertion that she would get better on her own) does indeed represent a degree of optimism since it takes up a quadrant also occupied by her ideal self and admired people (see Figure 7.10).

In this case, repertory grid technique has allowed us to understand the factors involved in Ms D's distress and to relate them to the results of her accident. We can see that her original rating of her former self suggested some ambivalence about her social self, and without effective help she has been unable, to date, to come through her adolescent problems and deal with her relationship difficulties compounded by the added burden of her amputation. Although she does not complain of physical disability, and spends her time not as an invalid but by caring for her child as well as she can (at the last assessment her Beck Depression Inventory score was 46), and so counts as successfully

Figure 7.10: Case Study 2, Element Plot of Final Grid

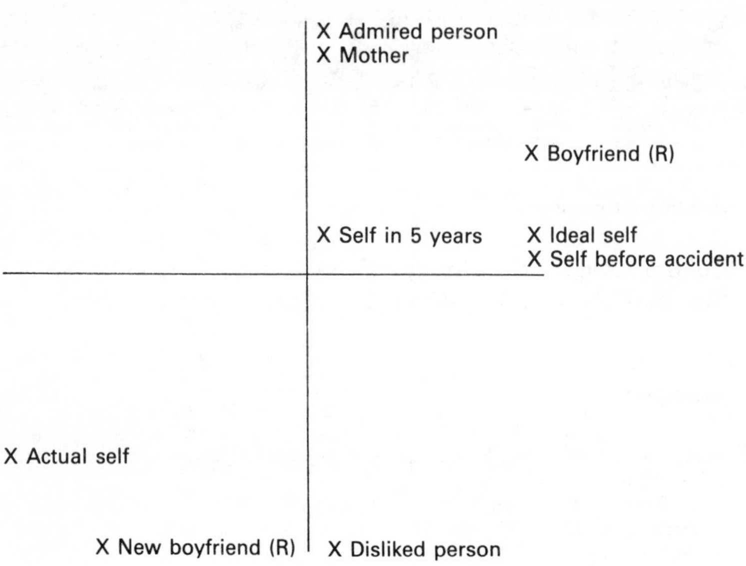

```
                              X Admired person
                              X Mother


                                              X Boyfriend (R)


                         X Self in 5 years    X Ideal self
                                              X Self before accident
 ─────────────────────────────────┼──────────────────────────────────


 X Actual self


            X New boyfriend (R)    X Disliked person
```

rehabilitated, psychologically she is close to helplessness. It is unlikely that this deterioration would have been so dramatic without the intervention of some major trauma, and we have been able to measure Ms D's change in her self-esteem which she represents as an increasing distance between her actual and former selves. We have enough information to plan an effective treatment programme by cognitive restructuring, and if she would agree to it we could measure our therapeutic success by looking for a reduction in her self-alienation and a widening of her construct system, and we could test the validity of her optimism for the future.

Conclusion

The Repertory grid technique seems extremely suitable for helping medical and therapy staff (physical and psychological) to understand the adjustment problems of individual patients following serious injury. It has the advantage of using the patients' unique experience, and makes no assumptions about 'appropriate' reactions at different stages. Furthermore, by examining the results of groups of patients, it may be possible to predict at an earlier stage those people who have certain psychological difficulties which will interfere with rehabilitation success.

Acknowledgements

To Mr J. Angel FRCS for permission to study his patients, and to Mrs Barbara Rose Freedman for excellent secretarial help.

References

Beck, A. (1978) *Depression Inventory*, Center for Cognitive Therapy, Philadelphia
———, Rush, A.J., Shaw, B.F. and Emery, G. (1979) *Cognitive Therapy of Depression*, Wiley, Chichester
Bender, L. (1938) *A Visual Motor Gestalt Test and its Clinical Use*, American Orthopsychiatric Association
Caine, D. (1973) 'Psychological Consideration Affecting Rehabilitation after Amputation', *Med. J. Aust.*, 2, 818-21
Cunningham, D.J. (1977) 'Stigma and Social Isolation', HSRU, Report No.27, Canterbury
Fitts, W.H. (1965) *Tennessee Self-concept Scale*, Nashville Mental Health Center, Tennessee
Fransella, F. (1972) *Personal Change and Reconstruction*, Academic Press, London
——— and Bannister, D. (1977) *A Manual for Repertory Grid Technique*, Academic Press, London
Katz, S., Shurka, E. and Florian, V. (1978) 'The Relationship between Physical Disability, Social Perception and Psychological Stress', *Scand. J. Rehab. Med.*, *10*, 109-13
Kelly, G. (1955) *The Psychology of Personal Constructs*, Norton, New York
Makhlouf-Norris, F. and Norris, H. (1972) 'The Obsessive Compulsive Syndrome as a Neurotic Device for the Reduction of Self-uncertainty', *The Brit. Jnl. of Psychiatry, 121*, 277-88
Murray-Parkes, C. (1973) 'Factors Determining the Persistence of Phantom Pain in the Amputee', *Jnl. of Psychosomatic Research, 17*, 97-108
Nie, N.H., Hull, C.H., Jenkins, J.G. Steinbrenner, K. and Bent, D.H. (1975) *Statistical Package for the Social Sciences*, 2nd edn, McGraw-Hill
Osgood, G.E., Suci, G.J. and Tannenbaum, P.H. (1957) *The Measurement of Meaning*, University of Illinois Press, Urbana
Weiss, S.A., Fishman, S. and Krause, F. (1970) 'Symbolic Impulsivity, the Bender Gestalt Test and Prosthetic Adjustment in Amputees', *Arch. Phys. Med., 51*, 152

8 USING REPERTORY GRID TECHNIQUE WITH SEVERELY DISABLED PEOPLE

Nigel Beail

Repertory grid technique offers us a way of investigating the meaning of a disability, both for a person with it and for those trying to relate to her or him. Yet very little use of grid methods has been made in either individual work or research with people who are physically disabled. In this chapter the reasons for the lack of use are discussed, and some suggestions on how grids can be usefully and successfully employed with disabled people are made.

Numerous studies have established that physically disabled people are construed in a more negative light than able bodied/'normal' people (Altman, 1981; Bender, 1981). This negative construction portrays people with physical disabilities as capable of only a limited range of ability and behaviour. In Personal Construct Theory terms an individual's 'being disabled' is construed in a constellatory or stereotyped way as it implies being less intelligent, less able to make the right decisions, less realistic, less logical and less able to determine his/her own life than a non-disabled person (Safilios-Rothchild, 1976). These attitudes are widely held and have remained unchanged over the last twenty years (Furnham and Pendred, 1983). Professionals (nurses, physiotherapists, occupational therapists, psychologists and social workers) engaged in rehabilitation have also been found to hold the same negative attitudes as those shown by the general population (Goodman *et al.*, 1963).

These negative attitudes seem to have placed a limit on the use of repertory grid technique with disabled people — particularly those who have severe disabilities. My own experience is that many researchers and clinicians believe that the grid method is not suitable to use with disabled people because the task involved is beyond their capabilities.

Similar views are put forward in relation to using repertory grids with people who have mental handicaps. Davis (1983) points out that mentally handicapped people are professionally and traditionally construed pre-emptively as nothing but 'unintelligent'. He goes on to argue that at best current views are constellatory in that the construct 'low intelligence' immediately defines other relevant constructs, for example 'socially maladjusted', 'uneducable' and we could add 'too limited to use grids with'. However, among the population of mentally handicapped people there exists a wide range of intellectual and social handicaps. From a Personal Construct Theory viewpoint it is argued that people with mental handicaps are like everyone else in that they have a personal construct system.

The possibility of exploring the personal construct systems of mentally handicapped people with grids was investigated by Barton, Walton and Rowe (1976). They used grid methods with 26 residents in a large mental handicap hospital, and found that it was possible to obtain reliable and valid pictures of their clients' construct systems using repertory grids. They found this technique to have several advantages 'as it requires little or no literacy, sustained concentration and does not use concepts which may not be understood and/or inappropriate' (Barton *et al.*, 1976). An illustration of the use of repertory grid technique with a person with mental handicap can be found in Chapter 1.

In the debate concerning the provision of psychotherapy for mentally handicapped people (for a résumé see Beail, 1984) arguments against seem to imply that there is a cut-off point on the IQ continuum where psychotherapy becomes unapplicable. Barton *et al.* seem to be making a similar suggestion in regard to the use of grids with mentally handicapped people in that they state 'As a general rule an IQ of 50 may be taken as the lower limit at which a grid can be completed unless the patient is verbally quite able and has lived in an environment encouraging verbal expression'. I would argue, however, that what is important is not IQ or verbal expression but communication in its variety of forms. If the clinician and client can find a way of communicating then construct exploration can be attempted.

Today very little use of grid technique is made by professionals working with mentally handicapped people despite the evidence showing its usefulness. Professional constructs are slow to change.

Professionals working with physically disabled people similarly have made little use of grids. However, the Personal Construct Theory approach leads one away from prejudicing people from without towards attempting to understand them from within their world. Therefore, taking a Personal Construct Theory approach one would seek to do this and use the tools for the job.

You Might Be Able To

Fransella (1968) was the first to suggest the use of repertory grid technique as a 'quantitative assessment of personality' of people with physical disabilities. In her paper she briefly outlined the Personal Construct Theory view and described the rank order and implications grid. She suggested how the theory and method might be used with disabled people but confessed that 'Experience with this technique is still relatively limited'. Indeed, she went on to state that her paper was 'highly speculative' and no applications of the method with disabled people were reported. Two years later Bannister (1970) contributed a chapter to P. Mittler's book *The Psychological Assessment of Mental and Physical Handicaps*. However, in this chapter grid technique was described and compared with the semantic differential, and no discussion on applications with people with physical disabilities was made. So one could only conclude from these early papers that one might be able to use grids with people with physical disabilities. Certainly, neither Bannister nor Fransella mentioned any difficulties.

You Can't

The first account that I can find of using grids with people with severe physical disabilities is that of Cunningham (1977). The respondents in her study were multiple sclerosis sufferers. She asked subjects to list family members, friends, liked person, disliked person, self, ideal self and so on, as elements. Constructs were then elicited by the triad method and elements were rank ordered on each of the construct dimensions.

Cunningham reported that she had little success and decided to abandon the method at the pilot stage. She found the procedure very time consuming and reported that respondents became bored with the process. She felt that these problems in administration had to be weighted against the problems of the grid alienating the respondent, and making it impossible to carry out a further interview in the same session. She also states that the respondent found the 'test' inappropriate and in some cases threatening to compare such elements as ideal self, etc. Some respondents also found it upsetting when asked about the past, present and future with respect to people they knew. Cunningham did not give her subjects a rationale for using the grid method as she felt this would invalidate the results.

Cunningham states that the problems she experienced with grid method may have been associated with the nature of the disease in that people with multiple sclerosis suffer from fatigue and in some cases appeared to be depressed. So she abandoned the method and did not seek to change the grid she used. She felt that this would invalidate the method in Kellyan terms. She argued that there seems to have been insufficient attention paid to standardising the method and training people to use it.

Cunningham's study was not widely circulated, but it did have considerable impact on people who were working with disabled people and those researching in the area of physical disability. Repertory grid technique became to be construed as 'not applicable' with this group. In fact, so little use had been made of grids in this area at that time that one could argue that her study confirmed what many had already thought. However, there are a number of points which should be raised about the way Cunningham construed and used repertory grid technique.

Test or Technique: Rigidity Versus Flexibility

In the context of using grids with people with physical disabilities, Fransella (1968) stated: 'It is a technique and not a test, which means it can be styled for whatever purpose one has in mind'. Cunningham, however, attempted to adhere to what she considered to be a 'Kelly Grid', therefore construing grids as a test — but a rather messy test in need of standardisation. Psychologists who work with disabled clients have found many of their standardised psychometric tests to be unapplicable without modification to a disabled population. Disabled people are not represented in the populations on which these tests are developed and standardised, and often the questions or tasks are inappropriate. Repertory grid technique, on the other hand, was designed to be flexible so that it can be tailored to a particular individual or group to meet the needs of the situation. Therefore, the person or group you are interviewing using the grid format will determine the form the grid takes. If an individual has many elements and a large repertoire of constructs then the resultant grid will be large. If that individual also has multiple sclerosis or cerebral palsy and suffers from fatigue then the grid could be constructed over a number of sessions. If the interviewee has a speech difficulty then communication boards and devices can facilitate communication. Some physically disabled people have poor eyesight; in such cases the interviewer should use materials that they can see (for example, large print), or be able to describe the procedure in clear and simple terms. Choice of element allotment procedure is also important. Cunningham used the rank order method. This is often more time consuming than rating or dichotomous procedures. Ranking also can become a very meaningless exercise when the grid has many elements.

An important issue raised by Cunningham is that of training. Repertory grid technique is a very flexible and diverse method applicable in a wide range of settings. Thus, when planning to use a grid one should be aware that it is not a 'test', and be familiar with its diversity and flexibility. Therefore, using grids involves planning — particularly when being used as part of a research project. We need to consider carefully what questions we are asking, and whether the answers would be better obtained with individually constructed grids or by supplying a set of elements you feel are particularly relevant to the investigation. Alternatively, you may wish to supply some constructs or supply both constructs and elements.

An Illustration

I started my own research investigating the self-image of physically disabled people after the publication of Cunningham's study. As I have pointed out, her findings did influence the attitudes of workers in the area, and there was a general feeling that it was not worth pursuing research with disabled people with this method. However, I was not sufficiently deterred as my understanding of the technique led me to question her reservations. I took heed of her findings and sought a grid format which could be administered to a cross-section of people with severe physical disabilities. In particular, I felt that the grid should be designed with brevity and ease of administration as an important feature. The population to be studied were residents of local authority homes providing residential accommodation for severely physically disabled people. In all 30 people were interviewed (14 male, 16 female). The disabilities of the interviewees covered a wide range, with types of cerebral palsy being the most commonly occurring (see Table 8.1).

Table 8.1: Subjects' Disabilities

Disability	Number
Cerebral palsy	11
Multiple sclerosis	6
Rheumatoid arthritis	3
Poliomyelitis	2
Friedreich's ataxia	2
Hemiplegia	2
Spina bifida	1
Scoliosis	1
Multiple congenital abnormalities	1
Paraplegia	1

No attempt was made to classify the interviewees as to degree of handicap. However, their disability was severe enough as to require admission to a residential unit as they cannot support themselves in the community. Three interviewees also had additional mental handicap. The age range was from 18 years to 57 years, with a mean of 33.4 years.

Elements

The study was concerned with the self-image of physically disabled people — particularly the relationship between the 'self' and the 'stereotype' (how the public see the disabled). I limited the number of elements to those I was specifically interested in: self, ideal self, public self, future self, self without my disability, and how the public see the disabled.

Constructs

Considering the length of time needed to elicit constructs and the fact that many severely physically disabled people suffer from additional fatigue, I considered whether to elicit or supply constructs. Cunningham's experience of eliciting constructs suggests that she may have had more success if she had changed her grid to one in which constructs were supplied. Taking into account the debate on this issue (see Adams-Webber, 1979), I decided to err on the side of caution and supply. Twelve bipolar constructs were employed, and these were derived from a list compiled from a survey of semantic differential and grid studies of self and body image.

Presentation

Several factors influenced the method of presentation. Many of the residents had problems with their eyesight, therefore the materials had to be presented in a form that they could see or that could be easily described. Also most of the residents had motor impairments which made it either difficult or impossible for them to write. Some also had speech difficulties. In order to overcome these I opted for the rating method of element allotment and presented each construct scale (5 point) in large black print on 6 in × 9 in (15 cm × 22.5 cm) white cards. Therefore, respondents were able to concentrate on each construct for each element. All but one subject could see the scales. The exception was blind, but had no difficulty understanding the procedure. The three subjects who had additional mental handicap had a little difficulty with some of the constructs labels. This was overcome by elaborating the meaning of the word and by giving examples.

All the writing was done by the interviewer, and those with speech difficulties could indicate on each scale their choice of rating for the elements. In Gary's case, however, there was the problem of his having both severe speech and hand motor difficulties. But when I arrived to carry out the interview he had arranged for a friend who could understand his speech to be there, and the interview was conducted with her assistance.

Completing the Grid

Overall, subjects had little difficulty completing this small grid. One problem which emerged was the choice of the element 'self without disability'. Five subjects, all of whom had a congenital disability, could not construe this element — it was outside their range of convenience. As Linda put it: 'I have no idea what it would be like to be able bodied and I don't want to know. I fear the day they find a cure.'

David felt that I would only understand what disability means by viewing the world from his position. When I arrived to conduct the interview he vacated his wheelchair and told me to sit in it. I obliged, and conducted the interview sitting in his chair.

If the subjects completed the grid without difficulty and were not feeling tired, then I asked them to complete a second grid. This second grid was a dyad grid (see Chapter 12) in which the elements were elicited (relationships with the five most important people in each subject's life) and the constructs were supplied and presented in the same way as for the self grid. All subjects went on to complete the second grid. Only Gary did not complete his dyad grid as one of the important relationships in his life was with the girl who interprets his speech. He felt that he could not discuss his feelings in relation to her through her.

The Self and the Stereotype

The aim of this chapter has been to illustrate how grids can be used with people who have severe physical disabilities. Therefore, I will only briefly mention some of the findings from my own research. I will focus on the relationship between the self and the stereotype as it is these data that I have made a thorough analysis, and these findings are most salient to the earlier discussion on attitudes towards disabled people.

Many theoretical positions argue that our perceptions of ourselves are the result in part of the reactions of others to us. This has important implications for people who are placed in a stigmatised group such as 'the disabled'. Studies indicate, and our own experience tells us, that attitudes to such groups are negative. However, repertory grid and semantic differential studies of people who have been placed in a stigmatised category have found that group members reject general identification with society's stereotype of their group (Bannister, 1965; Fransella, 1968a, 1977; Fransella and Adams, 1966; Hoy, 1973; O'Mahoney, 1982). Therefore, as Fransella (1977) proposes, 'It seems reasonable to suppose that we are unlikely to embrace the stereotype to *us* if it is evaluatively *bad*'. My own study sought to examine whether the same phenomenon could be demonstrated for a group of physically disabled adults by comparing how they see themselves with what they think is the stereotype of 'the disabled'.

The thirty individual grids were analysed by the PA1 method of sub-program Factor in the Statistical Package for the Social Sciences. This method of analysis provides an intercorrelation (Pearson's r) matrix and a principal components analysis which is plotted as part of the computer printout. The results showed considerable variation to exist between the 'self' and the 'stereotype' elements for this group. The values of Pearson's r ranged from -0.35 to $+0.82$ with a mean (z transformation) of $+0.31$ (NS). Statistically significant relationships at the 0.05 level or better occurred in only five cases.

As a further test, t tests, which take into account the variability in the subject's response, were undertaken to compare the response of all thirty subjects on each of the construct scales for the 'self' and the 'steroetype'. The means profile showed that in all but one case the 'stereotype' was rated overall more negatively than the 'self'. All twelve t tests produced a significant result at the 0.05 level or better.

These results demonstrate that this group of disabled people reject general identification with the stereotype of 'the disabled'. This relationship is similar to that reported in studies of other stigmatised groups, and supports Fransella's (1977) proposal. However, the fact that this group of disabled people reject society's stereotype of them does not mean that they are unaffected by it. The stereotype is imposed on a group by others and limits are set on their behaviour and alternatives open to individuals within the group. The idea that you cannot use grids with disabled people is held by professionals and imposed on disabled people, this being a minor example of a major problem. So, if disabled people are to become integrated members of society then it is for society to regard them in a more positive and less stereotyped way.

Conclusion

Repertory grid technique is a broad methodology providing flexible means whereby a person can communicate how he/she perceives his/her world. Little use has been made of this method in clinical work or research with people who have severe physical disabilities. The technique has been construed as not viable or beyond the limits of this population. This view was validated by Cunningham when she reported the results of her pilot study in which she used grids unsuccessfully with a group of multiple sclerosis sufferers. However, the conclusions drawn by Cunningham were based on a very limited definition of grid method. I have argued for a flexible construction of this method and have outlined ways in which it might most usefully be utilised in individual work and research with disabled people.

My own study illustrates that grids designed with brevity and ease of administration as an important component can be successfully used as a research tool with people with severe physical disabilities. However, the size of the grid would not appear to be the problem. What is important is how the grid is presented. Repertory grids do not need special case additions in order to be used with disabled people. As it is a technique, flexibility and diversity are standard aspects of its design. With this in mind repertory grid technique can be successfully and usefully employed with people with severe physical disabilities.

References

Adams-Webber, J.R. (1979) *Personal Construct Theory: Concepts and Applications*, Wiley, Chichester

Altman, B. (1981) 'Studies of Attitudes Toward the Handicapped: The Need for a New Direction', *Social Problems, 28*, 321-37

Bannister, D. (1965) 'The Rationale and Clinical Relevance of Repertory Grid Technique', *British Journal of Psychiatry, 111*, 977-82

—— (1970) 'Concepts of Personality: Kelly and Osgood' in P. Mittler (ed.), *The Psychological Assessment of Mental and Physical Handicaps*, Tavistock, London

Barton, E.S., Walton, T. and Rowe, D. (1976) 'Using Grid Technique with the Mentally Handicapped' in P. Slater (ed.), *The Measurement of Intrapersonal Space by Grid Technique, vol. 1*, Wiley, Chichester

Beail, N. (1984) 'Psychotherapy with Mentally Handicapped People', *BPS Division of Clinical Psychology Newsletter, 43*, 58-9

Bender, L.P. (1981) 'Changing Attitudes Towards Disabled People', *Developmental Medicine and Child Neurology, 23*, 103-8

Cunningham, D.J. (1977) 'Stigma and Social Isolation: Self-perceived Problems of a Group of Multiple Sclerosis Sufferers', Health Services Research Unit Report No. 27, University of Kent at Canterbury

Davis, H. (1983) 'Constructs of Handicap: Working with Parents and Children', *Changes, 1, (2)*, 37-9

Fransella, F. (1968) 'Quantitative Assessment of Personality' in P.J.P. Nichols

and W.H. Bradly (eds), *Proceedings of a Symposium on the Motivation of the Physically Disabled*, National Fund for Research into Crippling Diseases, London
—— (1968a) 'Self Concepts and the Stutterer', *British Journal of Psychiatry, 114*, 1531-5
—— (1977) 'The Self and the Stereotype' in D. Bannister (ed.), *New Perspectives in Personal Construct Theory*, Academic Press, London
—— and Adams, B. (1966) 'An Illustration of the Use of Repertory Grid Technique in a Clinical Setting', *British Journal of Social and Clinical Psychology, 5*, 51-62
Furnham, A. and Pendred, J. (1983) 'Attitudes Towards the Mentally and Physically Disabled', *British Journal of Medical Psychology, 56*, 179-88
Goodman, N., Richardson, S.A., Dornbusch, S.M. and Hastorf, A.H. (1963) 'Variant Reactions to Physical Disabilities', *American Sociological Review, 28*, 429-35
Hoy, R.M. (1973) 'The Meaning of Alcoholism for Alcoholics: A Repertory Grid Study', *British Journal of Social and Clinical Psychology, 12*, 98-9
O'Mahoney, P.D. (1982) 'Psychiatric Patient Denial of Mental Illness as a Normal Process', *British Journal of Medical Psychology, 55*, 109-18
Safilios-Rothchild, C. (1976) 'Disabled Persons' Self-definitions and their Implications for Rehabilitation', in G.L. Albrecht (ed.), *The Sociology of Physical Disability and Rehabilitation*, University of Pittsburgh Press, Pittsburgh

PART THREE

THE EVALUATION OF CHANGE

Personal Construct Theory is a theory of change. For Kelly the main concern of his theory building efforts was the psychological reconstruction of life. Kelly often used the term 'reconstrue' to more adequately describe what he felt should take place in psychotherapy. Man is viewed as a 'form of motion', developing and changing from the moment of birth. We do not stop developing when we cease to be construed as a child; development is a continuous process. Therefore, as Personal Construct Theory is a theory of change its methodological component — repertory grid technique — must also be capable of reflecting change.

In this section we examine how grids can be used to measure change in the clinical setting. First, in Chapter 9, Maureen Sheehan presents an account of changes in the self-construing of a depressed patient throughout 18 months of personal construct psychotherapy. Construing was monitored by repeated administrations of a grid every 3 to 4 months. In Chapter 10 David Winter discusses the appropriateness of repertory grid technique as a measure of therapeutic outcome. He reviews the work to date in which grid technique has been used to evaluate change in a variety of therapies. He then presents a framework for the use of the repertory grid as an individualised outcome measure.

9 THE PROCESS OF CHANGE IN THE SELF-CONSTRUING OF A DEPRESSED PATIENT — CLARE

Maureen J. Sheehan

Introduction

Clare was aged 22 when she came into therapy. She was a slim, pretty, intelligent young woman. She had been depressed for four years, and the referral letter stated that she had a depressive illness. She was living at home and had been unable to work for the previous 6 months. A great deal of her time was spent lying in bed staring at the ceiling. She had constricted her life to an alarming degree.

Clare was one of a group of depressed patients who were monitored during the course of personal construct psychotherapy. Personal construct psychotherapy has been described in detail by Kelly (1955) and elaborated by Fransella (1972), Bannister (1975), Bannister and Fransella (1980), Epting and Amerikaner, Leitner, Landfield, McCoy, Karst and Fransella (in Landfield and Leitner, 1980). A therapeutic procedure that was focal for depression, based on personal construct theory and described in Sheehan (1984 a, b) was used in this study.

Kelly (1955) suggests that a process of constriction is central to the disorder of depression. Constriction in Personal Construct Theory terms is the tendency to exclude events that are difficult or anxiety-provoking, and to attend to those few events that can be dealt with comfortably. For the depressed person it is rather like tunnel vision or tunnel living. The result is a construct system which is fixed, rigid and contains few contradictions.

One of the ways of assessing such characteristics of a person's construct system is through the use of repertory grids. For example, the absence of contradiction or ambivalence may be conceptualised in terms of the logical patterns of relationships between constructs. A method of 'conflict' assessment based on triads of constructs has been described by Slade and Sheehan (1979). Rather than giving the technical details of this measure, I

Figure 9.1:   An Illustration of the Two Possible Types of Imbalanced Triads of Constructs

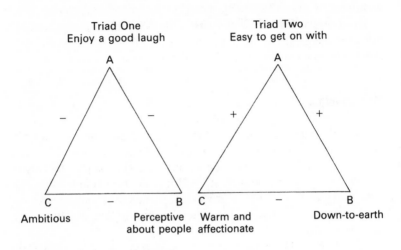

shall attempt to describe the concept in psychological terms taking triads of constructs from Clare's grids. Figure 9.1 gives two examples. Logically these patterns of correlations are inconsistent. In Triad One, if A is negatively correlated with both B and C, then B and C should be positively correlated. Similarly, in Triad Two, if A is positively correlated with B and C, then B and C should be positively correlated. We describe the triads shown in Figure 9.1 as imbalanced. Despite the logical inconsistency, these relationships can exist in psychological terms. Sometimes they can be a source of conflict. Clare's dilemmas may be interpreted as follows:

Triad One: People who are ambitious are not perceptive about others and do not enjoy a good laugh. But people who enjoy a good laugh are not perceptive about others.
Triad Two: I am seen as down-to-earth, easy to get on with and warm and affectionate. But down-to-earth people are not usually warm and affectionate.

These triads were obviously conflictual for Clare. She was worried about not being ambitious, but valued her sense of humour and her perceptiveness about others. She was confused about the implications of being ambitious. Likewise, she worried that her 'realism' got in the way of her warmth and affection and wondered if these feelings in her case were only superficial.

By contrast, a triad of constructs may be logically inconsistent but psychologically tenable in terms of a higher order construct. An example of such a triad from Clare's grids was:

Triad Three

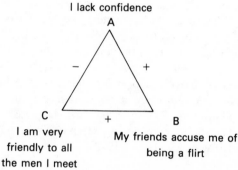

This seemingly inconsistent triad of constructs is explicable in terms of the higher order construct: 'I need constant reassurance that I am attractive'.

In a previous study of depressed patients Sheehan (1981) looked at various dimensions of their self-construct systems including 'conflict' and found that these covaried with mood. As the mood improved the level of 'conflict' increased. Seemingly, when not depressed the person's system is able to encompass a much higher degree of ambiguity or contradiction.

On the basis of this research, it was possible to make the following predictions in relation to the changes in self-construing of a depressed patient undergoing personal construct psychotherapy. The self-construct system would vary with the level of depression in the following ways. As the level of depression diminished, the construct system would become more differentiated, less tightly organised and the percentage of 'conflict' would increase. At the same time, the level of self-esteem would increase and the discrepancy between view of self and others' view of self would diminish. The dimensions related to these predictions are described below.

Changes in Clare's self-construing were studied using multiple perception of the self grids in which she rated how she believed the people who were important to her perceived her. These are referred to as 'looking-in' grids to distinguish them from the more traditional 'looking-out' grids. Twelve elements with the following role titles were selected: (1) self, (2) father, (3) mother, (4) boyfriend/girlfriend, (5) brother surrogate, (6) sister, (7) female friend, (8) male friend, (9) disliked person, (10) successful person, (11) boss, (12) ideal self. Ten constructs were elicited using the triadic method. Each element was rated on a 7 point scale. This grid was repeated at intervals of 3 to 4 months. The same role titles were used, but new constructs were elicited and these grids are referred to as process grids. At the end of therapy Clare completed a re-test grid containing the same elements and constructs as her initial grid.

The level of Clare's depression was assessed initially and at termination of therapy by a consultant psychiatrist using the Modified Hamilton Rating Scale for Depression (Hamilton, 1967). At each administration of grids, Clare completed a Beck Depression Inventory (Beck, 1978).

Analysis of Grids

At the end of 18 months of therapy each of Clare's grids was analysed into its principal components using the INGRID 1972 computer program (Slater, 1977). The INGRID analysis also provides a measure of the distance between elements. The observed distance between elements is computed and expressed as a ratio of the expected distance.

The grids were then analysed further using the CONFLICT program (Slade and Sheehan, 1979). The program provides not only a 'conflict' measure but also a measure of the overall amount of interrelationship between triads of constructs, namely the level of 'intensity'.

A comparison of the initial/re-test grids containing the same elements and constructs was carried out subsequently using the DELTA program (Slater, 1977).

Dimensions Related to Predictions

The following are the psychological dimensions related to the predictions referred to above. To avoid over-complication the technical measures associated with these dimensions are not discussed in detail. As part of the process of constriction, it was hypothesised that:

(1) Depressed persons think largely along one dimension only, and the self-construct system is therefore less differentiated. The percentage of variance accounted for by the first principal component was used as the measure.

(2) They appear to tighten their construing and the relationship between their constructs is greatly increased. The level of 'intensity' derived from the CONFLICT program was the measure selected.

(3) The level of 'conflict' would be low in depression and would increase as the mood improved on the grounds that the person seeks to eliminate contradictions or, in construct theory terms, fragmentation. The measure of 'conflict' from the CONFLICT program was used.

(4) It is generally agreed that a low level of self-esteem is one of the outstanding features of depression. The distance between the self and the ideal self elements was used as the measure and was derived from the INGRID analysis. On the basis of Slater's preliminary work of standardisation (Slater, 1972) any distance smaller than 0.8 and larger than 1.2 may be considered to be significantly similar or dissimilar.

(5) It was predicted that depressives view themselves differently from the 'self as perceived by others' and that this difference would diminish as the mood improved. The mean distance between the self element and all other elements (excluding the ideal self) was taken as the measure of self-discrepancy, and was derived from the element distances provided by the INGRID program.

For convenience these five measures are referred to as differentiation, tightness of construing, 'conflict', self-esteem and self-discrepancy. The first three measures are concerned with the structure of the system and the last two with the self-concept.

Initial Assessment

The level of Clare's depression had been rated by the referring consultant psychiatrist using the Hamilton Depression Scale (HDS), and Clare completed the Beck Depression Inventory

(BDI) at the beginning of the first session. The scores were HDS −25 (severe) and BDI −40 (severe).

Grid One

The constructs and elements of Clare's initial grid and the loadings on the first three components derived from the INGRID analysis are shown in Table 9.1.

Differentiation

The percentage of variance accounted for by the first principal component (52.83) is high enough to suggest a simple structure around one major dimension. This first component contrasts in particular 'care too much about what others think' and 'too willing to please' with 'think my relationships go well'. Clare's own view of herself is most clearly defined by this component (the self has a loading of 5.59).

This component represented one of Clare's major difficulties and underlay her perplexity. She was aware of her tendency to do what she felt would be pleasing to others and yet her relationships failed. The fact that her friends were unaware of her difficulties added to her sense of grievance and of being misunderstood. Perhaps even more fundamental and not yet articulated was that she had been able to please her parents for most of her life, but at the age of 18 their approval and affection became conditional upon her passing her A-level examinations. It was at this time that she became depressed.

Although the percentage of variance accounted for by the first principal component has been selected as the measure of differentiation, it is important to look at the other major components which may contain much that is of psychological significance.

The second principal component accounts for 20.66 per cent of the variance and contrasts 'needling in on their lives — a threat to them' and 'considerate'. She believes that her girlfriends (both liked and disliked) view her as ruthless and a threat to them. This component paints a very different picture from the first and highlights the marked discrepancy between the 'family view' of her, including her view of herself, and her 'friends' view' of her. The picture suggested is of an angel at home and a devil abroad.

Clare was very obviously confused at the start of therapy with regard to her reputation. One of her major presenting problems/

Table 9.1: Loadings of Constructs and Elements on the First 3 Components Derived from the INGRID Analysis Grid One

		1st comp. (52.83)	2nd comp. (20.66)	3rd comp. (11.27)
Constructs				
1. Big softie	— Strong enough to take it	3.78	0.56	2.24
2. Think my relationships go well	— Know that I don't have it easy	-4.18	1.76	-0.04
3. Think I'm a flirt	— Don't think I'm a flirt	1.38	-2.80	0.99
4. Care too much about what others think	— Caring in the right proportion	5.39	-0.29	1.01
5. Too willing to please	— Give and take	4.40	-0.08	0.13
6. Needling in on their lives (a threat to them)	— No threat to them	-2.68	-4.44	0.09
7. Lack of confidence	— Confident	2.42	-0.49	-3.55
8. Thought I would make it	— Not sure I'd use my potential	-2.66	-0.19	2.37
9. Think I'm easily manipulated	— Have my own opinions	3.93	-1.10	-0.27
10. Don't give a damn so long as I'm having fun (ruthless)	— Considerate	-1.11	-3.74	-0.18
Elements				
1. Self		5.59	0.59	-0.76
2. Father		4.07	-0.77	-0.36
3. Mother		3.55	-0.48	1.01
4. Girl/boyfriend		1.48	-2.96	0.21
5. Brother surrogate		0.72	1.32	3.33
6. Sister		-1.67	1.90	-2.30
7. A female friend		-4.55	-2.59	1.34
8. A male friend		0.08	1.24	-0.29
9. A disliked person		-3.94	-2.96	-1.02
10. A successful person		0.15	-0.41	-1.12
11. An authority figure		-1.81	1.88	-1.25
12. Ideal self		-3.67	3.23	1.22

complaints was that others misconstrued her. Also she felt that she did not get the sympathy she deserved as other people had no idea of the difficulties she experienced. Her friends had accused her of being lazy and had told her to 'snap out of it'. Always, her response to these accusations was to feel hurt rather than angry. To feel hurt was consistent with her view of herself as an injured, innocent victim, whereas to feel angry was to be like her sister.

Feeling hurt, however, was accompanied by loss of energy, depression and the conviction that she was physically ill. The behaviour designed to elicit sympathy was 'hostile' in the Kellyan sense, which is to attempt to force others to validate our behaviour or point of view even though we have been invalidated time and again. Although Clare had begun to recognise the pattern of invalidation and the subsequent increased desire for sympathy, the alternative behaviour (to be assertive or angry) ran counter to her view of herself as soft, eager to please and easily manipulated.

The third principal component accounts for 11.27 per cent of the variance and contrasts 'big softie' and 'lacks confidence'. Her surrogate brother's view of her loads most highly on the positive side of this component and her sister's view of her loads most highly on the negative side. It was clear from the sessions that Clare lacked confidence in many areas and that this was linked to her worry about not being ambitious. Her sister had managed to satisfy their parents' ambition but she had not.

Tightness of Construing

Contrary to prediction, Clare's self-construct system was comparatively loose possibly due to the confusion noted above. It is important to stress that tightness and looseness of construing are not in themselves either good or bad unless taken to extremes. (In this study, the two patients who improved the least had significantly tighter systems than the rest of the group throughout the period of therapy.) We need both kinds of construing in order to develop and to be creative. Kelly refers to cycles of tightening and loosening as creativity cycles. In any psychotherapeutic endeavour, unless the initial construing is very loose, it is necessary to begin by creating a looser structure in order that change can take place.

'Conflict'

The 'conflict' score of 3.37 was lower than the mean for the group. This suggests that Clare found it difficult to deal with ambiguity (or fragmentation) and had constricted her focus in an effort to reduce the amount to be organised.

As discussed earlier, a Personal Construct Theory approach leads us to view 'conflict' at various levels of the construct system. This enables us to see that at one level constructs may be employed in ways which are incompatible but which are logically consistent in terms of a more superordinate system. One may hypothesise that where the level of 'conflict' is low, the person lacks such higher level superordinate constructions. In the case of the depresssed individual, he appears to narrow his perceptual field in order to minimise apparent incompatibilities and to constrict his use of higher order constructs.

If we argue that the psychologically healthy person is able to deal with a certain amount of 'conflict' in his system by means of higher-level superordinate constructions, the absence of 'conflict' may be a warning signal. It may indicate that superordinate construction which transcends contradiction has broken down.

Thus, individual imbalanced triads of constructs may be conflictual and the patient may express difficulty in operating with the related constructs. The 'conflict' analysis of Clare's initial grid shows that the highest percentage of imbalance was attached to constructs 10, 3 and 6, namely:

C.10 Don't give a damn so long as I'm having fun (ruthless)
      — considerate
C.3   Think I'm a flirt — don't think I'm a flirt
C.6   Needling in on their lives (a threat to them) — no threat
      to them

Figure 9.2 illustrates three of the imbalanced triads involving these constructs. She seems to be saying the following:

Triad One: People who think I am a flirt, think I'm a threat to them and a big softie. But big softies are not a threat.
Triad Two: People who think I am a flirt, think I don't give a damn so long as I'm having fun (ruthless) and that I am a big softie. But big softies are not ruthless.
Triad Three: People who think I am a flirt, think I don't give a

Figure 9.2: Imbalanced Triads from Grid One

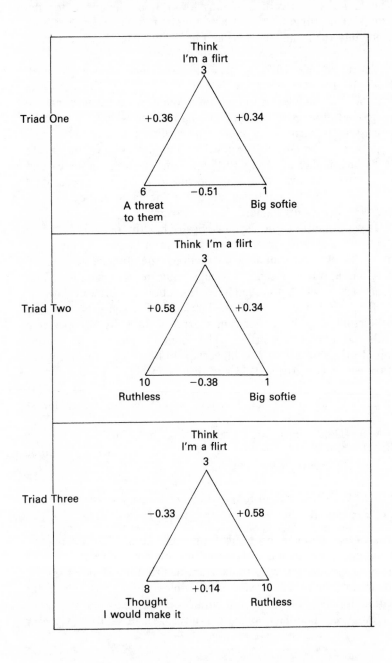

damn so long as I'm having fun (ruthless) and that I shall reach my potential. But flirts don't reach their potential.

Seemingly, the 'family' view of her as too kind and soft — in marked contrast to her friends' view of her as ruthless and a threat — has created the conflict represented by the first two triads. Her worries about her lack of achievement and her wasted potential are reflected in the third triad.

Measures of the Self Concept

The distance between Clare's ratings of self and of ideal self was relatively close (0.79). In this respect Clare was atypical of the group of patients most of whom had a very negative view of the self, and rated themselves at the opposite extreme from their ideal selves. The slight similarity suggested by this measure was perhaps to be expected. When Clare came into therapy she was convinced that in spite of stringent physiological tests a large part of her depression was due to lack of energy and her difficulties in sleeping, which in turn stemmed from an undiscovered physical condition. She had been treated with antidepressant medication for the first three years of her depression and said that this had not helped her. She did not feel that there was much wrong with her as far as her personality was concerned.

Self-discrepancy

The mean distance between Clare's view of self and others' view of self was 1.07. Looking at the individual distances of the 'self-as-perceived' elements, excluding the ideal self, four of them are at a distance greater than 1.2 (namely her sister, female friend, disliked person and boss).

Overview of the Process of Change as Reflected in the Grid Measures

It is not possible in such a short chapter to give details of the constructs and elements of the process grids nor an account of what happened in therapy. Instead, an overview will be given of the changes reflected in the formal measures discussed in relation to the initial grids.

It is clear from the DELTA analysis that the self-construct

system underwent a significant amount of change. The DELTA analysis compares two grids with the same constructs and elements and provides a general degree of correlation. It is assumed that the lower the degree of correlation the greater the amount of change. The correlation of the initial/re-test grids was r = 0.13.

A summary of the grid measures and depression scores is given in Table 9.2. As can be seen, after treatment the level of depression was reduced considerably. The rating scale scores were HDS = 4 (not depressed) and BDI = 14 (mildly depressed). Concurrent with this improvement in mood, the grid measures discussed below had moved in the direction predicted on the basis of previous research.

Structure

Looking at the trends in the structural measures over the course of therapy, we can see that these aspects of Clare's construing followed a variable course, and the direction (although not the magnitude) of these changes was consistent with the changes in her subjective levels of depression as measured by the BDI.

After treatment when the level of depression was reduced considerably, the self-construct system had become more differentiated, looser and contained more 'conflict'. A system such as this which is less rigidly organised should be more flexible and less vulnerable to invalidation. Theoretically, therefore, Clare has a greater chance of maintaining her improvement and is less likely to relapse.

Measures of the Self Concept

Although at the end of therapy the level of self-esteem had increased and the level of self-discrepancy had decreased, the changes over time did not accord with the predicted pattern.

Self-esteem

The self-ideal self distance widened during therapy. This is consistent with Ryle's finding (1975) that the gap between self and ideal widens (within his psychoanalytical framework this is conceptualised as the patient becoming less defensive) and then comes closer as self-dissatisfaction decreases. From the start of therapy with Clare it had been argued that such a move was necessary before the work of reconstruction could begin. Clare

Table 9.2: Summary of 'Looking-in' Grid Measures and Depression Scores

Grids	Structure			Measures of Self Concept		Depression Rating Score	
	% Variance 1st Comp.	'Intensity'	'Conflict'	Self-ideal self distance	Mean self-others distance	BDI	HDS
ONE	52.83	135.36	3.37	0.79	1.07	40	25
TWO	47.07	53.87	8.63	1.50	1.20	26	
THREE	38.89	21.26	9.59	1.14	0.98	23	
FOUR	49.79	84.65	2.36	1.45	0.94	28	
FIVE	40.38	32.71	8.65	0.57	0.64	14	4

had thought that she had a physical illness and that her difficulties in work and relationships were due mainly to her misfortune in being surrounded by people who were selfish, lacking in understanding, mystifying, or could not be trusted. Apparently once she had loosened her construing and had considered alternative constructions of her difficulties, the gap between self and ideal widened. At termination the distance between self and ideal had narrowed considerably to 0.57, and confirmed my clinical impression that Clare was more confident and realistic about herself.

Self-discrepancy

Table 9.2 shows the mean distances between Clare's view of herself and how she feels she is construed by others at each assessment point in therapy. As can be seen, this distance widened during the first 3 or 4 months of therapy and then narrowed to 0.64 at re-test.

It is important to realise that, in Clare's case, the reason for the greater distances initially were not that she perceived all the important people in her life as having a negative view of her. It was rather that there was a mismatch, both positive and negative, between her view of herself and her perception of how others construed her. For example, at that time she resented the fact that so many people saw her as stronger, less vulnerable and as having had an 'easier time' than she knew herself to have had.

Table 9.3: Table of Individual Distances Between Clare's View of Self and her Perception of Others' View of Self

| Elements | 'Looking-in' grids over time | | | | |
	G1	G2	G3	G4	Re-test
Father	0.56	1.19	0.74	0.65	0.69
Mother	0.56	0.93	0.67	0.55	0.74
Girlfriend	0.88	1.55*	0.85	0.80	0.98
Brother surrogate	1.04	1.17	0.96	1.12	1.01
Sister	1.23*	1.41*	1.19	1.25*	0.90
Female friend	1.71*	1.15	1.04	0.87	0.94
Male friend	0.96	0.96	1.12	1.14	1.04
Disliked person	1.61*	1.36*	1.41*	0.89	1.11
Successful person	0.98	1.13	0.66	0.99	0.83
Boss	1.22*	1.85*	1.19	1.17	0.78
Ideal self	1.56*	1.79*	1.44*	1.86*	0.64

* distances greater than 1.2.

Table 9.3 gives a breakdown of the individual distances between Clare's view of herself and how she perceived others' construing of her. At first assessment there were five 'self-as-perceived' elements at a distance greater than 1.2 from the self. None of the distances in the re-test grid are above the cut-off point of 1.2. At re-test, her girlfriends' view of her and her boss's view of her are very similar to her view of herself and her parents' view of her. The split between the 'parental' view of her and the 'outside world' view of her has disappeared. Moreover, the gap between her view of herself and her sister's view of her has been reduced from 1.23 to 0.90. These convergent perceptions suggest that Clare has developed a more integrated view of herself.

Discussion

Kelly linked depression with constriction. So far in this account we have looked at constriction mainly in terms of a number of selected grid measures which were thought to demonstrate this aspect of construing. The behavioural manifestations of constriction were, however, clearly evident. At the start of therapy Clare had constricted her life considerably in that she was not working, she had no social life, and most of her day was spent in bed. It is perhaps necessary to stress that each facet of the construct system has a purpose which may be viewed positively and negatively. Constriction enables people to avoid being faced with a largely unconstruable world. They shrink it to a manageable size and are then able to function if only to a limited extent.

By the end of therapy Clare had dilated her system considerably, and this was shown in her behaviour in that she worked full time, had a busy social life, was interested in cookery, and had joined a gymnasium. Shortly after termination of therapy, she became engaged to be married.

Subsequent to Kelly's formulation, attempts have been made to evaluate constriction in terms of the *application* of constructs (i.e. the number of instances when the person is unable to rate an element) and in the *content* of constructs (inferred from the presence of a greater number of concrete descriptions — Landfield, 1976). Constriction has also been inferred from difficulties in supplying elements (Ashworth, 1976). In Clare's case, evidence of constriction in these terms was less obvious than the gross behavioural manifestations. Initially, it is true, she took considerable time to supply the elements and the constructs. Some of the constructs were less abstract or more subordinate than those of the final process grid, which were all at a higher level of superordinacy, and she had no difficulty in supplying them or in rating the elements.

To avoid constricting this discussion, let me summarise what we know of the relationship between Clare's personal construct system and her experience of depression. It was clear from the start that her construct system was stuck in a side-track in that she viewed her depression as mainly physiological and therefore she had few means of helping herself. Ravenette (1980) gives an excerpt from a case analysis of a boy suffering from physical symptoms who came from a very moralistic family where it was considered wrong to have negative, angry, bad feelings. He asks: 'Is it simply that his proper and ordinary bad feelings are not allowed to exist unless channelized into a physical rather than a psychological form?' In Clare's case her core-role structure of a soft, yielding, moral person undoubtedly meant an inhibition of negative feelings, but in her family her sister gave expression to such feelings.

At the start of treatment, the evidence of loss of confidence and self-discrepancy suggest that it was not only her position on the physiological–psychological dimension which kept her depressed. Her unstable sense of self was one of the dominant factors throughout therapy in that she feared being defined by whoever was perceiving her at the time. It was only in the last months of therapy that she developed a core-role structure that remained relatively stable and which, together with the changes discussed, seemed to enable her to maintain a more balanced mood state.

We may speculate that for our core structure to develop in a stable manner, we must be validated for ourselves and not for what we do, otherwise the core structure is reliant on external validation. It seems likely that one of the major precipitants of Clare's depression was when she found that she was no longer valued for herself but was required to achieve academic success. This signalled the loss of unconditional love.

Follow-up

At follow-up 6 months after termination of therapy, Clare was feeling fairly contented and pleased with her progress. She completed a Beck Depression Inventory and the score was 6. At follow-up 12 months later she had maintained this progress. Her score on the Beck Depression Inventory was 3.

References

Ashworth, C.M. (1976) 'Psychological Studies of Mania and Depression', unpublished PhD thesis, University of Dundee

Bannister, D. (1975) 'Personal Construct Theory Psychotherapy' in D. Bannister (ed.), *Issues and Approaches in the Psychological Therapies*, Wiley, Chichester

—— and Fransella, F. (1980) *Inquiring Man* (2nd edition), Penguin, Harmondsworth

Beck, A.T. (1978) *Beck Depression Inventory*, University of Pennsylvania, Philadephia

Fransella, F. (1972) *Personal Change and Reconstruction*, Academic Press, London

Hamilton, M. (1967) 'Development of a Rating Scale for Primary Depressive Illness', *British Journal of Social and Clinical Psychology*, 6, 278-96

Kelly, G.A. (1955) *The Psychology of Personal Constructs*, Norton, New York (2 volumes)

Landfield, A.W. (1976) 'A Personal Construct Approach to Suicidal Behaviour' in P. Slater (ed.), *Explorations of Intrapersonal Space*, Wiley, Chichester

—— and Leitner, L.M. (eds), (1980) *Personal Construct Psychology: Psychotherapy and Personality*, Wiley, New York

Ravenette, A.T. (1980) 'The Exploration of Consciousness: Personal Construct Intervention with Children' in A.W. Landfield and L.M. Leitner (eds), *Personal Construct Psychology: Psychotherapy and Personality*, Wiley, New York

Ryle, A. (1975) *Frames and Cages*, Sussex University Press, Sussex

Sheehan, M.J. (1981) 'Constructs and "Conflict" in Depression', *British Journal of Psychology*, 72, 197-209

—— (1984a) 'Personal Construct Psychotherapy and Depression: a Process Study', unpublished PhD thesis, University of London

—— (1984b) 'Personal Construct Psychotherapy and Depression. Constructs, 2, 4, Centre for Personal Construct Psychology, London

Slade, P.D. and Sheehan, M.J. (1979) 'Measurement of "Conflict" in Repertory Grids', *British Journal of Psychology*, 70, 519-24

—— and —— (1981) 'Modified Conflict Grid Program', Royal Free Hospital, London

Slater, P. (1972) 'Notes on INGRID 72', St George's Hospital, London

—— (1977) *Dimensions of Intrapersonal Space*, Wiley, Chichester

10 REPERTORY GRID TECHNIQUE IN THE EVALUATION OF THERAPEUTIC OUTCOME

David A. Winter

There has been a singular lack of agreement amongst researchers or clinicians regarding the question of treatment outcome in the psychological therapies. However, differences in the conclusions reached by investigators of different theoretical persuasions may in many cases merely reflect variations in the design of the studies which they report. A major variable in this regard is the choice of outcome measure employed. Thus, as Malan (1973, 1976) has indicated, it may not be surprising if a researcher whose sole outcome criterion is symptom reduction or some other behavioural change concludes that behaviour therapy is more effective than psychotherapy. He has advocated the evaluation of psychodynamic therapies in terms of psychodynamically oriented measures of improvement and, in common with other researchers, has found changes on such dimensions of subjective experience to bear little relationship to changes on measures of external behaviour. He further suggests that outcome criteria should be tailored to the individual client, for clients differ not only in the dimensions of treatment response which are relevant to their difficulties, but also in what constitutes a positive direction of change on these measures. Yalom (1970) feels that such considerations may explain the unimpressive findings of studies which have applied the same outcome criteria to every client, and which therefore exemplify what Kiesler (1966) termed the 'uniformity myths' in psychotherapy research. Similar conclusions have been reached in reviews of outcome research by Truax and Carkhuff (1967) and Bergin and Lambert (1978), the latter authors stating that 'divergent processes are occurring in therapeutic change; that people themselves embody divergent dimensions or phenomena; and that divergent methods of criterion measurement must be used to match the divergency in human beings and in the change processes that occur within them' (p. 171).

It will be apparent, therefore, that an appropriate instrument for evaluating the psychological therapies would ideally combine objectivity of scoring, and sensitivity to psychological change, with sufficient flexibility to allow the derivation from it of individualised outcome criteria which are relevant to the focus of the therapies under study. Repertory grid technique may be considered to fulfil these requirements particularly well. Its scoring is facilitated by the various available hand and computer methods for individual grid analysis, and the comparison of pairs and groups of grids, and several measures thus derived have some apparent validity as indices of psychological disorder (Button, 1985). The assessment of change is an inevitable concern of any measuring instrument developed within a Personal Construct Theory framework, with its emphasis on the constant revision of constructions (Kelly, 1955). This contrasts with the traditional focus in psychological test construction on maximum reliability, apparently defined by Kelly as 'that characteristic of a test which makes it insensitive to change' (Bannister and Mair, 1968, p. 156). As Personal Construct Theory also emphasises the uniqueness of the individual, the repertory test is, almost by definition, a basically idiographic measure. Its grid form has little face validity, and therefore may tap areas of low cognitive awareness, as well as providing more direct measures of self-perception. Finally, it is not a fixed technique, but rather a framework which may be fleshed out in a way appropriate to a particular assessment problem. Something of its consequent versatility as an outcome measure will now be indicated by reviewing its uses in the evaluation of diverse forms of therapy.

Individual Psychotherapy

The use of conventional grid forms has allowed the monitoring of changes in construing during individual psychotherapy (Bannister, 1965; Fransella and Adams, 1966), while grid methods in which the elements are some aspect of the self on successive occasions of testing have also indicated the active ingredients of therapy (Slater, 1970, 1976; Ben Tovim and Greenup, 1983). However, Kelly introduced the repertory test primarily as a diagnostic tool which, by indicating channels of movement, could facilitate the planning of psychotherapy. It is fitting, therefore, that numerous studies have used the grid not only to evaluate the effectiveness of therapy, but also to define its optimum focus and to predict the reconstructions which are likely to accompany successful treatment.

Much of this work has been carried out, not by a personal construct theorist, but by Anthony Ryle, whose primary orientation is Object Relations Theory and who considers that repertory grids are able to tap unconscious processes. Many of his psychotherapy outcome measures, selected on the basis of clinical impressions and a pre-treatment grid assessment, involve the translation of psychoanalytical concepts into grid terms (Ryle and Lunghi, 1969; Ryle, 1975), while in his later work they are formulated as a reduction in the client's 'dilemmas, traps and snags' (Ryle, 1979a, 1979b, 1980). He has found that most of his predicted changes in grid scores during brief psychotherapy are confirmed, and show some correspondence with independent evaluations of treatment outcome. In one study, the most improved clients also showed somewhat greater changes on grid features which Ryle and Breen (1972a) had found to characterise neurotics, and which concerned construing of the self as dissimilar to the ideal self, parents and other people, and polarised construing, particularly regarding the self. Discussing his dilemma, trap and snag formulations, Ryle (1979b, p. 232) concludes that 'No other approach to the evaluation of change in dynamic psychotherapy offers a comparable degree of relevance and specificity'. However, the employment of a standard grid in his recent work, while allowing the collection of normative data, does not fully utilise the potential of the technique as an idiographic outcome measure and, as a study by Landfield and Nawas (1964) indicated, may lessen its likelihood of registering therapeutic change.

The focus of convenience of grid methods is, of course, personal construct psychotherapy, but there are few reports of its use in evaluating this form of treatment. Fransella (1972) employed implication grids to monitor her treatment of stutterers, finding reduction of disfluencies to be associated with an increase in the meaningfulness of fluency, and lack of improvement with premature tightening of constructions. Some association between repertory grid indices of positive outcome and independent measures has also been demonstrated in a study of fixed role therapy (Skene, 1973), while changes in construing have been related to clinical impressions of the response to personal construct psychotherapy of a client diagnosed as schizophrenic (Neimeyer and Neimeyer, 1981).

Marital Therapy

Ryle's use of the grid has by no means been confined to the individual psychotherapy situation, and his dyad grid, in which the elements are relationships rather than individual people, is particularly appropriate for the investigation of marital therapy. In its 'double dyad' form (where each member of the couple, in addition to completing his/her own grid, predicts his/her partner's grid), it allows the monitoring of changes in the couple's degree of mutual empathy (Ryle and Breen, 1972b). An additional variation, which has been used by Ryle and Lipshitz (1975, 1976a) to explore change during conjoint therapy, is the 'reconstruction grid', in which the elements are the couple's reciprocal relationships over the course of therapy. Further intriguing possibilities of grid technique in this area have been indicated by Bannister and Bott (1974), who showed how changes in the power balance in a couple during therapy may be revealed by, on successive occasions, correlating their individual grids with a 'duo grid' which the couple complete together. Finally, grids have also allowed Burns, Hunter and Lieberman (1980) to demonstrate the occurrence of reconstruing during sex therapy.

Group Therapies

Repertory grid technique has been used fairly extensively to monitor changes in construing which accompany group psychotherapy following Watson's (1970, 1972) introduction of a method in which all group members complete serial grids with each other as elements. The grids of the clients in Watson's groups changed more than those of the therapists, and the use of the same supplied constructs with all group members, as in studies by Fransella and Joyston-Bechal (1971) and Winter and Trippett (1977), allowed the demonstration of variations in construing which appeared to affect the whole group. Other studies have shown reconstruing during group therapy to be related to clinical improvement (Ryle and Lipshitz, 1976b) and to clients' group behaviour (Caplan, *et al.*, 1975; Fielding, 1983; Koch, 1983b). A particularly common finding is that, if therapy is successful, group members come to perceive more similarities amongst themselves, and between themselves and their significant others (Fielding, 1975; Winter and Trippett, 1977; Koch 1983a), providing some support for Yalom's (1970) view that 'universality' and 'family re-enactment' are curative factors in group psychotherapy. It might be thought, then, that such changes in construing could form the basis of general criteria of group psychotherapy outcome in grid terms. However, the studies by Winter and Trippett (1977) and Koch (1983a) demonstrated that general predictions, applied to every group member, of changes in grid scores which would accompany therapeutic improvement are less likely to be confirmed than are predictions which have been individually tailored to each client.

Grids have also been employed to monitor change in non-psychodynamic group therapies, including encounter groups (Lieberman, Yalom and Miles, 1973) and personal construct group psychotherapy (Morris, 1977). It might be thought that they would be particularly appropriate instruments for evaluating the outcome of cognitive therapies, and Neimeyer, Heath and Strauss (1985) have indeed demonstrated that, compared to waiting-list controls, depressives undergoing group cognitive therapy construe themselves less negatively, as well as showing symptomatic improvement.

Hospital and Medical Treatment Regimes

In-patient group approaches have been the subject of some repertory grid investigation, as in two studies which, with somewhat conflicting results, have attempted to relate clinical improvement in alcoholics to reconstruing of the self and of drinking (Heather, Edwards and Hore, 1975; Hoy, 1977). Changes in grid measures of self-construing, which showed some correspondence with clinical impressions, have also been found to accompany therapeutic community treatment, and in men, attendance at the community's group meetings (Norris, 1983).

Demonstrations of reconstruing during in-patient treatment are not limited, however, to hospital regimes which employ group-therapy methods. Thus, changes in repertory grid measures in clients with eating disorders have been found to accompany, and possibly to precede, weight change during hospital treatment involving dietary control and some individual psychotherapy (Mair and Crisp, 1968; Fransella and Crisp, 1970; Crisp and Fransella, 1972; Button, 1983). In hospitalised depressives, a lifting of depressed mood has been associated with loosening in clients' construing of affect (Silverman, 1977), and construing of the self as more similar to other people (Hewstone, Hooper and Miller, 1981). Similarly, Sheehan (1981) has found mood change in depressives receiving drug treatment to be accompanied by a more favourable self-construction, and reconstruing has also been shown to occur in depressed individuals who show clinical improvement following treatment from their general practitioners (Sperlinger, 1971).

Behaviour Therapy

Behaviour therapists are placing increasing emphasis on the role of cognitive factors, such as perceived self-efficacy (Bandura, 1977), in their treatments, and it may not be unexpected, therefore, that repertory grid studies have provided evidence of changes in construing during behaviour therapy. More surprising is the fact that the predictions of grid changes during therapy in one of the first such studies were derived from psychodynamic concepts, and focused on transference issues (Crisp, 1964). Caine, Wijesinghe and Winter (1981) demonstrated no differences in the degree of reconstruing exhibited by neurotic clients undergoing group psychotherapy and those receiving behaviour therapy, while Winter (1983a) has found considerable changes on grid measures in both clients and their spouses during the exposure treatment of agoraphobics. Both phobics and spouses came to construe the phobic more favourably, and symptomatic improvement was associated with changes in the implications of confidence, independence and the ability to go out, which became a less superordinate construct for the phobics. As predicted, the phobics came to differentiate more between others, who were no longer perceived as uniformly good, while symptom loss in the phobics was also associated with, and possibly facilitated by, an increase in the flexibility of their spouses' construing.

A Framework for the Use of the Repertory Grid as an Individualised Outcome Measure

It would appear, therefore, that repertory grid technique is sensitive to change in treatment approaches ranging from the symptom-oriented to the insight-oriented. However, some caution should be exercised in drawing such conclusions. The majority of the investigations reviewed above were essentially uncontrolled, single case studies rather than experimental tests of the validity of the grid as an outcome measure, and in many of them the grid was not independent of the treatment procedure, being used to plan therapy as well as to evaluate it. As Caine and Smail (1969) have noted, a rather more problematic issue if the grid is to be used in an outcome study is the question of its reliability, despite Kelly's views on this matter. Thus, some investigations (e.g. Koch, 1983a) have demonstrated changes in grid measures in untreated control groups and, when asked to specify the active ingredients of their therapy, clients have been known to attribute a major therapeutic role to the grid assessment itself. Such an assessment is an invitation to the client to elaborate his/her construing, and there is some evidence that it may lead to a tightening of constructions (Bannister, 1962; Bannister, Fransella and Agnew, 1971). Nevertheless, despite this reactivity of the grid, other studies have demonstrated a high degree of stability in grid measures, particularly those concerned with construing of the self (Bonarius, 1965; Sperlinger, 1976), and that when change in grid scores does occur this is often predictable. One course which is open to the outcome researcher, then, is to predict changes on grid measures which are likely to accompany successful therapy, and perhaps to take up Slater's (1969) suggestion of making control predictions of no change in certain areas. However, such an approach, in which the researcher derives predictions of outcome in grid terms from a pre-treatment grid, is fraught with problems involving what Anastasi (1968) terms 'scorer reliability'. This is because the investigator's interpretation of a client's grid, and consequent predictions, may be as much a reflection of his/their own construct system as of the client's. A certain standardisation of the process of predicting therapeutic changes in grid scores is therefore desirable, and with this in mind a study of reconstruing in neurotic clients during therapy attempted to provide guidelines for the researcher or clinician wishing to make such predictions (Winter, 1979, 1982, 1983b; Caine *et al.*, 1981).

In this investigation, 20 clients allocated to group psychotherapy and 20 receiving behaviour therapy were assessed pre- and post-treatment with a repertory grid using largely elicited elements and constructs, together with various questionnaires and rating scales. Grids were analysed by Slater's (1972) INGRID computer program, and the following four types of grid measure of therapeutic outcome were compared:

(1) *Individualised measures*: These were derived from predictions, based on inspection of a client's pre-treatment grid, of changes in grid scores thought to be conducive to greater psychological well-being.

(2) *General measures*: These were applied to every client in the sample, and mostly involved a reduction in those aspects of the content and structure of construing which Ryle and Breen (1972a) had found to characterise neurotics.

(3) *'Conflict' measures*: Two types of measure were used which do not require examination of construct content, but which have been considered to indicate conflict. One, proposed by Fransella and Crisp (1979), is the distance between a construct and element with the same verbal label (in this case 'self'); while the other, derived from Slade and Sheehan's (1977) CONFLICT computer program, involved logical inconsistencies in construct relationships.

(4) *'Extremity control' measures*: These involved a reduction in the extremity of any construct correlation reaching the 5 per cent level of significance, and any element distance of an extremity likely to occur less than 5 per cent of the time, i.e. above 1.50 or below 0.45 (Slater, 1972).

As in the previous study by Winter and Trippett (1977), a significantly greater percentage of the individualised grid predictions of outcome than of the general predictions was confirmed at post-treatment assessment. Those clients who did not drop out of therapy did, however, show significant change on two of the 'general measures', coming to construe themselves as more similar to their ideal selves and to other people in general, although no change was apparent on the 'conflict' measures. The percentages of individualised and 'extremity control' predictions confirmed did not differ significantly, suggesting that the improvement indicated on the former measures may merely have reflected a general reduction in the extremity of construing, regardless of its content. However, while predicted changes on the individualised, and to a lesser extent the general, grid measures were highly correlated with positive changes in symptom scores, neuroticism, and therapist ratings, this was not the case for changes on the extremity control measures. The significant correlations obtained between the individualised and general grid outcome measures and independent measures of change therefore provided some indication of the validity of these grid criteria of therapeutic outcome, but at the same time suggested that the usefulness of such criteria may be questioned in view of the fact that the grid is considerably more time-consuming than the questionnaires and rating scales employed. Accordingly, a principal component analysis of all change scores was carried out, and this revealed a considerable degree of separation of grid and questionnaire measures, possibly indicating that they are tapping rather different levels of cognitive awareness.

Several conclusions may be drawn from these findings. It appears that, while there is a tendency for regression to the mean in serial grids administered during therapy, these changes are not related to therapeutic improvement and so are of no value as outcome criteria. A similar insensitivity to therapeutic change is shown by conflict measures which are not primarily concerned with the content of construing, and therefore in order to devise grid measures which do have this sensitivity the content of the construct system must be considered in addition to its structure. Such measures may be used in the same way with every client, in which case increase in self-esteem and decrease in isolation of the self are likely to be particularly useful as indices of positive outcome, but therapeutic improvement or its lack is more likely to be detected using measures tailored to the individual client.

How, then, does the investigator arrive at these individualised grid criteria of therapeutic outcome? As this was very much an *ad hoc* procedure in the Caine *et al.* (1981) study, and therefore open to the charge of low-scorer reliability, its replicability was enhanced by the provision of a framework for the derivation of individualised outcome predictions from a client's pre-treatment grid. The predictions used in the study were categorised retrospectively, and all those which appeared to bear some relationship to therapeutic outcome, mostly showing a higher degree of change in clients who improved than in those who did not, are presented below. The following three types of construct will be considered:

Self-construct: 'like me' — 'unlike me';
Symptom construct: symptom pole (e.g. 'depressed') — contrast pole (e.g. 'happy');
Low desirability construct: pole describing undesirable characteristic (e.g. 'unkind') — pole describing desirable characteristic (e.g. 'kind').

Construing of the Self

(1) If the distance between the elements self and ideal self is initially high, it will decrease.
(2) If there is a high relationship (cosine or correlation) between the self element or construct and a symptom construct, this will decrease.
(3) If there is a high relationship between the self element or construct and a low desirability construct, this will decrease.
All of the above predictions concern an increase in the client's self-esteem and a reduction in the extent to which the self is construed as characterised by the symptoms. This latter is comparable to a decrease in scores on a symptom inventory, but may be of greater personal relevance to the client in that the symptoms are stated in their own terms.
(4) If the distance between the elements self and ideal self is initially low, it will increase.
(5) If there is a negative cosine/correlation between the self element/construct and a symptom construct, this will become less negative.
(6) If there is a very extreme negative cosine/correlation between the self element/construct and a low desirability construct, this will become less negative.
Predictions 4-6 concern a reduction in self-esteem, or in dissociation from the symptoms, in the client whose self-construing is much more favourable than might be considered realistic in view of their referral for psychological therapy. For example, reconstruing of this type was predicted in a woman presenting with marital problems and depressive episodes whose

grid indicated that she construed herself as the most ideal and attractive person she knew. Such changes are likely to occur in the initial stages of therapy, but may be followed by some degree of recovery of self-esteem.

Self and Others

(7) If the distance between the self and a parent element is initially high, it will decrease.

(8) If the self-opposite sex parent distance minus the self-same sex parent distance is equal to or less than -0.20, it will increase.

(9) If the sum of squares accounted for by the self element is initially higher than twice the average sum of squares, it will decrease.

Predictions 7-9 were made in view of previously demonstrated associations between psychopathology and both perceived dissimilarity of the self and others and cross-sex identification (e.g. Ryle and Breen, 1972a).

Dilemmas, Conflicts and Non-consensual Construing

(10) If there is an extreme negative correlation between symptom and low-desirability constructs, this correlation will become less negative.

(11) If there is an extreme negative correlation between two low-desirability constructs, this correlation will become less negative. These correlations may indicate the dilemmas faced by a client whose presenting complaints have certain positive implications, or payoffs, for them. As has been clearly indicated in the work of Rowe (1971), Tschudi (1977), and Ryle (1979a), therapeutic change in such an individual will require the resolution of the dilemma. Dilemmas of this type generally involve the association of the symptom with some quality of tenderness or morality, as in the following correlations between clients' constructs, all of which showed a predicted decrease during therapy:

> correlations of 'has libido' with 'inconsiderate', 'unconcerned about the family', and 'unkind' in a woman presenting with lack of sexual interest in her husband;
> correlation of 'sexually attractive' with 'likes to dominate' in an impotent man;
> correlations of 'always eating' with 'moral' and 'sensitive' in a compulsive eater.

(12) If there is a high, inappropriate correlation between a symptom construct and a low-desirability construct, this correlation will decrease.

An extreme and inappropriate negative construction of a symptom may indicate an elaborated view of the self as a failure or as ill, and thus be as indicative of psychological disorder as an inappropriate positive construction. A reduction in such a construct relationship, as in the case of the socially anxious client with a correlation of 0.75 between the constructs 'stupid' and 'unable to communicate', may therefore be associated with increased self-acceptance and positive therapeutic outcome.

(13) Any other non-consensual relationship between constructs will change in the direction of social consensus.

While these guidelines are based on only one of the many possible grid forms, using one particular method of analysis, they may point to areas to which the outcome researcher or clinician might usefully attend in scanning a neurotic client's pre-treatment grid, predicting a change if one of the grid scores concerned exceeds their criterion of extremity. If a fairly stringent criterion of an extreme construct correlation or cosine is required, this may be taken to be the magnitude of correlation which reaches the 5 per cent level of significance for a one-tailed test (i.e. $\pm$ 0.51 for n = 15 elements), while an extreme element distance may be taken to be one greater than 1.50 or less than 0.45. However, the particular criterion used by the researcher will vary in relation to the confidence with which a prediction is made, and in this respect questions of statistical significance are of less import than those of clinical significance, the extent to which a grid score indicates a deviation from 'normality' in content of construing, and the total configuration of the individual's grid. The framework therefore does not eliminate entirely the subjective judgements of the researcher, as is also apparent from the requirement that characteristics described by a construct be designated as desirable, undesirable, or neutral. However, as in predictions (10) and (11) above, such judgements may be considered to point to dilemmas at a low level of cognitive awareness, and so to the essence of a client's predicament.

Methods such as this may be thought particularly appropriate in studies of therapeutic change using single-case experimental designs. However, as has been seen, they may also be employed in extensive, group designs in which the percentage of individualised outcome predictions confirmed, or the percentage on which there is a certain degree of change (e.g. statistically significant change in a construct correlation) may be used as an outcome measure. The researcher using a group design may wish to standardise his or her grid measures by employing the same constructs and elements with every client, thus sacrificing the greater personal meaningfulness to the client which would be afforded it these were elicited. A partial solution to this problem would be to elicit constructs from the population under study, and then to pool these in a standard grid. In deciding whether to supply or to elicit constructs, however, the researcher may do well to remember that what are supplied are construct labels rather than constructs, and may in fact be construed in very different ways by different subjects. In some ways, therefore, a grid with elicited constructs may be considered a more standard procedure in that, with every client, it is likely to tap the more superordinate reaches of their construct system.

A further advantage of the use of grids with elicited constructs in monitoring therapy is that, as well as demonstrating changes on the client's existing construct dimensions, they allow some indication of the more fundamental reconstruing reflected in the emergence of new constructs. To quote Kelly (1955):

> psychotherapeutic movement may mean (1) that the client has reconstrued his self and certain other features of his world within his original system, (2) that he has organised his old system more precisely, or (3) that he has replaced some of the constructs in his old system with new ones. This last type of movement is likely to be the most significant, although the behavioural changes may not be as spectacular as in the first type. The second type of movement may be most impressive to those who always look to therapy to produce verbal consistency and 'insight'. (p. 941)

It is customary to end a review of applications of repertory grid technique with some comment on the relationship between the technique and Kelly's ideas. Depending on the orientation of the reviewer, this will either bemoan the divorce of the grid from its parent theory, or applaud as one of its strengths the capacity for testing hypotheses derived from alternative theoretical approaches. While the concern here has been to demonstrate that the grid may serve as an appropriate outcome measure for therapists of diverse theoretical backgrounds, the view is taken that Personal Construct Theory has considerable heuristic potential, which if drawn on will greatly facilitate the prediction of changes in a client's grid scores during therapy. To take just one example, Kelly's Choice Corollary indicates that a person will only move towards a view of the world which offers greater possibilities for the anticipation of events, and such considerations may allow the likelihood of changes in a client's use of particular constructs to be predicted (Levy, 1956; Hinkle, 1965; Hayden, 1975; Leitner, 1984).

However, whatever the theoretical perspective of the clinician or researcher who uses the grid to evaluate treatment outcome, they are likely to find, in contrast to the conclusions of Bergin and Lambert (1978, p. 177), that it is not just another self-concept measure which adds 'practically nothing to what is obtained from the MMPI or similar instruments'.

References

Anastasi, A. (1968) *Psychological Testing*, Macmillan, Toronto

Bandura, A. (1977) 'Self-efficacy: Towards a Unifying Theory of Behavioral Change', *Psychological Review, 84*, 191-215

Bannister, D. (1962), 'The Nature and Measurement of Schizophrenic Thought Disorder', *Journal of Mental Science, 108*, 825-42

—— (1965) 'The Rationale and Clinical Relevance of Repertory Grid Technique', *British Journal of Psychiatry, 111*, 977-82

—— and Mair, J.M.M. (1968) *The Evaluation of Personal Constructs*, Academic Press, London

——, Fransella, F. and Agnew, J. (1971) 'Characteristics and Validity of the Grid Test of Thought Disorder', *British Journal of Social and Clinical Psychology, 10*, 144-51

—— and Bott, M. (1974) 'Evaluating the Person' in P. Kline (ed.), *New Approaches to Psychological Medicine*, Wiley, Chichester

Ben Tovim, D.I. and Greenup, J. (1983) 'The Representation of Transference through Serial Grids: A Methodological Study', *British Journal of Medical Psychology, 56*, 255-62

Bergin, A.E. and Lambert, M.J. (1978) 'The Evaluation of Therapeutic Outcomes' in S.L. Garfield and A.E. Bergin (eds), *Handbook of Psychotherapy and Behaviour Change: An Empirical Analysis*, Wiley, New York

Bonarius, J.C.J. (1965) 'Research in the Personal Construct Theory of George A. Kelly', in B.A. Maher (ed.), *Progress in Experimental Personality Research, vol 2*, Academic Press, New York

Burns, T., Hunter, M. and Lieberman, S. (1980) 'A Repertory Grid Study of

Therapist/Couple Interaction', *Journal of Family Therapy, 2,* 297-310

Button, E.J. (1983) 'Construing the Anorexic' in J.R. Adams-Webber and J.C. Mancuso (eds), *Applications of Personal Construct Theory,* Academic Press, London

—— (ed.) (1985) *Personal Construct Theory and Mental Health,* Croom Helm, London

Caine, T.M. and Smail, D.J. (1969) 'A Study of the Reliability and Validity of the Repertory Grid Technique as a Measure of the Hysteroid/Obsessoid Component of Personality', *British Journal of Psychiatry, 115,* 1305-8

——, Wijesinghe, O.B.A. and Winter, D.A. (1981) *Personal Styles in Neurosis: Implications for Small Group Psychotherapy and Behaviour Therapy,* Routledge & Kegan Paul, London

Caplan, H.L., Rohde, P.D., Shapiro, D.A. and Watson, J.P. (1975) 'Some Correlates of Repertory Grid Measures Used to study a Psychotherapeutic Group', *British Journal of Medical Psychology, 48,* 217-26

Crisp, A.H. (1964) 'An Attempt to Measure an Aspect of "Transference" ', *British Journal of Medical Psychology, 37,* 17-30

—— and Fransella, F. (1972) 'Conceptual Change During Recovery from Anorexia Nervosa', *British Journal of Medical Psychology, 45,* 395-405

Fielding, J.M. (1975) 'A Technique for Measuring Outcome in Group Psychotherapy', *British Journal of Medical Psychology, 48,* 189-98

—— (1983) 'Verbal Participation and Group Therapy Outcome', *British Journal of Psychiatry, 142,* 524-8

Fransella, F. (1972) *Personal Change and Reconstruction: Research on a Treatment of Stuttering,* Academic Press, London

—— and Adams, B. (1966) 'An Illustration of the Use of Repertory Grid Technique in a Clinical Setting', *British Journal of Social and Clinical Psychology, 5,* 51-62

—— and Crisp, A.H. (1970) 'Conceptual Organisation and Weight Change', *Psychotherapy and Psychosomatics, 18,* 176-85

—— and Joyston-Bechal, M.P. (1971) 'An Investigation of Conceptual Process and Pattern Change in a Psychotherapy Group', *British Journal of Psychiatry, 119,* 199-206

—— and Crisp, A.H., (1979) 'Comparisons of Weight Concepts in Groups of Neurotic, Normal and Anorexic Females', *British Journal of Psychiatry, 134,* 79-86

Hayden, B. (1979) 'The Self and Possibilities for Change', *Journal of Personality, 47,* 546-56

Heather, N., Edwards, S. and Hore, B.D. (1975) 'Changes in Construing and Outcome of Group Therapy for Alcoholism', *Journal of Studies on Alcohol, 36,* 1235-53

Hewstone, M., Hooper, D. and Miller, K. (1981) 'Psychological Change in Neurotic Depression: A Repertory Grid and Personal Construct Theory Approach', *British Journal of Psychiatry, 139,* 47-51

Hinkle, D. (1965) 'The Change of Personal Constructs from the Viewpoint of a Theory of Construct Implications', unpublished PhD thesis, Ohio State University

Hoy, R.M. (1977) 'Some Findings Concerning Beliefs about Alcoholism', *British Journal of Medical Psychology, 50,* 227-36

Kelly, G.A. (1955) *The Psychology of Personal Constructs,* Norton, New York

Kiesler, D.J. (1966) 'Some Myths of Psychotherapy Research and the Search for a Paradigm', *Psychological Bulletin, 65,* 110-36

Koch, H.C.H. (1983a) 'Changes in Personal Construing in Three Psychotherapy Groups and a Control Group', *British Journal of Medical Psychology, 56,* 245-54

—— (1983b) 'Correlates of Changes in Personal Construing of Members of Two Psychotherapy Groups: Changes in Affective Expression', *British Journal of Medical Psychology, 56*, 323-8

Landfield, A.W. and Nawas, M.M. (1964) 'Psychotherapeutic Improvement as a Function of Communication and Adoption of Therapist's Values', *Journal of Counseling Psychology, 11*, 336-41

Leitner, L.M. (1984) 'An Investigation into Variables Affecting Self-change on Personal Constructs, *British Journal of Medical Psychology, 57*, 7-14

Levy, L. (1956) 'Personal Constructs and Predictive Behaviour', *Journal of Abnormal and Social Psychology, 53*, 54-8

Lieberman, M.A., Yalom, I.D. and Miles, M.B. (1973) *Encounter Groups: First Facts*, Basic Books, New York

Mair, J.M. and Crisp, A.H. (1968) 'Estimating Psychological Organization, Meaning and Change in Relation to Clinical Practice', *British Journal of Medical Psychology, 41*, 15-29

Malan, D.H. (1973) 'The Outcome Problem in Psychotherapy Research: A Historical Review', *Archives of General Psychiatry, 29*, 719-29

—— (1976) *Towards the Validation of Dynamic Psychotherapy: A Replication*, Plenum Press, New York

Morris, J.B. (1977) 'The Prediction and Measurement of Change in a Psychotherapy Group Using the Repertory Grid' in F. Fransella and D. Bannister, *A Manual for Repertory Grid Technique*, Academic Press, London

Neimeyer, G.J. and Neimeyer, R.A. (1981) 'Personal Construct Perspectives on Cognitive Assessment' in T.V. Merluzzi, C.R. Glass and M. Genest (eds), *Cognitive Assessment*, Guilford Press, New York

Neimeyer, R.A., Heath, A.E. and Strauss, J. (1985) 'Personal Reconstruction during Group Cognitive Therapy for Depression' in F.R. Epting and A.W. Landfield (eds), *Anticipating Personal Construct Theory*, Nebraska Press, Lincoln

Norris, M. (1983) 'Changes in Patients during Treatment at the Henderson Hospital Therapeutic Community during 1977-81', *British Journal of Medical Psychology, 56*, 135-44

Rowe, D. (1971) 'Poor Prognosis in a Case of Depression as Predicted by the Repertory Grid, *British Journal of Psychiatry, 118*, 297-300

Ryle, A. (1975) *Frames and Cages: The Repertory Grid Approach to Human Understanding*, Sussex University Press, London

—— (1979a) 'The Focus in Brief Interpretive Psychotherapy: Dilemmas, Traps and Snags as Target Problems', *British Journal of Psychiatry, 134*, 46-54

—— (1979b) 'Definining Goals and Assessing Change in Brief Psychotherapy: A Pilot Study Using Target Ratings and the Dyad Grid', *British Journal of Medical Psychology, 52*, 223-34

—— (1980) 'Some Measures of Goal Attainment in focused Integrated Active Psychotherapy: A Study of Fifteen Cases', *British Journal of Psychiatry, 137*, 475-86

—— and Lunghi, M.W. (1969) 'The Measurement of Relevant Change after Psychotherapy: Use of Repertory Grid Testing', *British Journal of Psychiatry, 115*, 1297-304

—— and Breen, D. (1972a) 'Some Differences in the Personal Constructs of Neurotic and Normal Subjects, *British Journal of Psychiatry, 120*, 483-9

—— and —— (1972b) 'The Use of the Double Dyad Grid in the Clinical Setting', *British Journal of Medical Psychology, 45*, 383-9

—— and Lipshitz, S. (1975) 'Recording Change in Marital Therapy with the Reconstruction Grid', *British Journal of Medical Psychology, 48*, 39-48

—— and —— (1976a) 'Repertory Grid Elucidation of a Difficult Conjoint Therapy', *British Journal of Medical Psychology, 49*, 281-5

—— and —— (1976b) 'An Intensive Case-study of a Therapeutic Group', *British Journal of Psychiatry, 128*, 581-7

Sheehan, M.J. (1981) 'Constructs and "Conflict" in Depression', *British Journal of Psychology, 72*, 197-209

Silverman, G. (1977) 'Aspects of Intensity of Affective Constructs in Depressed Patients', *British Journal of Psychiatry, 130*, 174-6

Skene, R.A. (1973) 'Construct Shift in the Treatment of a Case of Homosexuality', *British Journal of Medical Psychology, 46*, 287-92

Slade, P.D. and Sheehan, M.J. (1977) *Modified Conflict Grid Programme*, Royal Free Hospital, London

Slater, P. (1969) 'Theory and Technique of the Repertory Grid', *British Journal of Psychiatry, 121*, 45-51

—— (1970) 'Personal Questionnaire Data Treated as Forming a Repertory Grid', *British Journal of Social and Clinical Psychology, 9*, 357-70

—— (1972) 'Notes on INGRID 72', St George's Hospital, London

—— (1976) 'Monitoring Change in the Mental State of a Patient Undergoing Psychiatric Treatment' in P. Slater (ed.), *The Measurement of Intrapersonal Space by Grid Technique: Vol. 1 Explorations of Intrapersonal Space*, Wiley, Chichester

Sperlinger, D.J. (1971) 'A Repertory Grid and Questionnaire Study of Individuals Receiving Treatment for Depression from General Practitioners', unpublished PhD thesis, University of Birmingham

—— (1976) 'Aspects of Stability in the Repertory Grid', *British Journal of Medical Psychology, 49*, 341-8

Truax, C.B. and Carkhuff, R.R. (1967) *Towards Effective Counselling and Psychotherapy: Training and Practice*, Aldine Atherton, Chicago

Tschudi, F. (1977) 'Loaded and Honest Questions: A Construct Theory View of Symptoms and Therapy' in D. Bannister (ed), *New Perspectives in Personal Construct Theory*, Academic Press, London

Watson, J.P. (1970) 'A Repertory Grid Method of Studying Groups', *British Journal of Psychiatry, 117*, 309-18

—— (1972) 'Possible Measures of Change during Group Psychotherapy', *British Journal of Medical Psychology, 45*, 71-7

Winter, D.A. (1979) 'Repertory Grid Technique in Research on the Psychological Therapies', unpublished PhD thesis, University of Durham

—— (1982) 'Construct Relationships, Pyschological Disorder and Therapeutic Change', *British Journal of Medical Psychology, 55*, 257-69

—— (1983a) 'Constriction and Construction in Agoraphobia', paper presented at 5th International Congress on Personal Construct Psychology, Pine Manor College, Boston

—— (1983b) 'Logical Inconsistency in Construct Relationships: Conflict or Complexity?' *British Journal of Medical Psychology, 56*, 79-87

—— and Trippett, C.J. (1977) 'Serial Change in Group Psychotherapy', *British Journal of Medical Psychology, 50*, 341-8

Yalom, I.D. (1970) *Theory and Practice of Group Psychotherapy*, Basic Books, New York

PART FOUR

EXPLORING RELATIONSHIPS THROUGH GRIDS

Kelly's original grid form was concerned with how we construe significant people in our life. Thus, the constructs produced are in part derived from our experiences in relationships with these other people. But the grid did not investigate relationships *per se*. However, various modifications of the technique have been developed which enable more direct investigations to be carried out. In this section four such modifications are presented and illustrated.

Steven Mendoza presents in Chapter 11 an outline of the 'Exchange Grid' which enables two people to enter each other's phenomenological world by exchanging and using each other's constructs. The technique is illustrated through an administration to a married couple. Although the procedure is concerned with the elicitation of constructs and how two people use each other's constructs Mendoza uses the method within a psychodynamic framework. In Chapter 12 Anthony Ryle presents an overview of his work using the Dyad Grid in psychotherapy and psycho-therapy research. The Dyad Grid is similar to the standard grid format except that all the elements are relationships (self to mother). Like Mendoza, Ryle also works mainly within a psychodynamic framework.

In the *Psychology of Personal Constructs*, Kelly (1955) presented a development of the grid method called the Situa-tional Resources Repertory Test. This method was devised to explore dependency from a Personal Construct Theory point of view. In Chapter 13 Nigel and Sue Beail present this grid form, and discuss some ways that it can be used to evaluate dependency in the clinical setting.

In Chapter 14 Harry Procter presents some of his work using grids in family therapy and research. He begins his explorations using individual grids with each family member containing family members in the elements. On the basis of these he derives a family grid and then a common family grid, thus providing insight into the family construct system.

The chapters in this section suggest that there is no one way of exploring the nature of relationships with grids. There are probably many other ways in which grids could be used in this way; there is ample scope for further exploration.

Reference

Kelly, G. (1955) *The Psychology of Personal Constructs*, Norton, New York

11 THE EXCHANGE GRID

Steven Mendoza

As soon as I started to play with grids I wanted to look not only at relations between elements and constructs within the individual but also between individuals. It seemed to me an obvious step from an account of the individual which can be arithmetic continuous and multidimensional to such an account of two individuals in relationship.

My interest is not only in describing but also in mediating phenomenological action. To this end I assisted Laurie Thomas in development of the computer elicitation of the grid (Thomas and Mendoza, 1972). I sought to have the program interact with the construer so that it would put him into a heuristic relation with himelf. Now I wish for a grid game which will put the individual into heuristic encounter with another. The difficulties of administration of such games involving, as they do, so much conjuring with paper and arithmetic and the inherent appeal of computers to some, make me look for an exchange of constructs between people that is mediated by a computer which stores and presents the grids and which organises feed back in real time.

Meanwhile I can only describe the protocol of the Exchange Grid as it is so far. Its essentials are two:

(1) Both parties construe the same elements.
(2) Each party rates the elements on the constructs of the other and on the constructs of self.

So there is one set of common elements and two sets of constructs — one from each party. There are two sets of ratings — one from each party. Each set of ratings is on the constructs of both self and other.

For illustration I shall describe a pilot administration of the grid to a married couple. Both are qualified in the 'helping professions' and they have adolescent children. They have had experience of the roles of child, parent and adult. Thus, they seemed to me an exemplary couple for the purpose of looking at parenting *within* a relationship.

173

Elements

I believe that long-term sexual relationships and to some degree all other dialectical encounters depend for their survival on their ability to satisfy the infantile needs all adults have, and which are, for most of us, essentially problematic. Certainly, my recent experience of psychotherapy with a number of patients bears out the universality of regression, dependency, need and vulnerability as the source of emotional disturbance and woe. Accordingly, I specified a set of roles for the elements that I hoped would determine a range of convenience mapping onto the areas of caring and being cared for. The roles are:

WS	Wife as whole self	HS	Husband as whole self
WC	Wife as child	HC	Husband as child
WP	Wife as parent	HP	Husband as parent
WA	Wife as adult	HA	Husband as adult
WM	Wife's mother	HM	Husband's mother
WF	Wife's father	HF	Husband's father
FW	Friend who is a wife	FH	Friend who is a husband

C1
C2 } Participants' own children
C3

Participants agreed on a couple to stand for friends who are wife and husband (FW and FH). The remainder of the roles are uniquely occupied for this couple.

I have used the Berne ego states Adult Parent Child because they are appropriate, well known and comprehensible. I do not intend them to stand for an involvement with transactional psychology, much as I esteem it. My concern is with the emphasis Klein (1975), Guntrip (1968) and Balint (1968) lay on regression as a component in adult functioning, and with the Freudian principle of primary process as a primitive function that pervades the whole of life and complements the organised discriminating reality testing ego functioning we so easily mistake for the complete account of the psychology of the adult and his personal constructs.

Constructs

Triads were based on role pairs from the two participants in roles Parent Adult Child, with a third taken representatively from the remainder of the role set. This was intended to focus construing on the central relationships — in all roles equally.

One participant thus produced 9 constructs and the other 10. Each rated the elements on their own constructs but not the constructs of the other. Thus, there was *one* set of ratings. This *source grid* was then correlated by matching scores and 7 constructs each extracted for the purpose of exchange.

Selecting Constructs for Exchange

The purpose of extracting constructs is dual: to reduce the time involved in administration, and to maximise the heuristic value of the exchange by concentrating on constructs that do not correlate too highly with *any* of the partners. Accordingly, constructs were selected with the main criterion being the highest correlation with a construct of the partner. Another criterion of selection was the relevance of the construct to the purpose of the exchange: thus, two of the wife's constructs were excluded in favour of two having a higher maximum matching score with partner's constructs. A more difficult criterion to apply is high matching score between selected constructs: they may be orthogonal to partner's constructs, but match closely to each other.

Difficult as it is to apply a consistent protocol to the selection of constructs, the procedure is, in principle, an interesting one from the point of view of the heuristic and interactive use of the grid. I have applied it previously in the Demon grid elicitation program (Thomas and Mendoza, 1972), where the construer has the option of eliminating a construct with a high matching score or generating an element which would rate so as to reduce the high matching score.

This approach is to construing as a dialectical activity in interaction both with the world and particularly with the construct system of another — or even, more simply, with another. It is away from construing as the deployment of a constant and finite set of core constructs which mutually and inevitably define the world and the self. This is not to detract from the validity of core constructs as a conceptual indicator of personality, but to bring within the range of grid procedures the process of change in the construct system in the course of interaction.

Table 11.1 shows each construct with the construct of the partner which has the highest matching score to it. The scores are satisfactory in the degree of orthogonality but only one is strikingly low: calm/volatile. Correlations *within* each participant's set of constructs are even lower — there are 8 matching scores over 50 per cent as against 11 over 50 per cent of the equal number of matching scores of constructs with partner's constructs. So here are two systems of constructs which comprise an overall interpersonal semantic space, which is articulated but has consistent and real variance.

To orient us in this working through of the protocol: we have now elicited a source grid of 9 and 10 constructs, each with partner's own ratings. From the matching score matrix 7 constructs from each have been selected to make up the initial grid.

Exchanging

For the administration of the initial grid each partner was provided with the 14 constructs one week later and asked to rate all elements on all constructs both own and others. Then they were exchanging for the first time — using others' constructs as if they were their own. The duplication of ratings on own constructs enabled me to compare the reliability of ratings with the agreement of partners on constructing.

Agreement is a parameter of measurement designated by Laing, Phillipson and Lee (1978) in their book *The Interpersonal Perception Method*. Very simply put, this is an inventory of multiple-choice items referring to marital events. Partners are compared in their own choices and their attribution of partner's choices and, to a third level, of their realisation of how the partner thinks they would answer: The questions that define and explain these levels are:

Agreement: How do you answer?
Understanding: How would your partner answer?

Table 11.1: Constructs: Each with Partner's Highest Matching Construct

	%MC					
H1	←88→W1		X	Maleness / Femaleness	Male / Female	X
H6	←73 →		X	Intelligent / Non-intelligent		
H9	55	W5		Scholarly / Unscholarly	Carefree / Conscientious	
H8	52			Worldliness / Unworldliness		
H4	←61 →			Warm / Cold		
H5	61	W2		Motherliness / Non-motherliness	Overweight / Underweight	
H7	55			Wise / Not wise		
W3	←73 →		X	Energetic / Placid		
W6	58			Anxious / Relaxed		
W8	55	H3		Thrifty / Free-spending	Activity / Passivity	
W10	44			Keen on reading / Avoids reading		
W9	58		X	Walker / Sitter		
W4	←52 →H2			Expects to take / Expects to give	Interest Judaism / Minor interest	X

← →: denotes mutually selecting pair (each is partner's highest matching construct)
%MC: percentage matching score
X: construct excluded from exchange

Realisation: How would your partner think you would answer?

My ultimate goal was to adapt this method to a client-centred construct system from a fixed-choice repertory. These three levels of perception seem to me to give an account both of the Sociality Corollary of Kelly and Bateson's Theory of Logical Types. Agreement for the purpose of the exchange grid is measured by matching score between ratings of each partner on the *same* construct. Unfortunately, pilot results militates against this adaptation being at all easy: agreement scores are high to the point of being comparable with scores for reliability — that is to say they are often as high as they meaningfully can be. The partners assimilated each other's constructs as fully as if they were their own. The idea of the partner's construct system as a foreign semantic space is not supported. It remains to be seen whether this is a function of my selection of pilot respondents or a universal effect. I hope that participants selected for patho-logical relationships would show the impoverishment of agree-ment that *should* be definitive of disturbances in communication. But it does seem clear already that the range of convenience of these constructs is unsuitable to the focus of the exchange. The constructs are too much in the area of objective perceptions of others and not sufficiently in the anxiety laden areas of participant's feelings and attributions for one another — the area of disturbance in relationships.

These pilot results are unfortunate because my orientation is to the development of a grid based interaction using feedback to mediate an increase in agreement scores with assimilation of partner's construct system. Maybe this is a control couple with a mature communication that has already achieved the results offered by feedback. Were I looking for such a control couple I certainly could not wish for a more suitable one.

Using Feedback

The feedback protocol consists of pairing off the elements to form two split halves: one set for use in feedback; one set for experimental ratings after feedback. Feedback was generated by Apple II computer in basic: first, the constructs and elements are sequenced from lowest to highest agreement; secondly, the elements and constructs are presented in formats intended to give a graphic representation of the meaning of each in grid context, with disagreement emphasised to orient interaction to disturb-ances of communication. The four feedback formats are as follows:

Constructs: Element Profiles

Each construct of a partner is presented to the other partner with the elements laid out in rating sequence from pole to pole. Against each element the partner's own rating is given for comparison with the rating of the partner generating the construct.

Expects to give			Expects to take	
One	*Two*	*Three*	*Four*	*Five*
4 Wife's mother	1 Wife	4 Husband Friend		5 Child 2
3 Wife as child		2 Husband as parent		
		4 Husband's father		
		3 Husband as adult		

Note that elements on a given rating are listed in order of disagreement. Note also that agreement is *high*!

Constructs: Construct Sequence

For a given construct the other constructs can be listed in order of matching score with that construct to demonstrate its relation to the system as a whole. The partner's own matching scores on received constructs is given for comparison.

Elements: Polar Profiles

For each element the partner's constructs are listed in the order of *partner's ratings*. For ratings of 4 and 5, poles are inverted to give a clear profile from constructs generating extreme ratings to ones giving medium ratings. Partner's ratings are set out graphically in columns from 1 and 3. Own ratings are listed for comparison.

Husband as parent

Conscientious	2	1		Carefree
Calm	3	2		Volatile
Free-spending	1	2		Thrifty
Keen reader	2	2		Avoids reading
Overweight	1		3	Underweight
Expects to give	2		3	Expects to take

Elements: Element Sequences

For each element the other elements are listed in the sequence of matching scores to the element derived from *partner's* ratings. Again matching scores of *own* ratings are listed for comparison.

Computer capacity and duration of administration obliged me to select the two feedback modes of which examples are given. They have the advantage of being more graphic in layout. Respondents were disappointed by the comprehensibility and usefulness of the feedback, which was especially disappointing for me in view of the programming effort which went into them. Again it is possible that a higher level of initial disagreement would put more available information into the feedback.

I would like to see such feedback integrated into a fully interactive elicitation of the exchange in which feedback would be integrated with construing. Following feedback the participants rated the elements whose ratings had not been presented as feedback ratings. These I called the experimental grid, to contrast it with the other split half — the feedback grid.

Disappointing as the agreement scores are for showing learning from feedback, the matrix of element-matching scores does present a picture of the relationship that is consistent with emphasis on the child role in relationships comparable with marriage. The matrix of element-matching scores shown in Table 11.2, sets out the scores categorised into three groups for ease of scrutiny. The three categories, numbered 0, 1 and 2 are these:

0	100-75 %ME	% ME scores
1	74-50 %ME	below 25%
2	49-25 %ME	were not obtained

The elements are indicated only by the role initials. The key to these is the earlier table of elements. In the %ME matrix the elements are presented in these three *role groups*.

1   Child role: Participants in the role of child
                  Participant's own children
2   Parent role: Participants in the role of parent
                  Participant's own parents

	WC	MC	C1	C2	C3	WP	MP	MM	WM	HF	WF	WS	HS	FH	FW	WA
WA	1	2	1	0	0	1	0	1	1	1	1	0	0	0	0	0
	1	1	1	1	1	1	0	1	1	1	1	0	0	0	0	0
WA	0	2	1	0	0	0	0	1	1	1	1	0	1	0	0	
	0	1	1	1	0	0	0	1	1	1	1	0	0	0	0	
FW	1	1	1	0	0	1	0	1	0	1	1	0	0	0		
	0	1	0	0	0	0	0	1	1	1	1	0	0	0		
FM	1	2	1	0	0	1	0	2	1	1	1	0	1			
	0	1	1	0	0	0	1	2	1	1	1	0	1			
HS	1	1	1	10	1	0	1	1	1	1	1					
	1	1	1	1	0	0	0	1	1	1	1	0				
WS	1	2	1	0	0	0	1	1	0	1	1					
	0	1	1	1	0	0	0	1	1	1	1					
WF	1	2	1	1	1	1	1	2	2	1						
	1	1	1	1	1	1	1	2	1	1						
HF	1	1	1	1	1	1	1	1	1							
	1	1	1	1	1	1	1	1	0							
WM	1	1	1	1	1	1	1	1								
	1	0	1	1	1	1	1	1								
HM	2	0	1	2	1	2	1									
	1	0	1	1	1	1	1									
HP	1	1	1	0	0	1										
	1	1	1	1	0	0										
WP	0	2	1	0	1											
	0	1	1	1	0											
C3	1	2	1	0												
	0	1	1	0												
C2	1	2	1													
	1	1	0													
C1	2	1														
	1	1														
HC	1															
	1															

Notes: %ME: 0 = 100-75; 1 = 74-50; 2 = 49-25. Upper line: %ME wife; lower line: %ME husband. For key to element initial see p. 174.

3   Adult role: Participants in the role of whole self and adult
Husband's and wife's friends of the participants

Looking in this matrix at the degree of differentiation of elements
adults can be seen as a predominance of zeros especially *within*
the group. Participants' parents can be seen as a predominance of
1s running right through the matrix. Child roles show the two
younger children undifferentiated from adults and a slightly
higher level of discrimination by the wife.

I suggest these possible interpretations of this distribution of
variance which is so striking in its omission to show an elaborate
construction of the adult role:

(1) Participants' parents are the most highly constructed roles in
the exchange.
(2) Participants in the role of parents are not differentiated
comparably to their own parents. They differ in not sharing with
the real parents their differentiation from *adults* and the two
youngest children.
(3) Participants have a clearly differentiated construction of
themselves as children. In fact most of their discrimination is
concentrated in this role. As adults and parents they tend to
construct themselves as undifferentiated from other adults. This
seems to suggest the thesis that adults in the family, and perhaps
all adults, are predominantly aware of their child-like qualities.
(4) The wife shows a slight but clear predominance of highly
differentiated [25-40 %ME] [Category 2] scores over the husband
— especially in the construction of husband as child. This would
seem to favour some cherished prejudices about the role of the
mother and wife as caring.

The striking differentiation of participants' parents suggests a
strong persistence through life of the construction of formative
relationships. We may consider the idea that these relationships
predominate over currently significant others precisely because
they are formative. We may not share their constructs, but our
first construing emerged in reaction to their constructs and our
identity inheres in our construction of ourselves as separate from
them.

The Exchange Grid in Context

I have tried to present the protocol of the Exchange Grid in such a way as to enable a reader to imagine a clinical or training for education situation in which they might determine a range of convenience relevant to the relationship in question. Within this range they would ask the dyad to negotiate by discussion a set of appropriate elements. These might be roles or individuals or what Laurie Thomas suggests as a class of elements including the set 'marital events'.

Participants would construe these events — possibly on the basis of previous conversations from which the experimenter might infer constructs and offer them to the participants. I do not propose at this stage the introduction of a three-way exchange with experimenter as third party, but propose for now that inferred constructs are attributable to one party or the other. The source grid is analysed for matching scores of constructs, and the matrix of percentage matching scores [%MC] between own with each of others' constructs is selected for scrutiny.

It is my pleasure to fancy that this square matrix may be taken to stand for an interpersonal semantic space. Or rather, since it exists only in the arithmetic of intersecting constructs, an implicit interpersonal semantic space. It is the indication of the extent to which a construct is duplicated by a construct of the partner. Referring back to the table of constructs with partner's closest matching construct, it can be seen that the intersection is small. For most constructs neither the matching score nor the pole names suggest much duplication of constructs.

Thus in rating on partner's constructs each participant is making an act of discrimination foreign to his/her elicited construct space. Each is having to look at the elements in a new way: in the way that the partner looks at them. So even though agreement is initially as high as it could be the exchange is still an exercise in taking on the perceptual system of another.

Whether learning in an educational setting from didactic instruction or pursuing a relationship, taking on a perceptual system is precisely what has to be done. The constructs of the other have to be incorporated into constructs of the self. The implicit interpersonal semantic space has to be realised in the course of exchange.

The high scores for agreement show that these participants did this with ease. They did not omit to ask me one key question in the course of exchanging: 'Do I rate the elements as I would rate them or as my partner would rate them?' This I answered 'Rate on your partner's constructs as you think your partner would rate: on your own rate as you yourself rate'. I made this choice on the basis of an earlier exchange grid in which I had found that differences between ratings as self and as other were small. The extra effort of producing two sets of ratings was not justified in view of the high redundancy of the two sets. Indeed, the redundancy between own and other ratings is quite high enough!

Participants did find rating in the role of other an additional effort, and to this extent the protocol did succeed on putting them to the task of identifying with the other. The parameter of success in guessing how the other would rate is labelled 'Understanding' by Laing, Phillipson and Lee (1976). It constitutes the second level of logical types in the hierarchy of three they evolved.

In reality, of course, scores for agreement comprise two components: (i) The degree to which partners agree to rate elements the same, that is 'Agreement' as Laing, Phillipson and Lee designate the first logical type; (ii) Understanding: the second level. Participants found that for most ratings they were, genuinely, in agreement. Where they were not their understanding of how the other would rate was accurate.

I have tried to convey the idea of two intersecting grids and the process of expanding the personal construct system by assimilating the constructs of the other, and of having one's own constructs assimilated at the same time. I am trying to convey the idea that the exchange-grid procedure can function at three levels:

(1) As an operationalisation of concepts of human interaction which accommodates the range from emotionally charged attributions in relationships to the assimilation of concepts and information in the spheres of learning and co-operative work.
(2) As a potential method for measuring changes in relationships and the transactions which comprise them or for measuring lack of change.
(3) As a potential method for providing exercise in the practice of relating, for whatever purpose, and for providing a theatre in which the practise exercised is made manifest to the participants.

They can observe and talk to one another about the process of conversing.

Where I refer to the incorporation of one set of constructs into another I intend associations to Kleinian ideas of infant phantasies of incorporating and being incorporated in a more concrete sense of the corporal. Any familiarity with Kleinian ideas of oral aggression and paranoid anxiety can only dramatise the visualisation of the exchange grid as a phenomenological event in an appropriate way.

I want now to turn from the pilot grid to a brief event in individual psychotherapy where the processes the grid omits are more clearly displayed: a young woman speaks of her disappointment because her mother has expressed the wish to back out of a trip of a few days to visit old friends. The feeling of being tantalised and let down by her mother is a familiar theme, and her sometimes strong anger and sense of hurt are familiar too. We have explored her conflict between the extremity of her feeling of dependence on her mother and the hysterical symptoms which compel, or threaten to compel, that dependence, and on the other hand the feeling that her mother is envious, controlling and spiteful, and someone to get as far away from as possible. She has even achieved an understanding of how much her symptoms and anxieties are an identification with her mother, and hence can understand how her mother's reluctance to make the trip is an expression of fears they share.

Nevertheless, her reaction to her mother's reluctance is a petulance she cannot help but make plain to her. Her mother is surprised by this, having felt that her daughter wanted to make the trip only to please her mother. The event in question is this: the young woman has reached a stage of her work when she can, with difficulty, begin to see through her anger at her mother's spite to her mother's need to hear that her daughters loves her and values her company. The daughter struggles with her hate, her hate projected into her mother and her mother's own hate. Each of them struggles to affirm to herself and to the other the reality of their love in this face of the opposing reality of their hate and the fear of depending which underlines it.

The same theme of love and need feared and denied is acted out in their sexual relationships — the mother with the father — the daughter with her boyfriend. It is treated of by psychoanalytical

theorists in varying language and at different levels of disturbance: by Harry Guntrip (1968) as the schizoid in/out oscillation;
by Melanie Klein (1975) as the destruction of the object by
paranoid oral aggression and the consequent depression; by Bion
(1977) and Winnicott (1965) in different terms as the containment
by the mother in reverie of the infant's oral aggression — here it
seems is an infant who did not feel her aggression could be
contained without damage to the mother, or any other object
such as her boyfriend.

I hope this example conveys something of what I have called
constructs which are attributions of the other — and sometimes
too of the self. The other may be loved and hated, loving and
hating: to assimilate it or to be assimilated by it may be taken as
occasion for anxiety. There may be some merit in undertaking
the exercise in the safely bounded conditions of a tedious
construing and rating task. Desensitising people to the anxiety of
encounter may be helpful to some, perhaps in the course of
trying to improve a marriage, perhaps in reconciling ourselves to
the tasks of learning and teaching.

To continue this discussion of the exchange grid as mediating
relationships, it must be noted that it has emphasised more and
more the other: our attitude to it and its attitude to us. More and
more I am aware that Kelly's is a psychology of personal
constructs and, as he himself says, 'we do not attempt to employ
the notion of ego . . .'. It is not a psychology of mental events
different in nature from the act of construing. Indeed, it
proposes, I think, that mental events *can only be* acts of
construction, very much, I suppose, as gestalt psychology
proposes that the mental event can only be the discrimination of
figure from ground and refinements of that discrimination. In my
ignorance I think of man the scientist springing, equipped with
constructs as cupid with arrows, fully sentient from the loins of a
cloth mother, wearing as a caul, I suppose, the emblematic white
coat of his profession.

So what is Kelly's account of human development, of how the
neonate becomes competent to construe self as self and other as
other, to construe self as construing self and other as similarly but
enigmatically construing itself? I will not hide the fact that I do
not know. But in thinking about the exchange grid I can
conjecture what it might be.

I think that the construct system of the first months is a world of events which are alternatively welcome and unwelcome. Scrutinising the sensorium that is available to this nearly helpless infant, we can quickly agree that of the areas we now survey few are available to him. But of the detail and intensity of his construing we can demonstrate little, however much we may propose. We might as well assume that there is a time so early that the concepts of causation and agency are absent — events just happen — they are nice or nasty.

But all too soon the concept of agency intrudes on this empyrean vision. The will asserts its self-centred, increasingly self-aware intention toward events — intent either that they should happen or that they should not. But what the will proposes it must first suppose and suddenly one dimension of experience takes prominence: events are either imaginary or real.

Let us suppose that there is a time so early that there is a willing self that lacks the construct real/imaginary: fantasy is equated with reality, or more accurately, there are only events, no fantasy and no reality for one needs the other to define it. As the poor orphan comes more and more to realise that it has little control of events it comes to conceive of agencies that *do* control events — some are hated, some are loved.

Over this battlefield of conflicting emotions and plural objects there eventually appears a *deus ex machina*: The concept of events as caused by another agent — self-conscious like the infant's self and having intentions toward him as has he toward it. Kelly may choose not to employ the concept, but ego is a *convenient* word for an individual capable of operating the sociality corollary — of construing the construing of the other. Arriving at it has been a mythic journey as full of intensity as an opera. Nor have we begun to consider the role of the third person in this drama.

Obviously, these ideas are a ridiculous simplication of a very confused understanding of Kleinian and object-relations psychologies. They are an attempt to assimilate them into a profound ignorance of the psychology of personal constructs. I wish they would serve to convey how the exchange grid might encompass in one interaction a whole hierarchy of levels of experience and organisation of self — after all there is room in Kelly for a whole range of ontologies: flexibility is its byword.

I contend that when we relate to one another we have the opportunity to recapitulate the whole of our individual mental evolution. I suggest that the other is problematic — that you may not love me and that certainly I sometimes hate you and so must you me. But on the other hand, it is the other that calls us into being. It is the act of construing the other that creates the self-conscious intending agent that is the whole range of convenience of psychologies. If we can only get dealing with other people right then we have assembled a psyche in good running order — firing on all cylinders. If our fantasies of what we have done to the other are too dreadful to contemplate and we do not have the construct real/imaginary, then our terror of losing the other or of its revenge can make relating difficult.

Having followed the concept of interpersonal semantic space all the way down to some narcissistic tantric seed, it would be appropriate for us to complete with a look in the outward direction. Out of what Balint (1968) calls the 'interpenetrating harmonious mix-up' of mother and child, interpersonal semantic space becomes more and more articulate, self-aware and precisely discriminated until we have a world of society and culture. The constructs of many integrated and refined into a recorded system of knowledge that is received as having an existence in its own right and coming from somewhere else. But no information, however objective, precise, impersonal or neutral, can ever completely shed the quality of the other — vulnerable and yet also dangerous.

Conclusion

I wish I could offer here a properly developed experimental, diagnostic and therapeutic instrument, but I have only a vague notion of one. I have tried to suggest how one might be thought out and to what purpose. I have tried to show how the construction by the mother of the infant elicits its development: how this concept allows personal construct psychology to be developmental as well as existential.

I have tried to show how the exchange grid is for me the focus of an interest both practical and theoretical: an essay in the design of heuristic interactions and a theoretical specualtion on not only how our sentience operates, but how it comes to operate. To do this I have tried to assimilate the concepts of object relations psychology into those of personal construct psychology. For justification I can only propose the necessity to a psychology to include the developmental. Klein proposes that anxiety and guilt are concomitant to development: Kelly disposes of them with two elegant definitions. I propose that psychodynamic treatments of guilt and anxiety can be consistent with them, and that when Kelly postulates their mode of function in terms of construction that does not explain them away, but makes them available to investigation.

The threats of not having constructs to cover the impinging range of convenience and of dislodgement from core constructs, Kelly's postulates of anxiety and guilt, are hardly avoidable in exchange: assimilation with the other entails both. Whatever they be postulated as, they remain phenomonologically painful and to be avoided. From here I might continue into concepts of psychic defence and hence to the unconscious, but space and temerity persuade me to leave speculation at the heresy that scientists have mothers, and that people are systems that mothers program for sentience in the face of the threats of constructlessness, and loss of constructs that sentience involves.

References

Balint, M. (1968) *The Basic Fault*, Tavistock, London

Bion, W.R. (1977) *Seven Servants*, Jason Aronson, New York

Guntrip, H. (1968) *Schizoid Phenomena, Object Relations and the Self*, Hogarth Press, London

Kelly, G. (1965) *The Psychology Of Personal Constructs, vol. 2*, Norton, New York

Klein, M. (1975) *Envy and Gratitude*, Hogarth Press, London

Laing, R.D., Philipson, R. and Lee, A. (1976) *The Interpersonal Perception Method*, Tavistock, London

Mendoza, S. (1976) *Personal Construction of the World*, Centre for the Study of Human Learning, Brunel University, Uxbridge

Thomas, L. and Mendoza, S. (1972) *Demon And Double Demon*, Centre for the Study of Human Learning, Brunel University, Uxbridge

Winnicott, D.W. (1965) *The Maturational Processes and the Facilitating Environment*, Hogarth Press, London

For a detailed account of the ontology of development see:

Kernberg, O. (1976) *Object Relations and Clinical Psychoanalysis*, Aronson, New York

12 THE DYAD GRID AND PSYCHOTHERAPY RESEARCH

Anthony Ryle

Personal Construct Theory and repertory grid technique were developed in teaching and clinical settings, and the main applications have always been to the study of how people construe themselves and others. For this purpose, most studies have used a grid form in which the elements are people. Some limitations of this approach led to the development of the dyad grid (Ryle and Lunghi, 1970), and this chapter will describe the use of this modified form. The argument for the modification was set out in the 1970 paper as follows:

> In a clinical setting the constructs elicited from the patient refer largely to attributes relating to interpersonal behaviour and such constructs are of salient interest to the psychiatrist. These constructs, however, are applied to the elements in general and this may, at times, lead to a loss of information. For example, in rating John on the construct '*is understanding*' the rater must make an overall judgement which might not take account of John's relative lack of understanding of Jill, or of his exceptional understanding of Elizabeth. In order to overcome this disadvantage, we have developed a modified form of repertory grid testing which we call the dyad grid, in which the elements, instead of being individuals, i.e. John or Jill, are the relationships between pairs, i.e. John in relation to Jill, John in relation to Elizabeth and so on.

In the rest of this chapter various past applications of the dyad grid will be described and possible further uses considered; in the first instance the technique of administering the dyad grid will be considered.

Administration of the Dyad Grid

Elements

The elements of the dyad grid are relationships. Any pair relationship may be included in the grid, but it is for most purposes the person's own relationship patterns that are of most interest. Hence, the majority at least of elements of a dyad grid will be the various relationships between self and A,B,C etc., where A,B,C etc. are significant other people. Each relationship will generate two elements, self-to-other and other-to-self. To this may be added relationships with ideal figures and the relationship of self-to-self. For some purposes the relationship between real and imaginary other pairs who might be seen as role models may be of interest.

Constructs

Constructs must be in a form that describes interaction, for example, *is dependent on* or *finds fault with*. They may be elicited by the classical triadic method, but in practice contrasting pairs of dyadic relationships, for example, John-to-self with self-to-father, yields a satisfactory range of constructs and is less unwieldly. Constructs may be applied in a bipolar form, in which case the contrast pole must also be elicited, but it is my own view that it is best to deduce the contrast pole of a construct by discovering which constructs have high negative correlations with it in the completed, analysed grid. For example, the semantic opposite to *controls* is, to most people, *submits*, or *gives in to*. However, in grids using unipolar constructs, in which the subject rates how far each construct applies to each relationship in turn it is common to find positive correlations between *controls* and *submits*; a finding which could be concealed by the tendency of subjects to offer semantic opposites.

Standard and Semi-standard Dyad Grids

The whole range of constructs and elements may be elicited from the subject, and this will, as always, maximise the individual relevance of the exercise. However, other purposes may be served by providing some or all of the elements and constructs. For a great many purposes a standard form of grid, which provides an indication of the relationships to be included and some standard constructs, is the best solution. While this allows the additional elicitation of idiosyncratic elements and constructs, it provides a basis for standardised comparisons between individuals, and permits the development of some normative values for some of the grid measures. A standard set of instructions and a standard grid form has been the basis of much of the work to be reported later in this chapter. The provided constructs in this test were based upon those elicited in a large number of previous grids. The average percentage of variance accounted for by these supplied constructs is not significantly different from those elicited from the subjects themselves, which suggests that they are constructs which the vast majority of people are capable of using meaningfully. Many subjects are able to complete the test from the following instructions, but guidance through the elicitation process may yield a richer array.

Relationships Test

The purpose of this form is to help in the understanding of the patterns of your relationships with others. It is part of an ongoing research project and a similar form has proved useful in identifying difficulties and clarifying the goals of treatment. You are asked to rate a number of relationships against a number of descriptions; some descriptions are provided and some relationships named, but there are also spaces for you to add your own. First decide which relationships you are going to add, listing these people in the numbered spaces below, giving their initials, their sex, and their relationships e.g. boyfriend; female flatmate; hated male teacher; sister etc.

	Initials	Sex	Role in your Life
1.			
2.			
3.			
4.			
5.			
6.			

Now choose at random any two of these and jot down, on scrap paper, descriptions of how they feel and act towards you, and of how you feel and act towards them, noting both similarities and differences. Repeat this with different relationships, and go on until you feel the important descriptions have been noted. Now turn to the rating form Figure 12.1; you will see that 10 descriptions are provided and that a further 6 spaces are left blank. Write into these spaces the 6 most important of your own descriptions, leaving out any that are already provided. At the top of the form you will see the numbered relationships, these numbers corresponding to your list above. Each relationship is rated against each description by allocating a score between 5 (very true) and 1 (not true at all). Fill in the form fairly quickly, rating all the relationships on each description in turn (i.e. fill row by row, not column by column). After it has been processed we will discuss what can be deduced from the test.

Analysis and Display of Dyad Grids

A dyad grid can be analysed in precisely the same way as any other grid. My own practice has been to use Slater's INGRID 72 program (Slater, 1972). An example of the graph plotted from the first two principle components from such a grid, summarising the relationship of constructs and elements, is given in Figure 12.2. (Based on Ryle and Breen, 1974). In this plot the related elements of each dyad are joined by a line (the dyad line). This enables one to highlight the subject's perceived pattern of reciprocal roles. In this example a social work student is recording her relationships to her fieldwork supervisor, course tutor and to two clients.

It can be seen that the dyad lines in the grid are roughly parallel; this indicates similar reciprocal role relationships. The self, however, appears at opposite ends of the dyad in the self-client relationships and in the self-tutor and self-supervisor ones. This dyad grid could be seen as providing a visual display of the student's role modelling.

The Interpretation of Dyad Grid Data

As is the case with all grid data, it is up to the tester and the subject to make sense of what emerges. *The two-component graph* is usually the most accessible form in which to present the analysis of grid data to subjects. Many dyad grids displayed in this way show remarkably stereotyped patterns of relationship,

	Mother to Father	Father to Mother	Self to Father at age:	Father to Self	Self to Mother at age:	Mother to Self	Self to (1)
5 = Very true 4 = True 3 = ± 2 = Not true 1 = Not true at all Rate each relationship on each description with a number, scoring thus according to the degree to which the description applies. No: Date:							
1. Looks after							
2. Is forgiving to							
3. Respects							
4. Controls							
5. Feels guilty to							
6. Is dependent on							
7. Gets cross with							
8. Blames							
9. Gives in to							
10. Confuses							
11.							
12.							
13.							
14.							
15.							
16.							

Figure 12.1: Standard Dyad Grid

(1) to Self	Self to (2)	(2) to Self	Self to (3)	(3) to Self	Self to (4)	(4) to Self	Self to (5)	(5) to Self	Self to (6)	(6) to Self	Self to Self

Figure 12.2: Social Work Student: Simplified Two-component Graph of Dyad Grid

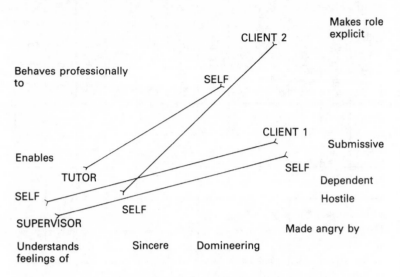

Figure 12.3: Dyad Grid: Two-component Graph Demonstrating Stereotyped Reciprocal Roles

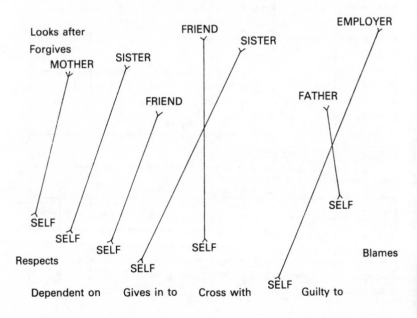

with all the dyad lines running in more or less parallel directions and with self-to-other always occupying the same pole of the dyad. Figure 12.3 gives an example of such a graph. In such instances it is usually the case that the pattern that emerges, which reflects the subject's ratings of his individual relationships, reveals a single higher-order scheme of which he is largely or wholly unaware.

In addition to providing this general view of the subject's perceived reciprocal relationships, the distribution in the construct space of the different relationships and the parallelism between particular relationships may be of interest. Figure 12.4 is the two-component graph of a woman patient who consulted because, after the experience of being raped, she was even more profoundly disturbed than might have been expected, feeling that in some way she had lost her grip of her life. She had many obsessional personality traits but no previous psychiatric history. Her childhood had been a stormy one, due to mother's numerous short-lived marriages and affairs. In the decade since leaving home she had lived an emotionally controlled, constrained and rather solitary life. The graph shows how closely the relationship with the rapist emerges as parallel to that with mother, something of which she was quite unaware. This suggested that the physical assault had been experienced as analogous to mother's earlier emotional assaults, and had thus served to disturb a personality structure formed in response to her earlier experiences of childhood and adolescence.

It is important to note that the first two components of the grid usually account for less than 70 per cent of the total variance, sometimes much less. In interpreting the two-component graph, therefore, it is as well to check the main loadings on the third component of both elements and constructs to note any important further discriminations.

The INGRID program yields direct measures of the relationships of elements and constructs in the whole construct-element space, and for some purposes it is preferable to rely upon these, especially when predictions of change are being made. Thus, *the table of construct correlations* provides a measure of how far an element rated high or low on one construct is likely to be similarly rated on another. This relationship is expressed in the INGRID program, both as a correlation and as an angular distance (an angle of 90° = no correlation; 0° a correlation of +1;

Figure 12.4: Dyad Grid: Two-component Graph Showing Similarity of Role Perceptions in Relation to Mother and Rapist

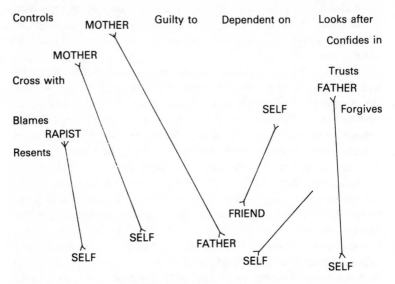

180° of −1). These construct correlations provide a way of looking at the implications of particular judgements, and this can be useful when comparing an individual's own view of his relationships on different occasions, or when comparing similar grids completed by different people. When grids are used which include standard provided constructs, population norms and standard deviations for the values of the angular distances between constructs can be calculated so that the degree to which a given individual departs from the consensual understanding of, say the association between *depends upon* and *gives in to*, or *looks after* and *controls*, can be identified. Data of this sort and its applications are discussed further below.

The table of element distances provides similar indications of the overall similarity, in terms of all the constructs used in the test, of any two elements. From this one can see which role is most or least similar to any other given role, a measure which can also be compared between testing occasions. In the INGRID program, element distances are calculated in terms of the mean expected distance, which is given the value of 1; values greater than 1 imply relative dissimilarity and values smaller than 1 imply relative similarity.

The percentage variance accounted for by individual constructs may also require interpretation. Certain constructs may be used more powerfully to distinguish between elements than others. Calculating the expected mean percentage variation (100 divided by the number of constructs) enables one to identify constructs accounting for very high or very low percentages of variance. It is important to refer back to the raw grid data in interpreting these figures. Very high variance may reflect a construct in which only one or two elements are rated at the extreme pole away from all others. (Such constructs are unsatisfactory and should be avoided.) Very low variance, on the other hand, may indicate that the construct is irrelevant, or misunderstood, or it may refer to behaviours or feelings with which the subject is ill at ease. If, for example, the ratings indicate that everyone is seen as trusting everybody equally, or nobody is angry with anybody, one suspects denial is operating in the completion of the test.

One other issue arises in the case of the dyad grid that requires additional interpretation. The assumption in any grid procedure is that all the elements fall within the range of convenience of all the constructs and can be presumed to be judged within the same system. Even in the standard grid, with individuals as elements, this assumption may not be true. The separate analysis of elements divided, for example, by sex or age, may produce two grids showing quite marked differences in their construct relationships (see Ryle, 1975). In the case of the dyad grid the separate analysis of self-to-other and other-to-self element grids frequently shows that the system of judgements applied differs markedly. The use of Slater's COIN program (Slater, 1972) to compare the self-other and other-self element grids, provides a measure of the degree to which the two systems are similar, in the form of a coefficient of correlation. When the value of this is low, the interpretation of construct correlations derived from the combined grid may be misleading. If, for example, for self-to-other, *looking after* is highly correlated with *controlling* and negatively correlated with *trusting*, while for other-to-self the reverse is true, analysis of the combined grid will produce an average result, concealing important information. Identification of those construct correlations which do differ markedly between self-to-other and other-to-self grids may be of considerable psychological interest. An example is given in the appendix of Ryle (1982). Where the angular distance between two constructs differs between the self-other and other-self grids by 40° or more, (corresponding to about two standard deviations) there is usually good clinical evidence to support the psychological significance of the difference.

Dyad Grids in the Study of Relationships

Although the study of an individual's construing of his roles is of clinical interest, a particular application of the dyad grid is to study dyadic relationships. Clinical applications of this approach to work with married couples is reported in Ryle and Breen (1972a) and a comparison of adjusted and maladjusted couples is described in Ryle and Breen (1972b). In this latter study the two members of each couple completed identical grids and also predicted how they believed their partners would complete the grid. The resultant grids were compared on the DELTA program (Slater, 1972). The main difference between adjusted and maladjusted couples lay in the perceived similarity of their relationship to each other to their relationship with their parents. Maladjusted couples

> differed from controls in that they were more likely to see the relationship with the partner as resembling the relationship with their parents, and more likely to report that, when the relationship was going badly, they perceived their own role as more childlike while that of their partner became less parent-like.

This last observation was based on the introduction of two ratings of their own relationship, 'when it was going well' and 'when it was going badly'. This procedure makes it possible to investigate conscious ambivalence.

Another application of the dyad grid in the dyadic situation was reported by Ryle and Lunghi (1971). In this instance a patient in therapy completed a dyad grid, and the therapist completed the same grid as he believed the patient would complete it. A comparison of the two resultant grids revealed substantial predictive accuracy (the DELTA index or general consistency was over 0.5), but it also identified areas of misperception of importance to the conduct of the therapy.

A different technique was used by Ryle and Lipshitz (1975) in the study of the progress of a couple in marital therapy. In this case the couple related their own relationship before each session, using a commonly elicited list of constructs. The elements of the resultant 'reconstruction grid' were therefore the same relationship as rated on different occasions. Analysis of this grid provided a record of the reconstruction of the relationship through time, which could be displayed graphically either on the two-component graph or against each component separately. Change, however, involves revision of the construct system as well as re-location of elements in it. This kind of change was investigated by dividing the grid into two, made up of the sessional ratings from the first and second halves of therapy respectively, the resultant two grids being compared on the COIN program. Significant changes in construct relationships between the first and second halves of therapy were, therefore, identified for each of the couple. For the wife, for example, *seeking comfort from the other* became less likely to be seen as associated with *dominating behaviour*, less likely to be seen as associated with *being helpful to the other*, and less likely to be seen as associated with *feeling affectionate*, but more likely to be associated with *feeling guilty*. *Attacking behaviour* was seen as less likely to be associated with *feeling guilty* and more likely to be associated with *feeling affectionate*.

Another study of marital therapy, illustrating grid manifestations of what in psychoanalytical terms would be called projection, is given by Ryle and Lipshitz (1976).

The Dyad Grid and Individual Psychotherapy

Psychotherapists working in the dynamic tradition are centrally concerned with how an individual construes himself and his relationships with important others, and the dyad grid is capable of yielding important data in this field. Despite this, it has been relatively little used, except by the present author. One can only speculate as to reasons for this; most probably they are to be found in the persistent conceptual schism of the psychological theories that underlie psychotherapy, and in particular in the isolation of psychoanalytical thought from the rest of psychology. The relationship of object relations theory to grid data has been considered in Ryle (1975) and an attempt to restate central aspects of psychoanalytical theory in cognitive terms is presented in Ryle (1982, 1985). This attempt grew out of the experience of combining repertory grid investigations with psychotherapy, an experience which served also to modify the method of therapy employed. The experience of translating between grid data and psychoanalytical concepts was a valuable aid to re-thinking and re-formulating many psychoanalytical insights into more acessible terms. Arising from this, the provision of simple, dense descriptions of patients' faulty assumptions, thought processes (conscious and unconscious) and behaviours became a central means of focusing therapy (Ryle, 1979a). Personal Construct Theory has tended to be more concerned with how the world and the self are construed than with the questions of the organisation of action, and grid technique cannot offer access to the full range of an individual's cognitive procedures. It offers a cross section of how reality is construed, but cannot illuminate the sequential unfolding of complex schemata, such as are involved in any aim-directed behaviour. The dyad grid is, however, of particular value in identifying the restrictive options imposed on an individual in his personal relationships by the particular form of his construct system. For the purpose of therapy these may be described as dilemmas (Ryle, 1979a, 1982), and expressed in the form of *either-or* (e.g. either *dependent* or *controlling* when the constructs are negatively correlated), or in the form of *if-then* (e.g. if *dependent*, then *submissive* when the constructs are positively correlated). Such dilemmas may be identified clinically from the patterns of an individuals relationship with others, and from the way in which he/she controls and cares for him/herself. It is in identifying these processes that normative data are of value; construct correlations expressed as angular distances for the relationships between four constructs with mean values of standard deviations are given in Table 12.1 (from Ryle, 1981). In practice, when the values of these angular distances are more than one standard deviation from the mean, it is nearly always the case that the individual shows relationship difficulties reflecting these non-consensual assumptions. The relevant values are those derived from analysis of the grid of self-other elements separately from other-to-self, at least where self-other and other-self grids show low agreement. In such cases, the other-to-self element grid will indicate the reciprocations expected from others.

Table 12.1: Mean Values and Standard Deviations of the Angular Distances between Four Constructs (43 Patients, 23 Controls)

	Gives in to		Controls		Is dependent on	
Looks after:						
Patients	73	20	74	25	73	23
Controls	73	21	70	24	67	17
Is dependent on:						
Patients	64	21	83	23		
Controls	65	18	74	17		
Controls:						
Patients	96	24				
Controls	91	21				

An example is provided by a man aged 35 who consulted because he was depressed and was unable to resolve the conflict between a residual attachment to his wife and a more passionate but stormy relationship with a lover, who was also worried about episodes in which he felt, and sometimes acted upon, violently angry feelings.

In the grid of self-to-other elements, the following construct correlations between *looks after, controls, dependent on, cross with* and *gives in to* are more than one standard deviation from the mean value. *Looks after* and *dependent on* (35°), *controls* and *cross with* (39°), *dependent on* and *gives in to* (40°), *gives in to* and *cross with* (49°). Expressing this in prose one could say that for this man to depend implies to look after and to give in to, to give in to implies to be cross and to be cross also implies to control. For the other-to-self elements the equivalent figures for correlation varying more than one standard deviation from the mean are as follows:

looks after and *dependent on*	119°
looks after and *gives in to*	117°
controls and *dependent on*	53°

controls and *gives in to*	59°
dependent on and *cross with*	44°
dependent on and *gives in to*	41°

The options open to this man on the basis of this personal 'theory of relationships' are limited, with no obvious possibility of a mutual relationship. For the 'self', to depend implies to give care and to give in to the 'other', which is associated with crossness. Dependency in the 'other' is seen as associated with being controlling, giving in to, and with crossness. To receive care from the 'other' implies another who is not dependent and not liable to give in to the 'self', so is a vulnerable role. Therapy in this situation must strive to alter this 'theory of relationships' which can be summarised in the relationship dilemma, *either* depend caringly, submissively or crossly on the non-dependent, non-submissive care of others, *or* offer cross, dependent, controlling care to cross, controlling and submissive dependent others.

The Dyad Grid and Outcome Research

In the above section it has been shown how a person's interpersonal behaviour can be limited by the terms within which he construes the roles of self and other. Clinically, problems of relationship are an important aspect of most neurotic patients' difficulties, usually being manifest in non-mutual, conflicted or diminished patterns of interaction. As suggested above, the description of these restricted role options as false dichotomies or dilemmas can be useful in focusing psychotherapy on the task of revising the assumptions about roles rather than as representing simply behavioural change (Ryle, 1979a). Moreover, if such dilemmas are identified on the basis of clinical and grid data, the aims of therapy can be defined as being the resolution of the dilemmas, and predictions of appropriate changes in construct correlations can be made and their fulfilment tested by repeating the grid after therapy. This method of assessing change in therapy has been reported in a pilot study (Ryle, 1979b) and in a series of 15 cases (Ryle, 1980). In the latter study patient ratings of change on the identified dilemmas were matched by changes in construct correlations in the appropriate direction in nearly every instance. In a current large-scale study of hospital outpatients receiving 12 sessions of psychotherapy, a similar result is being found, revision of grid measures being accompanied by changes also in symptom scores. The application of the dyad grid, therefore, permits the direct measurement of specific high level cognitive changes in areas of central clinical relevance.

Conclusion

The aim of this chapter has been to describe the basic features of the dyad grid and to give examples of various applications of this approach to the study of interaction, of psychopathology and of change. The flexibility of the method is, I hope, evident, and the clinical relevance of many of the reported findings is clear. Despite this, and despite the fact that the information yielded can be made sense of in terms of personal construct theory, cognitive psychology or psychoanalysis, the technique has been made use of on a very modest scale, and there is clearly scope for a more extensive and various application.

References

Ryle, A. (1975) *Frames and Cages: The Repertory Grid Approach to Human Understanding*, Chatto & Windus for Sussex University Press, London

—— (1979a) 'The Focus in Brief Interpretive Psychotherapy: Dilemmas, Traps and Snags as Target Problems', *Brit. Journal Psychiat.*, *134*, 46-54

—— (1979b) 'Defining Goals and Assessing Change in Brief Psychotherapy: A Pilot Study using Target Ratings and the Dyad Grid', *British Journal Med. Psychol.*, *52*, 223-33

—— (1980) 'Some Measures of Goal Attainment in Focused Integrated Active Psychotherapy: A Study of Fifteen Cases', *Brit. J. Psychiat.*, *137*, 475-86

—— (1981) 'Dyad Grid Dilemmas in Patient and Control Subjects', *British Journal Med. Psychol.*, *54*, 353-8

—— (1982) *Psychotherapy: A Cognitive Integration of Theory and Practice*, Academic Press, London

—— (1985) 'Cognitive Theory, Object Relations and the Self', *British Journal of Med. Psychol.*, *58*, 1-7

—— and Lunghi, M. (1970) 'The Dyad Grid: A Modification of Repertory Grid Technique', *British Journal Psychiat.*, *117*, 323-7

—— and Breen, D. (1972a) 'The Use of the Double Dyad Grid in the Clinical Setting', *British Journal Med. Psychol.*, *45*, 383-9

—— and —— (1972b) 'A Comparison of Adjusted and Maladjusted Couples using the Double Dyad Grid', *British Journal Med. Psychol.*, *45*, 375-82

—— and —— (1974) 'Change in the Course of Social Work Training: A Repertory Grid Study', *British Journal Med. Psychol.*, *47*, 139-47

—— and Lipshitz, S. (1975) 'Recording Change in Marital Therapy with the

Reconstruction Grid', *British Journal Med. Psychol.*, *48*, 39-48
—— and —— (1976) 'Repertory Grid Elucidation of a Difficult Conjoint Therapy', *British Journal Med. Psychol.*, *49*, 281-5
—— and —— (1971) 'A Therapist's Prediction of a Patient's Dyad Grid', *British Journal Psychiat.*, *118*, 555-60
Slater, P. (1972) Details of the widely available INGRID 72, DELTA and COIN programs are available from Dr Patrick Slater, St George's Hospital Medical School, London

13 EVALUATING DEPENDENCY

Nigel Beail and Sue Beail

Independence-dependence

Being 'independent' is highly valued as a personal attribute in our society. Growing-up is viewed as a process of moving towards independence. Some would go further and argue that the drive for the child to become independent is a force that is built into his maturational process' (Brazelton, 1979). People are judged along a dimension with independent as one pole and dependence as its opposite. Independence has the weight of the axiom, it implies strength, leadership and individualism and is upheld as a goal. Dependence, on the other hand, is devalued, and implies helplessness, indecision, weakness and childishness.

Kelly (1955), however, felt that this dichotomy was meaningless, and that it was misleading to emphasise dependency as an axis along which people vary. For him it seemed more a matter of how one's dependency relationships are distributed. Kelly argued that adults, like children, are dependent too, but they extend their dependencies discriminatingly to more people, to more things and to institutions. Similarly, arguments have been put forward by other writers. Wright (1960) suggests that we should extend the emphasis on dependency by submitting that dependence in itself is of value in that it is essential in many important kinds of interpersonal relations. She argues that we should be able to rely on others, to ask for help and accept help and know that there are many occasions when dependence is indeed laudable. For Caplan (1964), 'psychosocial supplies' are an essential ingredient of a person's social network. Similarly, Cassels (1974) lays emphasis on the availability of 'group support' for the person, and Bowlby (1975) states that people are happiest when they know that they can rely on someone they can trust who will provide a secure base from which to operate. The studies of Brown and his co-workers have shown that a poor, non-confiding marriage is a factor which increases the chances of developing depression in the presence of a stressful event (Brown and Harris, 1978). A study by Roy (1981) also found this to be true for men.

So the approach that therapists and other 'helping professionals' should take towards dependency should *not* be one of labelling people as dependent or independent, or helping them to move along that dimension but one where we 'throw emphasis upon variation in their dispersion' (Kelly, 1955) and see it as a salient aspect of a healthy person.

Evaluating Dependency

Kelly (1955) developed a grid method for investigating a client's dependencies from this alternative approach. This is the 'Situational Resources Repertory Test' — now called the 'dependency grid' (Fransella and Bannister, 1977). This grid is similar to the repertory grid, only in the dependency grid the sorting categories are situations which are essentially stressful, and the things to be sorted are resources upon whom we may call for help, or on whom we may lean and depend.

Kelly presented the dependency grid as a clinical tool, and this chapter will be concerned with investigating dependency in the clinical setting. This grid form, however, can also be used in educational settings and such an application is presented in Chapter 19.

Situations

When constructing a dependency grid we need to identify situations of different types which the client may have experienced, or may experience, which might be expected to be stressful. Kelly (1955, p. 314-15) suggests 22 such situations, for example:

'The time when you were most hard-up financially'
'The time when you were most lonely'
'The time when you had serious trouble with your parents or came nearest to having trouble with them'
'The time when you made one of the most serious mistakes in your life'

Any of Kelly's suggested situations can be used, or you may

know of some more appropriate situations for your client. Kelly made a note of where and when these situations were experienced.

Resources

The next step is to elicit a list of resources. These are people, things and institutions upon whom one may lean at one time or another in one's life. Kelly used his list of 24 role titles from the Repertory Test to aid the elicitation of resources. The client supplies the names for the role titles where appropriate, but you may feel that other resources not in Kelly's list are more appropriate and your client may produce some of his/her own.

Completing the Grid

The situations are written down the side of the grid and the resources are written along the top. To complete the grid the subject places a cross in those intersects showing to whom he or she turned to for help in that situation. For examples of completed dependency grids see Figures 13.1 and 13.3.

'If'

We may be interested in how our client would cope with certain stresseful situations 'if' they occurred now or in the future. To explore this Fransella and Bannister (1977) suggest that you elicit situations which your client may encounter and his/her possible resources, and ask the question '*If* this happened to whom would you turn to for help?'. The client then completes the grid in the same way.

In his presentation of grid technique Kelly only used a dichotomous scale for allotting elements to constructs and resources to situations. But subsequently other scales have been employed with repertory grids. These scales can also be used with '*if*' dependency grids. The client could be asked to rank order his/her resources for each situation from the person he/she would be most likely to turn to for help to the person he/she would be least likely to turn to.

Rating scales of say 5 or 7 points can also be used; one pole of the scale indicating that you would definitely go to that person through maybe/maybe not at the mid-point to definitely not at the opposite end of the scale.

Figure 13.1: David's Dependency Grid

SITUATIONS	Father	Wife	Boss	Sister	Close friend	Housing	Mother-in-law	Grandma	Social Worker	Mother
Children	X	X					X		X	X
Money Problems	X	X			X		X	X	X	X
Family Rows		X			X			X		X
Housing	X	X				X	X			X
Work	X	X	X		X		X	X		X
Can't Cope	X	X			X		X	X		X
Fighting	X	X			X		X	X		X
Drinking	X	X			X		X	X		X
Marital Problems	X						X			X
Police	X	X			X		X	X	X	X

Clarifying the Information in the Grid

Kelly (1955) suggested that factorial analysis indicates ways in which the person groups his human resources. For a detailed discussion of using Slater's principal components analysis with dependency grids, see Chapter 19. However, we have found that this type of analysis is often hampered by the fact that some rows or columns contain only one or two ticks (lopsidedness) which can give rise to spurious measures of association. We have also found that many people will identify resources but never use them, thus giving a column of blanks. In these cases Slater's INGRID program drops the row of blanks from the analysis, thus

Figure 13.2: David's FOCUSed Dependency Grid

RESOURCES

SITUATIONS	Mother	Wife	Father	Mother-in-law	Grandma	Close friend	Social Worker	Housing Department	Boss	Sister
Money Problems	X	X	X	X	X	X	X			
Police	X	X	X	X	X	X	X			
Work	X	X	X	X	X	X			X	
Can't Cope	X	X	X	X	X	X				
Fighting	X	X	X	X	X	X				
Drinking	X	X	X	X	X	X				
Children	X	X	X	X			X			
Housing	X	X	X	X				X		
Family Rows	X	X			X	X				
Marital Problems	X		X	X						

excluding information from the results. Sometimes no clarification is needed (see, for example, Figure 13.3), but if it is we suggest users simply FOCUS their grids by hand or by computer if that facility is available (see Chapter 18). This involves re-ordering the rows of situations and columns of resources to put like with like. We have FOCUSed David's grid to illustrate this (see Figure 13.2). It is easier to see to whom David turns to in each of the situations in the FOCUSed grid. In the clinical setting FOCUSing is often sufficient for the clinician's needs, but we would not want to deter users from applying other forms of analysis as they can supply considerable information (see Chapter 19).

The dependency grid provides information about our allocation of interpersonal dependencies. It shows whether our needs are specialised among a number of people. It reveals situations where we feel that we have no one to turn to; whether we turn to one or two people every time a problem arises, or whether we go to anyone — calling on everyone for everything.

David's main resources are his close family, except his sister who is listed as a resource, but he would not ask her for anything. One interpretation would be that David has not made the break from his parents on leaving home and starting his own family. However, David comes from a close-knit working-class family where family members live at most a few streets away and this kind of dependency is the norm. David has only one close friend on whom he relies heavily. He would like to be able to make more friends so as to ease the burden on his mate who he fears will eventually get fed up with him.

Undistributed Dependency

We have used the dependency grid to investigate the dependency relationships of a group of ex-psychiatric patients who were living in a hostel. One of the main aims of the organisation which runs the hostel is to 'encourage independence'. This is in line with the philosophy of rehabilitation work as Affleck (1975) states, for resettlement to be successful the patient must move from a position of hospital dependence to community independence. This view was held by the hostel warden. When a new patient arrives at the hostel he/she is encouraged to give up dependence on the hospital, and the role of the Social Worker is also played down. Residents are encouraged to turn to the warden for help and advice, and later they are encouraged to look after themselves.

From a Personal Construct Theory point of view this approach is doomed to failure, and we predicted that the residents' dependency grids would show what Kelly called 'undistributed dependency'. This is where a person turns to one or two people for help and is a less hopeful sign than a distribution which suggests a specialisation of needs amongst a number of people.

We were interested in how the residents would cope in stressful situations now and in the future, so the 'if' version was administered (by S.B.) with six residents. A list of possible stressful situations was drawn up. Resources were identified with the aid of a list of role titles including relatives, friends, hostel staff and residents and various members of the helping professions. The grids were scored by placing an X in each row under each person they felt they could turn to.

As predicted, all six grids showed undistributed dependency, and the person they most frequently turned to for help was the hostel warden. Table 13.1 shows that all the residents were dependent on a few people. However, they could identify at least twice as many resources than they would use.

Table 13.1: Number of Resources Identified by Residents and the Number They Would Use

Resident	Number of resources identified	Actual number would use
1	13	4
2	10	2
3	8	2
4	12	6
5	11	5
6	13	4

One of the residents, Elsie, organises her day around the whereabouts of the hostel warden. When he is in the hostel she gets out of bed, and when he leaves she goes back to bed, whatever the time of day. In the grid the warden appeared to be virtually the only person she felt she could turn to when a problem arose. Her grid (Figure 13.3) illustrates this 'undistributed dependency'.

According to the philosophy of rehabilitation the next step for Elsie would be to reduce her dependence on the hostel warden and start to look after herself. Thus, she would be left in isolation without resource — a situation she is unlikely to accept. Her dependence on the hostel warden cannot be reduced without alternative resources being made available to her. The next step, therefore, should be to explore how she may specialise her needs among a number of people and explore the possibility of there being even more resources available to her — for example she sees her daughter as a problem but not as a resource.

Figure 13.3: Elsie's Dependency Grid Showing Undistributed Dependency

SITUATIONS	Husband	Mother	Father	Sister	Brother	Daughter	Chief Warden	Hostel Warde	Care Assistant	Hostel Resident	Social Worker	Psychiatrist	G.P.
								RESOURCES					
Money								X					
Police								X					
Room-mate								X					
Arguments													
Parents								X					
Children			X										
Voices								X					
Feeling Ill								X					
Confusion								X					
Boredom													
Future													
Relationships													
Work								X					

Construing Resources

Having established to whom or what resources a person turns to in a number of stressful situations through the dependency grid, we should then establish why one person or group are used in preference to another. This information would tell us what qualities a client requires of someone they could depend on or confide in. To investigate this we write each resource on a card. These are then sorted into two groups according to the ticks and blanks in a situation row. So for each stressful situation in the grid there are a group of resources 'I would use' and a group 'I would not use'. We then ask the client 'Why do you prefer to go to these people; rather than these in this situation?' This is a form of construct elicitation as a construct is the basic contrast between two groups (Kelly, 1970).

When Tom has problems with money he goes to one group of resources because they are NOT AWKWARD whereas he does not go to another group because he feels it would be 'STICKY and COMPLICATED and may jeopardise his relationship with them'. Other constructs elicited from Tom were:

Won't think of me as peculiar	— would get the wrong end of the stick
Trustworthy	— frightened
Supportive	— wouldn't understand
Helpful	— would take over
Will listen to me and make suggestions	— would not listen
Easy to talk to	— not easy

We now know why one person or group are preferred to another. But the reasons (constructs) meaning may not be clear. For example, why does Tom prefer to go to people who are 'not awkward'?

Tom Less hassle, I don't want to be moralised at.
NB What sort of people moralised at you?
Tom People who try to impose and draw me into their world and imprison me.
NB Why do you prefer people who don't moralise at you — people who give you less hassle?
Tom They encourage you to be yourself and learn things in a gentle way so I won't be frightened of discovery.
NB Why do you prefer people who encourage you to be yourself?
Tom Because if I change I want to change by wanting to and not fear.
NB Why?
Tom It's more genuine.

No further constructs were elicited after genuine. This line of questioning is similar to Hinkle's (1965) laddering procedure for eliciting increasingly superordinate constructs. When you reach a point at which no further constructs are elicited, Hinkle states that we have elicited a highly superordinate construct, a construct which subsumes other constructs — an over-riding principle. If this line of questioning is applied to all constructs elicited Kelly's organisational corollary would lead one to expect a convergence of construction at higher levels of superordination. Indeed, Tom's constructs 'supportive' and 'not awkward' both converge at 'genuine'.

When a construct is already highly superordinate very little information can be elicited using 'laddering up' type questions. Tom's construct 'trustworthy' was found to be already highly superordinate; therefore, to find out more we can ladder down by using Landfield's (1971) pyramid procedure. This involves simply asking for example 'What more can you tell me about someone who is *trustworthy*?'

Tom: They respect the otherness of people.
NB: What sort of people don't respect the otherness of people?
Tom: People who treat others like objects.

The questioning is applied to both emergent and implicit poles of each construct and the pyramid builds up (see Landfield, 1971).

Conclusion

Through these methods the client's personal view of his dependency relationships are revealed and shared. We know to whom and what resources a person turns to in stressful situations and why some resources are used in preference to others. We can see whether the qualities they are seeking in others are of such a high standard that no-one could meet them or so wide as to include everyone. Alternatively, there may be literally no-one to whom the client may turn, or our client may need no help in this area, as his grid may show a specialisation of resources.

Hinkle (quoted in Fransella and Bannister, 1977) has suggested that the dependency grid can be turned on its ear by asking the question 'Who turns to you for help, or leans on you in what sorts of situations?' You can then follow this up with the construct elicitation procedure by asking 'Why do you think this group turn to you and this group do not?' The essential feature of these methods is that the therapist tries to learn and work in the client's own language.

The importance of confiding relationships and social-support networks are increasingly being stressed. Growing towards and being dependent — by specialising our needs among a number of people — is a positive strategy and a salient aspect of development. The methods presented here have a potentially wide range of application, to help reveal an individual's dependency network and his/her reasoning behind it. The dependency grid is not new, being first presented in 1955, but has been relatively ignored and unexplored. As Fransella and Bannister (1977) state 'This is a little-used but potentially valuable type of grid'.

References

Affleck, J. (1975) 'Rehabilitation, Resettlement and Support' in A. Forrest and J. Affleck (ed.), *New Perspectives in Schizophrenia*, Churchill Livingstone, Edinburgh

Brazelton, T.B. (1979) *Toddlers and Parents*, Penguin, Harmondsworth

Bowlby, J. (1975) *Attachment and Loss, vol. 2. Separation: Anxiety and Anger*, Penguin, Harmondsworth

Brown, G.W. and Harris, T. (1978) *The Social Origins of Depression*, Tavistock, London

Caplan, G. (1964) *Principles of Preventive Psychiatry*, Tavistock, London

Cassels, J.C. (1974) 'Psychiatric Epidemiology', in *American Handbook of Psychiatry, vol. 2*, Basic Books, New York

Fransella, F. and Bannister D. (1977) *A Manual for Repertory Grid Technique*, Academic Press, London

Hinkle, D. (1965) 'The Change of Personal Constructs from the Viewpoint of a Theory of Implications', unpublished dissertation, Ohio State University

Kelly, G.A. (1955) *The Psychology of Personal Constructs, vols 1 and 2*, Norton, New York

—— (1970) 'A Brief Introduction to Personal Construct Theory' in D. Bannister (ed.), *Perspectives in Personal Construct Theory*, Academic Press, London

Landfield, A.W. (1971) *Personal Construct Systems in Psychotherapy*, Rand McNally, Chicago

Roy, A. (1981) 'Vulnerability Factors and Depression in Men', *British Journal of Psychiatry, 138*, 75-7

Wright, B. (1960) *Physical Disability. A Psychological Approach*, Harper & Brothers, New York

14 REPERTORY GRIDS IN FAMILY THERAPY AND RESEARCH

Harry Procter

The repertory grid technique is ideally suited to the study of the family and might have been designed with such a purpose in mind. Many forms of the grid, including Kelly's original one, include as elements members of the person's family, with the invitation to find ways in which they are seen as similar and different. The grid is indeed a useful tool both in formal family research and in exploratory and therapeutic family interviewing. In a relatively brief period of time an extremely rich set of hypotheses can be generated. A second session using information gained from the first can yield an even more wide-ranging and evocative set of findings. The method has the advantage over many family assessment tools that have been developed in that it relies on the family members' *own* constructs and categories. And grids can also be developed, of course, which examine the way *therapists* and *research workers* construe families.

But, in spite of this, there has been relatively little use of the grid in family research and therapy. Why is this? It may have been because family therapists, in their attempt to build a systemic, interactional view of the family found it necessary to reject 'intrapsychic' concepts, and personal contructs were thrown out with the bath water. This is certainly true of the influential Jay Haley (1963, 1976).

The idea of the family constructing its reality can, however, be found in Minuchin (1974) and Reiss (1981). The Milan associates, drawing from Bateson, put much emphasis on the family's definition of their relationships. Family therapy from a psycho-dynamic and object-relations perspective contains many concepts of interest to construct theorists, particularly with their ideas of splitting (polarisation), sharing functions of the personality around the family, and the family as an internalised fantasy (Fairbain, 1952; Zinner and Shapiro, 1972, 1974; Laing, 1960, 1967, 1972).

Personal Construct Theory has epistemologically much in common with the thinking of Bateson (1972) and Watzlawick

(1976, 1984), Watzlawick, Bevin and Jackson (1967) and Watzlawick, Weakland and Fisch (1974). These authors have made an enormous contribution to our understanding of family processes with their emphasis on circular as opposed to linear causation. We are left, however, with a view which tends to underestimate the role and importance of subjective meanings and values.

The present author has attempted to redress this balance by using Construct Theory to elaborate and enrich systemic thinking about family and social processes (Procter, 1978, 1980). It is actually a relatively simple matter (in principle) to see how family members' constructs fit into and form a vital part of the interactional 'dance' that takes place in human relationships (Procter, in press). This makes available to the family researcher/ therapist the notion of constructs and grid methodology.

The view of constructs which emerges from this marriage of Kelly and systemic thinking is that they are an aspect of the interaction between a person and his or her environment, in particular the social or *semantic environment* that we create for each other in our relations. This moves away from the notion of constructs as traits, or attributes of the individual somehow in the brain or the mind of the person. The construct is seen as a much more transient entity, and if there is an apparent permanence in the way people construe it is because the constructs are being continuously *maintained* or *sustained* within the social interaction. The corollary to this is that construing can be changed and indeed is continually moulded by the interaction. Even the tone of voice we use to phrase a question can profoundly alter the other's view.

This all has important implications for Construct Theory and grid methodology. By its very nature the grid tends to over-emphasise the construct and construct system as attributes of individuals. Factor analysis of the results compounds this impression. Filling in the grid is in itself a series of social actions made in relation to the person's network — the information on the grid must be assumed to be a reasonable reflection of the person's repertory of social choices if the technique has any validity. But the grid is itself part of a conversation with the experimenter, an encounter involving much mutual elaboration and reconstruction — learning. The grid is, therefore, a measure of this social process, and this itself is embedded in a specific ecological context.

Having said this, I would like to present a grid methodology for examining families worked out some years ago (Procter, 1978). With proper computing facilities it has a part to play in the family therapy clinic as well as in research.

Three forms of grid were utilised. The first consisted of an ordinary individual grid, given to each of the family members. Constructs were then drawn from these to make up grids examining interpersonal perception (the family grid). Finally, information from the latter was put into a pooled grid (the common family grid). These will now be examined in more detail together with the kinds of hypotheses that can be derived from them.

The Individual Grids

The information gained from an ordinary repertory grid is of course fascinating, or there would not be a new book coming out thirty years after its invention. Giving a grid to members of the person's family, so that we see what the elements have got to say for themselves — and then comparing all the results — can be extremely interesting.

In my own work a 16 × 16 grid was used, similar to the one in Kelly (1955), with a role-title list and triadic sorts. A grid was given to each of four family members — the patient with two parents and one sibling. Trichotomous rating (including a 'neither' category) was used. A computer program was written based on Kelly's non-parametric factor analysis, Landfield's (1971) linkage analysis and various other measures. This would present the data graphically, making them a little easier to decipher.

Some interesting patterns of family construing emerge from the results. These in turn allow us to work out a kind of logic which governs the structure of the family and what happens, for example, when it goes through a transition in the family life-cycle (Haley, 1973).

In 25-year-old Henry's family, all four members appeared to be using a single evaluative 'us-them' construct. With one exception (see below) people in the family were seen as kind, considerate, happy, true, thoughtful and placid as against various unkind, lazy, two-faced, inconsiderate figures outside the family boundary. Perhaps we could even define the notion of boundary (Minuchin, 1974) in construct theory terms as being the cleavage line of shared us-them constructs.

This now raises the question of what happens during a transition. How do people leave and join a family like this with such a well-defined boundary? Some kind of revision of the construct or re-construing of the person must occur or there will be tensions. Issues of *loyalty* (Boszormenyi-Nagy and Spark, 1973) to the family culture could arise if a child leaves home and joins 'them'.

Both Henry's parents have included their fathers among the external bad figures. Mother sees her father as mean, unsociable and 'doesn't want to know'. Father sees his father as violent, two-faced and sullen. Now if part of being loyal to the family culture is to reject one's father, this puts Henry into a paradoxical position. The one exception to the monolithic construing mentioned above is that Henry has rated *his* father negatively — he is seen as unphilosophical, insensitive, unable to see another's point of view and lacking vision. This may give some clue to Henry's problems — to be loyal to his parents he has to reject one of them. Perhaps to cope with this contradiction he has blurred and loosened his construing and become thought-disordered (Bannister, 1960; Bannister and Salmon, 1966). His sister, who has left home successfully, has come up with another solution. She has preserved the shared family construct in her thinking, seeing family in the same positive light, but has come up with a second construct, a second orthogonal factor which discriminates herself as stubborn from her ideal self and her new husband (not stubborn).

The pattern of construing in another family with a son with problems at leaving-home time can be seen in Figure 14.1.

Even this small sample of information gathered from the four individual grids allows us to generate quite a rich hypothesis about what is occurring in this family. There is a shared main construct running through which discriminates mother, father and the patient (22-year-old Nigel) as kind, altruistic and home based from Nigel's sister, who is seen by the three as 'going out a lot' and by father as 'selfish'. Unlike Henry's sister, Nigel's has defined herself by contrast to her 'boring' family, involving herself in dance, drama and a gay life. There is tension as a result with her father who links 'going out a lot' with selfishness, like his

Figure 14.1: Construing in Nigel's Family (Selected from Individual Grids)

Perceivers:		Elements: Mother	Father	Patient (Nigel)	Sister	Externals +ve	-ve
	Mother	thoughtful	happy kind	happy kind	goes out a lot	MGF happy kind	Mother's brother gossips selfish
	Father	home based kind	home based kind	home based kind	selfish	Ideal PGM Br kind	Uncle PGF selfish
	Patient (Nigel)	conform	conform	conform	goes out a lot	Ideal conform	cold serious confident
	Sister	interesting confident	not confident not interesting	not interesting not confident	interesting confident	Ideal spouse likes drama music	

Figure 14.2: Construing in Peter's Family

Perceivers:		Elements: Mother	Father	Patient (Peter)	Brother	Externals +ve	-ve
	Mother	placid, happy quiet, doesn't like football	unhappy, temper, likes football	placid/happy	placid/ happy	Mother, Father, Sibling ideal happy, placid quiet	
	Father	sad argumentative shy proud	sad argumentative modest	sad argumentative shy modest	proud sociable happy talkative	Mother, Brother, ideal sociable happy	
	Patient	hard to please warm, loving babyish	cold not loving	warm shows feeling	cold not loving	Teacher ideal warm, loving	rejecting friend cold, not loving
	Brother	depressed introvert gentle	extrovert rough not clever	depressed introvert gentle not generous	extrovert	ideal trustworthy extrovert	

father and mother's brother. Sister has left the family, marrying a man who shares her interests; but how is Nigel to leave? Unlike his sister he 'conforms' loyally, shoring up the parents' reality. But sister sees mother as interesting and confident and she would perhaps like to have a more exciting life. Nigel's bizarre behaviour and apathy may be to detour the conflict from the parents' marriage. It is also interesting just how much similarity there is between constructs gathered totally independently.

This may be contrasted with another pattern (Figure 14.2), demonstrated in Peter's family: In this unhappy situation a construct of happy and extrovert versus sad and quiet runs through all four grids, but instead of all or most of the bad figures being seen in the *external* network, the very opposite is the case. Peter's brother sees the whole family as muddled and unhappy although trustworthy. There is a schism running through the family. The parents, Polish immigrants, contrast each other from their positively valued families of origin. Wife sees her husband as unhappy, with a temper, noisy and interested in football, in contrast to her mother, father, sister and two sons whom she sees as placid, happy, quiet and not interested in football. Husband sees himself, his wife and Peter (the identified patient) as sad, argumentative and shy. Peter's brother, however, he sees as happy, sociable, talkative and proud, like his mother, brother and ideal self. Both parents seem restricted to this monolithic cluster of constructs.

The sons, by contrast, have very elaborate and psychological construct systems. They have grown up with the language, of course, but maybe more than this, they have had to engage in more than the usual struggle to develop ways of surviving in the English-speaking culture. They both see much that is positive in the figures around them — teachers and friends who form large clusters in their linkage diagrams (see Figure 14.3 for Peter's element linkages). Peter rates his mother and himself as highly similar (warm, forthright, introvert, loving and unsure) as opposed to his father and brother who are cold and not loving. Peter has perhaps taken it upon himself to support his mother in her unhappy marriage. This constitutes a Construct Theory method of isolating that pattern which family therapists have emphasised — the coalition of two people across two generations against a third member of the family (Haley, 1965). It will be seen from Figure 14.2, though, that he is not totally happy with his mother — she is babyish and hard to please.

Figure 14.3: Peter's Element Linkage Diagram

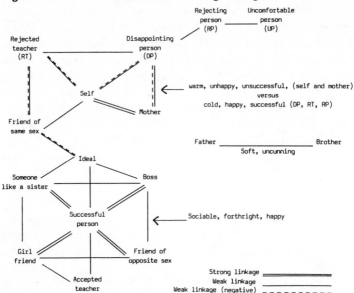

The Family Grid

The family grid is again 16 × 16 in size and uses sixteen constructs drawn from the individual grids. Four orthogonal constructs are drawn from each of the four family members according to various criteria (see Procter, 1978 for further details). The elements consist of the four members and twelve 'meta-elements' — how each one predicts the others would view the four members (see Figure 14.4). It is thus an interpersonal perception grid, rather like the IPM technique of Laing, Phillipson and Lee (1967), except that the family's *own* constructs are utilised rather than prescribed categories.

An identical family grid is given to each of the four members and, of course, it would be possible to adapt the methodology for smaller of larger groups. They are then processed by a second computer program developed by the writer, which derives a number or measures (Figure 14.5). These are all obtained from column (element) comparisons and will be described in detail

Figure 14.4: Peter's Family Grid (Peter's Family)*

FAMILY GRID

Name: Family P: Patient — Date 24/3/75

Number: √ = N, X

SORT No.	Construct	Contrast	How Steven sees himself	How Steven sees Paul	How Steven sees Fred	How Steven sees Mary	How Fred sees Steven	How Fred sees Paul	How Fred sees himself	How Fred sees Mary	How Mary sees Steven	How Mary sees Paul	How Mary sees Fred	How Mary sees herself	Steven	Paul	Fred	Mary
1	Placid	Temper	√	X	√	√	√	X	√	X	√	√	X	√	√	√	X	√
2	Quiet	Noisy	N	√	X	√	N	√	X	√	N	√	X	√	√	N	X	√
3	Happy	Unhappy	√	X	√	X	√	X	√	X	√	X	√	X	√	N	√	X
4	Generous	Not generous	√	X	√	√	√	X	√	N	√	√	X	√	√	√	√	√
5	Sociable	Reserved	√	X	√	X	√	X	√	X	N	X	√	X	N	X	√	X
6	Proud	Modest	√	X	√	N	√	X	√	N	√	N	N	X	N	N	X	N
7	Argumentative	Not argumentative	X	√	X	X	X	√	X	X	X	N	√	X	X	√	√	N
8	Talkative	Quiet	√	N	√	X	X	X	√	N	N	X	X	N	N	N	√	N
9	Confident	Unsure	√	X	√	X	√	X	√	N	√	X	√	X	√	X	√	X
10	Aggressive	Not aggressive	X	√	X	X	X	√	X	N	X	X	√	X	N	√	√	N
11	Cold	Warm, shows feeling	X	X	X	X	N	X	X	N	X	N	√	X	N	X	N	X
12	Hard to please	Easy to please	X	√	X	X	N	√	X	N	√	√	√	X	√	X	N	N
13	Depressed	Not depressed	X	√	X	√	X	√	X	X	X	√	X	√	X	X	N	√
14	Clever	Not clever	√	√	√	√	√	√	√	√	X	√	√	√	X	√	N	√
15	Shy	Not shy	N	√	X	X	X	√	X	X	N	X	X	X	N	N	√	N
16	Rough	Gentle	X	√	X	X	√	X	X	√	X	X	√	X	N	X	√	X

* Mary=mother, Fred=father, Paul=patient (here Peter), Steven=sibling

Figure 14.5: The Six Measures

Measure	Elements Compared	Example
1. Perceived Similarity	A — X/A — Y	Henry's view of mother compared to his view of his sister
2. Commonality	X — A/Y — A	Mother's view of Henry compared to sister's view of him
3. Perceived Commonality	A — X — B/A — Y — B	Henry's guess about how similarly his parents see him
4. Sociality	X — Y — A/Y — A	Henry's guess about mother's view compared with her actual view
5. Meta-commonality	X — A — B/Y — A — B	How much Henry and his sister agree about father's view of each of them
6. Comparison of self-concepts	X — X/Y — Y	The way Henry sees himself compared to the way father sees himself

Every possible value of A, B, X and Y is calculated by the program (average values for each element and the overall average are also provided). X and Y are the two elements being compared at any one time.

below. It is also interesting to put the family grids through the first program and examine the element and construct factors and clusters. The six measures will now be described. Examples from the families are included to illustrate the kind of hypotheses that can flow from the methodology.

1. Perceived Similarity

The first measure repeats information obtainable from the individual grids, except that the elements are now being rated on constructs elicited from all the family members. The program calculates all 24 possible pairings. It derives the average matching (a non-parametric type of correlation) for each perceiver — that is how much similarity or difference each member sees in all the dyads in the family. It also derives a score for each pair (averaged over the four perceivers) so that we can see at a glance which two are regarded as being most alike and which most dissimilar. Finally, an overall 'perceived similarity' score is calculated — the overall average.

Families vary on the amount of overall perceived similarity. As we might expect, Henry's and Nigel's families have higher values than Peter's. Distinctions tend to be made *within* the family in the latter, whereas they are made more across the family boundary in the other two families. There are also interesting variations across the four members in how much similarity they see. One member may see more than the others like Nigel's 'bad' sister who has left home. She sees the others as similar whilst making a strong bid to define herself by contrast to them.

It could possibly be helpful to Peter and his unhappy immigrant and split family, to help them notice more similarity between them — to strengthen their unique family identity. The measures show all four of them as seeing no signfiicant similarity at all. However, a closer look reveals one pairing of the 24 to stick out — mother sees herself and her crazy son as *identical*. This maybe signifies a projective relationship, perhaps clung to in the face of the general looseness and antagonism.

Scanning the measures in Nigel's family reveals another interesting pattern. Amidst generally low levels of perceived similarity, Nigel sees his parents as very similar. It is commonly said that symptomatology functions to keep parents together. The family grid findings may give us some insight into one way that this occurs. The patient sees similarity in the marriage even though his sister and both parents themselves do not. Could significant movement be accomplished by merely helping him to distinguish them, or for them to see what he means?

The same situation of one matching deviating markedly from the other 23 occurs a third time in Henry's family. His mother sees herself and her husband as identical. Remember that Henry and both parents saw their fathers in a strong negative light. She could be clinging to this view of her husband as identical to herself under threat of him flipping over to her son's view of him (insensitive, unable to see another's point of view, lacking vision) — strong medicine in the leaving-home transition.

2. The Measure of Commonality (Agreement)

This compares two people's views of each family member. Families may vary in how much overall commonality there is. Peter's family has a lower score, reflecting the split between the parents and the general disengagement in the relationships. Commonality seems to imply alliance and its contrast, hostility. But this is not necessarily the case. People with identical views can fight, symmetrically. Opposites can come together in a close complementary relationship. But in families differing views often do indicate conflict and this can be seen on the grid — marital, sibling and inter-generational differences.

In Henry's family the parent's score is the highest — they have forged a tight shared-construct system. The computer also tells us who is the most and least agreed about member. Significantly, Henry is the least agreed about member. Perhaps he is, in his crazy behaviour, successfully loosening the family's construing, helping them to adapt as they go through the changes in the life-cycle.

In Nigel's family it can be seen how the two children are elaborating contrasting 'slots' in the family construct system, Nigel being the 'home-based' one and his sister the sociable going-out-a-lot one. This is reflected in their low commonality (high individuality). It gives us an idea of how personality develops in the family. The children often have the tendency to find their own 'piece of territory' within the shared family reality and elaborate that. Development occurs through a dialectic of identification and differentiation.

It is interesting to compare the *fathers* in Nigel's and Peter's families. Both are the least agreed about members of their respective families. But Nigel's father is the most agreed *with* whilst Peter's is the least. The members of Nigel's family all agree with father although they do not agree with each other. He therefore appears to be a central figure, the hub of the wheel who holds them all together, but is also the bone of contention. Peter's father is much more peripheral. One might approach these two fathers very differently in therapy.

Coalition patterns can be detected clearly with this measure, for example if two members share a view of a third with concern (positive) or criticism (negative). It may even be possible to distinguish overt from *covert coalitions*, which family therapists have regarded as so important (Haley, 1965; Palazzoli *et al.*, 1978). Nigel's parents criticise their daughter, his sister, as thinking 'more of herself'. The content of her grid shows mainly a positive attitude towards them, so it may be that she is not aware of their criticism of her. We can, however, find out more about this from the family grid in the third measure — *perceived commonality*.

3. Perceived Commonality

This is the first of the three measures derived from the meta-elements on the family grid. These become fairly complicated conceptually and so a thorough analysis will not be attempted here. A more exhaustive exploration can be found in Procter (1978). The measures are interesting in themselves, but insight can also be gained by comparing them with each other.

Perceived commonality looks at how much each one *thinks* pairs of people agree or disagree rather than how much they actually do, as above. Thus, a family member can assume agreement between two members about someone. She may be right, or it may turn out that they do not actually agree so much. By contrast, disagreement may be perceived accurately or seen when the pair actually *agree*. The measure can thus detect the processes of pseudo-mutuality, pseudo-hostility, projection, secret coalitions and the like.

The program gives all 96 possible comparisons and also averages for each perceiver, for each pair and for each object of the agreement or disagreement. An overall measure is also calculated which indicates how much agreement or disagreement is assumed to exist in each family. Paralleling the commonality measure, Peter's family shows a lower level than Henry's and Nigel's.

In Henry's family, the mother tends to assume that everyone is in agreement. Father is ranked second on this measure, the sister third, with Henry himself the lowest. The parents assume that a family harmony exists in spite of actual disagreement, suggesting the presence of a family myth (Ferreira, 1963; Esterson, 1970; Byng-Hall, 1973). In Peter's family the parents are seen as having low levels of agreement compared to the other pairs. Henry's father is seen as being subject to the most agreement, Peter's the least.

4. Sociality

This measures how much one member's assumption about another's perception actually corresponds with that perception. The program calculates the measure for each of the 48 possibilities and gives overall averages for each pair (in each direction). Two useful scores are also calculated: the *empathy* score which gives each member's ability to predict the other's views, and the '*empathised*' score which shows how much each one's views are successfully predicted. Again an overall average is provided.

Scanning these tables can reveal some suggestive patterns. Henry's parents are very successful in predicting each other's views of the family members. Father is best at predicting and his views are most easily predicted. Henry's sister, perhaps because of her additional construct, is the most misunderstood. In Nigel's family the mother and sister have the highest mutual empathy. It will be remembered that this sister was seen as 'bad', having left the family in a disloyal way. Each parent has a good understanding of how Nigel sees the other parent, but not how he sees themselves.

Peter's family shows lower scores on this measure, some of them even being negative — i.e. the predictions are more wrong than right. Mother can predict father's views well though — even getting his view of the patient right on all 16 constructs, but he does not reciprocate.

5. *Metacommonality*

This measure compares two people's predictions of how another views the family members. It is not, therefore, concerned with the accuracy of the predictions as with the previous measure. If their predictions are accurate (high sociality)[1] then meta-commonality measures will be necessarily high. But an interesting and psychologically important situation arises when two people agree about another's view, but their prediction does not correspond with his actual view. There are instances of this in Henry's and Nigel's families. Henry's parents agree *perfectly* (on 16 constructs) on how their children view the family, and yet this prediction is not significantly related to their views. A similar situation exists between Nigel and his father about the mother's views. Whether these kinds of patterns are significant would, of course, have to be checked in interviewing and observing the family, but it may lead to a disconfirmation in which an innaccurate view is projected on to the other. This kind of process has been extensively reported in clinical studies of schizophrenic families (Laing, 1961; Palazzoli *et al.*, 1978; see also Watzlawick, Bevin and Jackson, 1967).

6. Comparisons of Self-concepts

This is the final measure derived by the program. One person's view of himself is compared with another's view of himself. It is possible that two (or more people) can see themselves in a similar way without either of them (or anyone else) seeing them as similar (as detected by the first measure, perceived similarity). Henry's parents are seen as similar by all except Henry himself. Henry and mother are seen as orthogonal by all, yet they share similar self-concepts. This may show in their life.

In Nigel's family there are no positive correlations here and no pairs are seen as similar except for him seeing his parents as highly similar, and in Peter's case no self-concepts are related although mother and Peter are strongly identified.

With this last measure we have begun to compare different members of the family rather than different views and meta-views of the same member. Further exploration can be achieved in the *common family grid*, pooled from all four family grids.

Common Family Grid

There is a rationale for pooling the grids in several ways — one with 16 straight elements (as viewed by each one). One could also construct a pooled grid to examine the perception and meta-perceptions of each of the four members. These grids may then be analysed like the individual grids with factor, person and cluster analysis.

There is an argument justifying pooling all the members' constructs and allowing all to rate them. Constructs have their origin in social and cultural context (Procter and Parry, 1978) and especially in a family context (Procter, 1980). The member knows unconsciously, if not in a verbally articulated way, how their intimates construe, and indeed many of their constructs are shared. Construct analyses of the common family grid allow us to examine the structure and interrelationships in the axes of the family reality. We can look at how they place themselves and each other in this space.

Two of the families had large clusters with some isolated constructs. Nigel's had two orthogonal clusters as shown in Figure 14.6. Each family member has constructs represented in

Figure 14.6: Linkage and Cluster of Constructs in Nigel's Family

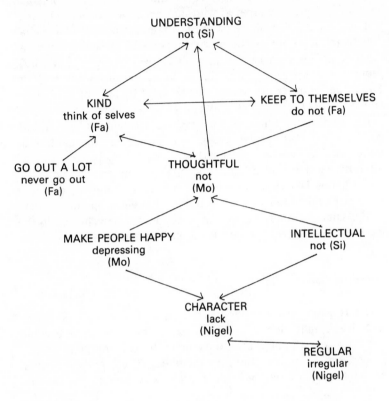

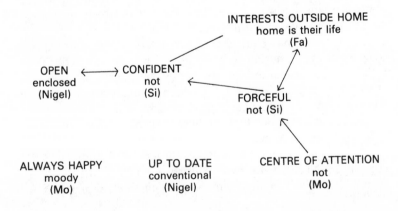

Figure 14.7: Linkage and Cluster of Elements in Nigel's Common Family Grid

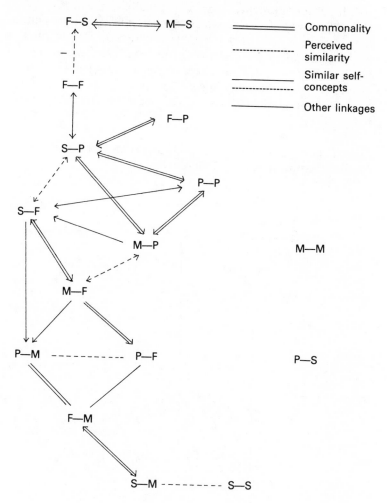

each cluster. This shows how a shared way of discriminating and identifying the elements is used by each, even though each has different ways of verbalising it. The parents' view of their daughter contrasting from the large family element cluster may be seen in Figure 14.7. Father's self-concept is the link between them. He sees himself above all as most different from her. Nigel sees his sister (P(atient) — S) orthogonally to the rest.

Another way of showing the common family grid is by plotting the elements in construct space (or vice versa). The distribution of the elements as seen by each of the four is shown for Peter's family in Figure 14.8. Only elements significantly loaded on these factors (outside the box) are shown. It gives us an immediate picture of the family.

Figure 14.8: Elements Mapped on Two Constructs From Peter's Common Family Grid

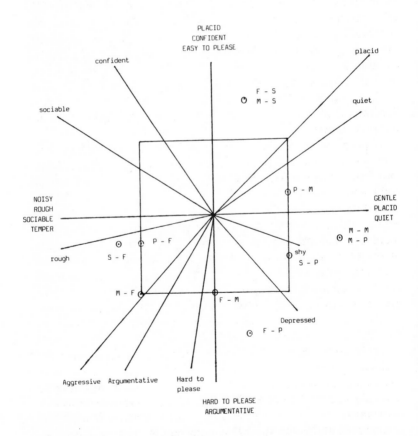

Other Measures

Various other measures can be carried out on the grids. Scanning the grid with a 'meta-construct', aligning the variance along a particular diagnostic dimension, can be a very useful measure. Kelly scanned his original repertory grid with sex and authority dimensions (1955, pp. 294-7). He also examined the distinctions generated by providing such elements as ideal self, successful person, ethical person and rejected person in the role-title list. Using these methods, we can learn how each family has negotiated unique ways of construing the universal of wider societal distinctions with which they are presented.

In the early 1940s, Bateson developed a theory or method for examining the way bipolarities (constructs) were assigned to role-relationships in different cultures. He called this *end-linkage* (Bateson, 1942; see also Mead, 1977). For example he compared the way spectatorship—exhibitionism was assigned to parents/children in England and in the United States. English children tended to quietly watch their parents perform at meal-times. The reverse situation tended to occur in American families. Spectatorship–exhibitionism is end-linked in opposite ways in the two cultures.

We can use the grid and family grid to study end-linkage and compare it in one family culture and another. What does it mean in a family to be a parent, a child, a man, a woman, a younger sister and so on?

Systems theorists have isolated certain dimensions of inter-action which they regard as of central importance in family therapy. Examples of these are hierarchy, proximity and being *in* or *out* of a sub-group or coalition. Together with observational data the grids could be used to show how family members construe themselves in the various possible positions. As the members move around the system they will systematically change in the way they are construed and possibly also how they construe as perceivers.

There are certain general social constructs which we all learn such as right versus wrong, good versus bad and ill versus well. Each family will negotiate its own version of these with its own particular set of implications. They may then be used to discriminate one or more members or positions from others. This is central in understanding problem formation and resolution. To be ill can thus be associated with raised or lowered positions in the hierarchy with the 'well' ones taking the complementary position. To be distant and quiet may mean one is sad, depressed or angry. The common systemic notion of symptoms regulating interpersonal distance (e.g. Byng-Hall and Campbell, 1981) can be understood to be mediated through implications in family constructs. Variations in one dimension will be accompanied by shifts in another.

A husband and wife in conflict may think of each other as hostile and angry, but in being so they may also be 'passionate' and 'trying hard to sort it out' as opposed to 'cold' and 'bored', as they are in other phases of their interaction. So, in systemic terms, their fighting regulates their distance. One may be able to locate some useful constructs to provide in therapy (re-frames) from the couple's *own* grid rather than some arbitrary adjective from the therapist's repertory.

The family's particular version of the general evaluative construct of good/bad is also useful to know. By sorting out all the evaluative constructs on the family grid one can look at each member's loading (who is seen in the best through to the worst light), and how much good or bad each one perceives in the family. This method is derived from Scott's and Ashworth's (1969) family relations test, which is a type of construct technique. Scott assumed that a bad image or 'shadow' can be passed down the generations.

Nigel (as object) has the highest loading on a cluster of seven bad constructs,[2] his mother the lowest. But Nigel sees the least bad in the four members. In Peter's family, mother sees high 'badness' in her husband, father sees it in his wife and in Peter (the identified client). Peter sees a lot in himself, and his brother Simon sees it in father and patient. If these correspond with blaming patterns, we likely can predict patterns of conflict in the family from them.

Measuring Change

Kelly said therapeutic change meant reconstruction. Our theory would suggest change in one person's construing will be accompanied by shifts in the whole family's pattern of shared and private construing (Procter, 1980), or certain aspects may remain constant even though the family may *think* that change in them was necessary for successful resolution of the problem.

In the family research, change could be examined during the six-month interval between the administering the individual and family grids. Sixteen measures come out (each of the four's views of the four members). In Peter's family, only one of these indicated significant change (indicating, from another point of view, the good *reliability* of the measures). Nigel has really shaped up over the six months — he has changed the most as perceiver and object, becoming more thoughtful (mother), more understanding (sister) and having more character (himself). But mother sees him and his father now as less happy. Henry (now out of hospital and better) has swapped poles with his father in his own eyes. His father now 'lacks motivation' and he himself has become 'forceful'. Father now sees him as *adaptable*, but mother complains he is now *untidy*.

Nomothetic Measures

The beauty of the grid is the rich ideographic picture it helps us to create. The family's own dimensions are used to plot the members. But some of the measures could be used in larger-scale studies to compare different families. The various measures discussed above could be used as dependent or independent variables to study nosological variations, identification patterns, choice of spouse and so on.

Conclusion

Hopefully, some of the possibilities arising from grid research on the family will have been demonstrated well enough in this paper to stimulate others to explore the possibilities and develop these further.

Acknowledgements

Thanks to Don Bannister, Andy Treacher, David Smail, George Irving, Tom Keen and of course to Nigel Beail for his interest and extreme patience during the preparation of the manuscript. I am grateful also to Ann Heesom for the typing.

Notes

1. The terms *commonality* and *sociality* chosen for these measures are not strictly accurate. High commonality means agreement on the sample of constructs, but the raters are constrained by the method to agree more than they may in practice, when only using their own repertoire. A better measure would be a boolean measure of overlap between two sub-sets of constructs. Also, sociality as Kelly meant it did not actually imply accuracy or empathy, but only the ability to *construe* another's construction processes (see Kelly, 1970). And mathematics forces the measures of commonality and sociality to be more interrelated than they are according to Kelly's original theory.

2. Not thoughtful, moody, depressing, think more of themselves, lack of character, not confident (negative poles only).

References

Bannister, D. (1960) 'Conceptual Structure in Thought-disordered Schizoprenics', *J. Ment. Sci., 106,* 1230
—— and Salmon, T. (1966) 'Schizophrenic Thought Disorder — Specific or Diffuse?', *Brit. J. Med. Psychol., 39,* 215
Bateson, G. (1942) 'Morale and National Character', reprinted in *Steps to an Ecology of Mind,* New York: Ballantine
—— (1972) *Steps to an Ecology of Mind,* Ballantine, New York
Boszormenyi-Nagi, I. and Spark, G. (1973) *Invisible Loyalties: Reciprocity in Intergenerational Family Therapy,* Harper & Row, New York
Byng-Hall, J. (1973) 'Family Myths Used as a Defence in Conjoint Family Therapy', *Brit. J. Med. Psychol., 46,* 3
— and Campbell, D. (1981) 'Resolving Conflicts Arising from Distance-regulation: An Integrative Approach', *J. Marital Fam. Ther, 7,* 321-30
Esterson, A. (1970) *The Leaves of Spring,* Tavistock, London
Fairbairn, W.R.D. (1952) *Psychoanalytic Studies of the Personality,* Tavistock, London
Ferreira, A.J. (1963) 'Family Myth and Homeostasis', *Arch. Gen. Psychiat., 9,* 475-83
Haley, J. (1963) *Strategies of Psychotherapy,* Grune & Stratton, New York
—— (1965) 'Toward a Theory of Pathological Systems', reprinted in *Reflections on Therapy,* Family Therapy Institute of Washington, DC
—— (1973) *Uncommon Therapy: The Psychiatric Techniques of Milton H. Erickson MD,* Norton, New York
—— (1976) *Problem Solving Therapy,* Jossey-Bass, San Francisco
Kelly, G.A. (1955) *The Psychology of Personal Constructs,* vol. 1, Norton, New York
—— (1970) 'Behaviour is an Experiment' in D. Bannister (ed.), *Perspectives in Personal Construct Theory,* Academic Press, London
Laing, R.D. (1960) *The Divided Self,* Tavistock, London
—— (1961) *The Self and Others,* Tavistock, London

—— (1967) 'Family and Individual Structure' in P. Lomas (ed.), *The Predicament of the Family*, Hogarth Press, London

—— (1972) *The Politics of the Family*, Random House, New York

——, Phillipson, H. and Lee, A. (1967) *Interpersonal Perception — a Theory and Method of Research*, Tavistock, London

Landfield, A.W. (1971) *Personal Construct Systems in Psychotherapy*, Rand-McNally, Chicago

Mead, M. (1977) 'End-Linkage: A Tool for Cross-cultural Analysis' in J. Brockman (ed.), *About Bateson*, Dutton, New York

Minuchin, S. (1974) *Families and Family Therapy*, Tavistock, London

Palazzoli, M.S., Boscolo, L., Cecchin, G. and Prata, G. (1978) *Paradox and Counter-Paradox: A New Model in the Therapy of the Family in Schizophrenic Transaction*, Jason Aronson, New York

Procter, H.G. (1978) 'Personal Construct Theory and the Family: A Theoretical and Methodological Study', unpublished PhD thesis, University of Bristol

—— (1980) 'Family Construct Psychology: An Approach Understanding and Treating Families' in Walrond-Skinner (ed.), *Developments in Family Therapy*, Routledge & Kegan Paul, London

—— (in press) 'A Construct Approach to Family Therapy and Systems Intervention' in E. Button (ed.), *Personal Construct Theory and Mental Health*, Croom Helm, London

—— and Parry, G. (1978) 'Constraint and Freedom: The Social Origin of Personal Constructs' in F. Fransella (ed.), *Personal Construct Psychology, 1977*, Academic Press, London

Reiss, D. (1981) *The Family's Construction of Reality*, Harvard University Press, London

Scott, R.D. and Ashworth, P.L. (1969) 'The Shadow of the Ancestor: a Historical Factor in the Transmission of Schizophrenia', *Brit. J. Med. Psychol.*, *42*, 13-32

Watzlawick, P. (1976) *How Real is Real?*, Souvenir Press, Bristol

—— (1984) *The Invented Reality*, Norton, New York

——, Bevin, J. and Jackson, D.D. (1967) *The Pragmatics of Human Communication*, Faber & Faber, London

——, Weakland, J. and Fisch, R. (1974) *Change: Principles of Problem Formation and Problem Resolution*, Norton, New York

Zinner, J. and Shapiro, R. (1972) 'Projective Identification as a Mode of Perception and Behaviour in Families of Adolescents', *Int. J. Psychoanal.*, *43*, 523-30

—— and —— (1974) 'The Family Group as a Single Psychic Entity: Implications for Acting Out in Adolescence', *Int. Rev. Psychoanal.*, *1*, 179-86

PART FIVE

PRACTICAL APPLICATIONS OF THE REPERTORY GRID IN EDUCATION

Personal Construct Theory has implications for the educational process itself. Indeed in 'Behaviour is an Experiment', Kelly (1970) described a school run along Construct Theory lines. He saw learning as a personal exploration, and saw the teacher as a facilitator who helped to 'design and implement each child's own undertaking. . . To become a fully accredited participant in the experimental enterprise he/she must gain some sense of what is being seen through the child's eyes'. Therefore, it is important for education, like psychotherapy, to be a joint venture between teacher and learner with each being aware of the constructs of the other.

In this section we focus on how repertory grids can be used in educational settings. Terry Honess (Chapter 15) show how grids can be used to generate case study material. He presents three applications of this approach in educational contexts. One of the main centres which applies Personal Construct Theory and grid techniques in education is The Centre for the Study of Human Learning at Brunel University. Laurie Thomas and Sheila Harri-Augstein (Chapter 16) of the Centre discuss the value of the repertory grid in teaching and learning. They present examples of the Centre's work to show how teachers and learners can be guided to become more aware of, and to more sensitively interact with each other in the teaching/learning situation.

Grids can be used as a classroom activity and examples of such applications are presented in the next two chapters. Estelle Phillips (Chapter 17) showed teachers how to use grids in a design lesson. Then, in Chapter 18, Laurie Thomas and Sheila Harri-Augstein illustrate how grids can be used to understand what students see as learning experiences. These classroom applications promote the learner to the position of explorer/scientist and the teacher becomes a facilitator who helps the learner articulate their personal perspectives.

The role of support during training is discussed in Chapter 19 where Bryn Davis provides an illustration of how the dependency grid can be used in an educational setting. In the last chapter of this section we turn to the issue of vocational choice. At some state the learner has to make a decision regarding vocation and Rob Davies discusses the advantages of using grids in this context.

Reference

Kelly, G.A. (1970) 'Behaviour is an Experiment' in D. Bannister (ed.), *Perspective in Personal Construct Theory*, Academic Press, London

15 REPERTORY GRIDS AND THE PSYCHOLOGICAL CASE STUDY

Terry Honess

Overview

It is argued that personal construct psychology techniques, in particular the repertory grid, provide a powerful yet sensitive means for structuring interviews in order to generate case study material. This is in contrast to such techniques being seen simply as a means to the end of obtaining quantifiable information. The argument for the *psychological* case study will be briefly stated, followed by an outline of general guidelines for constructing such studies. My position will then be illustrated with reference to three research projects, all concerned with applications in educational contexts.

The first project (Parsons, Graham and Honess, 1983) is predicated on the assumption that knowledge of a teacher's 'implicit model' of how children learn is an invaluable aid to effective in-service teaching, and describes the construction of such a model. The second (Honess, Murphy and Tann, 1983) involves two groups, infant schoolboys and male adolescents, all with reading difficulties. A case study strategy reveals that they each make sense of their poor achievement in specifiable but often idiosyncratic ways which generally relate to a group of 'core constructs' that constitute self-maintenance processes. The final project more fully meets the requirements of a full case study, and describes as yet unpublished work from a current three-year, ESRC-funded project directed by the author (A. Edwards is the project's Research Fellow). These three projects will demonstrate different variations of grid method, yet all have a case study focus.

The Psychological Case Study

Bromley's (1977) definition of what constitutes a case study is appropriate here:

243

The case study is essentially a reconstruction and interpretation, based on the best evidence available, of part of the story
of a person's life . . . (p. 163)

A case study, therefore, is really a theory about how and why
a person behaved as he (she) did in a given situation; this
theory has to be tested by collecting evidence and formulating
arguments relevant to the claims put forward in the theory (p.
165).

The study of individual cases outside of a clinical context has
recently seen the beginnings of fresh interest (e.g. Paranjpe,
1975; De Waele and Harré, 1976; Moriarty and Toussieng, 1976),
yet Bromley (1977, p. 168) is justified in arguing that 'It is a
serious criticism of personality study in psychology that it has not
yet built up a satisfactory body of psychological "case-law" '. The
reasons for this neglect cannot be explored here, but it is
necessary to summarise the advantages of the case study
approach:

(1) Allport (1942) argues that such an approach 'anchors a
discipline in the bedrock of human experience'. This is of
fundamental theoretical and methodological significance, if the
aim is to understand and intervene in particular aspects of the
teachers' and pupils' experiences, then an adequate description of
this is essential.

(2) Confronting mundane reality helps overcome implicit assumptions and stereotyping by researchers themselves. For example,
the argument that the young school leaver is 'alienated' (e.g.
Reeves, 1978) may partly reflect the preoccupations of the
investigator.

(3) The approach is an excellent source of hypotheses of both a
theoretical and practical kind, which may be amenable to further
exploration in more controlled conditions should this be necessary. Insight into subjective experience may also serve to re-
orient relatively mechanistic and functional analyses of the
educational process, since even these rely on implicit assumptions, often of a 'commonsense' type, concerning human
experience (Turner, 1974, provides general examples).

(4) An intensive study of individuals is the route *par excellence*
for developing and testing *general* propositions concerning
behaviour or experience. Drawing on the distinction articulated

by Bakan (1967), it may be further stated that the more familiar statistical comparisons between groups reveal only those properties which can be applied to a class considered as an *aggregate*. This distinction is important in so far as general propositions concerning such concepts as 'self', 'agency' and 'action' are increasingly put forward (e.g. the collections edited by Mischel, 1974, 1977).

(5) Case studies frequently require a longitudinal perspective which minimises the possibility of relatively static and hence spurious analysis because of an explicit concern with process and change. Dissatisfaction with the one-off study and a shift to truly longitudinal analyses is indeed evident within developmental psychology itself (see the critique of McCall, 1977; and the growing interest in 'life-span' developmental psychology).

Guidelines for Case Study Construction

It is several decades since Allport (e.g. 1942, Ch. 11), articulated desiderata for a 'scientifically acceptable' case study, and it is from this source as well as more recent works (e.g. Helling, 1975 and especially Bromley, 1977) that the author draws in summarising guidelines for case study construction. It should be noted, however, that not all these points will be relevant for every case study, as will be evident when we come to consider the three illustrative applications:

(1) The aims of objectives of the case study should be explicitly stated.
(2) The investigator must report fully and *be accurate in matters of detail*.
(3) The simplest explanation of the individual's reports and behaviour should normally be given especial consideration, but any lack of fit with available evidence will stimulate further explanations.
(4) There must be critical inquiry into the internal coherence, logic, and external validity of the whole network of argument.
(5) A close, fairly long and at times possibly difficult relationship with the subject should be anticipated (e.g. project 3 below).
(6) The person must be seen in an 'ecological context'; the proper focus of a case study is not so much a 'person' as a 'person in a situation'.

(7) The case study would involve a presentation of the subject's point of view in 'good plain English'.

(8) The case study should contribute to psychological 'case-law' in virtue of the general principles employed and, more importantly, inferred, in explaining the individual's behaviour.

For work with individuals, the identification of pertinent *themes* is often more appropriate than simple quantitative content analysis (see project 3 below). Here, a particular interview and transcript is listened to and read several times in order to identify any apparent integrative themes (this is close to what Bromley indicates in (3) above). Such themes, which may have been explicitly stated by participants themselves, are treated as hypotheses, and all statements are listed that refer to them (whether supporting or rejecting) in order to establish the apparent best fit. This strategy is one that Helling described (1976), but since a thematic analysis should encapsulate the participant's own perspective, her procedure does not go far enough. It is imperative to re-present such themes to individuals for further commentary as is the case in the research proposed here. Furthermore, individual's proneness to present a particular self-view should ideally be 'challenged' through the use of methodologies that situate the individual in different contexts, e.g. supplementing repertory grid data with other procedures. Finally, it is necessary to stress that thematic analysis is no less subject to estimates of inter-rater reliability and the like than is the case for quantitative content analysis (e.g. Honess, 1980, 1981).

Application 1. The Elaboration of a Teacher's Implicit Model

The starting point for this project was the recognition that teachers involved in in-service training frequently complain of the lack of relevance of psychology for their everyday teaching. Hence, we set out to develop a set of procedures that would allow a non-facile construction of a teacher's beliefs and assumptions about teaching in order than any academic psychology input would be maximally relevant and hence effective and durable for any training teacher. The 'case' described in Parsons, Graham and Honess (1983) was a 45-year-old primary teacher, Mrs C., with 15 years' experience.

Mrs C's first task was to complete a rating form of the repertory grid using photographs of children from her class as elements, and constructs were all elicited from triads of these elements in response to the instruction, 'State the way in which two of these children are similar in the way that they learn'. She was then asked to state the opposite of this characteristic. Mrs C. was able to produce 17 constructs in this way, and a factor analysis of construct intercorrelations was computed and two important clusterings of her ideas (accounting for 87 per cent of score variance) emerged. The first factor broadly encompassed the presence or absence of 'cognitive skills' (e.g. 'good memory', 'able to order thoughts in written work') the second factor concerned motivational/affective aspects (e.g. 'anxious when uncomprehending'). A graphical representation of which children were grouped together in terms of these two factors was also provided, but is not reported here. In addition, arrangements were made to observe and record twelve lessons in maths taken by Mrs C. with her class in successive weeks over one term. Eight were video recorded, and four audio recorded only. One researcher was present during each lesson, and issues arising from each lesson were discussed as soon as possible, using the researcher's notes and audio/visual replay as the basis for focused discussion. This discussion always had, as its focus, the articulation of the teacher's model; however, any account was always cross-checked against other aspects of the case material.

A detailed consideration of the implications of this one project is beyond the scope of this chapter. Nevertheless, it may be asserted that the repertory grid provided an extremely cost-effective input to the whole negotiation process. Indeed, any prescription for a package that could be used without expensive researcher time involves the following: (i) an expansion of the grid input, involving an explicit commentary on the meaning of elicited constructs through a 'laddering' procedure (see the projects below); (ii) elimination of video recording and a reliance on audio recording; and (iii) a reduction in the number of sessions that a researcher or possibly another 'in-service trainee' was present.

Application 2: Reading Problems and the Child's Identity

The theoretical framing for these studies was exclusively Kellyan. A Construct Theory framework has clear implications for understanding children's learning: 'the child . . . is seeking as all healthily curious individuals do, to elaborate on that which is partly strange . . . within the overall control of certain super-ordinate aspects of his (or her) system' (1955, pp. 494-5). The most important of these 'controlling constructs' are 'core' constructs which 'govern a person's maintenance processes', those by which 'identity and existence' are sustained (Kelly, 1955, p. 482). From this perspective the activity of reading might be interpreted by a child as positive and self-enhancing, in so far as existing 'maintenance processes' may be elaborated. Conversely, reading may be threatening in that the child's 'identity and existence' would require too radical a change, or reading may become 'anxiety' provoking in the sense that becoming a good reader is somewhat opaque and therefore potentially threatening (see Kelly's (1955) pertinent analysis of the concepts of 'threat' and 'anxiety'). There is finally the possibility that reading is essentially irrelevant for a particular child in that it holds no readily apparent implications for core construing.

The first study to be outlined here, which involved a comparison of two matched groups of 'good' and 'poor' 7-year-olds is a minimal example of a case study strategy as defined above, since grids were the sole procedural input, and there was only one interview with each child. Nevertheless, it is valuable in illustrating how an appropriate grid structure will readily allow the child to speak freely and easily about a potentially sensitive subject in a short period of time (generally within 30 minutes). After extensive piloting, an 8 × 8 rank order form of the grid was used in which the element situations consisted of 8 line drawings featuring e.g. 'a boy reading seated at a table' and 'a boy throwing a book'. The same 8 constructs were used for each child, and included 'The boy who likes reading best — the boy who likes reading least', and 'The boy who is most like me — the boy who is least like me'.

The first construct was introducd with the question 'Which boy likes reading best?' When a picture had been chosen its number was recorded as choice 1 on a score sheet, and the picture was turned face down on the table. In order to enable the child to keep in mind the bipolar nature of the constructs he was then asked to choose the picture that represented a child who least liked reading, and this picture was turned over. The first question was then repeated, and so on, until all 8 pictures had been rank ordered. All 8 constructs were similarly introduced and, during the procedure, but especially at the end, the child was helped to discuss his choices and to give his views on reading, in particular its place as an activity at home, and at school, and the difficulties encountered.

Full details of our findings are available in Honess *et al.* (1983), but for the present purposes I would particularly wish to argue that the 8 × 8 grid developed in that study should be of value to other researchers and practitioners. Both good and poor readers interpreted the elements/constructs in a similar fashion, but the personal ramifications of these was sharply distinguished in their responses. Thus, element relationships were generally similar within and between the groups, but the individual's own position *vis-à-vis* these groupings were markedly variable. This strategy of exploiting Personal Construct Theory techniques for providing a focused, but non-threatening structure to explore self/reading relationships is developed further in the study with male adolescents.

The observations of a number of remedial teachers led us to investigate the impact of three facets of the 'remedial context' for young male adolescents in their last year at school: the significance of one-to-one tuition, the teaching literature and the situation (school or FE college). Thirteen adolescent remedial readers were interviewed eight or nine times. The first interview was an introduction to the project and the process of getting acquainted. The remainder involved a series of construct theory techniques, followed by a final negotiation session:

(1) Construct elicitation using triads of elements drawn from groups of significant others and a 'self' card. The procedure for elicitation was as described for the infant school study. When a construct had been elicited the subject was asked with respect to which pole he preferred to be identified. The construct was then laddered by asking 'why' he preferred that pole. Upon each reply this procedure was repeated until the subject seemed to find the question meaningless or the answers became circular or excessively vague. This process was repeated, having the self card as a

triad element, but changing the other two.

(2) Self-characterisation sketch: the sketch (Kelly, 1955, p. 323) is a simple means of eliciting personal information concerning the self. Appropriate wording was developed using the pilot sample, and each subject was asked to provide a tape recording made in complete privacy.

(3) Constructs were selected from the above sources, and following further discussion with the adolescents a list was drawn up for input along with a group of supplied constructs into a repertory grid format (5-point rating scale for each construct) with 17 supplied elements. These were photographs of adolescent boys (faces 'blanked out') in a variety of contexts; e.g.

Boy at school reading a 'remedial book' receiving tuition.

(S+R+T)

Boy at FE college reading a 'newspaper'.   (FE+N)

Boy in a cafe reading a 'formal book'.

(C+F)

(4) Negotiation of interpretation (only one session was available for this, more would have been desirable).

A Case Illustration

The simplest way to illustrate the procedure is to describe some of the findings from one case. In his self-characterisation sketch Ian was essentially concerned with presenting himself as a valued person and also making an attempt to obtain affirmation of this presentation:

Ian D. is a boy of 15 who cannot read very well . . . [supplied prompt]. My name is Ian D. I live at [subject's address]. I like the work I am doing with Mr Murphy. I think it's really very interesting. I like going fishing best. I don't like anything in school very much except reading with Mrs H . . . but I don't like reading aloud. I used to go fishing with my Dad, but I live with my Mom and George now. He's my Mom's husband after Dad left home. George doesn't like fishing, so I go with the Gypsy's. [N.B. The Gypsy's is a fishing club run by a local pub, the 'Gypsy's Tent']. You're supposed to be eighteen to join, but I know some of the blokes there. I don't have to pay no 'subs' either. You have to meet the coach in town at the

Hall of Memory at 6 o'clock, but I get a lift from Frank. I like Frank. He can sort things out easy enough. I went round to his place last Saturday and the car was off the road. So he got us a taxi. It cost £3 but Frank says, 'That's what it's [money] for . . . enjoy yourself'. I don't like George much but I love my Mom. She gets worried about us but she loves us.

The constructs elicited from Ian using the triad procedure and laddering were consistent with the brief, but flowing sketch. For example:

Construct 5:	A person who has a good time
Triad:	self and John (peer) — George (stepfather)
Subordinate 1:	go fishing — doesn't
Subordinate 2:	something to do
Subordinate 3:	stops you getting bored
Superordinate:	better to have a good time (or have a laugh)

It was felt that, for Ian, to 'enjoy yourself' was synonymous with 'to have a laugh'. When asked 'why' he preferred to have a good time, he replied, 'To have a laugh' and vice versa. Four subordinate constructs, when laddered, implied this superordinate construct and is a theme in his self-characterisation sketch. Ian's grid was factor analysed and the output plotted on the first two principal components (programe devised by P. Coxhead, Management Studies, Aston University). With regard to element relationships, two clear clusters emerged.

These are at opposite ends to each other on the first component abstracted: the reading elements in the absence of a school setting and tuition are close to ideal self, being liked by others and being able to cope. The tuition elements are characterised by the contrasts of these characteristics in addition to liking being helped to learn.

The analysis is further clarified by reference to the higher of the construct inter-correlations:

self — likes school	(-0.60)
ideal self — persons whom others like	(0.75)
ideal self — person who can cope	(0.74)
ideal self — reads as well as he wants	(0.74)
likes school — has a good time	(-0.55)

likes school — likes being helped	(0.58)
person whom others like — can cope	(0.88)
person whom others like — reads as well as he wants	(0.83)
can cope — reads as well as he wants	(0.86)

In discussing the graph with Ian, his apparent dislike of tuition was the focus of discussion, and the following ensued:

Ian I like Mrs H., but it's boring . . . you can't have a laugh.
   — Why not?
Ian Well, it makes you feel daft. All the class can hear. They think you're daft.
   — You don't like people to know that you're not so good at reading then?
Ian I don't care . . . not really, no. I mean, if people out of school know they think you're daft . . . you can't get in the Army.
   — It's not nice if people think you're daft?
Ian Course not! But in any case you don't have to be good at reading. Dennis M's uncle makes a stack . . . works on the Cov (Coventry Road), got a 'tat' yard. If you can do things, that's all that matters. Frank says that's all.
   — What happens if people think you're daft, Ian?
Ian Well, they get on at you, don't they . . . they don't let you join in. . .
   — The 'graph' makes it seem like you think that people who get help in reading 'can't cope'. What do you think?
Ian Well, they can't can they, or they wouldn't need help!

Apparently Ian sees receiving tuition as a threatening activity. Being helped implies 'being daft' and daft people are not liked by others. Also people who need help evidently cannot cope. These constructions are in direct contrast to his ideal self, and suggest that Ian is most unlikely to improve his reading, since the idea of tuition is rejected, and variation in material or, indeed, situation (e.g. FE context) would not appear to be hopeful strategies. However, the ability to read is seen as desirable; although comments such as those with regard to 'Dennis's uncle' suggest that reading may be further devalued in the future. The stumbling block seems to be Ian's need to be seen to cope, hence a plausible strategy might involve Ian in a systematic remediation programme which he could self-monitor. This would give Ian more responsibility and esteemed 'coping'. Certainly reading aloud would be forsaken, since this is a highly aversive activity for him. Further details of this case and our general findings with respect to remedial teaching need not be pursued here, rather I now turn to the final application.

Application 3: Understanding the School-leaving Experience

This project is currently in progress and involves a longitudinal study of 160 poorly qualified school leavers, and the construction of detailed case studies for 28 of these. The case study group are involved in a number of different procedures, one of which is a repertory grid, given to them prior to leaving school and one year later (Honess and Edwards (1984) provide a detailed overview of the whole project). A 10 constructs by 8 elements rating form of the repertory grid has been used. Constructs were drawn from triadic elicitation (all elements 'self' in different situations) and laddering, as well as personal interviews. The 8 elements which are elaborated with each individual to ensure maximum relevance are based around the following themes: you working; you in school; you with girl/boy friend; you at home with your family; you on the dole; you alone in your free time; you in six months time; you out of school with friends. This procedure is relatively unusual in that it involves self-perception in a variety of situations, although Ravenette (1975) and Kitwood (1980) both find 'situations' a valuable focus for interviewing. As well as being theoretically sound, *viz.* the numerous challenges to the notion that individuals behave consistently irrespective of the situation, this strategy meets the common objection from respondents that rating single elements, devoid of context, forces them into a stereotypical judgement.

Half the case studies sample completed their grids in the normal fashion, and the other half of the sample were exposed to an entirely novel development of grid procedure in which each individual is imaginatively involved in each situation (element). This induction draws on the guidelines articulated by Yardley (1982) in the context of the use of role play in social psychology. It entails obtaining a full description of the relevant situation from the participant, making it highly specific in place and time, with the subject located in the psychological and physical centre of that situation. Once the individual becomes involved in her or his chosen situation, each construct of the grid is used as a basis for exploring that individual's feelings in that situation: 'Are you feeling predominantly happy or sad?' and so on for each construct in turn, and then on to the next of the remaining seven situations. We have found that this helps overcome the common criticism of grid techniques that they demand a too rational and detached analysis from respondents.

Conclusions

The central theme of this chapter has been to argue for the considerable merits of grid technique to help structure and focus interviews so that the *content* of responses ('thematic' analysis) is seen at least as significant as the *form* of responses that could be statistically analysed in a particular fashion. Moreover, it is argued that where more numerically sophisticated procedures are used these also should, where possible, be used as the basis for further negotiation and discussion. The use of a grid to structure an interview is most easily seen in 'application 2', the work with infant school boys. However, the other applications which were closer (applications 1 and particularly 3) to the desiderata for a good case study serve a cautionary note. Essentially, the grid might be seen simply as a sorting task, however flexible, and it is therefore incumbent upon the researcher to use a variety of methodologies to situate the individual in different contexts and to be prepared to negotiate different perspectives on the 'same' event. Hence, one is then able to prepare a good 'case' for interpreting part of a person's life in a particular way.

Acknowledgement

Preparation of this paper was helped, in part, by an ESRC grant (No. HR 8570).

References

Allport, G. (1942) *The Use of Personal Documents in Psychological Science*, SSRC, New York

Bakan, D. (1967) *On Method: Towards a Reconstruction of Psychological Investigation*, Jossey-Bass, San Francisco

Bromley, D.B. (1977) *Personality Description in Ordinary Language*, Wiley, Chichester

De Waele, J.P. and Harré, R. (1976) 'The Personality of Individuals' in R. Harré (ed.), *Personality*, Blackwell, Oxford

Helling, I. (1976) 'First Order Constructs in Occupational Biography; an Attempt to Apply the Sociology of A. Schutz', unpublished BPhil thesis, St Anne's College, University of Oxford

Honess, T. (1980) 'Self-reference in Children's Descriptions of Peers: Egocentricity or Collaboration?', *Child Development, 51*, 476-80

—— (1981) 'Girls' and Boys' Perception of their Peers: Peripheral versus Central and Objective versus Interpretative Aspects of Free Description', *British Journal of Psychology, 72*, 485-97

——, Murphy, C. and Tann, R. (1983) 'Reading Problems and the Child's Identity: A Construct Theory Analysis of Infant Schoolboys and Male Adolescents, *Human Learning, 2*, 187-208

—— and Edwards, A. (1984) 'Poorly Qualified School-leavers' Coping Strategies and Identity Development', *BPS Education Section Review*, in press

Kelly, G. (1955) *The Psychology of Personal Constructs, vol. 1*, Norton, New York

Kitwood, T. (1980) *Disclosures to a Stranger*, Routledge & Kegan Paul, London

McCall, R.B. (1977) 'Challenges to a Science of Developmental Psychology', *Child Development, 48*, 333-44

Mischel, T. (ed.) (1974) *Understanding Other Persons*, Blackwell, Oxford

—— (ed.) (1977) *The Self: Psychological and Philosophical Issues*, Blackwell, Oxford

Moriarty, A.E. and Toussieng, P.W. (1976) *Adolescent Coping*, Grune & Stratton, New York

Paranjpe, A.C. (1975) *In Search of Identity*, Halsted Press, New York

Parsons, J., Graham, N. and Honess, T. (1983) 'A Teacher's Implicit Model of How Children Learn', *British Educational Research Journal, 9*, 91-101

Ravenette, A. (1975) 'Grid Techniques for Children', *Journal of Child Psychology and Psychiatry, 16*, 79-82

Reeves, F.W. (1978) 'Alienation and the Secondary School Student', *Educational Review, 30*, 139-48

Turner, R. (ed.) (1974) *Ethnomethodology*, Penguin, Harmondsworth

Yardley, K. (1982) 'On Engaging Actors in As If Experiments', *Journal for the Theory of Social Behaviour, 12*, 291-304

16 TEACHING AND LEARNING AS THE NEGOTIATION OF PERSONAL MEANING

Laurie F. Thomas and Sheila Harri-Augstein

Introduction: Education as the Negotiation of Meaning

For the past two thousand years philosophers and teachers have discussed the processes of education. Plato reported the Socratic method, Locke suggested the *tabula rasa*, Dewey denied the existence of absolute knowledge and gave emphasis to our ability to achieve our own purposes in the real world, and both Russell and Rogers have advocated freedom-to-learn. Secular, Jesuit, Islam and Buddhist beliefs have each generated their own pedagogies. In our own time Freud has influenced many educators producing, for example, A.S. Neill's 'Summerhill'. Illich has taken a 'celebration of awareness' stance which again has had wide-sweeping influences. The theories of Piaget and Bruner have influenced nursery and primary education in the Western world, whilst Vygotsky and Luria and Mao have reformed the world of education in the Soviet bloc and parts of Asia.

In spite of their obvious differences all these approaches seem to focus on the notion that education can best be seen as an organised attempt to help *people attribute meaning to themselves*, to other people, to established knowledge, to our cultural and technical inheritance and to the objects and events around us. There is, of course, much controversy about what the 'right' meanings are, but there can be no question that most forms of education would be greatly enhanced by the development of more effective methods whereby *meaning itself* is attributed and exchanged.

Practitioners and theorists of education differ in their evaluation of the roles to be played by the teacher, and in their understanding of the form that the 'negotiation of meaning' should take. Each values *different states of knowing*. The negotiation of personally relevant meanings requires sensitivity, judgement and a positive touch. It can easily harden into a prescriptive handling down of established dogma, or it can easily degenerate and dissolve into the *laissez faire* assumption that all meanings are equally viable. Both positions negate the idea of negotiation by fixating the conversation into one restricted form. Teaching skill is notoriously difficult to acquire. It has often been assumed that one must be born with it. But our understanding of the purposes and processes of teaching is necessarily vague whilst it remains intuitive. If teaching is a skill, then the meanings needed to exercise this skill are inadequately defined. The contention here is that teaching is primarily concerned with *mediating the process by which significant, viable, personal meanings are achieved.*

Isolating 'patterns of meaning' as a focus of concern indicates the repertory grid as an appropriate method of investigation. A series of examples are reported in which the repertory grid has been used as a conversational tool for exploring, teaching, learning and the negotiation of personal meaning. These illustrate the various components of a developing methodology which has transformed our expectations about the possible levels of effectiveness which may be achieved in education.

For education to be an enriching experience the meanings that emerge must become *personal*, and they must be significant and important in some part of the person's life. Meanings must also be *viable*; that is they must prove useful and effective in mediating one's transactions; transactions with stored knowledge, with people and with the world around. A learner is offered access to many sources of knowledge, some of them as formal as a textbook, a lecture or a laboratory demonstration. Others are more general and spontaneous, from project work, job experience, educational visits to discussion and 'exploratory talk'. In each case it is difficult for the teacher to enter sufficiently into his or her pupils' thoughts and feelings to empathise with the problems that face each learner.

What is actually involved in attributing significant viable personal meanings to:

the structure of the nucleus of an atom,
a Mozart symphony,
a mathematical proof,
the theory of Natural Selection,
Jung's concept of synchronicity,

the assassination of Julius Caesar, or
Eliot's 'Wasteland'?

Each of these pieces of public knowledge arises out of the continually re-evaluated cumulative experience of major components of Western civilisation. The viability of the personal meanings attributed to each depends upon how richly the individual incorporates them into his or her experience and tries them out in living. Do they afford learners greater insight into their own processes, enhance their powers for communicating with others, or help them to identify and use more opportunities for rewarding transactions with objects and events? Do they help them to apply that knowledge effectively in predictable or unpredictable situations? Understanding how meaning becomes attributed and conducting conversations that elaborate, relate and extend personal meaning is the essence of effective teaching and learning. The repertory grid has been used as a powerful aid within such 'learning conversations'.

Learning and Construing

In any learning/teaching situation the same series of events will be experienced differently by each participant. A lecturer might be very surprised if he could hear tapes of the silent conversations going on in the head of each of his listening students. A young teacher baffled by the antics of children in her class might be scared and depressed, but not so baffled if she realised the strong and purposeful meaning systems within which each of them live. Many of the so-called motivational problems of learning arise in the differences in the purpose that lie between the teacher and the learner. Members of a seminar might be quite surprised to hear the silent monologue of their colleague who has become frightened and unable to break into the discussion. Occasionally in the lecture, the lesson or the seminar the silent conversations do break surface: usually to the embarrassment and impatience of the others who smooth it over or instantly suppress it, to carry on with the business in hand. It is for his kind of experience that the 'encounter'-type encounter is valued; it allows personal meanings to emerge in all their apparent irrelevance and by being heard and negotiated, to be incorporated into the personally viable meanings of each participant enlarging, freeing and enriching the developing meaning systems of all differently.

It is unfortunate that formal education too often insists on the well-established truths of yesterday rather than on tracing out why an initially rejected book such as *Ulysses*, Einstein's relativity theory or Darwinian Natural Selection, becomes negotiated into the personal meaning systems of the established figures of the next generation. There is more to resistance to change than resistance to change. In a more general but mundane context, each person within earshot of a radio reacts differently to the vibrations in the air as they impinge on the ear. 'The Archers', 'Any Questions', 'Talking About Antiques', 'Story Time', and 'The World at One' do not all attract us all equally. What goes on in people's heads when they are listening to the same programme clearly illustrates that *our capacity to attribute meaning is a major factor in determining our thoughts and feelings and the ways in which we live.*

Each individual approaches any event with some set of assumptions and expectations. These condition how they start to perceive, think and feel about it. As the interaction develops their assumptions and expectations change and the pattern of perceptual selectivity is altered. The guided perceptions feed back into the whole pattern of thought and feeling, changing further the basis of selectivity and the focus of attention. The relations between perceiving, thinking, feeling and acting are complex, but thoughts and feelings mould perception, and perceptions trigger thoughts and feelings and initiate actions. The study of skill and its relationship to craft, art and creativity throws considerable light on the structure of these processes. These mutually supportive processes very easily stabilise into concrete views and attitudes towards reality and into habitual ways of behaving within it. But each person's concrete view differs from every other. In everyday usage, words such as 'prejudiced', 'insightful', 'understanding', 'distorted', 'perceptive', 'dogmatic', 'revolutionary', 'veridical', and 'wrong', are used to designate one person's reality from within the pattern of personal meaning available to another.

The Kelly repertory grid is a method for exploring the pattern of selectivity which any one individual brings to a series of experiences. George Kelly (1955) developed a theory about how each person constructs his or her own version of reality and himself or herself in it; and about how he or she then lives within his or her own reality, revises it, tests it out, develops it and makes it viable within his or her range of experience. He called this 'The Theory of Personal Constructs'. The constructs are the more permanent scaffolding on which changing views of events can be supported. Kelly would claim that the whole system is hierarchical; at each level both the events and the constructs on which they are built are themselves earlier personal constructions.

Kelly saw each human being, operating as his own scientist having theories about reality, behaving on the basis of these theories, getting evidence from the outcomes of his actions, revising the theory in the light of his ongoing actions. Perhaps this is a rather optimistic view of science, but allowing for a fair degree of unawareness in our day-to-day transactions, not a bad view of the process of living. Given the body as one part of reality, Zen masters, football coaches, novelists and motor-cycle maintenance men might each describe their approach in much the same terms. Thus, for Kelly, the construction of reality is an active, creative, rational and pragmatic business. But it takes place in the human body, which is an infinitely rich sea of emotions and feelings. Thus each construct or particle of a person's view has both thought and feeling in it. Indeed he would go further and argue that thought and feeling are themselves constructs, the separation of which within a personal meaning system has its own dangers. T.S. Eliot had much the same view. The construing of reality is thus seen as primarily subjective and personal.

Kelly developed the repertory grid as a methodological component of his theoretical position. It is a method by which a person can be enabled to reveal the selective basis out of which he builds his construction of any part of the external and internal world. The repertory grid is a technique designed to elicit, systematise and exhibit personal meanings. Unlike the Osgood semantic differential (1957) it does not offer 'universal scales' or 'dimensions' within which to capture all meaning. In its most flexible form the content item and the dimensions of the descriptive structure emerge from the construer. Thus, the grid meets one of Maslow's (1962) criteria for the identification of a creative encounter. He claims that the terms in which a creative encounter is to be evaluated can be derived only from within the encounter itself. To impose previously determined criteria upon it is to ignore the truly creative component of the encounter by reducing it into the dimensions of the preconceived. So with the repertory grid. To enclose someone else's thinking and feelings in the straitjacket of your own preconceived explanation is to deny yourself a learning opportunity. The grid is therefore uniquely suited to become a tool for use in the continual negotiation and the development of expanding structures of significant personally viable meanings.

The grid and its derivatives, alternatives and developments (Thomas and Harri-Augstein, 1985) can be a powerful tool for the educator. It does not replace the older methods of, say, Socrates, the Jesuits of Montessori, nor does it obviate the need for skill and understanding in the art and science of teaching. What it does offer, by making the negotiation of meaning explicit, is an opportunity to see the process of learning more clearly and unambiguously. And this in turn offers the possibility for a very sensitive and detailed control of the learning conversation. Thus a Socratic-type dialogue, a Jesuit argument and a Montessori infant session are all learning conversations which can be illuminated by making the development of construing (i.e. personal meaning) explicit. It is a particularly sharp and precise additional instrument for use in situations where, for example, ignorance, attitudes, misunderstanding, incompetence or prejudice are disrupting the flow of the learning conversation.

The Repertory Grid in Teaching and Learning

Whenever a teacher, trainer, lecturer or psychologist talks about learning the likelihood is that they are thinking about teaching. It is often assumed that learning is the reception of teaching; but the learner knows differently. Learning is a reaction to teaching. It may take the form of an excited reception, or it can be the cynical sifting out of the odd 'useful' item from a welter of seeming rubbish. Many theories of learning are really theories of teaching, being simply systematic sets of rules for manipulating situations in which learning is expected to occur. 'Knowledge of results', 'schedules of reinforcement', 'spacing' and 'timing', 'presentation techniques', 'the design of materials' and 'systems for accessing resources' are all the prerogative of the teacher. They happen *to* the learner, not *in* them.

Learning is a change in construing. It happens inside the learner. When learners elaborate their meanings, they are learning; and when they change their pattern of meaning in any area, large or small, they have learned something. By considering learning as *changes in construing* an opportunity for a new approach to the categorisation of learning is created. Various techniques for measuring changes in construing have been developed (Harri-Augstein, 1979). These offer a new potential for understanding the experiential nature of learning difficulties.

Learning always involves simultaneous changes in perceiving, thinking and feeling. These are always linked intimately together and inevitably produce changes in behaviour. If the changes are valued then there is a perceived increase in competence. The simplest learning situation consists of a learner and some resource (Figure 16.1): a child with a yo-yo; a mathematician with a computer; a dog with a ball of string, or a student in a library. How the learners proceed will depend on their strategy and skills in identifying their needs and in accessing and manipulating the resource. Resources may be restricted or extensive, and the potential range of resources may be far greater than the learner appreciates. One application of the repertory grid is to explore the system of personal constructs which the learner uses in his dealings with the resource.

Figure 16.1: The Learner and the Resource

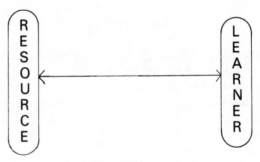

A study of how students construe books showed that much of their difficulty arose from construing books in ways that ran counter to their purposes. One student consistently construed books that were 'good for learning' as 'impossible for me to read'. This explained his ineffective use of the library. Staff members also revealed some unexpected constructs for books. For instance, one polytechnic lecturer construed *his own* learning experiences from books as 'to reflect on something', 'to clarify my own thoughts', 'involves creativity', 'unusual experiences', 'enjoyment' and 'involves self-evaluation' and 'elicitation of own view'. Yet another grid which explored his own values in assigning learning experiences for *his students*, showed that 'to answer factual questions', 'to instruct how to do something', 'to appreciate logic and argument', 'involves practical work', and to 'instruct on expert knowledge' represented what he expected them to learn from his recommended reading lists. In the same study students' grids showed an overwhelming 'dislike' for 'practical', 'work-orientated' and factual learning tasks set by their tutor (Thomas and Harri-Augstein, 1978).

Another example of learning from books illustrates how assumptions, often hidden from both teacher and pupils, give rise to conflicting priorities, negative feelings and blocks to learning. For instance, one comprehensive school teacher responsible for the reading curriculum in the 'middle school' was invited to use the grid to deeply explore her views on 'readability'. She had been consistently using various readability indices, largely based on the American school system, to match books to pupils without much success. Her *core constructs* showed that in her selection of books for 13-year-old boys with a reading age of 10-11, the readability criteria she consistently used were; 'short sentences', 'high frequency words', 'words not more than three syllables', 'paragraphs with one main idea expressed at the beginning', 'simplicity' and 'straight facts'. Yet grids elicited from five boys showed that 'good story line', 'pithy', 'dramatic', 'to do with scientists', 'peace', 'to do with conservation', 'excitement and originality' and 'clarity' were high on their criteria of 'readability'. Two boys were rather vague about what 'clarity' meant for them, but for one this was closely associated with a 'racy style'. None of these grids showed any concern or awareness of syntactical or grammatical factors as determinant of readability. Subsequent studies showed that provided *their own readability* criteria were met, these boys were able to effectively read articles and books well beyond those that they would have been given access to based on the structural and grammatical criteria used to determine their 'reading readiness'. They were able to create their own stories based on the books they had chosen, to discuss and critically appraise both their content and style, and to jot down a summary of the core ideas. Interestingly, they did not score effectively on the detailed multiple-choice-based factual questions set by their teacher on the very same texts (Thomas and Harri-Augstein, 1972).

These examples illustrate that guided-grid conversations can help teachers and pupils to explore together their assumptions about learning resources and to arrive at shared views and a better understanding of what can be learnt. Each learner builds up a personal system of meaning in his or her interaction with these resources. The meanings which are achieved by the learner may not relate exactly to the teacher's construing of the same material. Testing in the traditional way, as the last example has shown, may only reveal a poor learning performance.

Studies in the construing of maths questions provides another example which gives a much clearer picture of where in their own terms the students have actually got to. Repertory grids elicited from 22 students from one College of Education revealed the terms in which they construed 'command words' in maths questions. The elements in their grids consisted of twelve command words: prove, define, find, show, explain, calculate, sketch, state, express, solve, substitute, tabulate, and multiply. Construct dimensions reveal a profusion of emotionally loaded constructs including:

engaging	vs	disinterest
reassuring	vs	despair
challenging	vs	panic
homely	vs	alien
manageable	vs	downheartening
intriguing	vs	monotonous
fascinating	vs	frightening
rewarding	vs	infuriating
satisfying	vs	trivial

Thus, the repertory grid unerringly reveals the individual structure of each student's attitudes and preferences. It is therefore a highly effective diagnostic device and an aid to tutoring and counselling. Such findings are not obviously restricted to the construing of mathematics. Any subject, English literature, Biology, Woodwork, French or PE builds up idiosyncratic configurations of thoughts and feelings which may inhibit or facilitate processes of learning. Thus, the repertory grid is being displayed as a paradigm of an infinitely expendable set of meaning negotiating techniques which can be used to reflect upon, and challenge some of the more troublesome 'knots in construing learning'. As we have seen in our last example, the repertory grid used with elements selected as tests of subject content material, can be very revealing.

The teacher or staff member mediates the process of learning (Figure 16.2). His view of his students will condition how and when he intervenes as they interact with their resources. We are not surprised to discover that lecturers in Colleges of Art differ considerably in terms of the system of personal constructs they use when differentiating and evaluating students (Thomas and Pope, 1973). Teachers of reading (Thomas and Harri-Augstein, 1976), training officers (Thomas and Harri-Augstein, 1980), nursery school teachers (Thomas and Thompson, 1967) and members of a school of architecture (Glanville, 1978), all show

Figure 16.2: The Teacher Mediating the Process of Learning

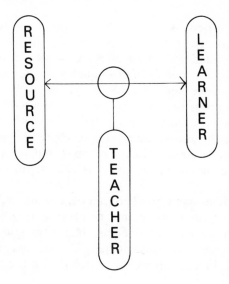

unexpected differences among themselves and between one group and another, in the terms in which they construe their learners, and in the ways in which they systematically intervene in the learning process.

Some teachers choose to isolate the learner from the resource, shielding him and interpreting everything for him (Figure 16.3). Often the learner remains completely unaware of the original resource and receives only predigested and packaged lessons. The repertory grid can be used to reveal the basis for some of the selectivites which they bring to the task.

Figure 16.3: The Teacher as Interpreter of the Resource

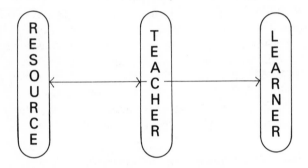

Some teachers encourage their learners to become more autonomous and many themselves retreat into the role of 'resource minder', abdicating all responsibility for presentation of material and for monitoring the quality of the learning (Figure 16.4). This role may be conceived narrowly as traditional librarian as in the case of some junior school teachers concerned with children's reading, or even sixth form teachers of chemistry and physics. It may be interpreted much more openly as adviser on how and where to access relevant and original resources, including people, books, models, visual aids, visits, events and so on.

On the other hand, teachers can degenerate under stress until they are no more than 'learner minders' who ignore everything but quiet or law and order (Figure 16.5). The grid has also been used to examine such pathologies (Thomas and Harri-Augstein 1976, 1984). In its positive connotation their role can become that

Figure 16.4: The Teacher as Resource Minder

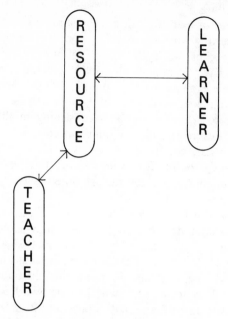

Figure 16.5: The Teacher as Learner Minder

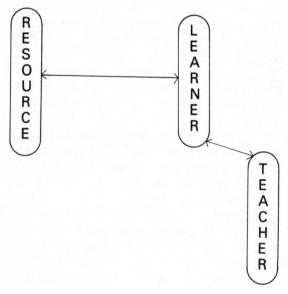

of supporting the learner's search for understanding through personal counselling.

The assessment of learning can also be studied using the grid. Some very interesting work has been done with our own students getting them to construe each other's laboratory reports. As examiners we have systematically explored the operational dimensions of our evaluations and compared and contrasted our examining techniques more rigorously. Some CSHL studies show that the degree to which a learner's construing of the subject agrees with the examiners, is a high-level predictor of examination performance (Blewitt, 1972). Similarly, grids have been used to explore self-assessment, for example one study showed how and why art students value certain art objects and not others (Thomas and Pope, 1973).

Pathologies of the learning/teaching situation have also been systematically examined. For example, one study shows that 70 per cent of the constructs used by students of mathematics about mathematics in a College of Education were totally emotional (Chapman, 1974). Approximately one hundred first-year college students were asked to write down the one word which best typified their reaction to mathematics. The results were pooled, classified, and placed in alphabetical order (Figure 16.6).

This simple study requires very little comment. The words can be seen to indicate the major constructs which this group of students bring to their understandings of mathematics. It would appear that the intellectual construing is outweighed by the emotional constructions.

There are many other ways in which the grid can be used to explore how learners construe other people, subject matter, objects and events. The ways in which social science students construe statistics, the ways in which domestic science students construe meals, and the ways in which children construe fairy stories all reveal new aspects of the learner. These examples show how the grid is not just a descriptive tool to be used for displaying a static state of affairs. It can be used diagnostically for negotiating the growth and development of meaning. Many grid tricks, added elements, added constructs extended range of convenience, sub-grids and so on are useful in creating greater awareness of the range of attitudes, prejudices, strategies, rules and methods involved in the teaching/learning situation. For example, in the study in which art students construed students,

Figure 16.6: Students' Constructs for Mathematics

Intellectual	Emotional		
A. abstract	abhorrence alienated apprehension	ambivalent	alright
B. brainwork	blank thought bewilderment bile boring	bearable	
C. complex complicated concentrated	chaos confusing crap crudish cruel	compulsory	challenging curious
D.	despair disapproval disgust disinterest dismal dislike doze dread dubious dull	doubtful	
E.			enjoyable enquiring essential
F.	fog frustration fuzziness		fascinating fun
G.			
H.	hate hopeless horror		happy hopeful humour
I. important	impossible indifference ignorance insecure incomprehen- sible		interesting
J.		Jesus	
K.			
L.	loathe		
M. measure mental	mental block maze		
N.			
O.			optimistic
P.		probing puzzled	pleasant
Q. questions			
R.	rugged		
S.	shit sorry stodge	sometimes	
T. technical	terror trepidation	tiring	
U.	ugh unattainable unbearable	uncanny uncertain unconfident	
V. vital	vomit	vacant vague	
W. work	worried		
X.			
Y.			
Z.			

three offered constructs were introduced into the grid of each teacher after the teachers' personal constructs had been elicited from them. These were:

Likely to be assessed highly at the end of year	vs	Likely to be assessed as unsuccessful
Likely to succeed as an artist	vs	Unlikely to succeed as an artist
Staff generally agree about him	vs	Staff generally disagree about him

This technique allows the investigator to study the teachers' assumptions about what goes with academic success, what goes with later vocational success, and how well each staff member is aware of others' opinions.

The grid has been used at the *perceptual level*. Industrial inspectors in a sweet factory 'did grids' to identify the sensory basis of their appreciation of the subtle properties of a first-class toffee. They were able to identify their areas of systematic disagreement and to negotiate an agreed meaning for acceptable high-grade toffee. The negotiating forms of the grid offer considerable potential for development in the area of subjective judgement. By introducing 'inferential grids' as a second level of reference it is possible to explore the structure of perception more insightfully than has previously been possible. For example, this technique has been used to explore the sensory basis of a skilled inspector's intuitive understanding of how various faults on the product relate to changes in the manufacturing process (Thomas and Harri-Augstein, 1980). Since inferential perception forms one of the central links in skilled activity there seems to be some likelihood that this technique will have implications for learning as seemingly different skills as the playing of association football, chemical-laboratory skills and play techniques in the nursery. In education the area of perceptual training is largely unexplored except for very specific topics.

The art and science of negotiating meanings is itself undergoing rapid development. Methods for analysing, reorganising and displaying the grids as *structures of meaning* (Harri-Augstein, 1978) open up a new set of tools for creating heightened awareness of one's own processes. Such *cognitive mirrors* reveal patterns in a person's thoughts and feelings of which he or she is not necessarily aware. The technique of cognitive mirroring is capable of massive development.

An on-line computer program, PEGASUS (Thomas, 1971, 1974, 1979, 1982) has been available for some time. It enables you to carry on a therapeutic, learning, or counselling conversation with yourself. It elicits both elements and constructs from the learner, processing the grid at each step. It offers the user feedback about his system of meanings, and can be instructed to lead the conversation in any one of a number of directions. The whole process is completely under the control of the user, who can preserve complete privacy about the whole interaction by deleting all trace of it upon completion. The work with this computer program has fed back into a series of paper-and-pencil hand-focusing and reflecting techniques. These enable learners to analyse and reorganise their grids without the need for complex statistical calculations.

'Exchange grids' (see Chapter 10) offer the opportunity for step-by-step negotiation of 'difficult' meanings. One person 'does a grid' and then offers the verbal descriptions of his constructs to another. They then discuss the meaning of each construct without referring to the elements which were in the original grid. When they reach verbal agreeemnt about the meanings the second person places the original elements on each of the constructs in turn, thus completing his version of the other's grid. The two completed grids are then compared and areas of specific disagreement identified. These focus attention on the points of inadequate verbal exchange. Exchanges about art objects produced some startling changes in the student's (and staff's) perceptions of pictures (Thomas and Mendoza, 1972). Similarly, exchanges about statistical concepts can break into the emotional blocks of learning this subject (Thomas and Harri-Augstein, 1972). Taste panels can be transformed by exchanges of this precision and exchanges about creative events can lead to increased creativity (Thomas and Harri-Augstein, 1984).

Change over a period of time can be studied by eliciting a series of grids and systematically comparing and contrasting them. For example, this has been done to help a trainee teacher improve her skills in teaching reading and a manager in developing skills in enabling his subordinates to learn more effectively. Suitable methods of comparison highlight various aspects of the change process (Harri-Augstein, 1979). Changes in attention and purpose can be studied by applying the Raiffa technique to a raw grid. This is a method for exploring how strongly each personal construct enters into a particular personal judgement or decision (McKnight, 1976).

Finally, one of the major inadequacies of grid techniques is that they are by definition concerned with verbal labels for what are often subtle non-verbal patterns of meaning. Sensory, inferential and exchange grids are concerned to help the construers exhibit their meanings in carefully negotiated verbal terms. Non-verbal grid games are designed to allow construers to communicate more directly without having to translate their experience into verbal irrelevancies in order to communicate. Non-verbal construing games takes one into direct contact with the texture, structure, taste, smell, form, sounds and appearances of another's view of reality (Thomas and Harri-Augstein, 1981, 1984).

Implications For Education

These selected examples from a whole range of CSHL action-research projects illustrate how teachers and learners can be guided to become more aware of, and to more sensitively interact with each other, within the teaching/learning situation. The main problem in our experience has been to articulate clearly a language in which *learning* can be discussed: teacher training is based almost exclusively on theories of teaching, and processes of learning are completely ignored. The teacher manipulates the learner and the situation. He or she organises the resources, then measures the results in his or her own terms, or those set by some external regulating agent. The internal processes of learning often go unobserved. One of the most productive uses of the grid is either individually, in pairs, or in groups, to explore directly the learning process itself. A 'learning incidents' or 'events' grid can serve to begin to create awareness of the deeply personal process of learning. It also assists to construct a 'process language' in which 'learning' as a topic in its own right can be discussed, reflected upon, reviewed and developed by all those involved in the enterprise (Thomas and Harri-Augstein, 1976).

Teachers can reflect upon their own methods to gain greater awareness of their often only partially articulated roles and thus be enabled to extend the range and effectiveness of their teaching skills. The greater the variety of methods mastered by means of such construing activities, the more flexible the individual can become as a teacher. Learners can reflect upon their ways of interacting with their resources to gain greater awareness of their own learning processes, to which often even the brightest pupils remain blind. Again, enhanced sensitivity to their needs, purposes, resources, strategies, tactics and evaluation by means of construing activities, facilitates flexibility and an enhanced capacity for learning.

To return to our argument in the introduction, we envisage the learning opportunities provided by an institution as a function of the ability of its teachers and learners to construe these adequately. In a broader context, parents, local authority advisers and Her Majesty's Inspectors can all be usefully involved in construing learning (Thomas and Harri-Augstein, 1977). These different evaluative perspectives of learning can be more fully integrated into a co-operative network whereby the process of learning and the construction of personal meaning can grow and develop into a more fully functioning and dynamic encounter.

References

Chapman, L.R. (1974) 'An Exploration of a Mathematical Command System', PhD thesis supervised by L.F. Thomas, CSHL, Brunel University

Blewitt, S. (1972) 'An Investigation, Using the Repertory Grid Technique, to Study the Thought Processes of Examiners and Students Who Evaluated a Set of Examination Scripts', project for BTech, Brunel University

Glanville, R. (1978) 'Architects' Construing of Space', CSHL symposium at Proceedings of the Second International Congress on Personal Construct Theory' in Fay Fransella (ed.), *Personal Construct Psychology 1977*, Academic Press, London

Harri-Augstein, S. (1978) 'Reflecting on Structures of Meaning: A Process of Learning-to-Learn', CSHL Symposium at Proceedings of the Second International Congress on Personal Construct Theory. Fay Fransella, (ed.), *Personal Construct Psychology 1977*, Academic Press, London

—— (1979) 'The Change Grid: A Conversational Heuristic for Self Development' paper presented at the Third Congress on Personal Construct Psychology, Utrecht, CSHL Publication, Brunel University

Kelly, G.A. (1955) *The Psychology of Personal Constructs, vols 1 and 2*, Norton, New York

McKnight, C. (1976) 'Purposive Preferences for Multi-Attributed Alternatives: A

Study of Choice Behaviour Using Personal Construct Theory in Conjunction with Decision Theory', PhD thesis, Brunel University

Maslow, A.H. (1962) 'Notes on Being-Psychology', *Journal of Humanistic Psychology, 1*, reprinted in A.J. Sutich and M.A. Vich (eds), (1969), *Readings in Humanistic Psychology*, New York, The Free Press

Osgood, C.E. (1957) *The Measurement of Meaning*, University of Illinois Press, Urbana

Thomas, L.F. (1971) 'Interactive Methods of Eliciting Kelly Repertory Real-Time Data Processing', paper presented to The Occupational Section of the BPS Annual Conference, CSHL Publication, Brunel University

—— (1974) 'DEMON and DOUBLE-DEMON: Computer-aided Conversations with Yourself', paper presented at BPS Annual Conference, CSHL Publication, Brunel University

—— (1979) 'Construct, Reflect and Converse: The Conversational Reconstruction of Social Realities' in D. Bannister and P. Stringer (eds), *Constructs of Sociality and Individuality*, Academic Press, London

—— (1982) 'The CSHL Reflective Learning Software Packages', Brunel University

—— and Thompson, B.F. (1967) 'Rejection and the Process of Control', CSHL Publication, Brunel University

—— and Mendoza, S. (1972) 'The Individual's Construction of His Visual World as Projected by the Repertory Grid', paper presented at the BPS Annual Conference, CSHL Publication, Brunel University

—— and Harri-Augstein, S. (1972) 'An Experimental Approach to the Study of Reading as a Learning Skill', *Research in Education, no. 8*

—— and Pope, N. (1973) 'On the Tutoring of Art Students Using Kelly Repertory Grid Techniques', First Report, St Martin's College of Art, CSHL Publication, Brunel University

—— and —— (1976) 'The Self-organised Learner and the Printed Word. Final Progress Report SSRC', *Further Development of Techniques for Studying and Influencing Reading as a Learning Skill*, a CSHL Monography, Brunel University

—— and —— (1977) 'Learning-to-Learn: The Personal Construction and Exchange of Meaning' in M. Howe (ed.), *Adult Learning*, Wiley, Chichester

—— and —— (1978) 'The Kelly Repertory Grid as a Vehicle for Eliciting a Personal Taxonomy of Purposes for Reading', *Journal of Research in Reading, vol. 1, no. 1*

—— and —— (1980) 'Using Reportory Grid Technique to Investigate Personal Aspects of Subjective Judgement in Quality Control', Kellogg Company of Great Britain. Final Report. CSHL Publication, Brunel University

—— and —— (1983) 'The Personal Scientist as Self-organised Learner: A Conversational Technology for Reflecting on Behaviour and Experience', in J. Adams-Webber (ed.), *Applications of Personal Construct Theory*, Academic Press, Ontario

—— and —— (1985) *Self-organised Learning: Foundations of a Conversational Science for Psychology*, Routledge & Kegan Paul, London

17 USING THE REPERTORY GRID IN THE CLASSROOM

Estelle M. Phillips

Introduction

The main aim of this chapter is to provide an illustration of how the grid technique can be used in the classroom. A lesser aim is to introduce readers to the application of Q-analysis as a method of making sense of problematic repertory grid data.

The work described was carried out in a London comprehensive school which has won many prizes for originality and achievement in the field of design. The original reason for visiting this school was because of its reputation for having escaped from the traditional 'handicraft'-and-'woodwork'-training approach to design education. It was thought that the staff might be able to suggest methods of teaching design which would help to develop pupils' creative abilities, and that these methods could be used to encourage teachers in more conventional departments to adopt a more design-centred approach.

The catchment area of the school was predominantly professional and middle class, but included a very large council housing estate. The pupils were of varying abilities and from different social backgrounds, which is not unusual for comprehensive schools. The school was visited on several occasions and pupils, ex-pupils and Design Department staff discussed their record of success. However, it was during the course of these discussions that some of the difficulties inherent in maintaining such high standards gradually emerged. The teachers requested help as they began to describe problems that they rarely discussed between themselves.

Members of staff discussed the problem of changing the teachers' role from one of being *in* authority to merely being *an* authority. They identified certain pupils' problems caused by having to cope with changing from the top of one school to the bottom of the next. Although this problem is common to all subjects and children one teacher commented that the age at

275

which it occurs in secondary education is particularly significant to the development of a stable 'self-concept'. He saw the design class as being the place where this area could be explicitly worked on as it was more feasible and open to negotiation with individual pupils than were other parts of the curriculum.

The staff made a distinction between getting prizes and teaching design well. They felt that the middling majority of pupils and the mediocre children needed help to develop both the ability and confidence to generate ideas by themselves. They also agreed that the degree of structure imposed by them had to be related to the ability of their pupils, but this had to be disguised so that the children would believe they were arriving at their own decisions. The staff agreed that the success of this strategy is entirely dependent on the teacher's skill. For example an ex-pupil, currently studying for a diploma in design, spoke of her eventual resistance to ideas coming from her teachers and the powerful feelings of rebellion she had come to terms with during her design lessons.

The teachers were willing to take part in any experiment that might help them to manage the middling majority better. Three areas of investigation — emotional characteristics, creativity and perception — were suggested. Of these the experiment concerning perception was chosen in which abstract questions such as 'How do we look at things?' and 'What do we see?' were considered of particular interest.

Some confounding variables present at the outset were:

(1) mixed-ability groupings meant that the group would contain some high and low-ability children as well as the middling majority;
(2) the school rule preventing girls from taking design until their third year meant the girls were having their first exposure to design while most of the boys already had two years' preparatory lessons behind them;
(3) therefore it would be difficult to discriminate between low-ability and new (female) students.

The experiment described was designed to encourage pupils to speak fluently and without inhibitions about some designed objects. In the experiment the teacher's role was to guide the children's thinking toward relationships between the objects.

The experiment aimed:

(1) to investigate how children construe designed objects;
(2) to see if children construe objects in a similar way;
(3) to compare a group of children with two years' design education with a group new to the subject;
(4) to compare the children's perception of the designed objects with that of their teachers, and to test the children's assessment of their teachers' perception of 'good design'.

It was hoped the practical results of this classroom experiment would be:

(a) to help the teachers direct a spontaneous but structured discussion among their pupils;
(b) to raise the level of awareness of the children regarding how they perceive objects;
(c) to help the children understand that other people perceive objects in ways sometimes different to their own;
(d) to promote discussions amongst the children to encourage more flexibility in and alternatives to their usual viewpoint;
(e) to help teachers and pupils become aware of the criteria used in assessment, in order to evaluate objects created by themselves and others.

Training Teachers To Use Grid Techniques

The teachers were trained to use grid techniques in order to help their pupils

(1) become aware of *their own and their classmates'* constructs which they themselves and their classmates use when they perceive objects; and
(2) assess their own efforts and also evaluate objects created by others.

The teachers were given the following detailed example to study for a week and then they discussed it at the next meeting. Only when they felt quite certain of what would happen did they begin to design their own experiment.

278 In the Classroom

Example Used by Teachers

The items (or elements) being rated in the examples are postcard reproductions of different objects. They are as follows:

Number 1	Two ancient figured Attic vases	(Museum of Rhodes)
Number 2	Gainsborough portrait of Col. John Hayes St Leger	(Royal Collection)
Number 3	Venus de Milo	(Louvre Museum)
Number 4	Mummy cover and coffin of Henutmehit	(British Museum)
Number 5	Slaughter Stone, Stonehenge	
Number 6	Manuscript with Hebrew characters of Moses Maimonides	(British Museum)
Number 7	Barbara Hepworth sculpture entitled 'Three Forms'	(Tate Gallery)

The pupils are shown three elements (postcards) from the set and asked to select two that are similar to each other and one that is different from the other two. Once the pair has been selected they have to say in what way they are similar, then they have to say in which way the single card differs from the pair. These reasons for the perceived similarities and differences for each group of three elements are the constructs. The following step-by-step example illustrates this procedure, the demonstration being done by a 13-year-old schoolboy.

The first triad of elements presented was postcards numbers 1, 2 and 3. The two that were selected as similar were (2) portrait and (3) Venus because they were 'human' and the one that was different was (1) two vases because they were 'inanimate'. His first construct therefore was human/inanimate. He was then shown another triad of postcards, 4, 5 and 6, and asked to select two that were similar and one that was different. He chose 4 and 5 as the pair and 6 as the single. He said that the pair were similar because they were heavy and the other one was light in weight. His second construct was, of course, heavy/light. The procedure was continued until he had been presented with all seven elements in a variety of groupings. The triads were presented as follows:

3rd presentation	1, 4, 7
4th presentation	2, 5, 7
5th presentation	3, 6, 7
6th presentation	1, 3, 5

No triad was ever repeated. The constructs elicited were as follows:

Similar =1 and 4	C3 representation of life	— abstract
2 and 5	C4 natural vegetation	— manufactured
3 and 7	CS sculptures	— writing
3 and 5	C6 incomplete	— nothing missing

Other class members grouped the same triads in different ways so that additional constructs could be added. Constructs supplied by other pupils included the following:

ancient	modern
British	foreign
priceless	possible to buy
useful	frivolous
has colours	not bright
rounded	has corners

At this point we have a series of construct scales, the first six being made from dimensions noted as important by one 13-year-old and the remaining six from his classmates.

The scale may be represented as follows:

1. Human	Inanimate
2. Heavy	Light
2. Represents life	Abstract
4. Natural vegetation	Manufactured
5. Sculptured	Written
6. Incomplete	Nothing missed
7. Ancient	Modern
8. British	Foreign
9. Priceless	Possible to buy
10. Useful	Frivolous
11. Colourful	Not bright
12. Rounded	Has corners

This first step, known as 'construct elicitation', has already shown the group how some people identify certain features of an object as significant while others are either not aware of them until the feature is made explicit, or else do not consider it to be a significant feature relative to that particular element (in this case postcard reproductions).

If we draw up a grid consisting of the seven elements and the twelve constructs we have the beginning of a matrix. Now, all that remains to be done in this simplified form of the grid is to ask the participants to give ticks (✓) or crosses (x) to each of the elements on each of the constructs. For example, on the first construct the schoolboy being used to illustrate the procedure rated elements 2, 3 and 4 as human, and 1, 5, 6 and 7 as inanimate. Therefore his first line looked like this:

x　✓　✓　✓　x　x　x

Another schoolboy disagreed with this because he thought that a mummy was inanimate, and it was only *before* the person being mummified was made into a mummy that it was human. He also said that the vases symbolised life for two reasons — one because they had drawings of people and animals on them, and two because they were used to store drinking water which sustained life and therefore he would have to tick human. Therefore, his first line looked like this:

✓　✓　✓　x　x　x　x

Once the matrix is completed for one person it is possible to see relationships between elements in the way that the individual construes them. By considering their personal grid, each individual can be made more aware of how they construct their reality.

When matrices from different people are compared it is a simple matter for the discussion to be directed towards those aspects of construing which are relatively stable across people, and those which are of importance to only a few members of the group. Such discussions help people to realise how things look from another person's point of view, and, possibly, make them more flexible in their judgements.

Another way of using the grid is to collect construct scales and draw up a large matrix on the blackboard. Then the ticks and crosses are filled in by the group as they reach consensus for each element. This exercise encourages discussions which educate people into seeing alternatives to their own preconceived ideas, while broadening the range of possible future ways of assessing and evaluating objects and ideas.

Thus, the repertory grid can be used to help clarify the way in which we perceive images, whether for appreciation as in a gallery, museum or showroom, or for examination as in assessing student's work or evaluating our own efforts.

Having had sufficient time to discuss what it was they were supposed to do and why they were doing it, the teachers were anxious to proceed with the experiment in their own classrooms.

Design of the Experiment

The teachers assembled a set of twelve available 'designed objects' which the children could see and touch (Table 17.1). Every pupil was given a blank (8×12) grid matrix with the names of the objects printed along the top, but the spaces for constructs as the side left blank. A giant (8×12) matrix was drawn on the blackboard before the experiment began.

The class was divided into two groups, those having two years' experience of design education and those having just joined the class. Because of the school rule preventing girls from taking design until their third year, the first group contained only boys and the second group only girls. The first group contained thirteen children and the second group contained seven. Each group had a teacher supervising the sorting procedure, and both groups were shown exactly the same group of 3 objects, or triads, from the set of 12.

The children were shown 6 sets of triads during the double lesson period of this experiment. The experiment took the whole afternoon, and no more than 6, out of the many triads possible could be accommodated in the time available.

The children individually sorted the triads into their own personal constructs. The children all acted independently at this stage. Having elicited a construct for a triad each child wrote his or her left-hand and right-hand poles in the vacant spaces on the next blank row of the grid. Having done this, each child went through all twelve objects putting a tick if it fell on the left-hand pole and

Table 17.1: The Set of Designed Objects

1. Saw	woodworking handsaw, wooden handle, metal blade
2. Candle display	made by one of the children out of translucent blue plastic, three cubic candle holders
3. Toy duck	yellow plastic duck, 15cm (6in) high with painted eyes and orange beak
4. Mask	elaborately ornamented party mask
5. Nutcracker	made by one of the children out of wood, screw type mechanism, contrasting colours
6. Bicycle	traditional gentleman's bicycle (used)
7. Spanner	mechanical spanner, 23cm (9in) long
8. Machine valve	valve from a machine, 5cm × 6cm (2in × 2½in)
9. Toy bat	cheap plastic toy bat, pink, 20cm × 12cm (8in × 8¾ in)
10. Housebrick	red housebrick, depression on top for mortar
11. Marmite jar	empty jar, dark glass, 5cm × 5cm × 5cm (2in × 2in × 2in), yellow metal screw top, coloured label
12. Drilling machine	fixed, free-standing, drilling machine used in the school workshop

a cross if it fell on the right-hand pole. This was repeated for 6 triads. In this way 13 grid matrices for boys and 7 grid matrices for girls were obtained, these being the children's personal repertory grids which show how the children construe the objects.

At the completion of this part of the experiment the children were asked to rate the objects on a scale between 1 and 10 as to how much they 'liked the objects' or to what extent they judged the objects to be 'good design'. They were also asked to assess how their teachers would rate the objects on the 'good-bad design' construct, the number 1 meaning *very bad* and the number 10 meaning *very good*. This provided two lines of numerical data per child. These lines gave the boys' assessments of the object, girls' assessments of the objects, and their guesses as to how the teachers would assess the objects.

Results

The data showed a marked difference between the boys' and girls' constructs. The boys' constructs tended to have logical opposites as poles while the girls tended to use more complex constructs. It can be seen that although there were only half the number of girls they generated more constructs than the boys. This remains true even after the constructs which were common to both groups are removed (Table 17.2). This table shows that none of the boys used a 'colour' construct and none of the girls used a 'work/home' construct. It seems rather surprising that this should happen, especially when these types of constructs recurred within the groups. The boys, with two years' of design education, generated several variants of the 'work/home' construct, and the girls, new to design, generated several variants of the 'colour' construct.

Table 17.2: Constructs With Duplications Removed

Boys and girls (n = 20)	Girls only (n = 7)	Boys only (n = 13)
To do with materials (e.g. metal/wood)	Transport/toys	Transparent/opaque
handmade/machine made	Flexible/hard	construction/not
curved/straight	heavy/light	mineral/non-mineral
container/not	ugly/nice	work-home
hollow/not	useful/not	* household/industrial
hard/soft	solid/(hollow)	domestic/not
shiny/not	has screws/doesn't	
mechanical/not	flat/bumpy	
tools/not	noisy/quiet	
mobile/static	ornaments/(tools)	
cutting (sharp)/not	brightly coloured/dull	
*	coloured/not	
	painted/not	
	floatable/sinkable	
	to play with/not	
	for children/for adults	
	mastered with hand/ not	
	force needed/not	
11 constructs	16 constructs	4 constructs

*Recurred within the group, but other groups not a single example.

In some cases, contrary to instructions, some children recorded objects as being related to both poles of a construct. In some cases, too, some children recorded a dash in a cell of their grid, indicating that the construct was not relevant to that particular object.

The tables show the range and variety of the children's individual constructs which they generated independently. Nevertheless, they were able to agree on constructs to be put on the blackboard. Table 17.3 gives the consensus constructs arrived at by the two groups separately. It can be seen that the boys did include a complex construct 'transparent/opaque' in their consensus grid but the girls did not include a single logical opposite type of construct in theirs, even though there had been several in their individual grids.

Table 17.3: Consensus Constructs

Triads	Boys	Girls
Mask, nutcracker, bike	Wood/not	Machine-made/ handmade
Saw, drilling m/c, mask	Tools/not	Tools/ornament
Marmite jar, brick, bike	Curved/not	Solid/hollow
Bat, candle display, spanner	Transparent/opaque	Metal/plastic
Toy duck, candle display, spanner	Handmade/not	Hard/soft
Drilling m/c, brick, Marmite jar	Constructional/not constructional	Ugly/nice

It was also apparent that although a dash, instead of a tick or a cross, appeared in the grids of both groups it occurred more often in the girls' grids. It is probably due to the fact that, although at first sight the girls' constructs appear to be more interesting, they are much more difficult to use than the boys. The complex constructs, which were perfectly meaningful when elicited from a specific triad, presented dilemmas for the children when they tried to apply them to other objects. An example of such a dilemma would be the need to decide whether to place a wooden-handled, metal-bladed saw on the right or left-hand pole of the construct 'wood/metal' and where a plastic bat fits along this construct.

Q-Analysis

A fundamental problem in repertory grid methodology occurs where bipolar constructs can be perfectly meaningful when elicited from a particular triad, but trying to apply them to other objects can create dilemmas. Such problems can be resolved by the use of Q-analysis (Johnson, 1981a, 1981b). Q-analysis of such problematic repertory grid data is done by splitting the construct (x/y) into two constructs (x/not-x) and (y/not-y) and resolving the single self-contradictory line of the matrix into two new lines.

In clinical psychology such practice is open to question because the investigator must not modify the elicitee's data in order to facilitate understanding in terms of the investigator's constructs; but the opposite could be argued for education. It may be that one of the purposes of education is to help children resolve their confusions by using clearer constructs. Sometimes this may refer to a wider body of knowledge (tried and tested constructs) which resolve the problems while retaining the meaning. The procedure used to handle illegal 'yes and no' data for Q-analysis also works for conventional repertory grid data processing.

Also, the children's responses included (illegal) dashes to mean 'I cannot apply this construct to this element', meaning the object is not in the constructs' range of application (or *range of convenience* (Kelly, 1955)). Conventional repertory grid methodology cannot properly deal with this case, the usual expedient of assigning the object to the 'middle of the scale' implies the construct can be applied to the object and that both poles apply equivalently. This can be a logical contradiction of the observed (and recorded) facts. These kind of data present no problem for Q-analysis, there being a number of methods available to represent such data according to what it means to the observer. The distinction between 'not applicable' and 'both poles equally' can be made explicitly. Such analyses have already been reported in Johnson (1981b), and Phillips and Johnson (1981), to which the interested reader is referred.

Q-analysis will be illustrated in this chapter using data concerning the children's and teachers' subjective opinions of the objects as expressed by their like/dislike ratings on a ten-point scale from 1 (very bad) to 10 (very good). As explained above (p. 282) the children each also gave their estimates of how much they thought their teachers would like the objects. The teachers, too, recorded their likes and dislikes of the objects on the 1-10 scale according to their criteria for 'good design'.

The Q-analysis involved a detailed interpretation of this scale, but for simplicity here consider only the interpretation 1, 2, 3 or 4 meaning 'dislike', and 6, 7, 8, 9, 10 meaning 'like'. In Figure 17.1 objects 9 and 11 are 9-connected because more than 9 boys disliked each of them. Object 2 is 7-connected to them because at least 7 of these boys also disliked it. The notion of connectivity is defined in terms of chains of connection: thus, objects 4, 6 and 12 are 10-connected because 10 boys liked each of objects 4 and 6, and more than 20 boys liked each of objects 6 and 12. These need not necessarily be the same boys, nor is it necessary (here) that more than 10 boys liked each of objects 4 and 12: they are 10-connected through object 6. Similar considerations apply to the girls' structure; for example, more than 4 girls liked each of objects 2 and 3. Objects 5 and 9 are 2-connected in the structure through chains of other objects determined by the girls' shared likes. Figure 17.1 gives more details than like/dislike as explained in the original analyses.

To summarise the original analysis (Phillips and Johnson, 1981):

> the bicycle was popular with both boys and girls, followed by the drilling machine for the girls, but the boys liked better the mask and the toy duck. All the children disliked the toy bat, and the boys also disliked the Marmite jar. The structures were relatively disconnected showing the children's opinions were quite different from each other, although the girls' structure showed they agreed more than the boys. (p. 446)

Alternative Analysis

I return now to more traditional methods of interpreting the data in order to show that no distortions occur through the introduction of Q-analytical techniques.

Table 17.4 gives the mean scores for all the like/dislike ratings. It can be seen that all the children liked the bicycle best and disliked the toy bat most, the boys also disliked the Marmite jar. The children's opinions were quite different from each other, although the girls agreed more than the boys. The teachers' ratings coincided exactly on only four objects — the nutcracker, bicycle, bat and Marmite jar, and differed by a maximum of 5 points on the toy duck.

Although there was no significant or 'only a weak' correlation between the boys' ratings of the objects and the teachers', there

Figure 17.1: A Summary of K Objects (Boys) and K
Objects (Girls) Like/dislike Structure

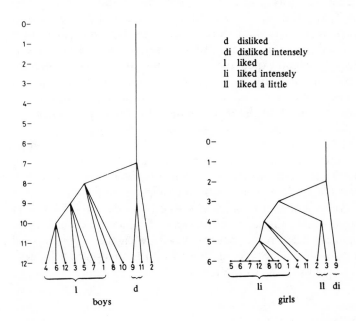

d disliked
di disliked intensely
l liked
li liked intensely
ll liked a little

was a significant correlation ($r = 0.61$; $p = 0.029$) between the
teachers' ratings and the boys' estimates of the teachers' ratings.
Therefore, it seems that the boys have learned what constitutes
good design in the teachers' eyes even though they themselves
may not like those objects very much.

There was a highly significant correlation ($r = 0.8$; $p = 0.001$)
between the girls' ratings of the objects and the teachers'. There
was also a correlation of $r = 0.8$ between the teachers' ratings
and the girls' estimates of the teachers' ratings. This may mean
that the girls could not handle the concept of putting themselves
in the teacher's place to make a decision and so their assessments
of the teachers' ratings may have simply been a reflection of their
own tastes. Alternatively, the girls, untrained as they were, were

nevertheless appreciating the elements of design that the teachers liked while also disliking objects that their teacher considered to be examples of poor design. The ratings in Table 17.4 show that the teachers' mean rating of both the Marmite jar and the saw was 8.5 while the girls' mean rating for each object was 7, and the boys' mean ratings were 2.4 and 5 respectively. Overall, the girls were more accurate in their assessment of the teachers' likes and dislikes than were the boys. This is curious since one would expect the boys to know the teachers better than would the girls after being taught by them for two years. The discrepancy could arise from the boys disliking the Marmite jar while the girls and the teachers thought it was well designed for its purpose, regardless of their likes or dislikes.

The data also show instances where the girls and the teachers marked lower than did the boys. The mean ratings for the mask were 8.1 boys, 6.5 teachers and 5.8 girls, while the bat, which was rated only 1 (mean score) by the teachers and 1.5 by the girls, was given a mean rating of 2.7 out of 10 by the boys. Why should this be so . . . that after two years of design education, the boys' personal tastes are not consistent with what they know to be the tastes of their teachers, while girls with no background in design have similar tastes to the teachers?

Discussion

Both sets (those relevant to the number and type of constructs as well as those relevant to the children's assessments of the objects) show differences between the groups. The groups were, of course, made up of boys who had two years' experience of design education and girls who were new to the subject. Unfortunately, it is not possible at present to disentangle these two factors, but let us assume that the differences were due more to what had occurred in the two years of design lessons than to any inherent differences between the sexes.

Personal Construct Theory includes two different cyclic processes in construing. One is concerned with learning, which Kelly saw as a general life activity, and the other he referred to as a creativity cycle. The creativity cycle involves using 'loose' constructs which can be linked to each other in different ways until one way is accepted as more useful than the others. When

Table 17.4: Mean Scores for Like/dislike Ratings

	Saw	Candle display	Toy duck	Mask	Nutcracker	Bicycle	Spanner	M/C valve	Bat	Brick	Marmite jar	Drilling m/c
Teachers' raw scores Y	8	6	5	5	7	10	8	7	1	10	9	5
Z	9	4	10	8	7	10	9	5	1	9	9	7
Mean scores												
Teachers	8.5	5.0	7.5	6.5	7.0	10	8.5	6	1.0	9.5	8.5	6.0
Boys	5.0	4.8	7.3	8.1	6.8	8.2	6.6	6.2	2.7	5.5	2.4	6.5
Boys/teachers	7.6	6.5	6.5	7.0	8.3	9.5	8.6	8.8	3.0	7.4	3.5	8.9
Girls	7.1	6.4	6.8	5.8	8.6	8.9	8.4	7.2	1.5	8.6	7.0	8.9
Girls/teachers	7.4	6.8	6.3	7.3	7.5	9.2	8.1	8.1	1.0	7.6	8.7	9.1

this happens the constructs are 'tightened' so that people can see where they have got to and try out the ideas. This can be interpreted to mean that, initially, when a person is new to an area and has very little knowledge of it most aspects are treated equally, that is, they are not differentiated.

Once the person starts to explore the area and becomes familiar with parts of it there is a period of high differentiation. At this time most aspects are treated separately, and difficulty might be experienced when attempts are made to coordinate all the individual components. This way of interpreting Kelly discriminates between learning (as a general life process) and learning *about* something specific. The suggestion here is that this happens once the area has been understood and the separate parts have been integrated. At this point, the way in which the subject area is differentiated in the individual's thoughts helps her to grasp the significant features without being confused by more trivial details.

In the present experiment, although the girls were new to design, the long list of constructs they generated suggests a very high level of differentiation. This is probably due to the fact that the objects were very familiar to them, being part of their everyday experience. What appears to be happening is that the girls were considering all parts of the objects as being equally important and so produced a heterogeneous list of constructs. The boys, on the other hand, tended to focus their attention onto significant features of the objects. In this way they produced a more homogeneous list of constructs which was less differentiated, as one might expect given their two years of exposure to design lessons.

An example of this way of focusing attention is the lack of a colour construct from any of the boys. This could be because they have a monochrome view of the objects compatible with drawing in one colour on the drawing board, perhaps thinking along the lines of 'make it first — paint it later'?

The children's constructs showed that there was a tendency for those new to design to use more complex constructs while those who had had two years in the design class tended more toward constructs made up of logical opposites.

The metal saw with wooden handle caused many children dilemmas, particularly those using a wood-metal construct. Most people would agree that the saw is part wood and part metal, and those children assigning it to both poles (contrary to instructions) of a wood-metal construct are consistent with the general (adult) convention. Those children plumping for either wood or metal on the wood-metal construct are not consistent with the (adult) consensus view since they either deny the saw is partly wood or deny it is partly metal.

Those who coded 'incorrectly' may have done so for the following reasons:

(1) they could 'see' only part of the object, for example the only important part of the saw was seen as its cutting edge, which is metal on the wood/metal construct. The saw has been perceived in terms of its function rather than in terms of what it is;
(2) they could not resolve the difference between parts of the object and the application of some constructs presented a real dilemma, i.e. the object could not be resolved into parts;
(3) although they were able to resolve the construct into parts, the application of some constructs applied to the parts differently. Rather than question their instructions, the children coded against their intuition and observations.

The children to whom the third explanation applies may have deliberately coded against their observations because this was the only way they could be consistent with the instructions they were given. These children could be encouraged to be more questioning, and to have more confidence in themselves.

To some extent the children who had received two years of design education did show more confidence than the others. In their estimates of how the teachers would assess the objects, the boys gave ratings they themselves had given to the objects. The girls, whose personal tastes coincided with those of their teachers, rated the teachers very similarly to themselves. It is possible that this showed an awareness of the correlation in their own and their teachers' estimates of good design. However, the more probable explanation is that these naïve pupils were unable to distance themselves sufficiently to imagine themselves in the teacher's place. The boys' confidence extended to stating explicitly, by giving different ratings for themselves and their teachers, that although they thought the teachers would not agree they still had their own ideas about what constitutes good and bad design.

In terms of the objectives, the experiment has given interesting insights into children's perception of designed objects, and shows they have different ways of construing things. The children with two years' design education used simpler constructs, and the composite constructs used by those without this experience caused them some problems. The children's perception of the designed objects did not appear very different from their teachers', but it was surprising to note that those less familiar with the teachers guessed their assessment best.

Those with two years' experience were able to focus their attention onto specific features of objects while those new to design were highly differentiated in their perceptions.

The Experiment as a Classroom Activity

The children made their own decisions about the grouped objects and wrote their personal constructs on their individual grids. They were then quite happy to select one of the constructs generated from their group to go on the blackboard as part of the consensus grid. There was no problem in agreeing, either as a result of discussion or by yielding to the majority on a show of hands.

They accepted other children's constructs as equally applicable and comprehensible. They were not surprised or disturbed to discover that others in their group were construing the objects in ways that were different from their own. In fact, the children thought of different ways in which they might construe the objects themselves. For example:

> 'Is wood a good way to describe it? You might not know it's made of wood, it *could* be plastic'. This was during the boys discussion about the mask which was covered in bright paint. Other examples show how certain ambiguities were made explicit and discussed in some detail.

> 'Is a nutcracker a tool?'
> 'Is a saw constructional when what it does is take things apart?'
> 'Do movable ears make the mask mechanical?'

The children were very interested in their teacher's assessment of the objects, which they were shown once the experiment had been completed. It might be that such an exercise, two hours of 'getting to know' a set of objects and then revealing how 'experts' rate them as examples of design, could increase children's design awareness and appreciation.

The teachers were able to listen to the children and guide their discussions without imposing their own bias on them during completion of the consensus grids. This suggests that such an exercise could be used to help teachers to make the difficult move from being *in* authority to being *an* authority, as discussed in the early talks with the teachers involved in this experiment. The teachers were controlling a spontaneous but structured discussion among their pupils, as had been hoped at the preparation stage of the experiment.

The children themselves enjoyed taking part in the experiment, but could not understand what it was all about or why they should have engaged in the activities they did. In fact, the teachers reported that the children thought it was 'a waste of time'. Nevertheless, the teachers have expressed a wish to try a similar experiment with younger children and with those of a lower-ability group. This is because they see the activity as encouraging the children to focus on some specific features of a group of objects and get them talking. With these younger, less able children, the main problem seems to be to get them to articulate anything at all. In fact, the teachers agree that it is the communication aspect of the activity that is important for them. They have requested that a similar activity be incorporated into the 'graphics' part of their teaching programme. In terms of integrating the kinds of activities undertaken during the course of this experiment into regular classroom procedures, there are some indications that both teachers and pupils might benefit. The teachers might be helped to *guide*, as opposed to direct their pupils' ideas; the pupils might be encouraged to talk about things they would not normally make explicit. This would eventually result in an increase in confidence on the part of both teachers and pupils.

Acknowledgements

I would like to thank the staff and pupils of the Design Department of the comprehensive school for their co-operation at all stages of this experiment; also members of the Barbican Research Group for their helpful comments during the planning stage.

References

Johnson, J.H. (1981a) 'Some Structures and Notation of Q-analysis', *Environment and Planning B, 8*, 73-86

— (1981b) 'Q-discrimination Analysis', *Environment and Planning B, 8(4)*, 419-34

Kelly, G.A. (1955) *The Psychology of Personal Constructs*, Norton, New York

Phillips, E.M. and Johnson, J.H. (1981) 'A Structural Investigation in Design Education', *Environment and Planning B, 8*, 435-48

18 EXPLORING LEARNING WITH THE GRID

Laurie F. Thomas and Sheila Harri-Augstein

Introduction

In this chapter some examples are offered of how the grid can be used to explore learning. A study is reported in which full-time technical college students studying A-level subjects used the grid to investigate their approach to learning. In the first part an individual grid of *significant incidents* in the life of a student is presented and discussed. In the second part nine grids are subjected to analysis, and the results systematically illustrate how these students were alienated from formal education. This study is used to illustrate how grids can tap the sources of individual understanding, and how by pooling the content of the grids from a group, attitudes in the group are clearly revealed in the terms in which the group feel them.

The Construing of Learning Events

Grids (elements, constructs and rated responses) were elicited from nine students studying A-level subjects full-time at a technical college. The names of the participant subjects have been changed but the grids remain unaltered. They volunteered to attend a course on *learning-to-learn*, and at the beginning of this course expressed strong but unclear dissatisfaction with their lot. This course formed part of an SSRC-sponsored project for the development of techniques for promoting self-organised learning.

Informal interviews indicated that learning was viewed very negatively and was always associated with being taught. Gradually in discussion a number of examples of really significant incidents were elicited, but these were viewed as having no relation to the concept/term/word 'learning'. Further discussion led to the acceptance of a repertory grid investigation.

The participant investigator introduced each individual elicitation with a conversational opening based on the following statement.

> I want you to think of any events which have had a real impact on you: in which you have learned something. It can be positive or negative and it can be any kind of event in formal education or outside.

The conversation following this statement gradually defined the universe of discourse.

When Harry Shard described the one event from which he had learned most during the past two years, he answered as follows:

> I was out in this dinghy and the wind caught me; I couldn't do anything. It was racing towards the bank and I tried to turn away, the boom swung over, I ducked, the boat capsized and I was trapped underneath. I thought my last moment had come.

Dick Archonad, in answer to the same question, described a visit to see 'The Merchant of Venice' at the Royal Shakespeare Theatre:

> I had studied the play for my O-level examinations and hated it; but seeing it acted like that was something else again.

Gwen Huston described how she had seen a man behaving very peculiarly:

> He was probably drunk, [she said], but it had a profound effect on me. I began to wonder what it would be like to be him.

Penny Fennel talked about a short history course:

> We had no history for one term, then this dishy young teacher arrived and we did an intensive course on the 18th and 19th century. I got really interested in the people and the issues. It's the first time I've seen anything in history.

> I learned most from being faced with a decision,

Mary Sinclair said:

> I didn't see it at first. I had this long discussion with my dad
> about his job and how he really hates it. We talked and talked.
> He had given me this electronics kit for Christmas and we
> made all kinds of things with it. I decided to study maths and
> physics for A-level, but the way they teach it is terrible. I
> really can't see what all that mathematical stuff has to do with
> designing computers. Early on I got very down. I really felt
> like leaving. In the end I gave myself a good talking to. Did I
> really want to suffer school for two more years so that I can go
> out and get the kind of job I want, or should I just leave and
> take a job where I can earn some money and have a good
> time. Deciding to continue my studies was really difficult for
> me.

Harry, Dick, Gwen, Penny and Mary were five of the young
adults attending the technical college. Their descriptions of
'significant learning events' as:

(a) being near death in a dinghy;
(b) seeing 'The Merchant of Venice' at the theatre after
reading it for O-level;
(c) seeing a man, possibly drunk;
(d) attending a short intensive history course run by an
enthusiastic young teacher; and
(e) deciding to endure the educational system so that I can get
a job in electronics.

surprised the researchers who were interviewing them. It also
surprised their teachers. Anything up to three quarters of an hour
was spent in negotiating the elements, which were, as illustrated,
obviously unique to each student.

The constructs were then elicited from each student by using
triads of elements. The students were asked to differentiate each
triad in terms of 'similarities and differences' and to describe
these briefly. This was done first by recording each element
description on separate cards, shuffling these and numbering
them E1 to E9, and then recording their descriptions of
similarities and differences on construct cards which were also
numbered. As a basic guide triads (i.e. sets of three elements)

are selected, so that all elements are used as often as each other and no pair of elements recur until all pairs have been used once. The construct elicitation conversation continued as follows:

> I want you to take yourself back into three of your learning events and really consider them deeply as personal learning experiences. Here are the first three E1, E2, E3. Now take your time, which two of these are most alike *as learning experiences* and which one was most different from the other two.

The subjects were encouraged to recall and re-live each event, and when they were ready they were asked to comment on the similarity (Pole 1) and difference (Pole 2). When the poles of the first construct have been elicited and recorded on the construct cards, the elicitation conversation continues: the two poles of the construct descriptions are laid in front of the subject with a space in between representing a 5-point scale. The similar pair of elements and the single one are placed against Pole 1 and Pole 2 respectively.

> I want you now to sort all your remaining element cards on to or between one or the other pole according to how similar or different these are. Try to imagine the space between Pole 1 and Pole 2 as one dimension of *your own thinking and feeling* about E1, E2 and E3.

When all the cards were distributed linearly on a 5-point scale, the results are recorded on a raw grid form. New sets of triads were selected until the grid is complete. Completion of a grid is achieved when all relevant constructs have been exhausted. In eliciting constructs the participant investigator must help subjects to clarify their thoughts and feelings into well-differentiated constructs. *Skilled conversation can avoid the use of constructs which confuse two or more meanings into a haphazard scale.*

The results of eliciting a series of personal constructs and assigning elements to their poles is then summarised in the grid. Conventionally, the elements are set out across the top of the grid defining each column, and each construct occupies one horizontal row. The poles of each construct are described on either side of each row and the scale (1-5) shows how each element has been assigned to one or other pole (Figure 18.1).

Whilst the raw grid contains all the data (verbal and ratings) it does not display the total pattern of personal meaning that lies within it. By re-ordering the elements and constructs the arbitrariness of the original sequence is replaced. The FOCUS technique (Thomas, 1976, 1978) uses a two-way cluster analysis based on a pattern recognition by defining items (elements and constructs) by their interrelationship. The FOCUSed grid displays the clusters of patterns of meaning in a person's construing compared with the raw grid, which offers a display of a person's constructs as if seen through a rough lens, the FOCUSed grid highlights and distils the pattern of meaning. This is a powerful tool for facilitating reflection upon personal meaning. Used conversationally to encourage personal feedback, it serves to offer a glimpse into the deeply personal process of construing.

FOCUSing can be done by means of a paper-and-pencil method which compares all elements (i.e. the columns) and all constructs (i.e. the rows), either visually by examining the pattern of responses or by systematically recording the cumulative difference scores (Thomas, 1976, 1978). The data in the raw grid are transferred onto strips of element and construct cards, and both element and construct strips can be compared, simply by physically sorting and re-sorting by eye to achieve an optimal re-ordering based on degrees of similarity and differences. If coloured pencils are used as follows to enter ratings (1-5)

Dark blue	Light blue	Grey	Light red	Dark red
1	2	3	4	5

the sorting procedure can be made speedily and fairly accurately. Although not as accurate as the numerical procedure it does highlight the pattern of meaning in the grid.

The FOCUS computer program (Thomas, 1976, 1981), provides a fast and accurate two-way cluster analysis procedures for re-sorting the grid. For the mathematically minded reader a more detailed description of the FOCUS procedure and comparison with factor-analytical methods is found elsewhere (Thomas, 1976; Thomas and Harri-Augstein, 1985). One important point for the practising teacher to bear in mind is that the process of visual focusing can be done *together with the participating subject*; they can play with alternate patterning and enrich their understanding of the meaning in the grid in doing so. The teacher has to decide whether the accuracy of the FOCUS program outweighs the advantages of the participative but cruder visual sorting methods.

Harry Shard's FOCUSed grid is shown in Figure 18.1. The display is enhanced further by using SPACEing to emphasise the pattern of responses. The distance between rows and the distances between columns *increases* as the mismatch, i.e. difference scores, between adjacent rows or between adjacent columns increases.

One Case Study — Harry Shard

Harry Shard's grid has been selected as an illustration because it is relatively simple, having only nine elements and six constructs. Harry's first element E1 (last in the FOCUSed grid, see Figure 18.1), might have been 'a short course', and he might have been trying to generalise his ideas about opportunities for learning by comparing and contrasting it with 'a trip abroad' 'learning from music' and 'personal adventures'. It is easy for an observer to read elements E1, E2, E7 and E4 in this way, but to do so is to already assume that *we know* how Harry experienced what he means when he writes down:

E1 A highly condensed history course with an enthusiastic young teacher who generated great enthusiasm.
E2 A month's visit to Finland.
E7 Musical outlook broadened by 'Deep Purple'.
E4 Near death in a dinghy.

To begin to interpret a grid in the learner's own terms it is useful to calculate difference scores. In Harry's grid we have calculated difference scores between each column of elements. This is part of the FOCUSing procedure referred to earlier. For instance, if we compare the responses (1-5 point scale) for Element 4 and Element 1 we get:

E4	E1	Diff. score
1	5	4
1	5	4
1	5	4

1	5	4
1	4	3
1	3	2
		21

giving a total cumulative difference of 21.

Now if we look at the elements on the extreme ends of the FOCUSed grid E4 'Dinghy' and E1 'Course' are rated extremely differently (diff. score = 21) on Harry's constructs. The dinghy incident is rated 1 on all six constructs. By reading down the left-hand (1) pole descriptions we begin to glimpse some of the terms in which Harry was thinking about this incident during the elicitation conversation. Reading down the right-hand (5) pole descriptions gives an idea of how he thought about 'the history course experience', keeping in mind that his ratings for it were 5, 5, 5, 5, 4, 3. The 3 is interesting, despite the positive verbal description of this element using words like enthusiasm, he sees it as *neutral* on

intellectual freak-out   vs   great use of intellect
    (no use)

One of the lessons to be learned from reading grids is that ideas and values which go together in the reader's mind do not necessarily do so in the author of the grid. Often, in retrospect, one wonders why certain ideas, values and events (constructs and elements) were not represented during the elicitation conversation. Sometimes the omission lies in the particular path taken by the conversation, i.e. in poor mutual control of the conversational process. Often the ideas are not there because they do not loom large in the participant subject's ordinary thoughts and feelings. Harry might well have been able to rate all his elements on a scale:

good learning experience   vs   bad learning experience

but the fact that he did not spontaneously offer it as a construct even within the context of a conversation about 'learning', is significant to our understanding of Harry.

The 'Visit to Finland' (E2) lies between 'Dinghy' (E4) and

Figure 18.1: Harry Shard's SPACEd FOCUSed Grid

NAME Harry Shard

SPACED FOCUSED GRID

	E4	E6	E3	E9	E5	E7	E2	E8	E1	
Individual activity ..looking after C2	1	3	3	1	1	2	2	4	5	* C2 Group Activity
myself .. self-reliance										
Spontaneous activity C5	1	4	3	5	2	1	1	5	5	* C5 Considered activity
Tense C4	1	2	2	3	4	5	5	5	5	* C4 Relaxed
Grudge against a person C6	1	1	1	5	5	5	5	5	5	* C6 No Grudge
External events (.. no control) C1	1	1	3	5	5	4	3	2	4	* C1 Emotions internally generated..control
Impinging on emotions										
Intellectual Freak Out (..no use) C3	1	3	5	5	5	5	1	1	3	* C3 Great use of intellect

```
* *
* *   * E1 A Highly Condensed History Course
* *   *         with an Enthusiastic Young Teacher
* *   *
* * * *   * E8 Coming to College Gave me
* * * *   *         a Surprised Freedom
* * * *   *
* * * *   *
* * * *   * E2 A Month Visit
* * * *   *         Finland
* * * *   *
* * * *   * E7 Musical Outlook Broadened
* * * *   *         by Deep Purple
* * * *   *
* * * *   *E5 Interest in Electronics
* * * *   *         Inspired by Father
* * * *   *
* * * *   E9 Determined to Endure Educational System
* * * *             to Obtain Ambition in Electronics
* * * *
* * * *   * E3 Learning How to Avoid Trouble
* * * *   *         when in Early Teens
* * * *
* * * *   * E6 Short Eyesight Made Me Give Up
* * * *             Playing Football for Team
* * * *
* *       * E4 Near Death in a Dinghy
```

'Course (E1). Like the 'Course' (E1) it is 'Relaxed' and 'No grudge' but like the 'Dinghy incident' (E4) it is:

individual activity, looking after myself, self-reliance;
spontaneous activity; and
intellectual freak-out.

A gradual easing of oneself into the grid begins to offer some insights into Harry's construing of significant learning experiences. If we now begin to look at 'what goes with what' in Harry's thoughts and feelings we see among the elements:

E5   interest in electronics inspired by father; and
E7   musical outlook broadened by 'Deep Purple' are rated similarly (diff. = 4) matching on two constructs and only mismatching by one point the other four;
E6   short eyesight made me give up playing football for a team; and
E3   learning to avoid trouble when in early teens.
     are also similar to each other (diff. score = 5).
Among Harry's constructs:

C4   tense vs relaxed; and
C6   grudge against a person vs no grudge
     are highly related (diff. score = 5).

The meaning of C4 and C6 is further illuminated when we realise that they group

E4 E6 and E3   in contrast   E9 E5 E7 E2 E8 and E1
                            to
near death in dinghy   education for electronics
short eyesight, give   'Deep Purple'
up football   Finland
                                             Technical College
avoid trouble in teens   history course

The ratings of the elements on a construct cluster adds specific meaning to the verbal descriptions of its poles, i.e.:

Element	Combined Rating	Construct/Cluster External Events (no control), emotional; Intellectual Freakout.
E4 near death in dinghy	(1 and 1)	1
E8 going to Technical College	(1 and 2)	
E2 visit to Finland		
E6 short eyesight: give up football	(1 and 3)	2
E1 history course	(3 and 4)	3
E3 avoid trouble in teens	(3 and 5)	4
E7 'Deep Purple'	(4 and 5)	
E5 electronics inspired by father	(5 and 5)	5
E9 endure education for electronics	(5 and 5)	emotion internally generated (control); great use of intellect.

Conversely, the ratings of an element on all constructs add personal meaning to its verbal description i.e. 'Musical Outlook Broadened by "Deep Purple" ', E7 is constructively defined by:

Ratings

     (1) very spontaneous activity;

     (2) individual activity: looking after myself: self reliance;

     (4) emotion internally generated (control);

     (5) very great use of intellect;

     (5) no grudge at all;

     (5) very relaxed.

Thus, my moving backwards and forwards between elements and constructs, seeing the construct in terms of the ordering of the elements and the elements in terms of its rating on the constructs, the pattern of meaning in the FOCUSed grid begins to emerge. To survey this whole pattern requires a scanning strategy which reveals the major lines of cleavage in the FOCUSed grid. The method of SPACEing is used to expose the structure further. With practice, the FOCUSed grid takes on 'gestalt-like' qualities that enhance this display of structure.

Harry was talked-back through his SPACEed, FOCUSed grid to help him become more aware of his views about learning. The elements elicited from Harry all seem to emphasise direct experience. This system of constructs begins to reveal how his thoughts and feelings about these learning events cluster into a simple pattern of relationships. Discovery of this pattern and of its significance for Harry lead to a deeper understanding about what learning really meant for him, and for the first time he began to reflect how studying at a technical college related to his deeply held views. This was the beginning of an ongoing series of 'learning conversations' which marked a turning point in his approach to study and in his educational career. Harry passed two A-level subjects with B grades and went on to study at a polytechnic. Similar experiences are also reported for each of the nine students who volunteered to participate in this study.

A Guide to Interpreting a FOCUSed Grid

Having examined one grid in some detail, it is possible to trace out a general approach to the exploration of a FOCUSed grid. The flowchart (Figure 18.2) should be seen only as a guide towards the examination of grids to be improved, changed, elaborated and discarded as the reader becomes familiar with them.

Comparing and Contrasting the Content of Grids

In our action-research studies we have used the repertory grid in many different ways. As an individual case study method it enables the teacher or educational psychologist to systematically explore a child's or student's thinking and feeling around a central topic within one universe of discourse. As such it is a tool of some considerable power since it allows a teacher, tutor or psychologist to elicit a whole series of experiences piecemeal and to get the learner to consider them in threes (triads) as described earlier. The results (elements, constructs and responses) are all entered onto one grid and FOCUSed so that they represent a

Figure 18.2: A Flowchart for Interpreting a FOCUSed Grid

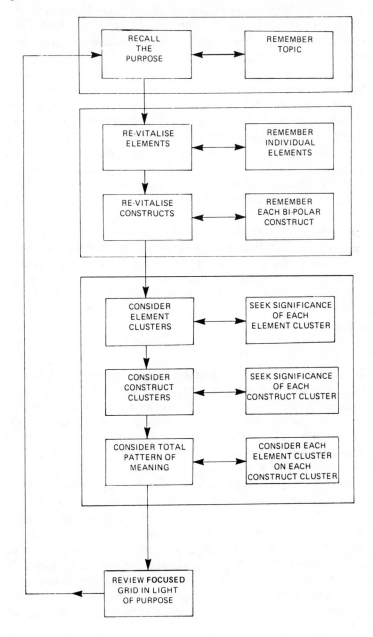

coherent pattern of relationships and meaning. The meaning is not in the grid; it is in the head of the subject. This is why grids seem both exciting and yet somehow rather more diluted than one would expect. A case study has been discussed to illustrate this use of the grid. This second part of the chapter compares and contrasts the results of the grids elicited from the nine students in the learning-to-learn group.

When the teacher is aware of a general issue or problem among a group of students, grids elicited from them can be used *to map out the extent and nature of the issues involved.* The grid has certain experiential advantages over the more seemingly objective techniques of questionnaire and semantic differential. But it is rather unwieldy as a group or comparative device. When grids are used in which everybody uses the 'same' elements (i.e. the same form of words at the top of the grid), it is possible to use factor analytical and cluster analysis methods to compare the constructs of different groups (Thomas, McKnight and Shaw, 1976). But when the elements within a given universe of discourse are unique to each subject, a less mathematical procedure has to be adopted. Here, the question is how to explore nine such grids and to discover what they imply as a whole.

Construing the Construings

This is achieved by construing the construings. It as well to make this method explicit. The procedure of construing another's construing is the nature of all human communication. Conversation works or founders on how well each conversationalist is able to test the validity of his interpretations, and upon how well each is able to tolerate and recognise the inevitable distorting selection and changes in emphasis that go on during an exchange.

Interviewing can make this process more explicit. The skill of an interviewer lies largely in focusing the discussion upon relevant issues without over-distorting the interviewer's thoughts and feelings about the topics discussed. Coding of interview material, the process by which the transcript of an interview is cut up into items and each item is classified, comes close to making the construing of construing explicit. But even skilled interviewers may attribute a false objectivity to the resulting numbers.

In the grids used in this study the elements were individually elicited giving 102 different experiences from nine subjects. The grids were first examined as a whole to get a feel for their content and structure. The elements and constructs elicited were thoroughly examined and an estimate of the range of constructs made. To give a flavour of the procedure, this is now briefly described. Towards the end of the chapter a detailed step-by-step guide is given.

The participant-investigators in this study shared their grid elicitation experiences to give a greater depth of understanding of the rather bare words used to describe the incidents in the element descriptions. For example:

> Guy in park
> Splitting up
> Reading when ill

were all shared in a ten-minute conversation. No attempt is made here to give more adequate descriptions, but the whole usefulness of the grid depends upon the depth of understanding brought to its interpretation.

Each of the 102 elements were written on a card and distributed 'randomly' on a large plain surface (floor or table). Investigators sorted them into groupings or clusters keeping notes and continually re-distributing the cards. The notes were then compared to evoke a series of 'investigator constructs'. These emerged from the interaction of the investigators' agreed purpose and the free-flowing data.

After considerable exploration and discussion six shared investigator constructs were agreed from within a much more varied range of possibilities. Some constructs were discarded because they were too vague, others because there were not enough elements that warranted their use, whilst others were discarded because although interesting and related to the data, they appeared unlikely to yield evidence related to the purpose of the investigation. When the six 'investigator constructs' were agreed, the investigators individually applied each one in turn to all 102 elements. The separate construings of the investigators were then compared and 'disagreements' discussed and re-negotiated. This process led to a refining and some redefining of investigator constructs: For example, the original description of:

'emotional   vs   cognitive learning'

was refined into a triple categorisation:

'attitude, intellectual and social skill learning'

and an originally:

'challenging positively   vs   challenging negatively'

becomes:

'good experience   vs   bad experience'
(anxious and disruptive)

Some of the individual elements also offered problems: for example,

is 'leaving school' a 'school' experience?

General agreement among investigators was arrived at fairly easily for most elements and after negotiation, unanimously for each element on each construct. The subject's own construing of his elements as revealed in each FOCUSed grid was always used as a guide to the implied personal meaning of an element.

Some Results

Table 18.1 shows the six investigator constructs and a raw frequency count of the number of items, i.e. elements in each sub-category.

Since the constructs were invented to differentiate among the items great circumspection should be exercised in attributing too much meaning to these absolute numbers. Category definitions tend to have been set to distribute the items fairly evenly among them. However, the proportion of C1 'school' (i.e. educational) items (28 per cent) is rather low given the opening remarks of the elicitation conversation. And the proportion of C6 intellectual (19 per cent) as against attitudinal learning (66 per cent) is perhaps also surprisingly low. It should be remembered that these items represent 'what have been important learning experiences in my life'. Most of the other frequency counts are

Table 18.1: Constructs for Six Investigators and a Frequency Count of the Number of Elements in each Sub-category

Dimension 1

Category	Freq.	Abrev.
School[a]	28	Sch
Peers	19	Prs
Events	17	Evts
Media	16	Mda
Family	13	Fam
Miscell.	9	Msc
total	102	

Dimension 2

Category	Freq.	Abrev.
Learning alone	49	Al
Learning with others	53	Oth
total	102	

Dimension 3

Category	Freq.	Abrev.
Felt free during learning	53	Free
Neutral	14	N
Felt constrained during learning	35	Constr.
total	102	

Dimension 4

Category	Freq.	Abrev.
Good Experience (exciting)	55	Exc.
Neutral	5	N
Bad experience (anxious and disruptive)	42	anx
total	102	

Dimension 5

Category	Freq.	Abrev.
Learning; positively valued retrospectively	54	V+
Neutral	23	N
Learning-negatively valued retrospectively	25	V-
total	102	

Dimension 6

Category	Freq.	Abrev.
Intellectual Learning	19[a]	Intell
Social skill Learning	16	Soc
Attitudinal Learning	67	
total	102	

unexceptional. The neutral 23 per cent in C5 include many experiences which had to be endured. They were neither positive nor negative, but they were significant.

It is the relationships between frequencies of the items in the investigators dimensions of construing that yield some interesting results. For example, C2 relates to C5 as shown in Table 18.2.

Table 18.2: Negative vs Positive by Valued Learning Events Compared in Terms of Learning Alone vs Learning with Others

	Negatively valued	Neutral	Positively valued	Total
Learning alone	19*	12	18	49
Learning with others	6	11	36*	53
Total	25	23	54	102

Thus, on the whole 'learning with others' leads to much more learning which is 'positively valued in retrospect' than does 'learning alone', which produces as much 'negatively valued learning' as 'positively valued'.

Table 18.3 shows an equal distribution of positively and negatively valued events for attitudinal learning whereas intellectual and social skills learning are more positively valued.

Table 18.3: Negative vs Positively Valued Learning Compared with Intellectual vs Social Skills vs Attitudinal

	Negatively valued	Neutral	Positively valued	Total
Intellectual	2	3	14	19
Social skill	1	1	14	16
Attitudinal	22	19	26	67
Total	25	23	54	102

Table 18.4 shows an interesting characteristic of this *attitudinal learning* (22). Much of the learning done 'alone' was experienced negatively whereas the positively valued learning was done with 'others'.

Good, exciting experiences tend to produce learning which is positively valued in retrospect; and bad, anxious and disruptive experiences tend to lead to learning which is negatively valued in restrospect as shown in Table 18.5.

Table 18.4: A Comparison of Positively and Negatively Valued Events with 'Learning Alone and with Others for Attitudinal Learning'

	Negatively valued	Neutral	Positively valued	Total
Alone	17*	9	10	36
With others	5	10	16*	31
Total	22	19	26	67

Table 18.5: Positive and Negative Events Compared for 'Anxious and Exciting'

	Negatively valued	Neutral	Positively valued	Total
Exciting	0	4	51*	55
Neutral	1	4	0	5
Anxious	24*	15	3	42
Total	25	23	54	102

The comparisons which can be made are endless. There are 15 comparisons between two constructs and 25 between sets of three constructs, but as the comparisons become more differentiated the number of items in each cell drops, and the implications become much more dubious.

Experience of Formal Education

Comparing School (Educational) Experiences with all Others, i.e. C1 vs C5

When the school learning experiences are compared with other events a number of interesting comments on these students' attitudes towards academic learning can be made. Table 18.6 shows that 'school' has an exceptionally high proportion of negatively valued learning.

Table 18.7 shows that there is no clear indication that negatively valued learning takes place whilst people feel alone, and positively valued learning takes place whilst they feel themselves to be working with others.

Table 18.6: School and Other Events Compared for Positively and Negatively Valued Learning

	Negatively valued	Neutral	Positively valued	Total
School	13*	4	11	28
Peers	3	5	11	19
Events	3	3	11	17
Media	1	4	11	16
Family	1	5	7	13
Miscellaneous	4	2	3	9
Total	25	23	54	102

Table 18.7: School Events: 'Learning Alone vs Learning with Others' Compared for 'Positively vs Negatively Valued Learning'

	Negatively valued	Neutral	Positively valued	Total
Alone	12*	2	2	16
With others	1	2	9*	12
Total	13	4	11	28

Within school, two thirds of all retrospectively important learning is attitudinal and nearly three-fifths of this is negatively valued.

Table 18.8: Negative Attitudes to Learning: School Events: 'Type of Learning' Compared for 'Positively vs Negatively Valued'

	Negatively valued	Neutral	Positively valued	Total
Intellectual	2	1	2	5
Social skill	–	–	5	5
Attitudinal	11*	3	4	18
Total	13	4	11	28

This is emphasised when we compared 'school' with 'remainder' on the attitudinal elements. Table 18.9 shows that when learning alone three-quarters of the 'school' events are negative whilst half the 'remainder' are positive.

If we compare 'learning alone' with 'learning with others' (Table 18.10), obviously these students remembered educational experience as feeling 'learning alone' (16) more often than as 'with others' (12).

Table 18.9: Negative Attitudes to Learning Alone in School

	Negatively valued	Neutral	Positively valued	Total
School	11*	3	4	18
Remainder	11	16	22*	49
Total	22	19	26	67

Table 18.10: Comparison of 'Learning Alone' with 'Learning with Others' — a Three-way Classification of Learning Events

'Alone'	Negatively valued	Neutral	Positively valued	Total
School	12*	2	2	16
Remainder	7	10	16*	33
Total	19	12	18	49
'With others'				
School	1	2	9	12
Remainder	5	9	27	41
Total	6	11	36	53

Finally, if we compare 'school' with 'peers' for all learning experiences (Table 18.11), it is obvious that school produces more negatively valued experience. It was no wonder that these students were alienated from formal education.

Table 18.11: Comparison of 'Learning in School' with 'Learning with Peers' for Positively and Negatively Valued Learning

	Negatively valued	Neutral	Positively valued	Total
School	13	4	11	28
Peers	3	5	11	19
Total	16	9	22	47

One should be careful in drawing conclusions from grid studies. They are about people's thoughts and feelings. These do not necessarily reflect what happened; only how it was and is experienced. But a systematic use of grids can reveal the scope of the topic or problem in a group. Reference back and forth between group findings and individual grids ensures reliability. The pitfalls of statistical studies can be avoided since individual grids can be used to appreciate connections between averages; and individual differences can be avoided since individual grids can be used to appreciate connections between averages and individual differences. To summarise, the grids reveal how each individual thinks and feels about his or her learning. The trend is for school or educational experiences to have been *bad*. They are overwhelmingly attitudinal as against intellectual. These bad school experiences are remembered as occurring when the students felt alone and anxious. Learning experiences outside education are more positively valued.

A Guide for Construing the Contents of a Group of Grids

It is assumed that elements and constructs have been individually elicited, as illustrated by the study reported. The first stages in comparing grids is to treat them holistically:

(1) Count the number of elements and constructs in each grid.
(2) Order the grids by noting the element number and the construct number for each grid.
(3) Grid structure: Note the pattern (or structure) as revealed by each FOCUSed grid.

Once a holistic comparison has been made, a more detailed comparison is possible.

Constructs

Stage 1 Write each pole description on a separate card, keeping a record of their original source on the other side of each card.
Stage 2 Do a free sort of the cards keeping notes about groupings. (Let the data produce the groups.)
Stage 3 Refer back to the original grids and elicitation notes to clarify ideas about the meaning of individual constructs to the participant subject (if possible discuss them with him or her at this stage).
Stage 4 List possible investigator constructs.

Elements

Stage 5 Write all elements on separate cards.
Stage 6 Do a sort of the cards, keeping notes about groupings. Try to let the data fall into the groups created in stage 4, but be prepared to add groups if this becomes necessary. Bear in mind the purpose of the comparisons.

Add constructs ⎫
Drop constructs ⎬ to suit data and purpose

Stage 7 Refer back to the original grids and elicitation notes to clarify ideas about the meaning of individual elements to the participant subject (if possible, discuss them with him or her at this stage.)
Stage 8 Revise list of all possible investigator constructs.
Stage 9 Assign all elements to all investigator constructs.
Stage 10 Review the construct descriptions, in the light of effort to assign all elements.
Stage 11 Finalise investigator constructs.
Stage 12 Finalise assigning elements to investigator constructs.
Stage 13 Use coded cards to explore relations between investigator constructs. Write down 2×2 tables.
Stage 14 Review tables for interest and relevance in the light of the purpose of the comparison.

Implications

This study illustrates:

(1) How repertory grids can produce data that can be used for individual tutoring, to encourage reflection and review of a given topic, or universe of discourse.
(2) How a group of grids can be compared to examine an issue which is considered to be of importance.

The procedures described are essentially content-free and can be used variously to explore learning contexts. In the study reported, 'learning events' were taken as the elements representing the universe of discourse to be construed and compared. In other CSHL research projects, 'purposes for reading', 'learning strategies', 'learning outcomes', 'books I read', 'command words in exam questions', 'lectures', 'essays', 'learning resources', 'learning difficulties', and 'people who teach me', 'pupils/students I teach' have been selected as the universe of discourse to be investigated. Again, topics such as maths, chemistry, art objects, statistics, PE apparatus, botanical specimens, rocks, buildings, stories and even musical scores have been used to elicit constructs. The possibilities are endless. Ultimately the onus is on teachers and learners together to recruit the repertory grid as a tool for exploring the whole context of learning, and to evaluate its usefulness in terms of their own needs and purposes. This fundamentally challenges the responsibilities of the teacher, and for those who so choose, it can serve to extend their skills and add a new, rich and exciting dimensions to the teaching/learning enterprise.

References

Thomas, L.F. (1976) 'The FOCUS Technique: "Focusing the Repertory Grid" ', CSHL Technical Paper, Brunel University, Uxbridge

—— (1978) 'Conversational Techniques: A Personal Construct Approach to Learning in Education, Training and Therapy', CSHL Symposium at Proceedings of the Second International Congress on Personal Construct Theory, Fay Fransella (ed.), *Personal Construct Psychology 1977*, Academic Press, London

—— (1981) 'CSHL Reflective Learning Software', CSHL, Brunel University, Uxbridge

——, McKnight, C. and Shaw, M.L. (1976) 'Grids and Group Structure', paper read at Social Psychology Section of BPS Conference, University of Surrey, CSHL Paper, Brunel University, Uxbridge

—— and Harri-Augstein, S. (1985) *Self-organised Learning: Foundations of a Conversational Science for Psychology*, Routledge & Kegan Paul, London

19 DEPENDENCY GRIDS: AN ILLUSTRATION OF THEIR USE IN AN EDUCATIONAL SETTING

Bryn D. Davis

Introduction: Dependencies and Resources

The very structure of society is based on relationships between its component parts. These parts include people and the situations within which they exist, as well as the physical aspects of the environment. In particular, it is relationships between individuals which provide the cohesion necessary for social organisation and intercourse. As Kelly (1955, p. 914) argues, the adult individual is concerned to develop role relationships in order to distribute his dependencies, which can be defined perhaps as the extent or kind of need that an individual has for others.

Maturation through any process of development, education or socialisation, for example, involves the discrimination between dependencies or types of need and allocation of these among the available resources. This involves in its turn an ability to recognise and differentiate between dependencies. Their effective dispersion is an important part of the process of developing an adequate or required view of the world.

The dependency constructs of children or the neophyte tend to be relatively impermeable and pre-emptive. This simplistic use of resources, where needs are allocated to the one and only resource, changes with experience and learning. As the individual develops, or as the educational or socialisation process is successful, there is greater discrimination and a more sophist-icated system of resource allocation emerges. The greater discrimination is also related to the changes in need or dependency, and to the availability of resources that occur during the experience.

Thus, any attempt to study interpersonal relationships, social structure or organisational functioning should properly be concerned with dependencies and resources, and their construing by the individuals or groups concerned. Kelly recognised the ubiquity of dependence — the second volume of his 1955 book can be seen as a dissertation on this subject — but felt that the issue was not that people have dependencies, but that it was the way in which they deal with them. 'Dependency', he argued, 'is not in itself an unhealthy state of affairs' (p. 671) adding 'It is the dispersion of dependencies that must be emphasised' (p. 914).

In adulthood, after the normal processes of socialisation in childhood and adolescence, change is essentially superficial (Becker, 1964). Such changes can be seen as situational adjustment, a process more flexible than adult-role learning as described by Brim (1960). Becker emphasises the importance of the situational structure and the relationships within it. Also important is the degree of commitment to it, and the sense of responsibility for it.

The stability of later life comes from the continuity over time of the significant others in the individual's life — those to whom dependencies are allocated (Brim, 1960). This interaction with others, in terms of dependencies, is important also in the development of the self in relation to others. This leads to the concept of 'self as process — becoming' (Glaser and Strauss, 1964).

So far in this introduction the relationships between dependencies and resources has been assumed to involve people as resources (role relationships). These must, of course, usually be seen as the key aspects of an individual's resource systems. However, it is possible to identify three classes of resource: physical, social and personal (Kelly, 1955). Physical resources include such things as toys, equipment (personal or communal), technology, wealth. Personal resources include skills, intellect, knowledge, health. This latter class of resources introduces an aspect of dependency the study of which can be of great value. This is the question of independence, or the use of self, or personal attributes as resources for coping with needs or situations.

The process of socialisation involves the development of different social selves, with changes in their nature and integration. As Schein (1971) has argued, these social selves are constructed to deal with the social environment. The self in a way may view these social selves, or situational aspects of self, as constructs or as construed events, allowing the individual to compare self or a particular social self with others perceived to be 'like me in character; or like I would like to be in character' (Bannister and Fransella, 1971). The use of self can be extended in this way to include temporal or ideal aspects — 'self as I was'; 'self as I want to be'. This point is discussed and illustrated in a later section.

The nature of dependencies, and the resource system that is developed for them will vary from individual to individual, and for any individual over time and over different aspects of his life and place in the social structure. The development of techniques to reveal this resource system, by Kelly, was with reference to the therapeutic role in the clinical setting. There the concern was with facilitating the development of a more effective system of resources, and of helping the client to cope with the anxiety and stress which may be associated with that process. The same approach can be seen as readily applicable to counselling roles, as in marriage guidance, social work or the student/tutor relationship for example. However, as well as being of great potential value in these professional settings, the study of systems of resource allocation, and of ways of facilitating or manipulating these, offers research potential. The next section of this chapter looks in some detail at these techniques, with illustrations from recent work in an educational setting.

Techniques

As Kelly puts it (1955, p.312), 'Everyone is dependent; the problem is to make appropriate allocation of one's dependencies'. He describes a method for the elicitation of problem situations, which asks the respondent to nominate personal problems. 'Everyone faces some personal problems at one time or another in his life. Here are some very general types of problem that everyone comes up against in one way or another' (1955, p. 313). Sample situations are then given, concerning for example, the kind of job or vocation to go into, or the kind of difficulty experienced in understanding how to get along with people of the opposite sex. The respondent is asked to identify the situation by year and place. Kelly offers 22 sample-problem situations. This technique ensures the personal relevance of the problem situations.

However, alternative procedures can be used: counselling

interviews, biographical data such as diaries. In research settings problems may be generated or collected by the researcher and then used experimentally. Such research may involve recruits, or children in an 'if this then what' setting, exploring, for example, moral issues or management ability.

The following procedure was used to devise a list of problem situations which could be presented to each member of a group of student nurses, and at the same time have personal relevance. Each student was asked to list up to five situations that she had found a problem during her first year of training. A list of 152 situations was obtained. After group discussions and the eliminations a final list of twelve problem situations was agreed, and a grid was prepared, using as elements a list of potential resource people from the nurse-training milieu.

The Situational Dependency Grid

The Situational Dependency Grid (Sitsgrid) suggested by Kelly (1955, p. 312) is a development of the Repertory Grid (Repgrid) where the constructs are replaced by situations which are problematical to the subject. The role titles were those defined by the structure of the organisation, a set of people defined quite narrowly in time and place. The Sitsgrid is completed by referring each problem to each element in turn, and indication made as to which would be used as situational resources. The indication may be by ranking the list of elements for each problem, or by rating each element for each problem (Figure 19.1).

Analysis of Sitsgrids

The matrices produced by the student nurses in allocating problem situations to various significant others are amenable to a form of analysis similar to one advocated and demonstrated by Kelly as a non-parametric factor analysis (1955, p. 277). The form of analysis used in the present example involves a computer program devised by Slater (1977). This analysis provides a picture of the relationships between the various role titles and the problems, from a principal components analysis (PCA).

INGRID is a program which undertakes a transposition of a graded grid into a D matrix, where the score in each cell is the raw score minus the mean score for that row. The program then undertakes a PCA of the D matrix, taking these adjustments into

Figure 19.1: Grid A, Completed by Student Nurse A at the Beginning of her Training

	Self as I am	Student nurse	Registrar	Ward sister	Allocation Officer	Houseman	Patient	Staff nurse	Nursing Auxillary	Clinical tutor	Tutor	Self as I want to be
Death	✓			✓							✓	
Old people			✓		✓							✓
Unsocial hours								✓		✓		
People in pain		✓		✓								
Acquiring knowledge				✓						✓		✓
Difficult patients		✓			✓	✓	✓	✓				
Fear of inflicting pain				✓					✓			✓
Battered babies			✓	✓		✓						
Bedpans	✓							✓				
Being in charge	✓	✓									✓	
Discipline						✓		✓				✓
Fatigue	✓		✓	✓		✓						

Figure 19.2: Grid B, Completed at the Beginning of her Training by Student Nurse B

	Self as I am	Student nurse	Registrar	Ward sister	Allocation Officer	Houseman	Patient	Staff nurse	Nursing Auxillary	Clinical tutor	Tutor	Self as I want to be
Death				✓				✓			✓	
Old people				✓	✓			✓				
Unsocial hours				✓				✓		✓	✓	
People in pain				✓							✓	
Acquiring knowledge				✓				✓				
Difficult patients				✓							✓	
Fear of inflicting pain		✓		✓				✓				
Battered babies				✓							✓	
Bedpans				✓				✓				
Being in charge		✓									✓	
Discipline												✓
Fatigue								✓			✓	

account. The PCA produces clusters of situations and resource people which had been graded in a similar manner, ordered according to the proportion of the variance accounted for by each clustering. Each person (or situation) is weighted in each cluster (called a component) according to the adjusted scores and the degree to which its adjusted score correlates with other situations or people for that component.

Analysis

The analysis of the Sitsgrid A (Figure 19.1) follows the procedure described above. A comparison, Grid B (Figure 19.2), is also analysed to show the different structures that may occur and reflect the patterns of dependency in similar situations as seen by different participants.

Principal Components. The components accounting for most of the variance in the two grids are shown in Table 19.1. The relative proportions allocated to the first few components reflects the simplicity or complexity of the structure within each grid. Thus, Grid A, showing a relatively complex resource system, has low proportions of the variance accounted for by the main components, whereas the opposite is the case with Grid B. These differences may be related to the relative strengths and weaknesses in the two systems, Grid B perhaps being a more vulnerable system. Grid A incidently indicates a degree of independence as well as dependence. This will be discussed further below.

Table 19.3 and 19.4 show the composition of the principal components from Grids A and B, and again this reflects the relative complexity or simplicity, and independence or dependence of the two resource systems. The most highly loaded elements and problems are indicated.

Important Elements. Those elements accounting for most of the variance in the two grids are shown in Table 19.2. The relative simplicity or complexity of the system is demonstrated. Also the importance of self in Grid A is highlighted. The vulnerability in Grid B is related to the likelihood of non-availability of the resource people, particularly ward sister and tutor. The latter, in many instances, is rarely seen by the student nurse in the wards where the problems are most likely to occur. The ward sister is

Table 19.1: PCA Analysis of Grids A and B Showing the Proportion of the Variance Accounted for by the Main Components

Grid A		Grid B	
Component	% variance	Component	% variance
1	29.58	1	54.98
2	18.79	2	20.70
3	15.96		
4	12.20		75.68
	76.53		

Table 19.2: Proportion of the Variance Accounted for by the Main Elements in Grids A and B

Grid A		Grid B	
Element	% variance	Element	% variance
Ward sister	14.64	Ward sister	25.76
Self as I am	11.41	Tutor	21.21
Staff nurse	10.76	Staff nurse	19.7
Self to be	10.76		
Houseman	10.11		
Registrar	8.17		

Table 19.3: Elements and Problems Loaded Highly on the First Three Components, Grid A

COMPONENT 1

Elements	Problems
Ward sister	Fatigue
Staff nurse	Battered babies
Houseman	Old people
Self as I want to be	

COMPONENT 2 (Bipolar)

Self as I am	Death
Self as I want to be	
/	/
	Discipline
	Old people

COMPONENT 3 (Bipolar)

Ward sister	Acquiring knowledge
	Fear of inflicting pain
/	/
Self as I am	Bedpans
Staff nurse	
Houseman	

Table 19.4: Elements and Problems Loaded Highly on the First Two Components, Grid B

COMPONENT 1

Elements	*Problems*
Ward sister	All except
Tutor	discipline
Staff nurse	

COMPONENT 2 (Bipolar)

Tutor	
	Being in charge
	Battered babies
	Difficult patients
	People in pain
/	/
Staff nurse	Old people
	Fear of inflicting pain
	Acquiring knowledge
	Bedpans

also frequently occupied with administration which prevents her from joining in direct patient care, in contact with the learners. Thus, student B has only the staff nurse to rely on in practice, and seems unable to be self-reliant, in the way that student A does. Also the houseman and the registrar are more frequently in contact with the student in direct patient care, than perhaps is the ward sister.

Those concerned with the progress of the students and their support during training could obtain valuable insights into the relative dependencies of their charges from such information as that provided by these grids.

Further Refinements

Use of Self as an Element

When exploring the range of dependency, an important factor may involve the capabilities of the subjects themselves. The inclusion of self as an element can put the significant others and their relative importance into a clearer perspective. What might seem a vulnerable system of resource people may be strengthened when self is included. The reverse may hold of course, or the allocation of problems to self may be unrealistic or over-ambitious, in the light of experience or relative maturity.

The element self may be extended in time to include, for example 'self as I am'; 'self as I want to be' (ideal self) ; 'self as I was when . . .', depending on the circumstances of the inquiry. Study of the element self over time can indicate changes as a result of therapy, education, socialisation, maturation. This can also be demonstrated with respect to changes in the relative significance of the other elements, but the inclusion of self gives a more dramatic picture of personal growth and development (or the opposite).

In the grids demonstrated above, the elements 'self as I am' and 'self as I want to be' were included. The aim was to obtain a picture of student nurses, becoming nurses as they coped with (or did not), various problems identified by them. As can be seen in the completed Grid A, the elements 'self as I am', and 'self as I want to be' play a part in the resource system, whereas in Grid B they do not (Figures 19.1, 19.2). This is demonstrated more clearly in the breakdown of the PCA where those problems allocated to and correlating significantly with self are shown (Table 19.3). This student nurse at the beginning of her training already shows a fair degree of independence, and also shows an awareness of her future self. The analysis of Grid B shows a student nurse who does not show this independence or awareness. Further interpretation is not recommended without reference to the students themselves, or to follow-up grids to monitor progress over time.

Element Profiles

In the study of a person's situational resources and their dependencies, it is sometimes advantageous to study one or a few elements in detail, with respect to the range of problem situations. Those problems for which a particular element is scored highly on the grid may be considered for example. However, it may be difficult on occasion to determine which of the problems are associated with which element, and which problem is more associated with a particular element than another. It may be necessary to consider the scoring in each cell, for any problem, along the row of elements, but also, the relative scoring of each of the problems for any particular element. Thus, the highest score in the row for a problem may refer to an element for which that score is not particularly high; other problems are scored more highly for that element. Which problem is more important for that element, the one scoring highest in the element column, or the one with its highest score along the row, in that element's column? A similar problem occurs when grids are graded dichotomously. In any column there will be dichotomous scores for problems, where there are many ticks in the row, and where there are relatively few ticks. It is important to discriminate between dependency for problems with many resources and dependency for problems with few resources.

The program INGRID offers as an option, the calculation of an index of the relationship between particular problems and elements, indicated by a cosine which utilises this two way perspective of the score in each cell, whether dichotomous, rated or ranked (Slater, 1977). Using the cosine as a correlation it is possible to assess the probability of that degree of correlation occurring by chance, with degrees of freedom being calculated as the smallest 'n' in the grid (number of problems or number of elements) minus one. With reference to suitable tables, the degree of correlation necessary to achieve a level of significance, at, say, P = <0.05 can be found. Those problems correlating with the selected element at that level or higher are then identified.

This procedure provides a statistical measure for making decision about the relative importance of the problems for a particular element, or vice versa. However, it must not be forgotten that there may be important psychological, personal, professional or research reasons for making decisions, depending on the grid and its purpose.

In Tables 19.5 and 19.6 are shown element profiles for those elements accounting for the most variance in Grids A and B respectively. Of particular interest, in Table 19.5, are the profiles of elements 'self as I am' and 'self as I want to be'. Also by comparing 'self as I want to be' with other elements in terms of their profiles, it is possible to pinpoint role models and to follow this up in later grids. Thus, in Table 19.5, it can be seen that both ward sister and houseman appear to be role models in that they share problems in common with 'self as I want to be'. In this grid analysis it can also be seen that there is an articulated system of resources, with each element being associated with a different range of problems, although there are a few held in common (e.g. battered babies and fatigue being shared between ward sister and houseman). With Grid B there is a more monolithic structure (Table 19.6), with the three main resources

Table 19.5: Element Profiles, Grid A

Elements	Problems
Ward sister	Death
	People in pain
	Acquiring knowledge
	Fear of inflicting pain
	Battered babies
	Fatigue
Self as I am	Death
	Bedpans
	Being in charge
Staff nurse	Unsocial hours
	Bedpans
Self as I want to be	Old people
	Acquiring knowledge
	Fear of inflicting pain
	Discipline
Houseman	Old people
	Battered babies
	Discipline
	Fatigue

Table 19.6: Element Profiles, Grid B

Elements	Problems
Ward sister	Death
	Old people
	Unsocial hours
	People in pain
	Acquiring knowledge
	Difficult patients
	Fear of inflicting pain
	Battered babies
Tutor	Death
	Unsocial hours
	People in pain
	Difficult patients
	Battered babies
	Being in charge
	Fatigue
Staff nurse	Death
	Old people
	Unsocial hours
	Acquiring knowledge
	Fear of inflicting pain
	Bedpans
	Fatigue

having most of the problems in common, and thus not being clearly discriminated.

The analysis of a single grid studied in isolation is difficult if not dangerous to interpret. What is best offered the person completing the grid in terms of counselling, or therapy, say, must depend on other aspects of the situation. Some of these may be revealed in the analysis of an associated Reptest and grid. If the same elements are used as in the Sitsgrid, then the nature and scoring of the constructs elicited may help to interpret the pattern of dependence that resulted from the Sitsgrid as shown below.

Construct Profiles

The analysis of Repgrids, completed by the student nurses who completed the Sitsgrids A and B, produced cosines of the scores for constructs in relation to each element. Using the procedure described above, those constructs correlating significantly with particular elements can be found, and construct profiles created. Tables 19.7 and 19.8 show such profiles for elements from grids A and B. In particular support for the role modelling identified in Grid A (Table 19.5) is provided by the use of the construct 'I have the same ambition'. The importance of the availability and accessibility of resource people is also highlighted in both grids by the use of constructs 'come into contact with', in Grid A (Table 19.7), and 'work together' in Grid B (Table 19.8).

With respect to both element profiles and construct profiles, the provision of a statistically based reason for decisions about relationships between problems/constructs and elements does not mean that there may not be other reasons for considering such relationships important. The client or the nature of the investigation will itself help to determine which factors should be considered in such decision making.

Table 19.7: Construct Profiles, Grid A

Elements	Constructs
Elements	*Constructs*
Ward sister	
Concerned with nurses' progress	
	I have the same ambition
Staff nurse	On the ward
	Taken for granted
	Come into contact with
Houseman	Superior to nurses
	Come into contact with

Table 19.8: Construct Profiles, Grid B

Elements	Constructs
Ward sister	More experienced
	Qualified
	Senior
	More responsibility
Tutor	More experienced
	Senior
Staff nurse	More responsibility
	In charge
	Work on ward
	Work together

Conclusion

It has been the concern of this all too brief chapter to show how the suggestion of Kelly (1955) that client dependency is an important consideration, can be put into practice using his proposed Situational Dependency Grid. Examples have been given to demonstrate the technique in an educational setting. Further examples and discussion can be found in Davis (1983). Other recent applications have been by Henderson (1984), with undergraduates, and Latham (1983), with mothers of young babies. These small-scale but important studies have produced information from Sitsgrids which would otherwise have been very difficult and time-consuming to collect and evaluate.

The concept of dependency has also been extended somewhat by the consideration of resources and resourcefulness. Kelly defined constructs as being related to action, to ways of dealing with people and events. If the application of Repgrids or Sitsgrids is used to type or categorise those who complete them, then the essence of the Theory of Personal Constructs would be lost. Dependency is not a quality or a totality which reflects a status, but should be seen as a plurality of dependencies which show how the individual evaluates his or her resources. When these include self, then the dependencies show how resourceful the individual sees him or her self.

This puts the individual in a more active orientation, in that it emphasises the grid as being a view of or a window on the world, with the client describing the scenery. It also recalls the description by Kelly (1970) of man as an experimenter. A situation can be seen as the social laboratory in which relationships in the social structure of the individual's world can be studied. A range of situations offers a range of linked experiments in which the self or various social selves may also participate. In therapy, education, counselling or research, the individual, under guidance can, with grids completed over time, reveal or manipulate his dependencies, and also himself — himself as part of the social process within which he lives and has his being.

Acknowledgements

Some of the material discussed in this chapter was developed with the help of a DHSS Nursing Research Fellowship.

References

Bannister, D. and Fransella, F. (1971) *Inquiring Man*, Penguin, Harmondsworth

Becker, H.S. (1964) 'Personal Change in Adult Life', *Sociometry, 27*, 40-53

Brim, O. (1960) 'Personality Development as Role-learning', in I. Iscoe and H. Stevenson (eds), *Personality Development in Children*, University of Texas Press, Austin, pp. 127-59.

Davis, B.D. (1983) 'A Repertory Grid Study of Formal and Informal Aspects of Student Nurse Training', unpublished PhD thesis, London University

Glaser, B.G. and Strauss, A. (1964) 'Awareness Contexts and Social Interaction', *American Sociological Review, 29*, 669-78

Henderson, M.J. (1984) 'Students and Their Problems: To Whom Would They Turn, a Dependency Grid Study', unpublished MPhil thesis, Edinburgh University

Kelly, G.A. (1955) *The Psychology of Personal Constructs* vols 1 and 2, Norton, New York

—— (1970) 'Behaviour is an Experiment' in D. Bannister (ed.), *Perspectives in Personal Construct Theory*, Academic Press, London

Latham, R.K. (1983) 'Parent's Questions Pertaining to Their Neurologically Impaired Children', unpublished MSc educational psychology dissertation, Edinburgh University

Schein, E.H. (1971) 'The Individual, the Organisation and the Carers; a Conceptual Scheme', *Journal of Applied Behavioural Science, 7*, 401-26

Slater, P. (1977) *The Measurement of Interpersonal Space by Grid Technique, vols 1 and 2*, Wiley, Chichester

20 USING GRIDS IN VOCATIONAL GUIDANCE

Robert Davies

Introduction

Vocational guidance seems destined to become more 'occupational', i.e. not more concerned with jobs but with how individuals structure their time. Hepworth (1980) found that the best predictor of mental health in unemployed men was whether or not they felt that their time was occupied. Hepworth concludes that, if unemployment continues to rise, one purpose of education should be to develop resourcefulness, so that people can find out what they want to do with their time and be able to do it.

This chapter describes the advantages of using grids in guidance. I hope it also demonstrates the possibilities afforded by grid techniques in helping people decide on 'occupations' which may or may not have anything to do with employment.

The Psychology of Vocational Choice

Two different traditions have developed in the theory and practice of vocational guidance. The differential approach uses mainly objective measures such as aptitude tests, interest guides and profiles in an attempt to simply match an available person to an available job. The developmental approach seeks to understand the growth and development of an individual's vocational maturity and ability to make career decisions. Repertory grid techniques have proved most attractive within the developmental tradition due to the extreme subjectivity of the technique and its underlying theory. This section offers a brief introduction to three of the most influential developmentalist theories, which should point up the relevance of Construct Theory to this type of thinking.

Ginzberg, *et al.*, (1951) suggested that occupational choice was a process beginning almost at birth, and potentially continuing throughout life. Three periods were differentiated within this process, *viz.* fantasy choices (pre-11 years), tentative choices (11-17 years), realistic choices (17 years plus). During the tentative period the person experiments with choices based on their interests, capacities and values. The realistic period is one when the person explores alternatives, progressively crystallising and delimiting his or her choices. The personal-construct perspective would see both these periods as crucial to the development of effective and realistic construct systems. Exploring alternatives is an obvious example of the 'personal scientist' approach originally described by Kelly. Ginzberg *et al.* went on to stress the importance of compromise during the occupational-choice process. The individual tries to choose a career in which as much use as possible is made of his or her interests and capacities in a manner which will satisfy as many of his or her values and goals as possible. The individual must weigh up the opportunities and limitations of the environment and assess the extent to which they will contribute to, or detract from, his or her chances of gaining the maximum degree of satisfaction in work and in life. Again, it should be obvious that accurate construal is essential to the making of an adequate choice.

Donald Super (1965) criticised the description by Ginzberg *et al.* of the choice process because it failed to emphasise the importance of adjustment. For Super, the individual is born with 'neural and endocrine tendencies or potentialities' (1965, p. 212), whilst the environment contains other potentialities and tendencies which are independent of the individual. The interaction between the tendencies and potentialities of person and environment constitute the process we call 'socialisation'. Interaction becomes the central device of Super's model of vocational development. This interaction may be intra-individual (self-exploration), or individual/environmental (reality testing). In both instances, development of the self-concept results. The use of repertory grids in clinical settings has demonstrated that a person's concept of self is a truly dynamic construction dependent upon the way he or she construes others as well as his or her view of self. According to Super's interaction model, reality testing begins early in life when the individual first begins to differentiate between 'self' and 'other' as part of the socialisation process. Also, a person's needs interact with his or her experiences to produce interests (if a child finds satisfaction for a particular need through playing a particular game, that game or games in general may become an interest which offers that satisfaction on tap); this process of interest development has its own built-in procedure for reality testing. To the personal-construct psychologist the term 'need' is itself a construct: Kelly stated that a person's processes are 'channelised' by the way in which they anticipate events, and that when confronted by the possibility for choice the individual will opt for that alternative which fits best within his or her existing system. Thus, we may consider this process of reality testing as simply a specific example of constructive alternativism (see Kelly (1963) for fuller description of Personal Construct Theory and its philosophical bases). Super (1965) describes four characteristics of the individual and four characteristics of occupations which determine occupational entry:

the *individual's*   occupational information
technical qualifications
social role characteristics
reward value hierarchy
the *occupation's* formal opportunities or demands
functional or technical requirements
non-functional or social requirements
and amount and types of rewards

The task of the vocational counsellor is often one of information dissemination, offering knowledge on the important characteristics of jobs. What is often difficult to assess is the corresponding information about the client: what occupational information does he possess, what sort of social role has he created for himself within his construct system, how does he perceive particular types of reward?

Holland (1965) attempted to explain the psychological procedures by which people developed preferences for particular types of occupational environments. Aside from the obvious importance of individual needs and interests, one has to take into account cultural and personal forces such as parental influence, social class, cultural and physical aspects of the environment, etc. Holland suggests that, through interaction with such influences, the person develops habitual or preferred methods for dealing with environmental tasks. Since there are usually several different possible preferred methods, the person comes to organise these into a preferential hierarchy. For Holland, then, making a vocational choice involves searching for situations which satisfy the individual's preferred methods of dealing with the world. This search can be described in terms of the possible occupational environments, the person and his or her development, and the potential for match and mismatch between the two. Again, the tasks facing the counsellor include assessing the habits and preferences of the individual, verifying the adequacy of his or her job knowledge, and encouraging exploration of the potential each job or occupational environment offers for personal satisfaction and reward. Repertory grid techniques have been shown to contribute to each of these.

Grid Techniques in Vocational Research and Guidance

Repertory grids have had a number of applications in the field of vocational psychology. Grids have been used to explore and to develop self-awareness and self-evaluation. They have also proved useful in elaborating the client's occupational knowledge and understanding. Some counsellors have used grids to encourage the client to broaden his or her ideas and aspirations with regard to employment. In addition, grids have played a useful role in studies of how people perceive educational alternatives and jobs at large, and in studies of decision-making.

This section will briefly describe applications in each of these areas, though readers interested in applying such techniques themselves in guidance are strongly recommended to consult Edmonds' (1979) paper, which presents some extremely useful detailed suggestions regarding specific grid-based methods.

Smith, Hartley and Stewart (1978) is probably one of the most commonly cited examples of the use of grids in vocational guidance. The paper presents a case study of a young man who felt unhappy with his chosen university course. One of the aims of the paper is to demonstrate some of the differences in approach between guidance based on differentialist and developmentalist orientations. Smith *et al.* offer a clear and practical description of how to use straightforward grid technique in guidance. The client was asked to list the jobs that people like him might possibly do, which were then used as the elements of his grid. Two elements were also supplied, *viz*. 'myself as I am at university' and 'myself as I would really like to be'. Constructs were elicited by the method of triads, and the resultant grid was composed of 17 elements (two supplied) and 16 constructs. Smith *et al.* point out that a certain amount of insight can be gained simply by studying the elements and constructs themselves, and the order in which they emerge. Personal Construct Theory would suggest that those elements elicited first reflect options or choices which the individual considers most realistic. Similarly, most important constructs would be expected to emerge first, and those which have most meaning for the person are likely to be repeated. In the case reported, the constructs produced were highly superficial, failing to reflect the intrinsic nature of jobs and concentrating on esteem-related qualities.

The next step in the procedure is obviously to complete the grid. In this case a 7-point rating scale was used, taking care to ensure that the client rated all the elements on each of the constructs consecutively. This helps to ensure that each construct is employed in a consistent manner across the sample of elements. Other practitioners have used ranked or dichotomous ratings with equal success, as described later in this chapter. It might also be said that 7-point scales offer little more accuracy than 5-point scales, which many people find easier to use.

Methods of analysis for grid data have proliferated as the technique has found application in more various contexts. Smith and his colleagues had fewer options, and employed the most widely used method of the day, the INGRID package (Slater, 1972). This yields three types of results: first, since the grid is a two-way matrix of ratings, variability within the grid can be explained according to either the elements or the constructs. INGRID shows the amount of variation due to each element and construct in turn, allowing identification of similarities and differences in the ways they have been used. Secondly, the program shows the interrelationships between the constructs and between the elements in terms of correlations. Finally, INGRID carries out a form of factor analysis known as Principal Component Analysis (PCA). This identifies the major dimensions of the cognitive space defined by the elements and constructs by means of factor loadings. That is to say, the way the person thinks about jobs is determined by the nature of the constructs they use in this domain. Each construct accounts for a certain amount of the variation within that space, but some account for more than others. PCA identifies those constructs, or combinations of constructs, which do most to determine the distribution within the space. This will become more clear when I describe a cognitive map.

Smith and his colleagues used this information to try to identify the source of their client's dissatisfaction. Constructs which account for the most variation within a grid are those which possess the most meaning for that person. The young man in question, Anthony P., used constructs such as 'being concerned with business and commerce' and 'being concerned with figures' in the most differentiating way. However, his ratings on these constructs tended to be at the extremes of the scale, implying that Anthony found it difficult to discriminate between jobs other than in gross or extreme terms. Anthony had distinctive elements including 'jet set executive' and 'climbing instructor'. PCA also showed a degree of simplicity in Anthony's thinking about jobs. It could be seen that Anthony's construct system was largely concerned with identifying 'big shot' opportunities, and those which offered a chance of 'outside adventure'. This was demonstrated most plainly in a cognitive map showing the distribution of Anthony's elements according to their weightings on his principal components. A cognitive map is constructed from the results of the PCA. The INGRID printout gives a table of 'loadings' for each element on each of the main components. These loadings can be used to represent the position of each element along a dimension defined by the component. Anthony had only two main components and these were used to define two axes (see Smith *et al.*, 1978, p. 101). Positions for the elements along these axes are given by their loadings, allowing them to be plotted like points on a graph. In cases where more than two main components emerge, it is possible to use any combination of components to give different views of the elements' distribution.

The cognitive map produced from Anthony's grid showed his dilemma quite clearly. He divided jobs in four distinctive categories, 'outdoor bigshots', 'indoor bigshots', 'outdoor small-shots' and 'indoor smallshots'. His ideal self was identified as an outdoor bigshot, though he felt that his present course (reading history) was making him into an indoor smallshot. Hence his request for vocational advice. As a result of the insight gained from completing the grid and seeing the dilemma, Anthony changed to a management sciences degree in an attempt to put his future prospects more in line with his ideal. Smith goes so far as to suggest that Anthony's motive may even be to use the management degree to enter the armed forces or the police force.

Another aspect of Anthony's difficulty was that he used many of his constructs in a highly similar way, failing to differentiate between jobs in any subtle way. This indicates a degree of immaturity in Anthony's vocational development which the counsellor might attempt to remedy by encouraging him to think about, discuss or even experience jobs which are not related to outdoor physical activities. As it turned out, Anthony made his decision to change course primarily as a result of completing the grid and seeing his cognitive map. It seems that often the process of eliciting the grid itself encourages the 'constructive alternativism' that Kelly believed to be essential to control of one's environment.

Earlier in this chapter I mentioned Edmonds' (1979) paper as having a useful set of recommendations on how to use grids in guidance. In fact, this paper describes a very ambitious series of experimental applications designed to assess the usefulness of grid techniques within the work of the Employment Service Division (ESD) of the Manpower Services Commission. Much of the work of the ESD is concerned with careers guidance, primarily for adults and often specialising in rehabilitation for the handicapped, etc. Edmonds describes a number of different approaches which were tested in approximately 80 guidance trials. He began by using an adaptation of the standard grid method described by Bannister and Fransella (1971).

Working with a client who was interested in training at a Skillcentre, but who could not decide on a particular course to follow, Edmonds was initially struck by the shallowness of the constructs obtained. He felt that the client was giving him 'generally acceptable ways of distinguishing between jobs, rather than constructs which were of particular relevance to the client' (p. 227). Edmonds goes on to make an interesting comment on the implications of this observation for Personal Construct Theory, 'while each person's perceptions of the world are unique, none of us lives in a social vacuum, so there is a tendency for people to have constructs which are related to a general perceptual concensus' (p. 227). This may in fact be the case, though this observation could well have reflected a lack of adequate vocational information due to poor careers education. Edmonds concludes that the client needs to be steered towards seeing possibilities in more personal terms, i.e. to elicit elements as 'jobs which the individual client might do' rather than 'jobs which people in general might do'. This is as might be expected from the point of view of Personal Construct Theory, since each person has his own particular arrangement of elements within any particular domain, depending on his experience. Edmonds also tried to overcome this problem by eliciting elements as occupational stereotypes (i.e. a list of elements comprised of 'the sort of person who is a clerk', 'the sort of person who is a labourer', etc.) Generally, the point is made that the particular method of eliciting elements has to be selected to suit the particular application in hand. A further difficulty centred around the use of triads, a problem which has beset a number of grid practitioners in a variety of fields. Basically, the triad method is the one advocated by Kelly, and which has the most sound methodological basis (see Kelly, 1963). However, it is quite legitimate to elicit constructs using pairs of elements, and is often advisable when working with young people.

Edmonds reports that in most of his trials of grid technique in guidance, simple hand scoring and cluster-analysis methods have proved sufficient since the role of the grid has been in providing a focal point for discussion rather than producing 'hey presto' magical answers. This point has been taken up by Jankowicz and Cooper (1982), who describe the use of the FOCUS programs (Thomas, 1975; Jankowicz and Thomas, 1982) in the slightly different context of personal counselling. Jankowicz and Cooper describe three case studies involving the use of grids. These include a client with problems regarding his attitudes to study, an art student suffering from a creative 'block' and a senior manager faced with a number of performance and goal-setting appraisals of his junior staff. They reinforce the notion of the grid as a physical basis for discussion, but go on to demonstrate that the FOCUSed grid can lead to a level of insight which could readily be labelled an 'aha experience', which is often more realistic than the 'hey presto' Edmonds found missing. Further details of FOCUS and a number of other computer techniques for grid analysis are given in Shaw (1980).

In his paper Edmonds also describes his attempts to train five occupational-guidance officers to use the technique for them-selves. Whilst there is an understandable preference to use such an intensive technique in second or subsequent interviews, Edmonds had encouraging reactions from his trainees. Officers do recognise that the main drawback to the use of grids in their work is the time taken to complete the procedure. Some people also have difficulty in taking on board the fundamentals of Personal Construct Theory in the short period of time available on a one-day course. However, Edmonds has concentrated on their being able to understand the technique and being able to apply it, and in this way has achieved a marked increase in the number of grid users within the ESD.

Aside from applications with clients who have sought voca-tional guidance, grids have also been used to explore how people perceive the actual possibilities open to them. Many researchers have studied the way in which people perceive jobs (e.g. Walker, 1958; O'Dowd and Beardslee, 1960; Gonyea, 1961; Fine-Davis, McGowan and Franklin, 1976). However, most of these studies have set out to identify the 'underlying dimensions' of job perception. That is, the researchers have obtained the detailed job perceptions of large numbers of individuals and used various data contraction methods (usually some form of factor analysis) to identify any components which are common to the perceptions of all. However, a strong case can be made for preserving the idiosyncrasies of such data, particularly if one gives credence to the notion that such perceptions arise out of the unique pattern of experiences of each individual. This can be particularly pertinent in the case of vocational development since, as Gonyea (1961) states, we might

> regard the process of occupational choice as essentially a matching operation, in which the individual matches himself with jobs. To the extent that he makes an occupational choice based on information about himself, whether gained from counselling or elsewhere, it is obvious that such information is useful only to the extent that he also has corresponding information about the world of work. Thus, a critical requirement for an intelligent choice is that the individual have an objective and accurate perception of relevant jobs (p. 305).

Taking an average of several people's perceptions is likely to shroud even fairly common inaccuracies. So could an idiographic technique like the repertory grid provide the sort of information lost in many factor analytical studies, and can it tell us any more about how jobs are perceived?

I attempted to tackle these questions in a pilot study of fifth-form pupils' perceptions of jobs (Davies, 1979). Twenty pupils (10 male, 10 female) from a comprehensive school in South Wales were interviewed individually and asked to complete grids using job titles as the elements. Two specific elements were elicited via the prompts, 'a job which you think you would most like to do' and 'a job which you would least like to do' (preferred and non-preferred jobs, respectively). The remainder of the elements came out of discussion of jobs they had thought about or knew something about, jobs they considered were available to them, parents' and siblings' jobs, etc. Constructs were elicited from comparisons of pairs of elements rather than triads, in the interests of simplicity. The grid was completed using a 5-point scale, and the INGRID package was used for analysis. Each interviewee produced, on average, approximately 8 elements and 9 constructs per grid, and a total of 76 different job titles emerged. One pupil found it impossible to state a preferred job, though all could readily name at least one non-preferred job. The range of job titles were classified as either professional, skilled, semi-skilled or unskilled according to the qualifications necessary to obtain that job and the status commonly ascribed it by the lay person (e.g. professional artist, professional civil servant, etc.); care was taken during the elicitation procedure to gain a clear impression of the level of job the interviewee was referring to. This classification could have been done on the basis of more standard criteria, but since the study was concerned with impressionistic data anyway, it was felt that this was unnecessary. This classification yielded 27 professional jobs, 19 skilled, 16 semi-skilled and 14 unskilled. There was a slight preference for skilled and professional jobs and a marked aversion for unskilled jobs. From the INGRID output it was possible to identify the most salient elements, i.e. those which stand out most clearly in the individual's thinking. Of the most salient elements, a large number were non-preferred (14), whilst only a few (4) were preferred.

In a similar way, the constructs were classified as relating to either personal factors (personal qualities or personal demands), work factors (aspects or attributes of the work done), and academic factors (academic abilities needed to qualify or used in the job). This classification yielded 31 personal, 43 work and 3 academic factors. Constructs relating to work factors were twice as likely to be salient than personal factors, and academic factors were hardly salient at all.

From the results of the analysis, and from looking at the cognitive maps produced for each grid, it was possible to draw several conclusions about the way these young people construed jobs. Their ability to distinguish preferred and non-preferred jobs suggested that they had reached a reasonable level of vocational maturity. Although most preferred jobs were either skilled or professional, this did not necessarily indicate naïve or unrealistic aspirations since the distinctions drawn between jobs at all levels were quite subtle. A boy interested in forestry work was also being encouraged to consider training in environmental health. He, however, doubted that the effort required in order to qualify for the latter job was likely to be repaid by what the job had to offer in terms of personal satisfactions. This was reflected in the way he construed these two jobs. Preferred jobs which were unskilled were ranged against other unskilled jobs which were non-preferred. Thus, the individuals seemed to be oriented towards specific jobs at this level rather than any kind of unskilled work. In general, the construct systems of all the participants were relatively complex and seemingly efficient. It was particularly interesting to note the extent to which non-preferred jobs were seen as more distinctive than preferred jobs. Such a result should influence the way in which we tackle vocational guidance with young people. Similarly, young people would seem to place greatest emphasis on the things they have to do in jobs, less emphasis on the demands the jobs might make on them personally, and little emphasis at all on the academic demands. When the sorts of constructs which distinguished most effectively between jobs were looked at, it became apparent that, whilst there was a certain degree of similarity in the construing of different individuals, there was also noticeable degree of variability. It was not obvious from the results that a number of common factors could be identified which described job perceptions, as has been suggested by factor-analytical studies. Rather, it seemed that individual perceptions varied in a meaningful and effective manner. Most strikingly, it had proved remarkably easy to tap these perceptions, yielding information of much more practical use in an individual counselling session than that which is often gained from instruments based on the notion of common factors.

Duckworth and Entwistle (1974) used grids to investigate pupils' perceptions of their school subjects. Interviews with sixth-form pupils showed that reasons for choosing or rejecting subjects fell into three catgories, *viz.* interest or lack of interest, difficulty or easiness, and the subject's 'worthwhileness' or social benefit. Constructs relating to these three categories were supplied to 142 second and fifth-year pupils, elements being the subjects offered at their school. Responses to the grids showed common factors operating which corresponded to the results of the sixth-form pilot results. This tended to confirm that notions of 'interest' and 'difficulty' were common to many children's construal of subjects. A third common factor differentiated those subjects which allowed one to express one's own ideas, this factor replacing the notion of social benefit expressed by the older pupils. Looking at the relationship between attitude to subjects and attainment, Duckworth and Entwistle found that, at least for fifth-formers, attainment correlated positively with interest and negatively with difficulty. There was general agreement on which subjects were most difficult — maths, physics, French and Latin. Even when pupils opted to specialise in science subjects, physics and chemistry were still perceived as difficult; the researchers are tempted by this result to question the demands made by science curricula on pupils. The paper goes on to investigate other aspects of attitudes toward subjects, and concludes that 'the grid offers a compact format, simple completion and scoring, and an activity which the pupils appear to perceive as important to themselves' (p. 81), and thus could play a useful role in advising on subject choice.

Reid and Holley (1972) used group administrations of grids to investigate applicants' choices of university. This study demonstrated that the 'image' of a university does help to decide whether or not it is chosen by applicants. However, this image is often composed of constructs referring to 'tradition' and other dimensions unlikely to relate specifically to the person's own experience. Reid and Holley suggest that perceptions of universities are, in a sense, 'given' since they are not dependent on experience. They also point out that a feature of such stereotypes is that they often persist in the face of rational information to the contrary. Thus,

> increasing the quantity or quality of information to candidates is not enough: it is important to have a better understanding of the perceptions of the receivers of information, of the development of these perceptions over time and of the extent to which selection for universities is, in effect, self-selection based upon responses to popularly accepted stereotypes. Repertory grid techniques applied on a group basis may provide one useful method of making a beginning in this complex field of enquiry (p. 59).

These sentiments would be shared by many people who have experienced the utility of grid methods in various aspects of vocational guidance.

Finally, Brook (1979) used grids to investigate school children's perceptions of various types of people who might be sources of vocational counselling or advice. Brook constructed a grid of representative role titles (potential sources of advice) and common constructs identified in interviews with school students. The 22 × 22 grid was then administered to 143 fifth-form pupils in a variety of schools in New Zealand. Analysis based on multidimensional scaling and hierarchical clustering techniques showed that discriminations of potential advisers were made on the basis of two main factors; an intimacy factor differentiated between liked, intimate and attractive individuals on the one hand, and disliked, remote and unattractive individuals on the other. A potency factor differentiated according to the amount of authority a person was seen to exert, though this was also related to the person's age. Further, older people worthy of respect due to their abilities, knowledge, prestige, etc. were seen as important sources of information about possible jobs and careers. Parents and other adults who display warmth and understanding were valued for their ability to help the young person make good decisions. Personal problems were unlikely to be discussed with either of these groups, but are likely to be reserved for peer-group discussions. Brook therefore concludes that there is a distinction between the vocational and personal counselling role which is accurately perceived by young people themselves. A further component of this study was to see if there was any relationship between a person's intellectual ability and their ability to complete the grid. Intellectual ability was measured by taking an average of recent examination results, and this was compared with whether or not the grid had been completed successfully. A total of 18 subjects had failed to complete their grids, but it was found that there was no significant relationship between intellectual ability and grid completion. This provides further evidence that grids can be incorporated quite easily into current guidance practice, the major drawback being the amount of time the procedure takes. This remaining problem can well be reduced by teaching grid technique to the youngsters themselves. Alternatively, grid practitioners in a number of fields are working on interactive computer programs which enable individuals to elicit and interpret their own grids privately, and at their own pace.

Conclusions

It is hoped that this account of the use of grid methods in vocational guidance has demonstrated the relevance and advantages of such methods to the field. Grid techniques are being revised and expanded at a remarkable rate, particularly methods of analysis and interpretation. As a result, I have not placed a great deal of emphasis on these aspects of the studies I have described. Rather, the prospective users of grids in any field are encouraged to take advantage of the tremendous flexibility of the technique, to adopt or even devise any form of analysis which suits the nature of their investigations.

As mentioned earlier, there are arguments in favour of 'giving away' grid technique, enabling individuals to use it to their own ends and in a variety of contexts. Many of the people I know who have used grids professionally also use them personally; self-understanding, relationship difficulties, work planning, decision-making — all these and countless other psychological domains are the natural subjects for exploration of one's construct system. It would be heartening to think that such a useful tool would be offered to the public at large as an aid in coping with the transition to new values and ideas about work, new societal roles, realignment of the individual's conception of self, and all the other psychological ramifications of the sudden restructuring of our society. People are being left to find their own ways through the transition: it is unrealistic to expect the fields of psychology, including occupational, to continue to be relevant in the ways they have been practised in other times. Kelly demonstrated that each person operates as a psychologist in the way he or she attempts to understand his or her world. We may well not have enough 'experts' to cope with the imminent demand, so why don't we reconstrue repertory grid technique as a set of skills akin to literacy and numeracy?

References

Bannister, D. and Fransella, F. (1971) *Inquiring Man: the Theory of Personal Constructs*, Penguin, Harmondsworth

Brook, J. (1979) 'A Repertory Grid Analysis of Perceptions of Vocational Counselling Roles', *Journal of Vocational Behaviour, 15*, 25-35

Davies, R. (1979) 'A Preliminary Investigation of the Use of Repertory Grid Technique in the Study of Fifth-form Pupils' Perceptions of Jobs', unpublished undergraduate project, Dept. of Applied Psychology, UWIST, Cardiff

Duckworth, D. and Entwistle, N.J. (1974) 'Attitudes to School Subjects: A Repertory Grid Technique', *British Journal of Educational Psychology, 44*, 76-83

Edmonds, T. (1979) 'Applying Personal Construct Theory in Occupational Guidance', *British Journal of Guidance and Counselling, 7*, 225-33

Fine-Davis, M., McGowan, J. and Franklin, M. (1976) 'A Factor Analytic Study of Students' Perceptions of Occupations and their Characteristics', *Irish Journal of Psychology, 3*, 146-58

Ginzberg, E., Ginzberg, S.W., Axelrad, S. and Herma, J.L. (1951) *Occupational Choice: an Approach to a General Theory*, Columbia University, New York

Gonyea, G.C. (1961) 'Dimensions of Job Perceptions', *Journal of Counselling Psychology, 8*, 305-12

Hepworth, S.J. (1980) 'Moderating Factors on the Psychological Impact of Unemployment', *Journal of Occupational Psychology, 53*, 139-45

Holland, J.L. (1965) 'A Theory of Vocational Choice' in Adams (1970) *Counselling and Guidance*, Macmillan, London

Jankowicz, A.Z.D. and Cooper, K. (1982) 'The Use of FOCUSed Repertory Grids in Counselling', *British Journal of Guidance and Counselling, 10*, 136-50

—— and Thomas, L. (1982) 'Algorithm for the Cluster Analysis of Repertory Grids in Human Resource Development', *Personnel Review, 11* (pt 4), 15-22

Kelly, G.A. (1963) *A Theory of Personality*, Norton and Co., New York

O'Dowd, D.D. and Beardslee, D.C. (1960) 'College Students' Images of a Selected Group of Professions and Occupations', report, Cooperative Research Project No. 562(8142), Wesleyan University

Reid, W.A. and Holley, B.J. (1972) 'An Application of Repertory Grid Techniques to the Study of Choice of University', *British Journal of Educational Psychology, 42*, 52-9

Shaw, M.L.G. (1980) *On Becoming a Personal Scientist: Interactive Computer Elicitation of Personal Models of the World*, Academic Press, London

Slater, P. (1972) 'Notes on INGRID', St George's Hospital, London

Smith, M., Hartley, J. and Stewart, B. (1978) 'A Case Study of Repertory Grids Used in Vocational Guidance', *Journal of Occupational Psychology, 51*, 97-104

Super, D.E. (1965) 'Vocational Development: the Process of Compromise or Synthesis' in Adams (1970) *Counselling and Guidance*, Macmillan, London

Thomas, L. (1975) 'FOCUSing: Exhibiting the Meanings in a Grid', Centre for the Study of Human Learning, Brunel University

Walker, K.F. (1958) 'A Study of Occupational Stereotypes', *Journal of Applied Psychology, 42*, 122-4

PART SIX

CONSTRUCTS OF HANDICAP

In this section our focus is the constructs which parents and teachers hold about mentally handicapped children. The emphasis on early intervention makes studies of parents' constructs of their handicapped child essential. In Chapter 21 Sue Vicary examines the development in mothers' construing of their handicapped one-year-olds. Like Sheehan (Chapter 9), she administered grids every few months. The grids provide information on how these mothers see their children, and how their perceptions change over a period of a year. Such information is particularly useful to professionals providing early intervention, as an attempt is made to understand how she sees things, her needs and her concerns.

The emphasis in education on parents as partners suggests a need for methods which enable parents to understand teachers and teachers to understand parents. In Chapter 22 Judith Middleton presents a single case of an ESN(M) boy to illustrate how grid technique can be used in conjunction with other methods to compare the perspectives of teacher and parent for the same child. Her case clearly shows the need for greater understanding between teachers and parents.

21 DEVELOPMENTS IN MOTHERS' CONSTRUING OF THEIR MENTALLY HANDICAPPED ONE-YEAR-OLDS

Susan Vicary

When a child is identified as mentally handicapped it is inevitably an enormous shock to parents who have expected a 'perfectly normal' baby. Each parent will have formulated his or her own personal construction of the anticipated baby, although, as Bannister (1981) points out, the 'able or normal' contrast to 'disabled or handicapped' is extremely difficult to define.

In cases where the knowledge of delayed development comes later in the child's development, the distress is no less significant; whenever such a diagnosis is made the implications of the newly applied construct will be uniquely disturbing for every parent (McConachie, 1985). Few parents will have sufficient experience with handicapped individuals to hold but the vaguest notion of the ramifications for their own child, and, accommodating a particular child within the culturally based meaning of 'handicapped' will be a time of upheaval and distress, the extent of which has been widely documented (Crnic, Friedrich and Greenberg, 1983; Stevenson, Graham and Dorner, 1978).

Despite the initial shock, most parents acknowledge the new construction of their child as 'handicapped' within months of the confirmation of the diagnosis. The extent to which this is the case is usually demonstrated by the 'acceptance' of involvement in programmes of early intervention, meeting with other parents of similarly handicapped children, and establishing contacts with whatever local professional services offer (Beveridge *et al.*, 1982).

For many parents, however, the process of really understanding the nature and extent of their own child's disability involves prolonged appraisal of their child's behaviour and characteristics, in the light of information gathered from a number of sources. Frequently, the degree of delay cannot be fully appreciated until the second year, when the characteristic discrepancy in development typically emerges. Whilst development in some areas may

351

be age appropriate, much of the child's behaviour will be appropriate to a much younger age group.

So, parents are faced with the dual task of adapting to all the needs of a growing child, but also responding to new information about the extent of the delay. There is a chance that the handicap will be construed as not only slowing down the child's development, but also somehow changing the child, making the child fundamentally different from the normally developing child which the parents anticipated. The extent to which the construction of the child as 'handicapped' carries implications for the construction of other child characteristics may be of great importance to the success of programmes of early intervention aimed at minimising the effects of the disability. Further, daily interactions with a handicapped child may be influenced by the construed implications of the handicapping condition. In the study to be described, a repertory grid has been designed specifically for the purpose of exploring the construed implications of handicap.

The focus in this study is the mother, since it is mothers who are traditionally the principle care-givers, and to whom programmes of early intervention are predominantly aimed. The mother also usually spends most time with the child, so it is the mother who knows the child best, and who might be expected to have most clearly elaborated her personal system for construing the handicapped child. Further, it was following early discussions with mothers of handicapped children attending parent group meetings, that the decision to include an imaginary child element was made. Mothers dissuaded me from using elements, such as an 'ideal' child, an 'average' child or a 'perfect' child, as these were irrelevant to the way they thought about their own handicapped child — there could be 'no such thing as an ideal/perfect/average child'! These mothers insisted on 'being realistic' and acknowledging that the imagined normal child would not have been 'perfect', but just an 'ordinary' child. I shall proceed now to the details of the grid finally used for the investigation.

Design of the Grid

Elements

A modified version of Kelly's Minimum Role Context Grid was used for the investigation. The element set was modified to include several child elements, including a single imaginary child — the handicapped child as he or she would have been without the handicapping condition. Adults included were mother herself, father, a liked adult and a disliked adult. This group of elements were selected to provide a representative sample of significant persons occupying the mother's social network.

The minimum number of elements totalled 10, but siblings of the handicapped child were included, where present, as extra elements. The role titles used, as they were presented to the mothers, are listed in Figure 21.1. The choice of role titles for normally developing children known to the mother was designed to encourage a broad range of constructs in the elicitation procedure concerning personality and temperament characteristics, rather than focusing on child competence and disability.

Figure 21.1: Role Titles

Your child ....
Your child .... as you imagine he or she would have been
   without the developmental delay
Yourself
Your husband
A child you know who is sociable, or with whom you get on well
A child you know who is independent
A child you know who is difficult, or whom you do not get on with
An adult you know whom you get on well with
An adult you know whom you do not get on well with
Siblings, (1,2,3...) as they are now.
A brother or sister as you remember at the same age as your child
is now

The Constructs

To ensure that each mother's grid employed a highly salient sample of the many constructs available, Kelly's method of triads was used to elicit constructs from the subjects of this investigation. This method reflects the emphasis from within Personal

Construct Theory, on the idiosyncratic nature of each mother's system of cognitive dimensions used for construing others. The most commonly used triads are listed in Figure 21.2, although this was not rigidly adhered to. Mothers occasionally suggested triads themselves, or generated an important construct during discussion of their own handicapped child. Also, where mothers found the triad exercise difficult, they were asked to consider only two elements. Laddering techniques were used to ensure the salience of the constructs elicited, and to facilitate a more thorough understanding of the way any particular construct was applied. For more details of the techniques see Fransella and Bannister (1977).

Figure 21.2: Triads Used in the Construct Elicitation Procedure

---

Your child ....
Yourself
Your husband

Your child ....
Your child .... imagined normally developing
Another developmentally delayed child you know

Your child ....
Another developmentally delayed child you know
A difficult child

Your child ....
Yourself
A sociable child

Your child ....
Your child .... imagined normally developing
An independent child

Your child ....
A sociable child
An independent child

A liked adult
A disliked adult
Yourself

A liked adult
A disliked adult
Your husband

A difficult child
A sociable child
An independent child

Your child ....
Your child .... imagined normally developing
A difficult child

Optional Extra Triads

Your child ....
Your older child now
Your older child, as you remember him/her at the same age as
.... now

Your child ....
Your child .... imagined normally developing
Your older child, as you remember him/her at the same age as
.... now

Procedure

When between eight and ten constructs had been elicited, mothers were asked to make a rating of each element on a 5-point scale. Number 1 represented the construct extreme, and 5 represented the contrast extreme. A score of 3 was mid-way between these two extremes except when the mother could not be certain of how to apply a particular construct, in which case a score of 3 was recorded, but a special note was made of this. Where an element fell outside the range of convenience of a construct, a blank space was left on the grid.

For each of 9 mothers, a total of five grids were completed at three-monthly intervals over a one-year period. An incomplete set of three grids was obtained from a tenth mother who dropped out of the study. On each occasion, the original set of elements and constructs were re-presented, and others were asked to repeat the rating task. Mothers were also invited to add any new constructs which arose during the ensuing discussion.

Subjects

The subjects of the investigation were 10 mothers of mentally handicapped one-year-olds, contacted through Handicap Service Teams in the London Boroughs of Tower Hamlets, Hackney and Newham, Redbridge and Waltham Forest. One mother was living apart from the child's father at the start of the study, but they were reunited during the course of the study. The remaining families were 'intact'. All the fathers were in full-time employment, and two mothers were working part-time whilst their shift-working husbands took care of the child.

Eight of the children had been identified as having Down's syndrome, and the remaining two were brain-damaged at time of birth. All had been identified as 'handicapped' at or shortly after birth. The mean age of the children at the start of the investigation was 15.3 months (range 12-20). Only three of the group were girls, and the remaining boys included the two non-Down's children. Five of the children had older siblings, and one mother had another child during the one year of the study.

Analysis

For the purposes of this study, the rated score of each element at each separate time point was treated as an independent element, and included in a single grid analysis. Slater's BIG GRID program, a recently adapted version of INGRID Principal Components Analysis (1964) enabled such large grids to be dealt with. One major assumption underlying the treatment of the repeated grid data in this way was that the constructs used on repeated occasions throughout the investigation remained stable in their meaning. Some statistical support for this assumption was provided by the results of a COIN analysis (Slater, 1972), providing a measurement of the consistency of repeated grids. Thus, variations in the placement of elements within the construct space indicated variation in construing of elements, rather than variation in the way constructs were being used.

For the investigation of construed similarity between elements, the element distances, derived from the BIG GRID analysis have been used in a variety of statistical tests of relationship. Element distance scores can range from 0 to 1.999. A distance of 0 represents no difference in the construing of two elements, whilst 1.999 represents no similarity in construing. Slater's GRANNY analysis (1977) gives estimates of 'significance' boundaries for element distances derived from grids of a given size. For this investigation, element distances of less than 0.7, and greater than 1.30 can be considered significant at the 5 per cent level.

Results

For the whole group, the mean of element distances between the handicapped child (HC) and the same child — imagined normally developing (IN) were generally smaller than the element distances between the handicapped child and each other element (see Table 21.1).

Table 21.1: Mean Element Distances Between the Handicapped Child and Other Elements in the Role Set

Handicapped child imagined normally developing	0.6862*
Mother	0.9248
Father	0.9520
Another developmentally delayed child	0.7676
Sociable child	0.8280
Independent child	0.9504
Difficult child	0.9572
Liked adult	0.9827
Disliked adult	1.1486

* Significantly small at 5%.

However, four mothers each construed the handicapped child and the imagined child as very similar, and it is these mothers who account for the low group-mean element distance between (HC) and (IN) (see Table 21.2).

The extent to which the discrepancy in maternal construing of the handicapped child and the imagined child was related to other element distances was next considered. Statistically significant positive correlations were found between the (HC)—(IN)

Table 21.2: Mean Element Distances (HC) and (IN) for Each Mother

Subject	
1	0.7922
2	0.881
3	0.2532**
4	0.8332
5	1.1366
6	0.7802
7	0.5062*
8	0.2354**
9	0.9906
10 (3 visits only)	0.4440*

** Significantly small at P <0.01
* Significantly small at P <0.05

Table 21.3: Correlations Between (HC)—(IN) Discrepancy and Mean Element Distances Between (HC) and Other Elements

	Rho
Mother	0.767*
Father	0.767*
Another developmentally delayed child	0.61
Sociable child	0.58
Independent child	0.3
Difficult child	0.1
Liked adult	−0.06
Disliked adult	−0.2

Critical value for Rho P <0.05 is 0.65

Table 21.4: Correlations Between (HC)—(IN) and Mean Element Distance Between (IN) and Each Other Element

	Rho
Mother	−0.01
Father	0.24
Another developmentally delayed child	0.32
Sociable child	−0.3
Independent child	−0.15
Difficult child	−0.68*
Liked adult	−0.31
Disliked adult	−0.32

Critical value for Rho P <0.05 is 0.65

distance scores and the element distances between the handicapped child and mothers and fathers. Thus, the more similarly a child was construed to itself when imagined normally developing, the more construed similarity with both parents (see Table 21.3).

In contrast, a similar analysis looked at the relationship between the (HC)–(IN) child distances and the element distances between the imagined normally developing child and each other element. The pattern of interrelationships is entirely different, particularly for the three normal-child elements. A significant negative relationship emerges between the (HC)–(IN) distance and the (IN)–Difficult-child distances. Where the handicapped child and the imagined child are most dissimilar, the imagined child is construed as most like the difficult child known to the mother (see Table 21.4).

A comparison of element distances between mothers and fathers, with male and female children revealed a slight but non-significant tendency for girls to be construed as more similar to mothers than fathers, and boys to be construed as more similar to fathers than mothers (see Table 21.5).

Table 21.5: Mean Element Distances Between Mothers/Fathers ×
Girls/Boys

	Girls	Boys
Mothers	0.8411	0.9606
Fathers	1.0193	0.9283

Applying a trend test to element distances between the handicapped child and mothers and fathers respectively resulted in significant values — for mothers (568) and for fathers (569), demonstrating that the handicapped children were construed as becoming more like both parents over time (critical value = 271, Jockheere's Trend Test).

Further analysis of changes over time looked at the (HC)–(IN) distances. When mean element distances between the first and the last two grids were compared with the overall mean element discrepancies, a significant positive corellation resulted (Rho = 0.77, P <0.05). This suggested that where discrepancies were largest, they remained so, or increased. But, where discrepancies were low, they decreased over the year of the study.

Discussion

For the group as a whole, the mean element distances between the handicapped child and the imagined normally developing child were lower than the mean element distances between the handicapped child and any other element. This tends to suggest that the handicapped child is construed as most like him/herself 'imagined' normally developing, and as such, that the handicapping condition is not carrying enormous implications for maternal construing. However, broad individual variation in the distances between the handicapped and the imagined normal child element show that the low group-mean in element distance is accounted for predominantly by those four mothers whose grids demonstrated consistently low discrepancies between the handicapped and the imagined child elements. The remaining six mothers construed their handicapped children as differing from the imagined normally developing child on a number of constructs. For these 'discrepant' mothers, the handicap is carrying broad implications for construing the developmentally delayed child. Further, these mothers were more likely to maintain the discrepancy in construing the handicapped child, over the one year of the study. This contrasted with the less discrepant mothers, for whom the discrepancy was likely to decrease during that period.

The extent to which a mother construes discrepancy between the handicapped child and the imagined child could be interpreted as evidence of differing implicit theories about the meaning of the handicap. For the 'discrepant' mother, the handicap continues to make her child *different*, whereas, for the less discrepant mother, the handicap merely slows down development, leaving the child *essentially* unchanged. If this is the case, then one may be concerned for the child of a 'discrepant' mother who, in focusing predominantly upon the 'handicapped-ness' of the child, may be missing characteristics of the child him/herself.

Of much more particular concern is the effect of such a focus upon the child's developing sense of him/herself as an individual (Shotter, 1974). If even a few of those characteristics or behaviours, particular to the child, are simply attributed to the handicap, and therefore assumed to be *not* child-self directed, then a crucial aspect of the early parent-child interplay may be disrupted.

Further, for the 'discrepant' mother, concern arises from the significant positive correlations which emerged between the (HC)–(IN) discrepancy and the extent of construed similarity between the handicapped child and either parent. Where the handicapped child was construed as less like the 'imagined' child, he/she was also construed as less like either parent. Whilst there is little professional agreement about the precise nature of 'parental acceptance' of the handicapped child, it could be argued that one critical dimension of 'acceptance' might involve the ability to construe the handicapped child as alike yourselves, as parents, at least in certain respects. A significant trend for the whole group of mothers suggests, however, that there is a gradual tendency for the children to be construed as more like parents as they grow, although this is more marked for the less 'discrepant' mothers. Clearly, the changes in construing are related, at least in part to the increasing skills of the children, and all the children made some developmental progress during the year of the study. However, some comments made by the least 'discrepant' mothers also suggest that there are fundamental changes in the cognitive dimensions which mothers feel are appropriate to apply to the handicapped child, away from the focus on the developmental delay. Clearly, each of these mothers, is not simply 'denying' the problem, but getting to know the child him/herself minimises the construed impact on the child's person-ness! For example:

> I just can't imagine him any different now, not now his personality shows through, I sometimes forget he's even slow!
>
> He's such a character now, a real boy. . . I know he should be doing more, but now he's just part of the family and I can't picture him any other way!

Some findings concerning mothers' theories about normally developing children throw a different light on the discussion so far. Most mothers have had some experience with at least a few normally developing children, although not necessarily their own. There is some evidence which suggests that the elaboration of such theories come to play a part in the way the handicapped child is construed. There was a significant negative relationship between the (HC)–(IN) distance and the (IN)–Difficult child distance. Where the imagined normal child was construed most like the difficult child known to the mother, the handicapped child was construed less like the imagined child. This suggests a positive construction of the handicapped child for the more discrepant mother. One mother's comment on this subject provides a good illustration: 'Intelligent children are usually creative or artistic, but that also means they're likely to be difficult — my oldest is bright, that's why he's difficult on occasions!'

It is worth noting at this point that many of the distinctions made between the handicapped child and the imagined child presented the handicapped child in a positive light — as more friendly, less selfish, more loving, etc. Whether or not these children are actually more loving and less selfish than other children the mother knows is impossible to say, but construing a handicapped child in a positive light has obvious benefits for these mothers. But such positive construing of the 'handicapped-ness' of the child confirms and maintains the discrepancy in construing. By continuing to construe the handicapped child as essentially different from the child who might have been, each of these mothers is probably optimising her own 'acceptance' of the child.

This tendency to emphasise such positive characteristics of the handicapped child could be a major factor in the maintenance of stereotypes of handicapped children, particularly Down's syndrome children, as friendly, easy and cheerful (Belmont, 1971; Smith and Wilson, 1973). But evidence to suggest this has little empirical foundation (Gunn, Berry and Andrews, 1981).

The hypothesis which spurred this exploratory study concerned the construed implications of a handicapping condition. There was a suggestion that the more 'discrepant' mother might be in danger of allowing the child's handicap to predominate in her relationship with the child, and thus undermine the parent-child interaction. Within even this small sample of mothers, a broad range of construing has emerged, but it suggests that both discrepant and non-discrepant construing contributes significantly towards the acceptance of the child. The most discrepant mothers have adopted a pattern of construing which highlights the negative characteristics of normally developing children, and in turn fosters a positive disposition towards the handicapped child. The least discrepant mothers have each reorganised her system of construing to de-emphasize those constructs which might discriminate between her handicapped child and the child she might have had. There can, and should not be, any conclusion as to which, if any, of these mothers have the 'correct' attitude to the handicapped child. There can be as many correct ways to construe the handicapped child, as there are parents to construct them. However, what repertory grid technique has provided is a dimension with which to further explore the parental relationship with the developing handicapped child, which may contribute towards greater parent-professional rapport.

References

Bannister, D. (1981) 'Construing a Disability' in A. Brechin, F. Liddiard and J. Swain (eds), *Handicap in a Social World*, Hodder & Stoughton, London

Belmont, J.H. (1981) 'Medical-Behavioural Research in Retardation' in N.R. Ellis (ed.), *International Review of Research in Mental Retardation, vol. 5*, Academic Press, New York

Beveridge, S., Flanagan, R., McConachie, H. and Sebba, J. (1982) 'Parental Involvement in Anson House', Anson House Pre-school Project Paper 3 (1982), Barkingside, London

Crnic, K.A., Friedrich, W.N. and Greenberg, M.T. (1983) 'Adaptation of Families with Mentally Retarded Children: A Model of Stress, Coping and Family Ecology', *American Journal of Mental Deficiency, 88(2)*, 125-38

Fransella, F. and Bannister, D. (1977) *A Manual for Repertory Grid Technique*, Academic Press, London

Gunn, P., Berry, P. and Andrews, R.J. (1981) 'The Temperament of Down's Syndrome Infants, A Research Note', *Journal of Child Psychiatry, 22*, 189-94

McConachie, H. (1985) 'How Parents of Young Mentally Handicapped Children Construe Their Role' in D. Bannister (ed.), *Issues and Approaches in Personal Construct Theory*, Academic Press, London

Shotter, J. (1974) 'The Development of Personal Powers' in M.P.M. Richards (ed.), *The Integration of the Child into a Social World*, Cambridge University Press, Cambridge

Slater, P. (1964) *The Principal Components of a Repertory Grid*, Vincent Andrew, London

—— (1972) 'The Measurement of Consistency in Repertory Grids', *British Journal of Psychiatry, 121*, 45-51

Smith, D.W. and Wilson, A.A. (1973) *The Child With Down's Syndrome*, Saunders Philadelphia, Pennsylvania

Stevenson, J., Graham, P. and Dorner, S. (1978) 'Parental Reactions to the Birth of a Handicapped Child', *British Journal of Psychiatry, 132*, 105-15

22 SO WHERE DOES THIS LEAVE SIMON? A MOTHER'S AND A TEACHER'S PERSPECTIVE OF AN ESN(M) BOY

Judith Middleton

One of the advantages of the repertory grid is that it is a flexible technique which can be used in a variety of ways, and yet still relate back to personal construct psychology, from which it is derived. Reflecting the philosophy of constructive alternativism basic to personal construct psychology, we can use repertory grids as if they will be useful in the research and clinical fields, and test out whether they bring additional clarification to our questions. In terms of clinical work, they are used to clarify the patient's underlying construct systems.

Rowe and Slater (1976) have shown how grid technique may be used to help a psychiatrist to understand his patient more clearly. Their study underlined that there were areas of the patient's inner world which the psychiatrist misconstrued, partly through misinterpreting the patient's behaviour in hospital. Rowe and Slater point out that the limited behaviour observed on the ward might not reflect the full repertoire of behaviour open to the patient in different and less restricted environments, which might reveal the real nature of the patient's attitudes. This important point will be highlighted in the case study presented below, where a mother and a teacher construe a child based on their knowledge of his behaviour in two separate environments where he displays different behaviours.

Ravenette (1977) has also pointed out that people often do not know what their constructs are. They live their lives without conscious deliberation or reference to their constructs or construct systems, and may assume that the constructs they employ are the same, or are used in a similar manner to everyone else. When this is the case, misunderstandings may occur because common meanings to language are assumed. Ravenette illustrates this in reporting a mother who described her child as 'showing off', but when asked for clarification described behaviour more expressive of anger.

These two papers illustrate the importance of understanding individual descriptions of behaviour in both a clinical and an educational setting. Nash (1973) has shown that teachers can create different psychological environments in the classroom for individual pupils, based on the different ways they construe each child. This in turn affects the children's behaviour.

The case history below describes the use of repertory grids in trying to unravel the individual perspectives held by a mother and form teacher about an ESN(M) boy of 13. The child was taken from a group of subjects who were used in a research study considering the different perceptions of mothers and teachers of ESN(M) and normal children's social and independence skills.

Methodology

Simon Jones (this and other names in the case history are fictitious) was an English child of 13 years who went to an ESN(M) school in London. His mother was in her fifties, and worked as a school-bus attendant. She was divorced, and had one other son who was 20 years old. Mr Smith, Simon's teacher, was in his thirties, and had been teaching Simon for two terms, although he had known him for eight terms.

Simon was observed for an hour on two separate occasions, both at home and in his classroom, when a running record of his interactions with his mother and his teacher was made. Only the records of the second hour of observations were used. In addition, Simon's mother and teacher completed a questionnaire about his social and independence skills, and were also asked to complete a repertory grid.

Both the mother's and teacher's grids were made up of the same ten constructs and the same 10 element roles. Simon's name appeared on both the mother's and teacher's repertory grids, but they individually supplied the names of people who fitted the other 9 element roles. These roles were: normal, older, younger, dare-devil, good, problem and mature children, and a disliked and liked adult. The constructs had come from a common pool, and were the 10 which had been considered most representative in describing someone who was mature. The constructs were:

(a) Decisive — indecisive

  (b) Helpful — unhelpful
  (c) Friendly — unfriendly
  (d) Responsible — irresponsible
  (e) Independent — dependent
  (f) Calm — anxious
  (g) Sense of humour — no sense of humour
  (h) Positive — negative
  (i) Understanding — insensitive
  (j) Practical — impractical

Each element was rated along each construct on a 5-point scale. Grids were analysed using Slater's (1977) INGRID and DELTA programs, of which the latter enables a comparison to be made between two similar grids.

The observation and questionnaire data will be considered first, before discussing how Simon was construed. This will illustrate how the grid data considerably enhanced the interpretation of what was observed and reported by more conventional methods.

Observations

When Simon was observed in his classroom there were 16 other children present, and from time to time Mr Smith was helped by a teaching assistant. Desks were arranged in rows across the classroom, with all but the back row facing the board. The back row was at right angles to the board. Although Mr Smith taught from the front of the class, i.e. near the board, his desk was at the back. Simon sat immediately in front of Mr Smith, with his back to the teacher.

It is worthwhile commenting on Mr Smith's style of teaching. He tended to begin by teaching or talking to the children from the front of the class (near the board) for about 10 to 15 minutes. The children were then told to get on with their work, while Mr Smith sat at his desk and marked books or helped individual children as and when they came up to him. He only occasionally glanced round the classroom to check if all was well with the rest of the class.

Analysis of an hour's observations showed that Mr Smith taught or talked to the class generally during 10 minutes of the total hour observed. He told the class what to do during 4 minutes; and asked general questions of the class during 6 minutes. He spoke to Simon specifically on only three occasions, once to ask a question, to which Simon replied; once in reply to a question from Simon; and once to tell Simon off. Apart from that, Mr Smith appeared to take no notice of Simon throughout the period observed, although it is possible that as Simon sat so close to him Mr Smith was able to watch him unobtrusively out of the corner of his eye.

Simon tried six times to get Mr Smith's attention by raising his hand, each time in vain. During 43 of the 60 minutes Simon appeared to be listening to Mr Smith or getting on with his work for some of the time. However, during 44 of the minutes Simon glanced around the room; played with his books, or chatted to his neighbour.

In summary, it would appear that Simon was wasting a lot of his time by not attending or doing as he was told, or, if he was working, he did so for a short time and then went off task. Mr Smith's attention was focused on more disruptive children, or those who were eager to get help, so that Simon was virtually left to his own devices, which were divided between working, staring aimlessly about the room, and occasionally talking to his neighbour. His attempts to get Mr Smith's attention by raising his hand were unsuccessful, and most of the time he was fairly quiet.

Simon was observed at home with his mother later the same day. The section below illustrates what seemed to be typical of the interactions observed between Simon and his mother, and it will be seen that Simon's quietness at school was not reflected by his behaviour at home.

5.12 p.m. Simon comes downstairs and enters the kitchen, where
Mrs Jones is cooking.
Mrs Jones says he is a silly boy (for no apparent reason).
Simon asks to go out to play.
Mrs Jones says 'No'.
Simon asks again.
Mrs Jones slaps him.
Simon says he wants to go out to play.
Mrs Jones says he knows he can't (she had already told me 'he always gets into trouble').
Simon asks to go out again.
Mrs Jones says he'll have no supper.

Later on, Mrs Jones and Simon watched TV, during which time they chatted to each other. Simon also asked his mother a barrage of questions (during 27 of the 60 minutes), most of which she ignored or did not reply to directly. (This appears similar to Simon's school environment, where his attempts to get attention also failed.) During 10 minutes Mrs Jones told Simon what to do at least once, and during 13 minutes she told him off at least once. In contrast, Simon answered only one of her questions, and either ignored her, or verbally refused to comply with her requests. Here again, it appeared that Simon's non-cooperation at home on a number of occasions was reflected by the frequency with which he went off task at school.

During the time at school earlier in the day, Mr Smith had explained about school reports, and also a proposed school trip to which half the class could go. In discussing these two subjects that evening, it will be seen how Mrs Jones seems to treat Simon as if he is a younger, irresponsible child:

5.45 p.m. Simon tells Mrs Jones about the school holiday
Mrs Jones asks him to explain about it.
Simon tells her that the children will help to look after themselves.
Mrs Jones tells him he can't go in that case.
Simon continues to talk about the school holiday.
5.46 p.m. Mrs Jones again says he can't go. She asks who's going and says it will be too dangerous.
Simon asks why.
Mrs Jones tells him he can't swim.
5.47 p.m. Mrs Jones tells Simon he must be grown up.
Simon gives more details about the holiday.
Mrs Jones says she'll see Mr Smith about it.
5.48 p.m. Mrs Jones picks up Simon's report (which she opened earlier) and says it is not good, although his last teacher had been very pleased with him.

The issue of the report was quite important, because at school the next day Mr Smith told me that Mrs Jones had written to him complaining about the report. Mrs Jones had indicated that she saw Simon as a problem child, and suggested that if he misbehaved at school he should be slapped. Mr Smith saw many of Simon's problems in terms of his mother's handling.

Questionnaires

The specific aspects of independence and social skills covered by the questionnaires are listed in Table 22.2. Questions were of four types: (1) occurrence of behaviour; (2) frequency of behaviour; (3) ability/competency; and (4) explanations why some behaviours did not occur or occurred rarely.

Mrs Jones indicated that Simon was incapable of carrying out 20 tasks. These included dressing and washing himself without help, spending his own pocket money without direction, helping in the house, cooking, travelling anywhere alone, having a front door key, or being left alone at home. She also saw him as socially inept. In the majority of cases, the reason Mrs Jones gave to explain Simon's incapacity was in terms of his handicap (see Table 22.1).

Mr Smith, however, considered Simon was incapable of carrying out a task on only eleven occasions. His explanations are summarised in Table 22.1. The summary of these figures indicates that, while Mrs Jones felt Simon's inability could be explained in terms of causes within Simon, Mr Smith considered that Simon's restricted environment tended to play a more important role in explaining some of his incapacity.

Table 22.1: A Summary of the Explanations Given for Non-occurrence of Behaviour in Simon's Repertoire

| | Innate | | | | Environment | | |
	Handicapped	Normal	Total	School	Home	Social facility	Total
Mrs Jones	16	3	19	–	–	1	1
Mr Smith	2	1	3	2	6	–	8

All the rated questions common to both questionnaires were totalled. The discrepancies between Mrs Jones's and Mr Smith's ratings (on a 5-point scale) of Simon's competence are shown in Table 22.2.

Although this simple addition and comparison of the scores given by Mr Smith and Mrs Jones oversimplifies the discrepancies in their judgments of Simon's capabilities, the overriding trend shows that Mrs Jones felt that Simon was generally less competent than did Mr Smith. This was particularly so in those

Table 22.2: Summary of the Discrepancies Between Mrs Jones's
and Mr Smith's Ratings of Simon's Competence

Practical Self-care	Number of questions	Difference between mother's and teacher's ratings	+ = mother rates child as more competent
Personal care	1	+ 2	
Economic skills	3	− 5	− = teacher rates
Domestic skills	4	− 5	child as
Total	8	− 8	more competent
Independence			
Autonomy	2	− 3	
Self-sufficiency	3	− 7	
Total	5	−10	
Social awareness			
Relationships	7	− 3	
Social sensitivity	6	− 4	
Total	13	− 7	
Unexpected crisis situations			
Personal	6	− 8	
Social	2	+ 1	
Total	8	− 7	
Occupation			
General alertness and interest	3	+ 4	
Work skills	3	− 4	
Total	6	0	
Grand total	40	−32	

questions where Simon's general social awareness and his
independence skills were considered. The latter included travelling alone, or being left alone in the house for specific lengths
of time. However, both mother and teacher generally rated his
performance as very poor to average.

The brief descriptions of Simon's behaviour at home with his
mother and in the classroom with his teacher, along with the
questionnaire results, appear to indicate that Simon was seen as a
problematic child. His inappropriate behaviour was explained by
his mother as due to the fact he was handicapped, although his
teacher considered that his social environment was a contributory
factor. Mrs Jones appeared to treat Simon as younger child, so
that she curtailed his freedom both in his play activities and

school outings because she felt he was irresponsible and incapable of taking care of himself. This contrasted with Mr Smith, who seemed relatively unaware of Simon as an individual in the classroom, and felt that Simon was not as incompetent as Mrs Jones thought.

Repertory Grids

In completing the repertory grids the above was shown to be only part of the picture. By first giving a somewhat lengthy description of Simon's observed behaviour, I hope to emphasise how a repertory grid can then be used to probe how a child is construed by his mother and his teacher which may explain their behaviour towards him and their assessment of his abilities. This information is not clearly apparent from either the observations or questionnaire data. The repertory grids clarify some of the observed interactions and the apparent lack of understanding which may have arisen between Mrs Jones and Mr Smith. With the information from the grid analyses a deeper understanding of the dynamics of the situation can be gained.

Comparing Mrs Jones's and Mr Smith's grids, the DELTA program shows that the general degree of correlation between the grids was 0.454. While this indicates that mother and teacher are not in total agreement, they do use some constructs to judge some of the elements in similar ways. This is illustrated by looking at Figure 22.1, which gives a two-dimensional picture of the comparison between Mrs Jones's and Mr Smith's repertory grids. The elements and constructs lying closest to the intersection of the two principal components indicate that there is close agreement between mother and teacher. The further away from the intersection each construct or element is placed, the more Mrs Jones disagrees with Mr Smith.

Simon is apparently judged in much the same light by his mother and his form teacher within this framework. There is similar agreement over a typical normal child of the same age. However, Simon is the only child who is actually common to both grids, as the other elements are similar roles but not actual people. Because of this, it is perhaps not surprising that, with the exception of the normal child, there is closest agreement between teacher and mother over Simon than over other elements.

Looking at the two elements closest to Simon, normal and problem children, it appears that Mrs Jones and Mr Smith are in

Figure 22.1: Comparison of Mrs Jones's and Mr Smith's Grids (DELTA Program)

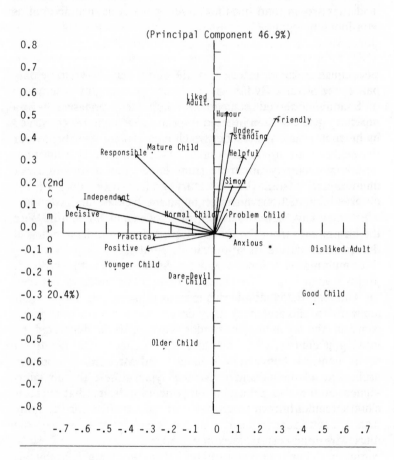

Negative poles of the constructs have not been given except * Anxious
for clarity of text

general agreement about how they construe these three children. Mrs Jones, however, consistently if not strongly, sees Simon and a typical problem child, as having more humour, understanding and friendliness than does Mr Smith. Mother and teacher differ considerably in the types of people they like and dislike. Mrs Jones shows greater preference than Mr Smith for people with a sense of humour who are sensitive and understanding. There are also considerable differences in the way they construe older and mature children.

Examining the constructs, it can be seen that mother and teacher seem to use the constructs calm/anxious, practical/impractical, and positive/negative, in much the same way. However, their use of descriptions such as friendly/unfriendly, understanding/insensitive, responsible/irresponsible, humour/no humour are more disparate.

This may well be an important factor when considering what they say about Simon. When Mrs Jones talks of Simon in terms of being irresponsible she may not be conveying as much information about Simon to Mr Smith as she anticipates, unless Mr Smith understands her particular use of the word as compared to his own.

Although the comparison of Mrs Jones's and Mr Smith's grids appears to show that they perceived Simon in terms of the constructs in much the same way, it was apparent that their views were not identical.

To consider their individual ways of perceiving Simon more clearly we can look at their grids separately. Figure 22.2 is a two-dimensional representation of how Mrs Jones judged the various children and adults in terms of the given constructs. It should be noted that the variation in the component space comprised by these two dimensions accounts for only 70 per cent of all variation. Thus, one-third of the information in the grid is not accounted for in the diagram.

Even so, it is clearly apparent that Simon is seen to lie close to both the good and problem children and the disliked adult. The table of distances between elements in the INGRID analysis gives the most accurate indication of how Simon is seen in relation to other elements. There he is closest to the disliked adult and the good child, but less close to the problem child. This underlines the fact that only 70 per cent of the grid is represented in Figure 22.2.

Figure 22.2: Two-dimensional Representation of Mrs Jones's Component Space (INGRID Program)

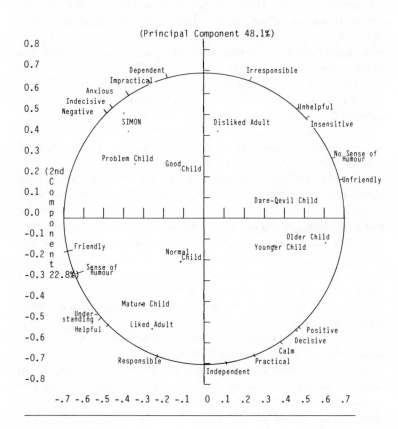

Simon and these other three elements, good and problem children and disliked adult, are seen to lie in the section of the diagram towards an apparently related group of constructs. These are negative, indecisive, anxious, impractical, dependent, and irresponsible. This is borne out in the questionnaire data in which, it will be remembered, Mrs Jones rated Simon as very poor in many areas of independence and social skills, and considered him as a problem. In contrast, Mrs Jones does not judge Simon particularly in terms of being friendly/unfriendly, understanding/insensitive, or having a sense of humour. He is most unlike (is farthest from) the liked adult, also the mature and older children.

Taken together, this tells us something about Mrs Jones's perception of Simon. It seems that she sees him both as a good and problem child. This is not easy to interpret. However, as he is like them in terms of being dependent, indecisive, anxious and impractical, which might all be regarded as fairly negative qualities, it is possible that the similarity between Simon and these children is that children with these attributes are in need of control, but still biddable and dependent, etc. Observations of Mrs Jones with Simon had been interprepted as showing that her control over Simon indicated she saw him as a much younger child, but he is not construed as such by his mother (i.e. they lie in the opposing halves of Figure 22.2). Perhaps Mrs Jones's interaction with her son is better seen as evidence she is construing him as a problem child needing to be kept under firm control.

More interesting is the fact that Simon is likened to the disliked adult, particularly when one appreciates that in Mrs Jones's grid the disliked adult was her ex-husband. This immediately throws a different light on Mrs Jones's antagonism towards Simon, particularly in view of the fact that the liked adult is seen as highly responsible and helpful. It is possible that Mrs Jones's expressed anger and frustration displayed towards Simon in her controlling behaviour, and in her letter to the school about Simon's report, reflects something of her attitude towards her ex-husband. He, like Simon, is construed in terms of being dependent and irresponsible (qualities Mrs Jones does not like), and also as unhelpful and insensitive. Thus, although Mrs Jones likens Simon to a good child because he is dependent, irresponsible, etc. and so perhaps controllable, these attributes also remind her of her husband who has left her, and whom she dislikes.

The present study did not pursue the interpretations made from grids, nor intervene in the individual cases, so the above interpretation is speculative and has not been checked out with Mrs Jones. Even so, the conclusions seem feasible, and could be seen as a way to explore and encourage more positive attitudes towards Simon in line with programmes to help to increase his independence and practical skills. It is also unlikely that this kind of information would come to light in more direct approaches, or from general conversation with Mrs Jones. It is here that the use of the grid can be seen to have benefits.

Briefly looking at Figure 22.3, which illustrates the two major dimensions in Mr Smith's component space, Simon is seen to be construed as most similar to the problem child, in terms of being indecisive, irresponsible and dependent. It will be remembered that Mr Smith had said at one stage that he did not see Simon as a problem because he felt his behaviour and low abilities were partly due to his restricted environments. The discrepancy between what he had indicated in the questionnaire and general conversation compared to evidence in the grid may be for a number of reasons. It is possible that all children whom Mr Smith construed as having problems are seen to have their problems caused by their environment, and that, given different environments, the problems would be considerably reduced. Alternatively, Mr Smith may construe Simon as a problem, but prefer not to admit this openly.

Although both Mrs Jones and Mr Smith did not agree about the attributes they liked in adults — particularly in terms of whether people had a sense of humour — both Mrs Jones and Mr Smith seem to construe Simon as opposite to the kind of adult they like. It is again probable that this kind of information would not be revealed in general discussion.

So where does this leave Simon? The dislike for him revealed in both his mother's and teacher's grid is likely to affect their interactions with him, and their assessment of his behaviour. There is agreement that Simon is seen as a problem child who is irresponsible and dependent, and observations at home show that to some extent his behaviour confirmed this view. Yet the reasons given for dependence and lack of social skills etc. differ between mother and teacher. Mrs Jones feels Simon's inability is

Figure 22.3: Two-dimensional Representation of Mr Smith's
Component Space (INGRID Program)

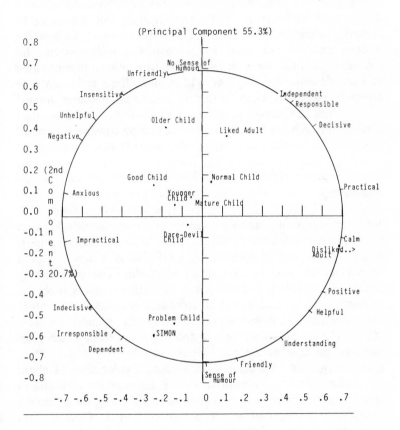

related to deficiencies within him; while Mr Smith feels Simon's psychological and social environment (in terms of a restrictive mother as well as the school itself) prevent opportunities for Simon to learn independent and social skills.

To some extent both these views may be correct, for there is likely to be an interaction of many factors. For Simon to be helped in learning the skills he lacks, it would seem that both his mother and teacher need to reconstrue his behaviour, and communicate their views to each other so that they at least come to a shared understanding. From there the difference in how they assess his capabilities can be discussed, and programmes devised to give him the opportunity to learn. In this way Simon may confirm through his behaviour that he can be construed in more positive, independent and, hopefully, likeable terms.

Summary

The importance of parents as partners in terms of the education of children with learning difficulties has been one of the corner-stones of the new Education Act (1981), as has the regular assessment of children in special education. The case history described above has indicated how a mother's and a teacher's assessment of a child based on questionnaires and observation data may differ. The use of the repertory grid reveals that there are underlying dynamics or construct systems from which both mother and teacher operate which may be reflected in their assessments and interactions with him. Exploration of these constructs, as well as behavioural assessments of the child would appear necessary in order to understand the individual child's capabilities as opposed to the construct system of others who interact with him and affect his behaviour.

References

Nash, R. (1973) *Classrooms Observed: The Teacher's Perception and the Pupil's Performance*, Routledge & Kegan Paul, London

Ravenette, A.T. (1977) 'Personal Construct Theory: An Approach to the Psychological Investigation of Children and Young People', in Bannister, D. (ed.), *New Perspectives in Personal Construct Theory*, Academic Press, London

Rowe, D. and Slater, P. (1976) 'Studies of the Psychiatrist's Insight into the Patient's Inner World', in Slater, P. (ed.), *Exploration of Intrapersonal Space*, John Wiley, Chichester

Slater, P. (ed.) (1977) *The Measurement of Interpersonal Space by Grid Technique, vol. 2*, Wiley, Chichester

PART SEVEN

CAVEAT

In 1979 I wrote a review of critiques of Personal Construct Theory (Beail, 1979). I was surprised to find so little and such weak criticism. At the same time I searched around the literature for critical appraisals of grid technique; again I found very little. There are numerous passing comments which are rarely substantiated, for example Vernon (1964) commented that the grid seems so flexible as to be almost unmanageable. If we substitute interview for grid the nonsensity of the comment becomes apparent. Some grid users have commented on the limits of the grid and pointed to the needs for developing further measures of construing. But this is not really a criticism. I found only one paper which critically evaluated some methodological aspect of the grid, and that was by D.M. Yorke (1978).

Being aware of the enthusiasm that many people feel for grid methods, I felt that the book would need a word of caution. Yorke has continued his critical appraisal of repertory grid technique and so I invited him to make a contribution to this book in order to provide a caveat.

References

Beail, N. (1979) 'Critiques of Personal Construct Theory: A Review', paper presented to the British Psychological Society, London Conference, University College, London

Vernon, P. (1964) *Personality Assessment; a Critical Survey*, Methuen, London

Yorke, D.M. (1978) 'Repertory Grids in Educational Research: Some Methodological Considerations', *British Educational Research Journal, 4*, 63-74

23 ADMINISTRATION, ANALYSIS AND ASSUMPTION: SOME ASPECTS OF VALIDITY

D.M. Yorke

Validity

> While it is eminently reasonable to question the validity of a *particular* grid format constructed to try and yield particular information, it is not sensible to dispute the validity of *the grid* as such. (Fransella and Bannister, 1977, p. 93: authors' emphasis)

Fransella and Bannister are asserting here that the diversity of possible elements, constructs, and ways of relating the two precludes a general discussion of the validity of repertory grids, whilst allowing the validity of specific grids to be appraised in terms of their particular contexts. This chapter, whilst accepting their argument at the level of the specific grid format, argues that serious questions regarding grid validity *do* arise at the general level, and that users of repertory grids need to probe beneath the surface of their chosen variant in order to ascertain whether the information to be collected is likely to be congruent with that which is sought.

Cronbach and Meehl (1955) construe the validity of psychological tests in four ways:

(1) predictive validity — in which future performance is the criterion against which the test data are set;

(2) concurrent validity — which depends upon the correlation between the test and another, established, test;

(3) content validity — which depends upon the demonstration that the test is composed of a representative sample from the relevant universe;

(4) construct validity — which refers to the extent to which the

383

> test can be taken as a measuring instrument for a particular attribute or quality.

Whilst it is acknowledged that a repertory grid is rather different from the typical psychological test, Cronbach and Meehl's categories provide a convenient point of departure for a discussion of grid validity.

Kelly is quoted by Frensella and Bannister (1977) as saying that validity 'refers to the capacity of a test to tell us what we already know' (p. 92). This is tantamount to defining validity in terms of concurrency — the extent to which the information derived from the repertory grid correlates with some acceptable yardstick of the attributes or characteristics being measured. Kelly was well aware of the circularity of construing validity in terms of concurrency, and preferred to view validity in terms of usefulness — in which is embedded that central tenet of his theorising, the notion of prediction. However, a grid may also be useful in an explanatory capacity, thus nudging the concept of validity back towards concurrency.

It is difficult to say much about construct validity since many grid users do not seek to measure a particular attribute or quality — and, when such a measurement is attempted (of 'cognitive complexity' or 'intensity', for instance), the meaning of what is measured proves to be as elusive as plankton in a shrimping net. The content validity of a grid is also problematic, as will be argued below, since the sampling of elements and constructs can rarely be shown to be representative of their respective populations.

There is a further aspect of validity, bearing upon the notion of usefulness, which has not yet been addressed and which is neatly illustrated in Fransella and Adams' (1966) grid study of an arsonist. A series of grids were administered, and the sequential unpacking of his construct system allowed the clinician to work towards a possible motive for the arsonist's behaviour which could not have been anticipated in the light of accepted rationales for arson. Viewed in more abstract terms, the grids were valid in the sense that they told the authors *what they did not know*, thereby contributing to the building of theory about the individual concerned. Should not validity, then, also be open to construing in terms of enlightenment?

Cronbach and Meehl's categorisation largely focuses upon validity at the level of the purpose for which a test — or grid — is being used. Validity can, however, be considered from a more fine-grained, but no less important, point of view: that of the potential of a grid to capture accurately the construing of a respondent. It is towards technical aspects of the collection and analysis of grid data that this chapter is mainly addressed: issues here include the definition of the grid's context, the sampling of elements and constructs, the nature of constructs, and the manner in which a grid matrix is built up. In the interests of completeness, the analysis of grid data is discussed towards the end of the chapter: validity here takes on a different colouring in that it refers to the processing and interpretation of grid data, rather than to its inherent quality.

Restriction on space has meant that much of this chapter's content has had to be presented rather baldly, occasionally in the form of unsupported assertion. This chapter is, in essence, a distillation (and, I hope, a valid sample) of a much fuller treatment of the issue which is given in Yorke (1983a), to which the interested — and substantially committed — reader is referred.

Grid Context

Various writers on grid methodology emphasise the importance of giving a clear indication of the context within which grid data are to be collected. Mair (1967), for instance, points out that failure to do so may result in the respondent flicking from one context to another as he or she works through the grid — a danger against which Nash (1973) failed to guard in his studies of the ways in which teachers construed pupils. To the construer, pupils in the classroom may appear very different from when they are in the playground or on an outside visit.

More serious, and particularly likely in grids containing elicited elements, is the problem of vagueness. Pope — in work reported in Pope and Keen (1981) — asked student teachers to provide as elements 'a list of things which come into your mind when you think about teaching' (p. 120), and thereby elicited elements of considerable heterogeneity: for example, one respondent's set included children, books, chalk, headmaster, classroom, ability, worry and attitudes. As associations of the word 'teaching', these elements might have been of substantial interest. However, as the starting-point for the collection of grid data they present considerable problems, as some respondents observed. One has only to try to produce a construct capable of subsuming 'chalk', 'headmaster' and 'worry' to recognise the difficulties involved — and it is worth recording that some of the grids collected by Pope were notable for the small number of constructs which they contained. Contextual vagueness is also particularly noticeable in a study by Kevill, Shaw and Goodacre (1982), whose evaluation of a diploma course in Literacy Development used grids in which the elements were aspects of the job of teaching which did not necessarily have any relevance to the purpose of the evaluation.

It is often difficult, however, to specify grid contexts with sufficient precision to eliminate ambiguity of response, for tightening the context narrows the focus of construing towards particular instances and thus reduces the generalisability of the findings. On the other hand, the broader the grid context, the greater is the opportunity to give generalisable but 'averaged-out' responses. The dilemma is an analogue of Heisenberg's uncertainty principle in physics.

Elements

The preceding discussion has indicated the importance of the grid elements in defining the context of the typical repertory grid — in fact, one of the key determinants of the validity of a grid is the 'goodness of fit' between the grid's context and its elements. Implicit in this argument is that, given a specific context, 'homogeneous' elements (i.e. elements of the same kind) enhance validity since such elements are likely to stimulate the elicitation of constructs relevant to all of them. In other words, the chance of an element falling outside the 'range of convenience' of a construct is thereby minimised. The resulting grid matrix should then contain few — if any — blank cells, a distinct advantage where statistical analysis is concerned.

Homogeneity should not be too easily assumed, since elements which at first glance appear to be of a similar type may turn out to exhibit important differences. Hopwood and Keen (1978) describe grids in which the elements comprise 'self', one effective and one ineffective teacher personally known to the respondent, and eleven unfamiliar teachers who are shown in short video-recordings of scaled-down teaching encounters. Whilst all of the 14 elements are teachers, the first 3 differ markedly in existential terms from the 'video-elements' and, in responding to this grid protocol, I found it difficult to engage meaningfully with the latter group (Yorke, 1978).

When, in my own work, I elicited grids from science teachers I found that they tended to construe 2 of the provided aspects of teaching ('homework' and 'achievement testing') as differing in kind from the remaining 13, in which teacher-pupil interaction was a more obvious component. Whilst *I* saw all 15 aspects as homogeneous in my research, the respondents — whose construing, after all, was the focus of my inquiry — clearly often did not.

A number of grid studies, including that mentioned in the previous paragraph, have included elements which were irrelevant to either the respondent or the thrust of the grid. As to the former, I found that both 'science club' and 'outside visits' were satisfactory in pilot work, but these proved to be of little or no importance in the teaching of those with whom I later worked. Where the thrust of the grid is concerned, the problem is exemplified by Perrott *et al.*, (1976), who asked teachers on an in-service course to construe 'two other specific teachers whose work you know' (p. 26), as well as five role-specified teachers. The data pertaining to these two teachers was, in practice, useless. Elements which have no clear purpose in the grid merely provide statistical 'noise'.

Vague elements may also give rise to statistical noise. Bannister and Mair (1968) showed that the construing of 'concrete', inanimate objects is likely to be highly stable. However, as elements become more complex and/or abstract, stability of construing may decline. There is little evidence to support this suggestion, save that from a small-scale study which I undertook. Students on an in-service Diploma in Counselling completed test and re-test grids with self-chosen elements of differing types: pupils, specific teaching situations (akin to critical incidents), and general teaching situations. Although numbers were too small for a statistically significant gradation to be fully established, the stabilities of the three types of grid were found to decline in the order listed. The findings are interpretable in terms of a gradation of increasing vagueness.

The validity of the sample of elements used is often problematic, though difficulties are avoided when the sample is identical with the population from which it is drawn — as when a whole class of pupils is used. Where the population of elements is indeterminate it is impossible to show in statistical terms that the sample of elements is representative, and the researcher has to justify the sample on qualitative grounds.

Finally in this section, the question of whether to supply or elicit elements must be raised. This issue is often debated among grid users — inconclusively, since the answer depends upon the purposes of the research. It is, of course, open to the researcher to use both methods of identifying elements in the same grid, in which case elicitation should precede supply in order to avoid 'contamination' of the list of elicited elements. Given the need to identify elements according to the problem to be investigated, there can be no simple relationship between the source of the elements and the validity of the grid.

Constructs

As with elements, a decision has to be made whether to elicit or supply constructs, or to use a combination of elicited and supplied constructs as Olson (1980) did. Whilst there are frequently good reasons for supplying elements, the supplying of constructs makes massive assumptions regarding shared meaning. A construct like 'extrovert/introvert' is not as simple as it seems, since the way that the respondent uses the polar labels is determined to a large extent by idiosyncratic associated meanings: whilst you and I may both use the same words, there is no guarantee that the meanings which we attach to them will be in substantial agreement. Put another way, the uncertainty that attaches to a respondent's construing of a supplied construct places the supplying of constructs upon distinctly uncertain foundations.

Kelly (1955) made a strong claim for the dichotomous nature of constructs, yet it seems unlikely that all construing is dichotomous: for instance, colour terms, whilst capable of being construed in terms of a series of dichotomies, constitute a 'contrastive set' within a given semantic field (Miller and

Johnson-Laird, 1976). It can be argued against Kelly that the construing of an object as 'red' involves a kind of pattern-matching procedure against internalised standards (or 'proto-types': Rosch, 1977) of redness, and may not involve — except implicitly — oppositional contrast. When the constructs are nouns and verbs, opposition (save in the set-inclusion/exclusion of classical logic rejected by Kelly) is often hard to specify in dichotomous terms: what, for example, might be the Kellyan contrast poles of 'sex' and 'acclimatise'?

Respondents often produce 'peculiar' constructs (Resnick and Landfield, 1961), in which the oppositions would not easily be recognised in terms of dictionary meaning. It would seem probable that such constructs represent the emergent poles of two conflated 'logical' oppositions. 'Peculiar' constructs seem more likely to be produced in response to elicitation procedures which stress the difference between elements, rather than to procedures which ask for the opposite characteristic to that evidenced by the pair of elements during the construing of triads (for a discussion of the 'difference' and 'opposition' approaches to triadic elicitation, see Epting *et al.*, 1971). Each approach has its virtues, but these tend to be related inversely: the 'difference' method may produce the more personally mean-ingful discriminations, though the production of 'peculiar' constructs creates problems in the completion and analysis of the grid matrix; the 'opposition' method tends to pro-duce 'logical' constructs which are easier to treat as scales, but at the risk to the communication of personal meaning.

Whilst triadic elicitation is widely used it does not always facilitate the production of constructs, since some respondents appear to find the cognitive demands of the procedure alien to the way they think, or would prefer to respond. The construing of *pairs* of elements ('dyadic elicitation') in terms of similarity or contrast is not inconsistent with Kellyan theory, and is often found easier: its relative simplicity is of advantage when a grid is administered to a group of respondents, seeming to minimise the errors associated with group administration (see Yorke, 1978, for some of the errors found in respect of triadic elicitation). 'Freer' forms of elicitation (such as interviewing) have been used, but in general the resulting constructs have not been incorporated into grids. However, their potential for eliciting richness of meaning suggests that they may be of considerable value in elucidating the dimensions of a respondent's thought.

Kelly's insistence on a relevance-conditioned contrast theory of meaning led him to prefer 'X/Y' to 'X/not X' constructs, where X and Y are oppositional poles within a specific semantic boundary. However, experience shows that simple negations are often given (whether the elicitation is 'difference' or 'opposition' in character), thus leaving the researcher the problem of interpreting the 'not X' pole.

'X/Y' constructs are not necessarily pairs of functional antonyms, for 'X' and 'Y' may constitute the emergent poles of two different constructs. Sometimes there seems to be no superordinate beneath which such separate poles may be subsumed: 'difference' triadic elicitation might, for instance, produce the construct 'happy/businesslike'. This would be a relatively extreme instance, but functional antonymy may be compromised in a 'bent' construct in which the contrast pole is not a 'logical' opposition but is selected from a group of possible poles which includes both a superordinate contrast and its subordinate implications (for a discussion of 'bentness' see Yorke, 1983b).

This problem draws attention to the inherent portmanteauism of many construct poles: what, returning to an example given earlier, does 'extrovert' actually *mean* to a respondent or to a researcher? I am prepared to argue that a term such as this is highly polysemic, composed of a host of associations and implications, and that its meaning evaporates under the fierce glare of rigorous appraisal unless the researcher is prepared to undertake, by further inquiry, the daunting task of unpacking its semantics.

Save for grids containing elements such as 'self as I am', 'self as I was' and 'self as I expect to be', there is little evidence in the literature that researchers have been aware of whether the constructs which they have elicited have been oriented to the past, the present or the future. Without appropriate specification, the verbal labels supplied by respondents may imply any of 'what was', 'what is', 'what is expected to be', 'what ought to be', and their subvariants.

The construing of people would seem to be predominantly of the 'was' and 'is' types, for individuals speak as they find, or have found. Predictive construing can obviously be built into a grid, but this requires the specification of a future-oriented context.

When situations comprise the elements — as in some of my own work — the basis of the construing is more uncertain, and there is an increased possibility that 'ought' constructs will enter the grid. The grid itself will not contain sufficient information to resolve any ambiguities: looking back on some of my own grids, I am unable to say whether a construct stressing *opportunity* (for example, 'strong . . ./little opportunity for feedback from the pupils') refers to the actual condition of handling a class, to a received wisdom, or to potential yet unfulfilled. Ambiguities such as this were not the fault of my respondents; the blame for them lies with a researcher who did not recognise them until he reflected upon procedure long after the grids were completed.

Completing the Grid Matrix

The majority of grid researches require the rating of elements on constructs: this emphasis will be reflected in the content of this section, but some of the points made have general applicability to the various ways of relating elements and constructs.

The dichotomous allocation of elements to construct poles, whilst of advantage in some circumstances (notably where simplicity of procedure is especially desirable), allows no scope for the communication of shades of meaning. As Bannister and Mair (1968) point out, 'lopsided' element allocation renders problematic analyses based upon matching scores: the 'split-half' grid suggested as a possible remedy overcomes some of the difficulties, but meaning may be compromised by this procedure's forced even-handedness of allocation.

The ranking of elements along a construct dimension is advantageous where respondents such as children might find rating too complex, but this becomes more difficult as the number of elements increases. Relationships between constructs can be shown through the use of rank correlation coefficients, but any relationships computed between elements are likely to have little meaning (Humphreys, 1973).

Rated grids, too, are not without their problems. It is easy to assume that a given oppositional continuum is used in a broadly consistent way across respondents or, at a cruder level, that all oppositional continua are metrically equivalent. Yorke (1983b) showed that such assumptions were highly unlikely to be justified in that respondents would bring to each continuum idiosyncratic meaning structures and evaluative loadings. Whilst poles of constructs may be relatively easy for respondents to construe, and hence use, mid-points may suffer from considerable vagueness in conceptualisation. This is not to claim — as some writers do — that the mid-point is unmeaningful: it *may* be unmeaningful, but it is not necessarily so (consider, for instance, any construct of the 'hypo-X/hyper-X' type). It is easy to demonstrate that the mid-point of an oppositional continuum is open to a considerable number of interpretations, thus undercutting the notion of a simple linear metric (Gaines and Shaw, 1981; Yorke, 1983a).

When an element falls outside the range of convenience of a construct (this can be expected to occur in 'situations' grids or when constructs are 'peculiar' in character), no rating should be entered into that particular grid cell. As far as the matrix itself is concerned, blank cells present no problems — indeed, they may be informative. A difficulty arises when one wishes to subject the matrix to statistical analysis, and the analytical tail is suspected of wagging the whole canine matrix if one is enjoined to use the mid-point whenever a construct cannot subsume an element (see, for instance, Thomas and Shaw, 1976).

The process of rating, then, cannot be construed as unproblematic. Relatively little is known about the ways in which individuals respond to scales, yet this would seem to be essential knowledge if the respondent's communicative intentions are to be adequately received by the researcher. Aspects of semantics and personal affect can be expected to influence ratings, but these are confounded with what appears to be an enduring personal response style (Yorke, 1984). Extremity of rating has been coupled with the notions of personal meaningfulness and pathology (see the reviews by Warr and Coffman, 1970, and Chetwynd, 1977), but my own experience suggests that there are occasional instances when respondents appear to be using extreme ratings in a manner close to dichotomous allocation in order to get the grid procedure over as soon as possible.

Perhaps the question of rating should be tackled from a different point of view. The annals of research using the semantic differential provide considerable evidence for — in Kellyan terms — element X construct interactions (see, for example, Mann, Phillips and Thompson, 1979). Put another way, constructs may be operationalised differentially according to the element being considered. If, as I would argue, verbal labels are a kind of shorthand for complexes of meaning (rather than representing unique, isolable and scalable attributes), and elements themselves are complex (whether people or situations), it seems improbable that the respondent will be able to remain consistent in the way in which a particular meaning-complex is being used. Various writers (e.g. Hollingworth, 1913; Underwood, Ham and Ekstrand, 1962; Mair, 1967) suggest that respondents may switch attention to different parts of an element, yet investigations have hitherto been sparse into the complexity of what might naïvely be construed as simple construct dimensions.

This line of thought can be pressed further. One can speculate that, instead of using a scale in a quasi-physical manner, a respondent may take the scale as providing an orientation towards particular properties of an element and then interrogate his or her experience of that element for relevant material. This material, which would be idiosyncratic to the element being considered, could then be 'processed' into a rating on the scale. As an example, I can identify two people whom I would rate as extremely generous, but for very different reasons: one offered me the indefinite use of a house, whilst the other stood back and let me take the credit for a piece of academic work which I had initiated but on which we had collaborated. This is a far cry from the physicalism of the ruler, and is much closer to the tenets of existential phenomenology — and its implications for research based on Personal Construct Theory are profound.

Analysis

The two methods of analysis most accessible to grid users are INGRID (Slater, 1972; 1977) and FOCUS (Thomas and Shaw, 1976). Each implicitly assumes that the rating scales are equal-interval in character (a matter open to debate, on the argument of the previous section), and each contains its own assumptions regarding the most appropriate method of reducing a large bulk of grid data to a more easily interpretable size.

INGRID uses principal components analysis to produce a set of components of the data matrix which are orthogonal (i.e. independent of each other). The algorithm extracts as a first component that which accounts for the greatest proportion of the total grid variance, and then proceeds to extract successive components in the same way from the variance which remains. In a typical grid, three components account for some 80 per cent of its variance, the remaining 20 per cent being distributed over a long 'tail' of minor components. Incorporated in INGRID is a test for the number of components to be deemed significant, but this should be treated with caution since (as Slater, 1977, is aware) this can produce enigmatic results: as a case in point, one of my grids produced nine significant components, the last of which contributed a mere 0.52 per cent of the variance in the matrix! Slater (1972) sees the most important advantage of principal components analysis (PCA) as lying in the orthogonal nature of the components produced, but Fiske (1971), writing generally about factor analysis, suggests that in personality research many observed dimensions exhibit considerable covariation, and that it is an open question whether the greater conceptual simplicity of orthogonal structure will prove to have theoretical advantages over structures produced by way of oblique factor analysis.

At the heart of INGRID is the product-moment correlation coefficient which has been widely criticised for its failure to take into account both the level and scatter of the data to which it is applied. Where, however, ratings are spread across the full scale length (and not concentrated, say, at one end), spatial inter-relationships between elements turn out to be similar to those produced by other methods, and it seems reasonable to assume that serious distortion of the output is unlikely to occur. In computing a table of correlation coefficients and angular distances between constructs, INGRID normalises the set of ratings on each construct. Whilst there are statistical advantages in minimising skewness in the distribution of scale ratings, such a procedure inevitably removes some of the original meaning from the data. Normalisation can be extended to the full PCA, and Slater (1977) indicates that the arguments for and against exercising this option are finely balanced.

FOCUS takes a different approach to the data matrix. An element similarity matrix is produced, the similarity scores being derived from transformations of inter-element distances computed according to the 'city block' metric[1]. A construct similarity matrix is also computed along broadly cognate lines, but the bipolarity of constructs enables similarity scores to be maximised by 'reflecting' (i.e. reversing the labels, and hence the scoring of) constructs, where appropriate.

Shaw (1980) gives the 'city block' metric a somewhat inadequate justification, and it can be argued that one large difference, say, of six scale divisions between a pair of elements in respect of a particular construct is of greater psychological significance than six single-unit differences spread out over a number of constructs. Whilst the 'city block' metric would accord the two types of discrepancy the same distance score (or FOCUS would indicate identical similarities), a Minkowski metric of higher power-coefficient would indicate a higher distance score in respect of the case exhibiting the single large difference. Constructs often refer to attributes which are not easily measured in physical terms, and Garner (1974) suggests that in such circumstances the 'Euclidean distance' (with its power-coefficient of two)[2] is more appropriate than the 'city block': however, the Euclidean distance metric is not available on FOCUS.

The FOCUS and INGRID algorithms present their output in very different manners. FOCUS rearranges the original grid data in such a way that elements and constructs are rendered contiguous according to the criterion of maximal similarity. The advantages of so doing are that the grid data are presented in essentially the same format as the original matrix (thus not mystifying the respondent), and that the clustering of both elements and constructs can be seen at a glance. These desirable features obscure two difficulties, however. First, some elements or constructs may be represented as distant from each other because their similarity is overridden by other requirements within the algorithm: here the element and construct similarity matrices can be consulted to cross-check the visual presentation. Secondly, the previously mentioned variations in both personal rating style and the semantics of scales vitiate any attempt to suggest a general criterion by which one might 'cut' the dendrograms and thus identify specific clusters of elements and clusters.

FOCUS necessarily presents element and construct relationships separately, whereas an advantage of INGRID is that both elements and constructs can be shown on a single diagram. Where three principal components are chosen for depiction, the plotting of elements and constructs on a globe, using polar co-ordinates, allows subsidiary similarities to be shown in a manner impossible with FOCUS. It should be pointed out that the compression of a hyperspace (often of high dimensionality) into three dimensions inevitably introduces some distortions: it is, as with FOCUS, always worth checking back against the original similarity data to see if the plotting is seriously misrepresentative. Some respondents do find geographical projections difficult to relate to the original data which they provided, thus reminding the researcher that the existential view at the surface of the world is not always commensurate with that of the astronaut.

Neither FOCUS nor INGRID completely overcomes the problem of missing data. The use of the mid-point rating as a 'dustbin' response category may allow statistics to be computed, but it has potentially serious implications for interpretation. Slater (1977) takes a more puritanical view of the problem in his advocacy of the elimination of rows and/or columns in which blank cells exist. To follow Slater's prescription for 'gappy' grids (particularly likely to result when situations comprise the elements) can lead to severe emaciation of the data matrix, again with serious implications for interpretation.

Before drawing this section to a close, two gross errors must be mentioned. First, no analysis of a repertory grid can give an indication of the hierarchical relationships between constructs: the elucidation of these requires that further evidence be imported from outside the grid. The point is made because a number of researchers have made mistakes of this kind, by confusing the phenetic with the phyletic, or by failing to differentiate the meaning of 'hierarchy' in the separate fields of construct theory and cluster analysis. Further, large clusters and factors do not necessarily imply dominance in a construct system despite the claims often made in the literature.

The second error is to assume that superficially identical grids can be combined or averaged to produce some kind of consensus grid. This procedure typically leads to the identification of two principal components accounting for the vast bulk of the variance in the combined grid (see Perrott *et al.*, 1976, for an example) — an unsurprising finding when one realises that the idiosyncratic aspects of the component grids have in effect been eliminated, for one is dealing with the means of the ratings whilst quietly forgetting their standard deviations. It has to be pointed out, too, that the aggregation of grids makes large assumptions of meaning-equivalence when verbal labels are treated as identical across a range of respondents, or when a role title is implicitly construed as invariant despite the fact that respondents select different individuals to match the specification.

Conclusion

Fransella and Bannister (1977) suggest that the repertory grid is a technique which 'is only limited by the user's lack of imagination' (p. 59). Within their contextual horizon, the point is a fair one. However, the literature bears witness to a slippage towards 'anything goes' as far as grid design is concerned. Put another way, a grid's validity has often been taken as axiomatic, thus leading the user away from a rigorous scrutiny of method.

This chapter does not pretend to be a complete inquiry into grid validity: for example, little has been said regarding the adequacy of a grid's verbal labels in capturing a respondent's construing, and regarding the stability of the data matrix. These, and other aspects of validity, await further exploration. Nevertheless, the issues discussed in this chapter indicate that the validity of a repertory grid cannot be taken for granted, and that serious questions regarding validity can be raised regarding grid methodology in general. I am not claiming that any grid will be subject to all of the flaws that have been discussed. As with any technique of research in the human sciences, all grids are flawed to some extent: the problem is to decide whether, all things considered, the particular grid in question can be regarded as an acceptable instrument of inquiry.

For some, this brief review will make disquieting reading: the state of the timberwork of the repertory grid ship clearly leaves something to be desired. Adapting Neurath's metaphor (Popper, 1972), can the construct theorist crew get away with the odd patch here and there, or must whole timbers be replaced as the ship sails along whilst trust is placed in the structural integrity of the remainder? Or is the situation such that the crew should take more drastic action?

Notes

1. The 'city block' distance between two elements A and B in a repertory grid is calculated by summing the differences, for each construct taken separately, in the ratings given to A and B. The arithmetical sign of the difference is ignored. The same procedure can be used in respect of constructs.

2. The 'Euclidean distance' is computed in a similar manner to the 'city block' distance, save that in this case each difference in rating is *squared* before the summation. Both the city block and Euclidean distances are special cases of the general Minkowski distance metric (see Everitt, 1974). Where comparison between grids of different size is desired, there are advantages in dividing the inter-element (or inter-construct) distance by the number of rating differences being taken into account, for this puts the distance measures for the different grids on an equal footing.

References

Bannister, D. and Mair, J.M.M. (1968) *The Evaluation of Personal Constructs*, Academic Press, London

Chetwynd, S.J. (1977) 'The Psychological Meaning of Structural Measures Derived from Grids' in P. Slater (ed.), *The Measurement of Intrapersonal Space by Grid Technique vol. 2*, Wiley, Chichester

Cronbach, L.J. and Meehl, P.E. (1955) 'Construct Validity in Psychological Tests', *Psychological Bulletin, 52*, 281-302

Epting, F.R., Suchman, D.I. and Nickeson, C.J. (1971) 'An Evaluation of Elicitation Procedures for Personal Constructs', *British Journal of Psychology, 62*, 513-17

Everitt, B. (1974) *Cluster Analysis*, Heinemann, London

Fiske, D.W. (1971) 'Strategies in the Search for Personality Constructs', *Journal of Experimental Research in Personality, 5*, 323-30

Fransella, F. and Adams, B. (1966) 'An Illustration of the Use of Repertory Grid Technique in a Clinical Setting', *British Journal of Social and Clinical Psychology, 5*, 51-62

—— and Bannister, D. (1977) *A Manual for Repertory Grid Technique*, Academic Press, London

Gaines, B.R. and Shaw, M.L.G. (1982) 'New Directions in the Analysis and Interactive Elicitation of Personal Construct Systems' in M.L.G. Shaw (ed.), *Recent Advances in Personal Construct Technology*, Academic Press, London, pp. 147-82

Garner, W.R. (1974) *The Processing of Information and Structure*, Lawrence Erlbaum Associates, Potomac, Maryland

Hollingworth, H.L. (1913) 'Judgement of Similarity and Difference', *Psychological Review, 20*, 271-89

Hopwood, W. and Keen, T. (1978) 'TARGET: A New Approach to the Appraisal of Teaching', *Programmed Learning and Educational Technology, 15*, 187-95

Humphreys, P.C. (1973) 'A Review of Some Statistical Properties of the Repertory Grid (and their Cognitive Implications)', in *Repertory Grid Methods*, The British Psychological Society (Mathematical and Statistical Psychology Section) Leicester, pp. 7-28

Kelly, G.A. (1955) *The Psychology of Personal Constructs* (2 volumes), Norton, New York

Kevill, F. Shaw, M. and Goodacre, E. (1982) 'In-service Diploma Course Evaluation Using Repertory Grids', *British Educational Research Journal, 8*, 45-56

Mair, J.M.M. (1967) 'Some Problems in Repertory Grid Measurement, I. The Use of Bipolar Constructs', *British Journal of Psychology, 58*, 261-70

Mann, I.T., Phillips, J.L. and Thompson, E.G. (1979) 'An Examination of Methodological Issues Relevant to the Use and Interpretation of the Semantic Differential', *Applied Psychological Measurement, 3*, 213-29

Miller, G.A. and Johnson-Laird, P.N. (1976) *Language and Perception*, Cambridge University Press, Cambridge

Nash, R. (1973) *Classrooms Observed*, Routledge & Kegan Paul, London

Olson, J. (1980) 'Innovative Doctrine and Practical Dilemmas: A Case Study of Curriculum Translation', unpublished PhD thesis, University of Birmingham

Perrott, E., Applebee, A.N., Heap, B. and Watson, E.P. (1976) 'An Investigation into Teachers' Reactions to a Self-instructional Microteaching Course', *Programmed Learning and Educational Technology, 13*, 25-35

Pope, M. and Keen, T.R. (1981) *Personal Construct Psychology and Education*, Academic Press, London

Popper, K.R. (1972) *Objective Knowledge*, Oxford University Press, Oxford

Resnick, J. and Landfield, A.W. (1961) 'The Oppositional Nature of Dichotomous Constructs', *Psychological Record, 11*, 47-55

Rosch, E. (1977) 'Human Categorization' in N. Warren (ed.), *Studies in Cross-cultural Psychology, vol. 1*, Academic Press, London, pp. 1-49

Shaw, M.L.G. (1980) *On Becoming a Personal Scientist*, Academic Press, London

Slater, P. (1972) 'Notes on INGRID 72', St George's Hospital (mimeo), London

—— (ed.) (1977) *The Measurement of Intrapersonal Space by Grid Technique, Volume 2: Dimensions of Intrapersonal Space*, Wiley, Chichester

Thomas, L.F. and Shaw, M.L.G. (1976) *FOCUS: A Manual for the 'Focus Computer Program'*, Centre for the Study of Human Learning, Brunel University, Uxbridge

Underwood, B.J. Ham, M. and Ekstrand, B. (1962) 'Cue Selection in Paired-associate Learning', *Journal of Experimental Psychology, 64*, 405-9

Warr, P.B. and Coffman, T.L. (1970) 'Personality, Involvement and Extremity of Judgement', *British Journal of Social and Clinical Psychology, 9*, 108-21

Yorke, D.M. (1978) 'Repertory Grids in Educational Research: Some Methodological Considerations', *British Educational Research Journal, 4*, 63-74

—— (1983a) 'The Repertory Grid: A Critical Appraisal', unpublished PhD thesis, University of Nottingham

—— (1983b) 'Straight or Bent? An Inquiry into Rating Scales in Repertory Grids', *British Educational Research Journal, 9*, 141-51

—— (1984) 'Rating Style in Repertory Grids', Centre for Educational Development and Training, Manchester Polytechnic (mimeo)

AUTHOR INDEX

SUBJECT INDEX